D0898137

CONFIGURATIONS OF A CULTURAL SCENE

McGill-Queen's Iberian and Latin American Cultures Series

Series editor: Nicolás Fernández-Medina

The McGill-Queen's Iberian and Latin American Cultures Series is committed to publishing original scholarship that explores and re-evaluates Iberian and Latin American cultures, connections, and identities. Offering diverse perspectives on a range of regional and global histories from the early modern period to twenty-first-century contexts, the series cuts across disciplinary boundaries to consider how questions of authority, nation, revolution, gender, sexuality, science, epistemology, avant-gardism, aesthetics, travel, colonization, race relations, religious belief, and media technologies, among others, have shaped the rich and complex trajectories of modernity in the Iberian Peninsula and Latin America.

The McGill-Queen's Iberian and Latin American Cultures Series promotes rigorous scholarship and welcomes proposals for innovative and theoretically compelling monographs and edited collections.

CONFIGURATIONS OF A CULTURAL SCENE

YOUNG WRITERS AND ARTISTS IN MADRID, 1918–1930

Andrew A. Anderson

McGill-Queen's University Press

Montreal & Kingston · London · Chicago

© McGill-Queen's University Press 2023

ISBN 978-0-2280-1386-0 (cloth)
ISBN 978-0-2280-1479-9 (ePDF)
ISBN 978-0-2280-1480-5 (ePUB)

Legal deposit first quarter 2023
Bibliothèque nationale du Québec

Printed in Canada on acid-free paper that is 100% ancient forest free
(100% post-consumer recycled), processed chlorine free

LIBRARY AND ARCHIVES CANADA CATALOGUING IN PUBLICATION

Title: Configurations of a cultural scene : young writers and artists in Madrid,
    1918–1930 / Andrew A. Anderson.
Names: Anderson, Andrew A., 1953– author.
Series: McGill-Queen's Iberian and Latin American cultures series ; 6.
Description: Series statement: McGill-Queen's Iberian and Latin American
    cultures series ; 6 | Includes bibliographical references and index.
Identifiers: Canadiana (print) 20220419434 | Canadiana (ebook) 20220419485 |
    ISBN 9780228013860 (cloth) | ISBN 9780228014799 (ePDF) |
    ISBN 9780228014805 (ePUB)
Subjects: LCSH: Authors, Spanish—Spain—Madrid—History—20th century. |
    LCSH: Artists—Spain—Madrid—History—20th century. | LCSH: Artistic
    collaboration—Spain—Madrid—History—20th century. | LCSH: Friendship—
    Spain—Madrid—History—20th century. | LCSH: Youth—Spain—Madrid—
    History—20th century. | LCSH: Interpersonal relations—Spain—Madrid—
    History—20th century. | LCSH: Madrid (Spain)—Intellectual life—20th century.
Classification: LCC DP357 .A53 2023 | DDC 306.4/709464109042—dc23

CONTENTS

TABLE AND FIGURES

Table

Figures

ACKNOWLEDGMENTS

I originally conceived the idea for this book while sitting in the lobby of a small hotel in old Cádiz, and I would not have been there had it not been for the urgings of my friends Joel and Pam Rini. Over the course of the book's composition, I peppered other friends and colleagues – Almudena de la Cueva, Melissa Dinverno, Nieves García Prados, Michael Gerli, Laurie-Anne Laget, Christopher Maurer, James Valender, Fernando Valverde – with numerous requests for diverse kinds of information and for help with interlibrary loans, and they always responded with great generosity, sharing their expertise and offering practical assistance. Miguel Valladares-Llata and Alfredo Valverde facilitated access to some rare bibliographical items, and Nora Benedict and Brandon Butler offered valuable practical advice toward the end of the project. I am very grateful for the support and enthusiasm shown throughout by the general editor of the series to which this book belongs, Nicolás Fernández-Medina, and by my editors at McGill-Queen's University Press, Richard Ratzlaff, Ryan Perks, and Kathleen Fraser.

NOTE ON TRANSLATIONS

The titles of books, magazines, newspapers, articles, plays, websites, etc. published in Spanish are given only in their original form; likewise the names of commercial establishments, cafés, buildings, streets, etc. The names of key institutions, organizations, significant historical events, set phrases, etc. are given in the Spanish (and sometimes French) with, when necessary, a literal translation or explanation included in parentheses on their first appearance. Quotations originally in Spanish are normally only given in English translation, except where a word or phrase is crucial to the meaning and is therefore included in brackets. All translations are my own; in general, I have aimed for fairly literal accuracy while trying to avoid any overly stilted constructions.

CONFIGURATIONS OF A CULTURAL SCENE

INTRODUCTION

At the end of the 1910s and through the 1920s, a remarkable number of young writers, painters, sculptors, musicians, and other artists were to be found living and working in Madrid, resulting in an atmosphere of effervescence and an upsurge in creativity that has rarely been equalled. Some of them had been born in the capital city, some moved there with their families, and some came alone to study or pursue their nascent careers. During that decade of the 1920s, they were typically in their twenties or early thirties, and within the space of a few years most of them had met and become familiar with each other. The result was a youthful, tightly woven community in which it seemed that everybody knew just about everybody else.

The documentation and analysis of this community and its constituent members could be extended to all areas of cultural production, but in what follows I limit the discussion to various writers and artists and their close interactions with one another. There are practical reasons to do so, given the very considerable range of individuals and forms of artistic expression that could potentially qualify for inclusion, but there are also compelling reasons specific to this period and this cohort. During these years writers and artists often formed very close friendships, and consequently it was very rare for their social circles to be composed exclusively of practitioners of the same discipline. Indeed, on occasion some artists counted among their friends more writers than fellow artists of the same medium, and vice versa. Furthermore, we find instances of individuals firmly based in both camps – a case in point would be that of the writer-artist José Moreno Villa – and also a number of others who either started out in one camp and then transitioned to the other – as exemplified by Rafael Alberti's transformation from artist into poet and dramatist – or those whose principal identity was located in one but who made incursions into the other – prominent examples being the

drawings of Federico García Lorca or the early writings of Salvador Dalí
and Luis Buñuel.

This close-knit community can be thought of as a network or a system
with commonalities of age and involvement with some form of innovative
artistic creation. It is one that existed and developed separate from,
but still very much in contact with, the group comprised of the older,
more established figures of the period. Because of their age, status, and
professional activities, these latter individuals had progressed beyond
that phase in their lives when they were engaged in formal education,
apprenticeship, or training. Likewise, because most of them had achieved
some form of economic stability, either in their chosen field or by
pursuing more conventional careers to support their artistic callings, and
also because many of them had by this stage started to form families, their
living arrangements would normally involve a private home rather than
the kinds of rented and/or shared accommodations to which younger
individuals, of economic necessity, would typically have recourse. While
sociability certainly was an ongoing factor, with their maturing careers,
outlooks, and reputations, these older writers and artists would, in general,
have been less influenced by others and be less given to collaboration.[1]

Since Madrid was, comparatively speaking, a small city at this time,
since writers and artists only formed a very small subset of the population,
and since in this pre-technological age direct social interaction was
highly valued and much fostered,[2] it is not hard to understand how
in-person encounters between these young people would have led to
a web-like network of relationships, relationships whose nature falls
on a scale ranging from passing acquaintance to intense friendship or
amorous involvement. Further, given their professed vocations, it is not
surprising that these connections were not only personal or social but
also artistic in nature, and there are many documented cases from the
period of inspiration, influence, exchange, collaboration, and debate, as
well as rivalry and attempts to outdo one another.

The initial encounters between these writers and artists, and the
subsequent development of their relationships, would have taken place
in what were often identifiable locales. Indeed, the study of many
individual cases has shown me that there were three principal types of
sites of engagement where these contacts occurred: places where people

interacted socially, in both informal and formal contexts; places where people studied; and places where people lived communally. These loci are, I would contend, equally or sometimes more important than other points of intersection that are typically judged worthy of scholarly attention, such as publishing houses, bookstores, anthologies, little magazines, etc., where personal, face-to-face encounters are largely infrequent and in some cases non-existent. Writers and artists have always tended to congregate together, whether at royal or noble courts, in academies, or at alehouse gatherings, and the three kinds of site just listed are those most likely to be in evidence here given the period, the culture, and the age of the aspiring writers and artists who form the principal focus of the following chapters.

Networks are made up of an indeterminate number of hubs with direct or indirect linkages between them. In the present instance, each hub is an individual writer or artist,[3] the radiating linkages are the friendships or collaborations between them, while one or two "degrees of separation" exist between individuals not directly acquainted but who are nonetheless connected with others who are.[4] The sites of engagement identified above constitute the physical locales where these relationships were first forged and then deepened, but it is important to recognize that they are far from constituting mere backdrops to the event of social interaction. Rather, more often than not they are actually the reason why an initial encounter occurred and why subsequent encounters followed: because they share a course of study, certain people may go to the same lecture hall; because the same arrangements for accommodation have been made, they may live in the same residence; or because they are attracted to a certain intellectual atmosphere, they may attend the same café gathering.[5]

In *Configurations of a Cultural Scene*, then, I concentrate on a number of young artists and writers in a way that emphasizes certain aspects of their lives and careers: how they entered and began to establish themselves in the world of art and letters, the encounters that they had and the friendships that they formed along the way, and the physical places where these occurred. At the same time I recognize that these particular features are only one constitutive part of the complex overall notion of a "cultural scene," and furthermore that there exists a considerable body of often theoretical scholarship on the subject, much of it coming from writers whom one might characterize as literary sociologists. For instance, in *The Field of Cultural Production*, Pierre Bourdieu provides acute commentary on the topic, but the system that he analyzes is conceived of more in terms of the different agents involved – aspiring and consecrated writers, reviewers, publishers, editors, patrons, readership, etc. – and from the point of view of competition and the acquisition of power and the exercise of control (or what he terms "symbolic capital").[6] In *The Rules of Art* his approach is again socio-political and ultimately diachronic in nature, tracing the historical evolution of the field of French letters through the nineteenth and twentieth centuries.

What I am interested in here is different and more specifically focused: my primary concern is with the creative practitioners themselves, rather than the numerous other kinds of people and professions operating within the cultural sphere and upon whom it ultimately depends. In this study, then, I seek to examine a dynamic interpersonal network, one made up of beginning artists and writers, lying at the heart of a particular cultural scene and whose youthfulness, specifically, has often been claimed as one of its most salient features. When we think of the Roaring Twenties, the Jazz Age, *les années folles* (the crazy years), the Bright Young Things, the Lost Generation, or even the so-called Generation of 1927,[7] one of the most basic defining traits is always the youthfulness of their members. I am interested in how such a network comes into being and how it operates on both the human and the creative levels, stressing companionship, sharing, and co-operation over competition and occasional strife. Certainly, by the time we reach the middle of the 1920s we can talk of a distinctive and complex world of youthful arts and letters in Madrid within which we can discover multiple points of engagement, of lived experience, a web that grows and expands in the space of just a few years and that comes to involve an increasingly large number of individuals.[8]

The dates 1918 and 1930 bracket the period under scrutiny for a number of reasons. Modernist and avant-garde movements in art and literature had gotten under way in several European countries prior to the outbreak of the First World War: the *fauves* in France or *Die Brücke* movements in Germany, both groups dating to 1905, followed in rapid succession by Picasso's *Les Demoiselles d'Avignon* and then Braque's *Maisons à l'Estaque* and all that flowed from those two revolutionary paintings. Italian Futurism was launched in 1909, followed shortly thereafter by German Expressionism and British Imagism.⁹ However, in Spain the impact of these movements, and of the trend toward radical renewal more broadly, was not registered until years later. Some exiles and émigrés arrived in neutral Spain during the war years, though in more general terms cultural influences arriving from abroad were relatively few during this time. Thus, with the partial exception of Barcelona and the Catalan avant-garde, innovative change came late to both literary and artistic production in Spain. The poetic movement of *Ultraísmo* was launched at the beginning of 1919, and around the same time painters like Celso Lagar were beginning to experiment with strikingly new forms and artistic languages.¹⁰

The years 1918–30 were turbulent from the point of view of politics, society, and economics. The October Revolution in Russia in 1917 was followed just over a year later by the end of the First World War. Spain had maintained its neutrality throughout that conflict but was very much divided between supporters of the Allies and those of Germany and Austro-Hungary. Internally, it was beset by deep-rooted labour troubles: after the major strikes of the Semana Trágica (Tragic Week) in 1909 and again in 1917, there was another significant one in 1919. The Rif War (or Second Moroccan War) had started in the Spanish protectorate in 1911, and ten years later the Spanish suffered the so-called Desastre de Annual (Disaster of Annual), with the army routed and over ten thousand killed. Also in 1921, Prime Minister Eduardo Dato was assassinated by anarchists. All these factors, and several more, combined to bring about the bloodless coup launched by General Primo de Rivera in September 1923, whose dictatorship lasted till the beginning of 1930, having resisted gradually intensifying opposition throughout the latter half of the decade. The effects of the Wall Street crash of late 1929 were also, predictably, soon felt in Spain.

Despite all this, over this period the lives and career trajectories of most of the young Madrid-based writers and artists were not much affected. Some of them came from bourgeois families and were supported by them throughout. Others were from more disadvantaged backgrounds, and in general seem to have accepted the reduced economic means that so often are the lot of the bohemian artist. Some individuals were interested in politics and contributed to contemporary debates – as was the case with Ernesto Giménez Caballero, for example[11] – but the majority were largely apolitical, which is why political and economic considerations do not figure more prominently in this study. Doubtless current events were one of the subjects discussed during informal conversations among writers and artists, but rarely were they determinative in affecting life choices or career paths. This would change toward the end of the decade, with the increase in resistance to Primo coming (in part) from student, professorial, and intellectual circles, among others. And yet widespread politicization, and its reflection in literary and artistic production, would really only occur with the advent of the Second Republic in 1931.

The structure of this book is fairly straightforward. Chapter 1 provides a documentary survey of the many possible sites of engagement. These are the places where encounters *could* occur and friendships *could* develop. As might be expected, not all of the relationships described in subsequent chapters can be traced back to all the locales first mentioned here; there is no guarantee that circumstances will combine to produce the necessary spark, and moreover, our biographical knowledge of all but the most famous figures of the period is still highly incomplete.

Chapters 2 through 6 offer five diverse case studies based on the application of the approach described in the preceding pages. The case studies that I have chosen are representative in their variety, and they appear here for several reasons: the individuals involved, while they were all important players on the cultural scene, have not received the close attention previously reserved for those most squarely in the limelight; each case showcases, to varying degrees, some form(s) of interaction and/or interconnectedness between writers and artists; some of them emphasize place ("sites of engagement") and others the individual or individuals involved (the network "hubs"); several foreground artists and some of them foreground writers; and finally, many of the individuals profiled here knew one another, and all of them would at the very least have been aware of the others, given that they were all part of the cultural fabric of 1920s Madrid.

As regards the various loci of social interaction, it is clear that informal contact occurred chiefly at *tertulias*.[12] The great majority of these were held in cafés, but sometimes at magazines' editorial offices, artists' studios, and other such suitable locations, and also occasionally in private homes. More formal contact occurred at lectures, readings, recitals, meetings, art openings, homage banquets, and other similar events, sponsored by entities such as the Ateneo de Madrid (Athenaeum of Madrid), the Residencia de Estudiantes (Residence for Students), the Residencia de Señoritas (Residence for Women Students), the Lyceum Club Femenino (Women's Lyceum Club), state and municipal museums, private art galleries, and other institutions and organizations. Sites of study include the university in Madrid, the Universidad Central, as well as colleges, professional schools, conservatories, research centres, and various other institutions; places of residence were principally boarding houses (*pensiones*) and state- or privately administered student residences.

In my choice of subjects, I have avoided the most famous writers and artists of the time (thus, Lorca and Dalí appear only as "supporting characters") in order to foreground other figures of substance who have previously received less critical scrutiny. Likewise, by far the most obvious selection for a site of engagement would have been the Residencia de Estudiantes, where students lived, studied, and socialized, all in a single locale, but because it has already received the lion's share of attention, I prefer to diversify the scope of my treatment. Chapter 2, then, is concerned with the Uruguayan artist Rafael Barradas and the *tertulia* with which he was associated, held at the Café de Oriente in the Atocha neighbourhood. Barradas's circle of friends and his fellow *tertulia* members illustrate particularly well the radiating pattern mentioned above. Furthermore, his table at the Café de Oriente was the locus where many of their most important discussions took place, where Barradas's ideas were formulated and reformulated, where new projects were conceived, and new friendships forged. The principal focus in chapter 3 is the studio located on the top floor of an apartment building in the Pasaje de la Alhambra (an alleyway with courtyard) in the centre of Madrid, and the two painters who occupied that space: Manuel Ángeles Ortiz and Julio Moisés. During Ortiz's time in the studio, it became the "hang-out place" for friends from

Granada who were either living in or visiting Madrid. When Moisés later took it over, it became the home of a "free academy," and consequently an even greater number of people passed through, attending lessons but again also socializing in and around that specific locale.

Chapter 4 is interested in the intersection of two locations and institutions, one of learning and one of residence, respectively: the Escuela Especial de Pintura, Escultura y Grabado (Special School for Painting, Sculpture, and Engraving – the Madrid art conservatory) and the Residencia de Señoritas (the equivalent for women of the Residencia de Estudiantes). The Escuela Especial had a certain percentage of women students studying there, and while many of them lived with their families in Madrid, a few found accommodation at the Residencia de Señoritas. It is hard to categorize Gabriel García Maroto, the subject of chapter 5. While he might be remembered today primarily as an artist, he was also a very prolific writer, critic, printer, and publisher, as well as playing a number of other secondary roles throughout the decade. Of the figures treated here, he comes closest to that model – personified by José Moreno Villa – of an individual with one foot planted firmly in each of the principal camps of cultural production, and hence tending to dissolve the generic classifications of "writer" and "artist." Finally, chapter 6 addresses the trajectory and vicissitudes during the latter half of the 1920s of the close friendship, romantic relationship, and collaboration between the artist Maruja Mallo and the writer Rafael Alberti (who during his first years in Madrid had professed a calling as a painter).

There are not many studies of the period that approximate this particular kind of approach.[13] One that comes quite close is Miguel García-Posada's *Acelerado sueño*. Although his avowed purpose, stated in the subtitle, is to write a "memoir" of the poets associated with the so-called Generation of 1927,[14] he tends to stress Andalusia and, within Andalusia, the city of Málaga, where Moreno Villa, Vicente Aleixandre, Emilio Prados, José María Hinojosa, and Manuel Altolaguirre all lived during their childhoods, and Lorca and Alberti spent some holidays.[15] The biographical documentation that Posada provides therefore allows the reader to follow the life experiences of the poet José María Hinojosa, and to extrapolate the multiple connections with other writers and artists that he made as he moved between Málaga, Madrid, and Paris.

As its title indicates, Aranzázu Ascunce's *Barcelona and Madrid: Social Networks of the Avant-Garde* concentrates on the two cities and the ties that existed in avant-garde circles between them in the 1920s. The network theory deployed in that monograph is drawn from the worlds of business, human resources, and sociology,[16] though as Ascunce acknowledges, "network analysis, in the strictest sense of the discipline, is much more analytical than what I intend to do here."[17] Ascunce's principal aim is to question the idea of separate avant-garde cultures in Castilian Madrid and Catalan Barcelona, and consequently she is much interested in the "bridge figures"[18] who she says connected the poles of the two cities. Naturally enough, what underpins many of the contacts and connections are encounters, acquaintanceships, friendships, and collaborations between certain individuals, as exemplified in the "cluster" of Federico García Lorca, Rafael Barradas, and Sebastià Gasch.[19] However, the three substantive chapters (chapters 4–6) devoted to particular nodal points[20] take as their objects of study little magazines, certain art exhibitions (held in 1925, 1926, 1929), and Ernesto Giménez Caballero, his magazine *La Gaceta Literaria*, and events that he and it sponsored. Ascunce describes magazines as "centers of information and its dissemination,"[21] and argues that "avant-garde art shows functioned as pivotal moments for contact, knowledge, education, and exchange among the members of the artistic and literary vanguard networks of Barcelona and Madrid."[22] However, as proposed above, little magazines mainly provided fora for indirect, mediated contact, with few if any face-to-face encounters. Similarly, I would contend that showing work at an art exhibition functioned in a way more analogous to the publication of a poem, article, or book than to an extended conversation at a *tertulia*. As a result, the final chapter of Ascunce's book, in which she focuses on Giménez Caballero's many and diverse interactions in person and in print with a number of Catalan writers, entrepreneurs, and politicians, comes closest to the sort of historical reconstruction that interests me here.

Alison Sinclair's book *Trafficking Knowledge in Early Twentieth-Century Spain* can also be read profitably in parallel with the two volumes just mentioned. Ultimately, her focus is more international, centring as it does on the relationship between Spain and other countries, but her study of how Spanish institutions, intellectuals, writers, and artists received influences from abroad, and the analysis, in her terminology, of the "centres of exchange" through which these were transmitted and negotiated, complements my examination of the "sites of engagement" for writers and artists. Sinclair also points out that "it would be impossible to chart the various cross-relations of individuals and institutions in Spain in the early decades of the twentieth century."[23] Taken as a blanket statement about the feasibility of exhaustive, comprehensive coverage, one must inevitably agree, because of the sheer numbers involved. And yet, that is also precisely why I believe that case studies are the best solution: they allow us to tunnel laterally and longitudinally, through space and time, into the multiple interrelations of notable artists and writers and the social clusters in which they were embedded.

CHAPTER 1

SITES OF ENGAGEMENT

Social Interaction

Many first encounters occur, and many pre-existing friendships deepen, at gathering places where people come to interact socially. Sometimes people will seek them out with the sole or principal purpose of seeing and talking with others, while on other occasions social interaction is more a by-product of the nature of the event (for example, the opening of an art exhibition). Likewise, these gatherings exist on a sliding scale between the informal and the formal, on a spectrum that runs from an entirely impromptu encounter all the way to attendance at a highly structured ceremony with a predetermined guest list.

In this section, I review a number of the leading sites and events where innumerable instances of sociability took place.[1] For many, the deliberate coming together of a number of literary and/or artistic figures for the purpose of conversation may be most closely associated with the salon, a practice that flourished in Italy and France for several centuries and which was frequently organized and hosted by women. A well-known and more recent example would be Gertrude Stein's Saturday evening salon in Paris.[2] In Spain the salon tradition was never as strong as in some other European countries, but we should note an important example in the forum hosted by Carmen de Burgos during the 1910s.[3] One of the regulars at those gatherings, Rafael Cansinos Assens, provides a number of details: they were held on Wednesday afternoons, in her apartments on calle Eguilaz and later on calle San Bernardo, and brought together men and women of different ages and professions, though principally writers.[4] With his unique perspective and style, Cansinos offers his evocative versions of various conversations that he either participated in or overheard.

THE *TERTULIA* AND THE CAFÉ

In Spain, the most characteristic gathering of this sort is the *tertulia*, which in turn is associated primarily with the café, though a number of other kinds of site could also host *tertulias*.[5] The *tertulia* admits of no absolute definition. It tended to involve a fairly regular group of people, some of them perhaps the "core" members and others more occasional participants, who would normally meet at the same place in order to engage in some mix of conversation, discussion, and the exchange of recent news and gossip. Over time, new members might join, often introduced by a current member, and others might leave. Individuals often belonged to several *tertulias*. Many *tertulias* revolved around a central figure, a leader or head who might stamp a distinctive character on the gatherings, though sometimes there could also be two principal figures, and sometimes none at all. Members might all belong to one profession or similar professions, or there might be a considerable mix of occupations and interests. The site where they met was fixed, usually a café, though a *tertulia* might move for various reasons (e.g., closing of the establishment, change of opening hours, change of proprietorship, or change of clientele) to a different location.[6] Some popular Madrid cafés (e.g., La Granja El Henar) hosted several *tertulias* that were associated with different sets of tables or areas within the commercial space. Commonly a *tertulia* would meet weekly or daily. Some *tertulias* had a more or less fixed start time, some maintained a kind of unspoken consensus so that members knew when attendance would reach its peak, and some operated on a more casual, drop-in basis over the course of the day and/or night. There were *tertulias* that met after lunch, in the afternoon, evening, or late at night.

In England, coffee houses were common in the seventeenth and eighteenth centuries, but gradually gave way in popularity to the tea house. In Austria – specifically Vienna – the height of the coffee house came later, starting at the end of the seventeenth century and only peaking around 1900. Not surprisingly, then, scholars interested in this phenomenon have focused on Austria, along with France and to a lesser extent Italy.[7] A recent study also explores the contribution of coffee houses to the development of Jewish culture in six diverse cities – Odessa, Warsaw, Vienna, Berlin, New York, and Tel Aviv–Jaffa – over several decades in the earlier part of the twentieth century.[8] As far as Spain is concerned, Bonet Correa has documented the appearance of cafés there, beginning toward the end of the eighteenth century.[9] From that point on we witness a steady rise in popularity through the nineteenth century, with the zenith of café culture coming in the last third of that century and the first years after 1900. By the 1920s, fashions had begun to change, with the emergence of the beer-oriented *cervecería* (bar or beer hall), the modern bar (*bar americano*) that served cocktails, and the tea room (*salón de té*), though many cafés endured. *Tertulia* culture was perhaps starting to decline in the 1930s, though the near total societal rupture caused by the outbreak of civil war in July 1936 makes the identification of a long-term trend problematic.

The fundamental difficulty with the study of *tertulia* culture is the breadth and depth of the topic, as it encompasses more than two hundred years and involves hundreds of *tertulias* with thousands of members. Ramón Gómez de la Serna was a pioneer in this field: in 1924 he published an extensive and wide-ranging history and survey of cafés and *tertulias*, a project that occupied the first third of his *La sagrada cripta de Pombo*.[10] As someone who mythologized the notion of the *tertulia*, as well as his own gathering, held on Saturday evenings at the Antiguo café y botillería de Pombo (Pombo's Old Café and Liquor Store), Gómez de la Serna also was acutely aware of the long and varied tradition into which he was inscribing himself. Later in the same decade a journalist – Santiago de la Cruz – also realized the importance of these groups. He published a series of more than a dozen articles that appeared in the newspaper *Heraldo de Madrid* from August to November 1929, dedicating each one to a café and its corresponding *tertulia*.[11]

In a volume of literary memoirs from 1941, Manuel Forcada Cabanellas includes a chapter on cafés and their *tertulias*; after briefly evoking several, along with their principal members, he describes in more detail those who met at Pombo and El Colonial.[12] In other chapters there are also short but tantalizing references to a number of other places and groups, as well as the Madrid Ateneo. In the post–Civil War period, two small books by Antonio Velasco Zazo demonstrate acutely the kinds of methodological problems mentioned above. His volume on cafés (1943) overlaps with the later one on *tertulias* (1952), and both present overwhelming lists of names, people, and places, with very little concrete historical context.[13] As with later books, these are evidently based mainly on first-hand familiarity, and to some degree also on transmitted memories, so they end up being more broadly evocative than strictly documentary in nature. This points to another basic problem with research on *tertulias* – namely, the lack of reliable, detailed sources. Obviously, neither cafés nor *tertulias* kept records, registers, or journals,[14] their meetings were not documented in official archives or even noted in newspaper announcements, so what sketchy information is available derives from personal or transmitted reminiscences, or from passing references in memoirs or sets of correspondence. As Bonet Correa observes, "For café specialists only the few authors of memoirs, of almanacs, of city guides and travel books provide them with the necessary pieces of information,"[15] though "necessary" is overly optimistic: while pertinent, the information to be gleaned is always far from adequate.

Employing a somewhat more scholarly approach, Gallego Morell chose to focus exclusively on *tertulias* from an earlier period,[16] while Pérez Ferrero, who was a direct participant in the cultural scene of the 1920s, was able to offer his own first-hand accounts.[17] Unfortunately, most of the more modern works on the subject follow the catalogue-like pattern described above. Thus Tudela's book abounds in names of cafés and names of *tertulia* members, but the time frames involved are indicated only very broadly, and no sources are cited anywhere in the volume.[18] Díaz's book is much the same, and while Río López's offers rather more solid information and a greater array of dates and locations, the characteristic feature of dozens and dozens of café names also reappears here.[19] Espina's posthumously collected writings concentrate on the different types of sites where *tertulias* might take place, and focus attention on the nineteenth and early twentieth centuries, but they touch on the bohemian 1920s only briefly and sporadically.[20] Díaz-Playa addresses a broader topic, the proverbial loquacity of Spaniards, and dedicates one chapter to *tertulias*.[21] Toral Madariaga updates the discussion somewhat with a book on *tertulia*-like gatherings, often attached to news programs, which are broadcast over the radio.[22] Doubtless there are many small nuggets of information here for researchers to compile, but they still fall far short of providing anything like a complete, historically grounded picture.

One way to tackle the formless sea of incomplete information is to concentrate exclusively on the history of just one *tertulia* or café. The Café Gijón has been the primary recipient of this kind of treatment, and consequently we have more detailed data about this establishment than any other, with the possible exception of Pombo.[23] Unfortunately, the Gijón, founded in 1888, was far from the most important café or meeting place in the 1920s, and only achieved its now iconic status during the Civil War and in the postwar period. Although the Pombo café is treated in many studies about Gómez de la Serna, it has only very recently been the subject of an entire monograph, by Alaminos López.[24] One book has also been dedicated to another important café, the Lyon d'Or (founded in 1898).[25]

The most serious and extensive panoramic work to date is Bonet Correa's *Los cafés históricos*, which reprints his "Discurso de recepción en la Real Academia de Bellas Artes de San Fernando" of 1987 and then follows it with a much longer treatment of the topic.[26] The "Discurso" provides a rapid treatment of coffee and coffeehouses in Europe before turning its attention to the history of the café in Spain from the eighteenth to the twentieth centuries. Bonet Correa also mentions the different modalities of the establishment, like the *café suizo* (Swiss café), the *café cantante* (café with singer[s], often flamenco), the *café concierto* (café with music), the *cafetín* (the small/local café), and so on. Part 2 of Bonet Correa's book offers a much more comprehensive treatment of essentially the same topics. He also picks out some individual cafés and the people associated with them for specific coverage.

Palomares-Salas includes in his recent study a useful chapter on the function and representation of cafés and *tertulias* during precisely the period that concerns us here.[27] Finally, one very valuable source is the website maintained by M.R. Giménez (http://antiguoscafesde madrid.blogspot.com/). Here, individual posts provide information on a single café, its history, its location, and the *tertulia* members associated with it. The internet-based format also allows for the posting of many period photographs.

Overall, when one charts the location of these cafés on a city plan of Madrid, it becomes strikingly clear how many of them were clustered around the Puerta del Sol, the city's main square, with several located in the plaza itself and numerous others in the various streets that lead off from it in different directions. Much café life was therefore concentrated in a small and highly walkable area in the very centre of the capital.

In the 1920s, café *tertulias* were the single most important element in the collective social life of writers and artists. Young, aspiring individuals would meet others with similar experiences and struggles, and the *tertulia* also often served as the place where they could be introduced to established figures, who might then take an interest in them and their work. During the discussions, opinions could be aired, theories tried out, and new poems tested on a sympathetic audience; plans for events, for the founding of little magazines, and for other initiatives emerged and crystallized in the context of an infectious group enthusiasm; news of cutting-edge ideas, recently published books, and upcoming exhibitions could be acquired. In short, it was a site not only of relaxation but also for the sharing of information and inspiration.

THE *TERTULIA* IN OTHER LOCALES

Although the *tertulia* and the café are intimately linked, *tertulia*-like gatherings certainly occurred before the emergence of the café itself, and over the last two hundred years many *tertulias* were also held in other locations. Antonio Espina reviews some of these, essentially any spot, indoors or outdoors, where a certain number of people could congregate and converse.[28] Among many such places and gatherings, he mentions *tertulias* in the open air, as, for instance, in a park or square; pleasure gardens (*jardines de recreo*);[29] private academies; social centres known as *casinos*;[30] various clubs, associations, or societies that adopted the name of athenaeums (particularly the Ateneo de Madrid), circles (particularly the Círculo de Bellas Artes, a centre for the fine arts), or lyceums (e.g., the Lyceum Club Femenino) – to say nothing of the constellation of taverns, inns, bars, and popular eateries (with another complex and overlapping nomenclature: *tabernas* [taverns], *botillerías* [liquor stores often also selling wine refills from the barrel], *mesones* [taverns/inns], *posadas* [inns], *figones* [modest cafés], *fondas* [modest eating spots], *ventas* [inns/taverns], *ventorrillos* [small inns/roadhouses], etc.).[31]

Several kinds of locale that were neither entirely public (such as the café) nor entirely private (an individual's home) also functioned as sites for *tertulias*. The artist's studio is a good example. Many young artists shared their space with one or more of their colleagues, while established figures were able to afford their own work area. Either way, such a bohemian environment provided an excellent environment for a *tertulia*. These studio-based *tertulias* could be important and were quite common. Victorina Durán, for example, gives a graphic description of the relaxed and distinctly louche atmosphere at Romero de Torres's workspace,[32] while some of the young painters associated with the Academia Libre (Free Academy) of Julio Moisés also frequented *tertulias* at shared studios on the Travesía del Horno de la Mata and on the Paseo del Prado.[33]

The offices of various magazines sometimes had large rooms that could function as the sites of *tertulias*, with many attendees being either members of a given magazine's editorial board or regular contributors. The gathering held at the headquarters of the *Revista de Occidente* was particularly famous; a Monday afternoon *tertulia* associated with *Cervantes* is also documented,[34] and no doubt there were others. Similarly, space in the editorial offices of a newspaper could fulfill an identical purpose: there was a room at *La Tribuna* that some of the journalists dubbed Atenas (Athens), and Ramón Gómez de la Serna formed a *tertulia* there with other staff members immediately before founding Pombo.[35] Cansinos Assens gives a lengthy account of the meetings held in the main office of *El Motín*, where the journalists were joined by friends and acquaintances with similar literary or political leanings.[36]

Other kinds of establishments were also equipped with rooms where *tertulias* could be held. Many theatres had a common space – often referred to as a *saloncillo* (small private room) – where playwrights and actors tended to congregate.[37] The *saloncillo* of the Teatro Español, on the Plaza de Santa Ana, is often mentioned,[38] as well as similar ones at the Teatro de la Princesa, Comedia, Cómico, Eslava, Lara, Apolo, and Zarzuela. Likewise, the back rooms or storerooms of some shops – known as the *trastienda* – could serve a similar function, and more than one bookshop was home to a *tertulia*.[39]

Finally, we need to mention *tertulia*-like gatherings in people's homes. These were not common, especially since, as noted above, the salon tradition was not strong and had largely petered out by the 1910s. But they did exist, some perhaps as a result of frugality, others because of unusual hospitality. As a young man, Ricardo Baeza held an impromptu *tertulia* in his lodgings on calle Campomanes.[40] When Vicente Huidobro arrived in Madrid in the summer of 1918, he took an apartment at Plaza de Oriente, 6,[41] and the fact that he invited Guillermo de Torre and others to his home surprised the young man:

> In that flat with light wood furniture and pleasant light I had my first contact with South American domestic hospitality. This was an event that was in no way extraordinary in and of itself, but much more exceptional, comparatively speaking, than one might suppose, for in a city like Madrid, where social life, and even more so literary life, was carried on solely in the cafés, with the rigorous exclusion and permanent concealment of people's residences, the fact that a writer should invite you to his home was indeed far from usual, and even more so that, breaking with the established pattern of all-male attendance ... , he should include in his gatherings individuals of the fair sex.[42]

As with Carmen de Burgos before her, Concha Espina held a salon-like *tertulia* at her home at calle Goya, 77, on Wednesdays. Darío Pérez reports that Cansinos Assens was a frequent and highly esteemed visitor at these events;[43] Fernández Gallo suggests that the idea of one fixed day per week was suggested to her by a friend, María de Hazas, in order that she might have the other days to dedicate to her writing, and she notes that the day appeared on the reverse of her calling cards.[44]

As Torre indicates, women rarely attended café *tertulias*. Indeed, at many such gatherings, they were no doubt explicitly made to feel unwelcome, but more generally it was just not a common social practice. Some of the more adventurous young women of the time did participate, of course, including Victorina Durán, Rosa Chacel, Concha Méndez, Maruja Mallo, and Remedios Varo.[45] In another gesture of nonconformity, the González Rodríguez sisters became members of Buñuel's Orden de Toledo (Order of Toledo, an imaginary order of knights), whose exclusivity and group mentality was evidence of its strong links with the *tertulia* ethos (see chapter 4). This may also go some way toward explaining the persistence of the salon-like *tertulia* presided over by women writers such as Burgos and Espina.

Another variant became possible as of late 1926 with the foundation of the Lyceum Club Femenino (initially installed in the so-called Casa de las Siete Chimeneas, bordered by calle Colmenares, calle de las Infantas, and the Plaza del Rey, and subsequently located at calle San Marcos, 44). The new club was organized into seven sections covering literature, sciences, visual and industrial arts,[46] social concerns, music, international affairs, and Hispano-American culture and politics, each of which had a committee and arranged a variety of activities.[47] But another less high-profile amenity that the club was able to offer its members was daily afternoon teas in a dedicated *sala de té* (tea room).[48] Durán recounts how the members split off into groups that congregated at different tables. The "regulars" at Durán's table were Trudi Araquistáin, María Baeza, Carmen de Mesa, Isabel Espada, Julia Meaba, and Matilde Calvo Rodero, and they were sometimes joined there by others.[49] How these "teas" operated, then, was basically no different from a *tertulia*, save that they were held in a members' club with limited access rather than a public café.[50]

FORMAL SOCIAL EVENTS

Although the *tertulia* operated within certain boundaries, it still had a free-flowing nature: who attended on a given day, how long they spent there, what was talked about, etc. – these features were rarely predetermined. Furthermore, the *tertulia* spread over months and years, on a daily or weekly basis. However, there were many other times when people had cause to come together and interact socially, on more formal or "structured" occasions where that social interaction was not the explicit or primary goal of the event but rather a by-product of it; these occasions were usually "one-off" occurrences, or at most infrequent and sporadic.

There were, for instance, a great many lectures, readings, and recitals given at many different locales; attendance at such events was for many as much a form of entertainment as it was one of self-education. It is easy to imagine that before and particularly after such a gathering, groups of friends or of people with similar interests might form informally in a vestibule or lobby, or indeed spill out into a nearby café, perhaps initially to discuss what they had just heard, but then quite possibly diversifying to other topics.

Another constant on the cultural landscape was art openings. There were numerous venues for exhibitions, which tended to run for ten days or, most typically, two weeks, so there were many "inaugurations" of shows throughout the year. Usually there would be some kind of reception to mark the opening, with the presence of the artist and perhaps other luminaries; occasionally speeches were made. Such events were inevitably social, with groups of people forming and re-forming, in the normal way found at receptions and cocktail parties, with discussions of the work on display and then often topics beyond that.

Homage banquets constitute a third important category. These gatherings – lunches or sometimes dinners – were a very frequent event during this period. They marked a range of special occasions, often the publication of a book, the premiere of a play, the launching of a new magazine, or the successful conclusion of an art exhibition, but also the visit of a distinguished figure from out of town or abroad, to mark the departure of a local luminary, and a host of other noteworthy occurrences. Often an organizing committee would be formed, whose job it was to coordinate the event, and tickets for the banquet would be put on sale by the restaurant that was to serve as host venue or at other suitable locations. Newspapers were filled with announcements of upcoming homages, and they also covered the event itself, often in great detail if the honouree were considered important enough. These, therefore, would have been the site of much conversation among attendees, as well as the occasion for initial encounters between individuals seated beside each other.

Ramón Gómez de la Serna made something of an art form out of the practice, embroidering on it and even parodying it. Among his more memorable stunts were the "Ágape en honor de Fígaro," held at the Fornos restaurant on 24 March 1909,[51] and then at Pombo the "Banquete a todos los pombianos por orden alfabético" on 14 October 1920, the "Banquete en honor de Don Nadie" on 6 May 1922,[52] the "Primer lectisternio pombiano" on 17 October 1922, and the "Banquete de fisonomías y trajes de época, o cena de antepasados" on 13 February 1923.[53] In a similar vein, on 12 March 1923 a banquet was held for Gómez de la Serna at the Lhardy restaurant, while simultaneously a number of his friends staged a less costly "budget version" at the Oro del Rhin restaurant; during the proceedings Gómez de la Serna dashed from one event to the other transported in a motorcycle sidecar.[54] Still, Ramón was not alone in dreaming up new and surprising ways to celebrate these congratulatory meals, as is demonstrated by the "Banquete en un vagón de ferrocarril" (Banquet in a Railway Carriage) offered on 17 January 1923 to Eduardo Zamacois by the Sindicato de Actores Españoles for his book *Memorias de un vagón de ferrocarril*.

Indeed, the vogue for banquets reached such a fever pitch that a months-long polemic broke out on the subject in 1923. It led to the creation of the semi-serious "Liga contra el banquete" (League against Banquets) headed by Mariano Benlliure, who declared himself to be against this spate of self-serving homages, the true purpose of which, he contended, was mutual promotion.[55] Gómez de la Serna was the principal target, accused of fomenting an epidemic of what *El Sol* termed "banquetmania." In response to Benlliure's formal announcement of the Liga in March, April became "the Month of Banquets," with both sides intensifying their publication of newspaper articles on the subject. Eventually, the debate collapsed under its own weight, with a couple more middle-of-the-road articles suggesting compromises. On the one hand, the whole affair demonstrates the precarious distinction between seriousness and ironic parody, but on the other it does show how conscious people were of the proliferation of banquets and of the different and not always altruistic functions that they served.

SPECIFIC CULTURAL ORGANIZATIONS

The Ateneo de Madrid presents a very important case, because of the multiple functions that it combined in a single institution and locale. It was founded in 1835 as the Ateneo Científico y Literario (Scientific and Literary Athenaeum), occupying a building – the Antigua Casa de Abrantes – at calle del Prado, 28.[56] This was just two years after the demise of the absolutist king Fernando VII and the succession of Isabel II; the Ateneo de Madrid was created out of the earlier Ateneo Español, which had functioned briefly during the so-called three-year liberal period (*trienio liberal*) of 1820–23, during Fernando's reign. In 1860 it adopted its current full name of Ateneo Científico, Literario y Artístico (Scientific, Literary and Artistic Athenaeum). Over the period 1835 to 1884 it was based at various addresses; in that latter year it was finally able to occupy new, purpose-built headquarters at calle del Prado, 21, where it remains today.[57] By the 1920s, besides the governing body, the following sections had been established: Moral and Political Sciences, Natural, Physical, and Mathematical Sciences, Literature, Historical Sciences, Philosophy, Visual Arts, Music, Ibero-American, Pedagogy, and Medicine, each with a committee structure of several administrative officers. Among its many facilities, the most notable was its remarkable library and reading rooms, which many favoured over the Biblioteca Nacional (National Library) for its unusually long opening hours, the range of its collection, and the up-to-date books and magazines that it received. In addition, there was the main auditorium – the Salón de Actos, plus a small exhibition space referred to in the press as the *saloncillo*, other multi-purpose rooms, and a space, nicknamed La Cacharrería (literally, the crockery shop), suitable for smaller talks but whose main purpose was to host *tertulias*. The range of events organized there was remarkable, not only for their number but also for the openness to "newfangled" ideas in all of the section areas; thus, the *ultraísta* group held one of their *veladas* (soirees) there, and many young and unrecognized artists had their first exhibition there.

It was a private institution, and to join one had to be nominated by two existing members, but the membership was large and quite diverse; notably, women were able to become members, and indeed a good number did.[58] There was something going on there almost every day, and so the chances of intersecting with friends and acquaintances were very high.[59] Very close by, at calle del Prado, 16, at the confluence of calle del Prado and calle del León, stood the Café del Prado, which had its own *tertulias* but which also was a convenient stopping-off point for people leaving the Ateneo.

The Círculo de Bellas Artes was founded in 1880 by a small group of artists who met at a *tertulia* at the Café Suizo in Madrid, and it was initially located at calle del Barquillo, 5 (1880–82), before subsequently occupying a variety of other premises. From 1913 to 1926, it was situated at calle de Alcalá, 14, in the iconic Palacio de la Equitativa, where room had become available thanks to the Casino de Madrid's move to new quarters. Here, the Círculo was close to the Puerta del Sol and very close to the Real Academia de Bellas Artes de San Fernando (Royal Academy of Fine Arts of San Fernando). However, needing greater space for its many exhibitions, in November 1916 it established a separate "Salón Permanente" on the ground floor of the Palace Hotel, located at Plaza de las Cortes, 4 (since renumbered), which operated until 1926. After experiencing a series of economic ups and downs, the Círculo was able, thanks to the introduction of gambling at the beginning of the twentieth century, to finance the construction of the current structure at calle de Alcalá, 42, which it moved into in 1926 and still occupies today.

The Círculo functioned as a social and cultural centre. Its Carnival balls, for which it ran yearly poster competitions, were famous, and there were also many concerts and lectures. It offered a range of free art lessons, including life drawing and engraving, mostly in the evenings. There was a library and space for *tertulias*. It was perhaps most in the news for the very numerous exhibitions that it sponsored, a good number of which constituted cultural or artistic landmarks of one sort or another. The new building, opened toward the end of 1926, was ambitiously large and luxurious and offered a wide range of facilities. There was exhibition space (the Sala Goya), six workshops, five studios, lecture halls, a theatre, library, reading rooms, study rooms, rooms designated for *tertulias*, as well as a bar, restaurant, private dining rooms, a ballroom, a rooftop terrace, a room for gambling (although banned during the Primo de Rivera dictatorship), a swimming pool, chess rooms, billiard rooms, a barber, hot and steam baths, manicure and massage facilities, gymnasium, rooms for fencing, radio installations, and so on.[60]

The first PEN Club was established in London in late 1921; the PEN Club Español was founded in Madrid in the summer of 1922. A number of people were involved in this endeavour, including Ramiro de Maeztu, Melchor de Almagro San Martín, Enrique de Mesa, Ramón Pérez de Ayala, Enrique Díez-Canedo, José María Salaverría, and Melchor Fernández Almagro. They chose Azorín to be the first president, while Ramón Gómez de la Serna occupied a post that he later described as "sommelier secretary" (*secretario sumiller*).[61] Gregorio Marañón and Pérez de Ayala were later sent to a meeting in London as representatives of the Madrid branch. Its inaugural session took place at the Lhardy restaurant on 5 July 1922, and other gatherings followed, approximately one per month, either at Lhardy or other restaurants (Hotel de París,

Molinero-Sicilia, etc.). In a sense, then, the way the Spanish PEN Club operated was just a variation on the banquet culture described above. Two printed lists of members were made, the first in 1922 showing 115 members, the second growing a year later to 155.[62] They were all writers and/or journalists; they did span a wide age range, but the majority were established figures. This first incarnation of a Madrid branch of PEN International did not thrive; it struggled on, holding events of decreasing frequency, through to 1925. Many writers who were not members were critical of it, especially for its exclusivity, economic and otherwise (the expensive meals in well-known restaurants, the overwhelming presence of establishment figures).[63] Its relatively brief existence overlapped with the polemic about banquets, in which, as we saw, Gómez de la Serna was also a central figure, and the necessary atmosphere of community and solidarity within the club failed to materialize.[64] Gómez de la Serna offers a very positive account of confraternity at the first meeting, only to then acknowledge that significant splits soon began to appear.[65]

Places of Study

Many young writers and artists followed some kind of program of higher education. In certain cases, this would be directly connected with their chosen vocation – art, music, theatre – while in other instances they would be engaged in some sort of study in deference to parental wishes or pressure while pursuing at the same time their own creative interests. This being the case, it is understandable that some initial encounters, along with the development of pre-existing friendships, would have occurred in the halls, classrooms, corridors, or general environs of places of learning.

UNIVERSIDAD CENTRAL

In the 1920s and '30s, Madrid had just one university, the Universidad Central. After the death of Fernando VII, the Universidad de Madrid opened in fall 1836 with a limited range of areas of study that had been transferred from the Universidad de Alcalá.[66] Alcalá was gradually reduced in size before being shut down in 1843. Meanwhile, the university in Madrid grew; various additional faculties were installed in temporary quarters, including the so-called Noviciado de los Jesuitas, on calle San

Bernardo. In 1842, this building – also known as the Caserón de San Bernardo – was designated as the main centre of operations, which led to a variety of changes involving the demolition of certain parts of the original Noviciado (which since disentailment had been used as a barracks) and the construction and extension of several others, at different times over the period 1842–81.

Major reforms in 1845 (under the banner of the Plan Pidal) led to significant changes to university admissions, the organization of university studies, and the centralization of the granting of advanced (doctoral) degrees, as well as a change of name, with the institution henceforth called the Universidad Literaria de Madrid; its catchment area was also expanded to include the provinces of Madrid, Toledo, Ciudad Real, Cuenca, Guadalajara, Ávila (soon reassigned to Salamanca), and Segovia.[67] In 1847, the Faculty of Philosophy was established as a kind of catch-all for studies not falling within the purview of law or medicine; it was divided into four sections covering literature, philosophy, natural sciences, and physical and mathematical sciences, though the latter two were subsequently split off into their own stand-alone faculties. Another name change – the school having been rechristened Universidad Central in the fall of 1850 – endured until 1970.[68] In 1859, six faculties were established: those of Law, Sciences, Philosophy and Letters, Medicine, Pharmacy, and Theology.[69] Notable, too, was the reactionary decree (the Decreto Orovio) enacted in the wake of the restoration of the monarchy in 1875, which led to the exodus from the university of many liberal professors and, months later, to the foundation of the Institución Libre de Enseñanza (Free Institution for Education). A subsequent law of 1885 established freedom of teaching for university professors, soothing some tensions between the remaining professors and the administration. The reformist legislation known as the Plan Silió of 1919 granted autonomy to universities, but governmental instability prevented its implementation, a process that in any case was soon rendered moot by the arrival of the Primo de Rivera dictatorship in 1923. However, it was under Primo that construction started, in 1929, on the new university campus in Moncloa, the Ciudad Universitaria, an ambitious building plan that continued on into the 1930s, but whose completion was interrupted by the outbreak of civil war.[70]

Through much of the nineteenth and twentieth centuries, it was extremely common for students, especially those with no clear career plans, to "hedge their bets" and enroll in degree programs in both law and philosophy and letters. As far as literary study was concerned, the Faculty of Philosophy and Letters was reorganized in 1900 and divided into three sections covering philosophy, literature, and historical studies. Common subjects for the three tracks leading to a four-year *licenciatura* (bachelor's degree) were established. In addition, the Escuela Superior de Diplomática (Higher School of Diplomatics, for training librarians, archivists, etc.) was dissolved and its various offerings folded into the newly reorganized faculty. Further revisions to the Faculty of Philosophy and Letters followed in 1913 and 1928, the latter creating separate degrees in philosophy, literature, and history. For the 1920–21 academic year, there was a total of 889 students enrolled in the faculty, though only 330 were "official" students while 559 were preparing for exams on their own. Of the 889, 831 were men and 58 women. Only twenty-three degrees were conferred. A decade later, in 1930–31, there was a total of 1,727 students in this faculty, of whom just 539 were officially enrolled; of those 539, 304 were men and 235 were women. Fifty-eight degrees were conferred.[71] Guillermo de Torre specifically locates in the university cloisters a couple of his first encounters with the other young writers José Quiroga Pla and Juan Chabás.[72]

ART, MUSIC, AND DRAMA

The official art conservatory in Madrid was the Escuela Especial de Pintura, Escultura y Grabado (EEPEG), the teaching arm of the Real Academia de Bellas Artes de San Fernando, located at calle de Alcalá, 13. Historical and other details about the school can be found in chapter 4.

The equivalent conservatories of music and drama in Madrid had a rather checkered history by comparison. Theatre in particular did not fare well, and for much of these schools' existence drama was combined with music as its distinctly poorer relation, as a "section" within what was essentially a music conservatory. The Real Conservatorio de Música y Declamación de María Cristina (Royal Conservatory of Music and Declamation/Recitation of María Cristina) was founded in 1830 and started operating in 1831 in the Palacio del Marqués de Revillagigedo, situated in the area of the Plaza de los Mostenses and calle del Álamo. In

1847, it moved to the Casa del Conde de Torrejón, at calle de Alcalá and calle de la Virgen de los Peligros, but needed to borrow the nearby hall of the Sociedad Museo Matritense for concerts. In 1852, the conservatory was installed in the then two-year-old Teatro Real (Royal Theatre), which was used principally for opera performances; this remained its home for over seventy years. Shortly after the September Revolution of 1868 came further reorganization and a change of name, after which it was known as the Escuela Nacional de Música y Declamación. Upon the restoration of the monarchy in 1875, the name was not changed back, but further reorganization in 1901 saw it named the Conservatorio de Música y Declamación. This was followed by further waves of reform in 1911 and then in 1917, when the institution once again became the Real Conservatorio de Música y Declamación. Major structural problems with the foundations of the Teatro Real in 1925 were responsible for the conservatory's exit from that building, which had to be closed for safety reasons. It would lack permanent quarters for the next fifteen years, through to the end of the Civil War. Its administrative offices found temporary accommodations at calle del Marqués Viudo de Pontejos, 2, and at the Teatro de la Princesa (as of 1928 renamed Teatro Nacional María Guerrero, at calle de Tamayo y Baus, 4), while lessons, rehearsal spaces, and concerts were spread over a large number of other locations. In 1931, with the advent of the Second Republic, the school was renamed again as the Conservatorio Nacional de Música y Declamación. In 1933, the main offices were once more moved, this time to the Palacio Bauer at calle San Bernardo and calle del Pez.[73]

The lack of up-to-date and comprehensive instruction for actors, directors, and other theatre professionals had been a long-term complaint in many artistic and intellectual quarters, and this issue became particularly pressing in the 1920s and '30s, in light of the many advances and innovations occurring in other countries, especially Russia, Germany, and Britain.[74] As the second half of the conservatory's name makes clear, the preparation for students hoping to enter the theatre tended to emphasize diction and recitation rather than the many other aspects of modern stagecraft.[75] This deficit led Cipriano Rivas Cherif to found the Estudio de Arte Dramático and then the Teatro Escuela de Arte during the years of the Second Republic in a brief and less than fully successful attempt to remedy the situation.

MULTIDISCIPLINARY RESEARCH

The opening pages of chapter 4 treat the creation and development of the Junta para Ampliación de Estudios e Investigaciones Científicas (Board for the Expansion of Studies and Scientific Research) (founded in 1907), which *was* a government agency but which operated outside and mainly independent of the regular university and professional school system. It set up some twenty-five units variously dedicated to research, teaching, conservation, and the housing of students.[76]

Of these, the most relevant for literary and art history studies is the Centro de Estudios Históricos (Centre for Historical Studies), founded in 1910. Different models for its internal organization were adopted at different times, but basically it was divided into a number of broad sections of research interests, such as philology,[77] medieval institutions, archaeology, history, contemporary philosophy, Arabic philosophy, Arabic institutions, Semitic studies, law, and art. Some of these sections were later additions, and some closed after a few years, but each pursued specific research projects (referred to as "lines of work") and also offered graduate seminars. By 1919, the Centro was down to four departments, with a very large philology section, followed at a distance by archaeology, then art, then law. From 1910 to 1919, the centre occupied a lower level in the Biblioteca Nacional (then formally known as the Palacio de Bibliotecas y Museos Nacionales, or Palace of the Library and National Museums, on the Paseo de Recoletos). Beginning in 1920 it was then housed in a large, stately house at calle Almagro, 26,[78] before moving again, in 1931, to the building known as the Palacio de Hielo y del Automóvil (Ice and Automobile Palace), which stands at calle del Duque de Medinaceli, 2–8, right beside the Palace Hotel.[79]

DIPLOMACY AND LANGUAGES

In 1911, the Instituto Libre de Enseñanza de las Carreras Diplomática y Consular y Centro de Estudios Marroquíes (Free Institute of Education in Diplomatic and Consular Careers and Centre for Moroccan Studies) was created as an affiliated institute of the Real Academia de Jurisprudencia y Legislación (Royal Academy of Jurisprudence and Legislation). In 1928, its name was changed to Instituto Diplomático y Centro de Estudios Marroquíes, and in 1932 it was absorbed into the newly founded Instituto de Estudios Internacionales (Institute for International Studies). Given the length of its formal title, it was generally known simply as the Instituto Diplomático y Consular. Its purpose was the training of diplomats who would work in Spanish America and Africa. After completing his law degree in 1923, Guillermo de Torre was enrolled there from 1923 until 1926, when he received the institution's diploma.[80]

The Escuela Central de Idiomas (Central School of Languages) opened in 1911 and offered classes in English, French, and German. Spanish for foreigners and Moroccan Arabic were added in 1912, and a little later Italian, Portuguese, and Esperanto. It was housed in a building belonging to the Condesa de Medina y Torres, at Cuesta de Santo Domingo, 3, and rented by the government. Classes proved to be very popular; they employed the "direct method" and were coeducational, with women students outnumbering men. Under the Primo de Rivera regime, the Escuela Central was attached to the Universidad Central in 1927, in response to the creation of a new degree, the *bachillerato universitario de idiomas modernos* (bachelor's in modern languages).[81]

PEDAGOGY

The Escuela Normal – Seminario Central de Maestros (Normal School – Central Seminary for Primary School Teachers) dates back to 1839, when it was installed in the expropriated Franciscan convent of Santa Clara, at calle Ancha de San Bernardo, 80; it was the first training college for primary school teachers in Spain. The Ley Moyano of 1857 codified practices already in place there. Economic pressures at the very end of the nineteenth century and beginning of the twentieth led to various changes in the plan of study and in the qualifications offered. Further reforms enacted in 1914 led to what was generally a more rigorous and longer period of study.[82]

The corresponding Escuela Normal de Maestras Central del Reino (Normal School for Women Primary School Teachers – Main Campus of the Kingdom) was not set up until 1858. It first occupied a building on calle Valverde, and in 1861 was transferred to calle del Arco de Santa María, 4. Its internal organization and plan of study underwent one major reform, updating, and expansion in 1882, and in 1883 it was able to move to more suitable quarters at calle del Barco, 24, where it remained until 1939.[83]

The Escuela de Estudios Superiores de Magisterio (School for Higher Studies in Teaching Training) was founded in 1909, in part to provide a place of study for those who had previously qualified in the Escuelas Normales at the level of "normal grade," a qualification that had been scrapped in 1901. It was located at calle de Montalbán, 12, in the large building that today houses the Museo Nacional de Artes Decorativas (National Museum of Decorative Arts). Its role was to train instructors to teach in the regular regional Escuelas Normales and also to become primary school inspectors. Initially coeducational, in 1914 it was divided into sections of *alumnas* and *alumnos*. It attracted a very distinguished set of professors who taught classes there. As it evolved, it became a centre for progressive and indeed experimental teaching practices, looking abroad for much of its inspiration. In 1932, it was closed and absorbed into the newly formed Pedagogy Section within the Faculty of Philosophy and Letters of the Universidad Central.[84]

Alongside these state-funded institutions, there were also a number of non-governmental initiatives, such as the schools set up by the Asociación para la Enseñanza de la Mujer (Association for the Education of Women), founded in 1870. Fernando de Castro had created the Ateneo Artístico y Literario de Señoras (Artistic and Literary Athenaeum for Ladies) in 1869, which was reorganized the following year into the National Association of Spanish Women and the first of its dependent schools, the Escuela de Institutrices (School for Governesses). Both institutions were initially installed in a building then also being used by the Escuela Normal Central de Maestras. An Escuela de Comercio (School of Commerce) followed in 1878. In 1881, given the success of these endeavours and their subsequent growth, they moved to larger quarters at calle de la Bolsa, 14. In a further flurry of expansion, an Escuela de Correos y Telégrafos (Post and Telegraph School) was added in 1883, in 1884 Escuelas de Profesoras de Párvulos (School for Kindergarten Teachers), de Primaria Elemental, and Primaria Superior (Schools for Lower and Upper Elementary Teachers), and in 1885 an Escuela Preparatoria (Preparatory School). They needed to move again, to new headquarters at calle San Mateo, 15, and two more schools were added, the Escuela de Segunda Enseñanza (School of Secondary Education), in 1894, and the Escuela de Taquígrafas y Mecanógrafas (School of Stenographers and Typists) in 1907.[85]

VOCATIONAL TRAINING

Drawing, applied arts, design, technical drawing, and draftsmanship as part of various forms of vocational training were taught at the Escuela de Artes y Oficios de Madrid (Madrid School of Arts and Trades), established in 1871 by the Real Conservatorio de Artes de Madrid (Royal Conservatory of Arts of Madrid); founded in 1824, the conservatory's role, despite its name, was to teach applied sciences and industrial engineering. In 1886, there was an expansion, with the creation of an Escuela Central de Artes y Oficios and seven "district" schools, and at the same time they became independent of the Real Conservatorio. In 1900, these eight bodies, together with a variety of Escuelas Provinciales de Bellas Artes (Provincial Schools of Fine Arts), were brought together under a single umbrella as Escuelas de Artes e Industrias (Schools of Arts and Crafts). In 1901, further organizational differentiation was introduced with the creation of four branches: Escuelas Superiores de Artes Industriales, Escuelas Superiores de Industrias, Escuelas Superiores de Bellas Artes, and Escuelas Superiores de Industrias y Bellas Artes. At the same time, Escuelas de Artes e Industrias were retained for elementary instruction, while the various Escuelas Superiores offered more advanced and specialized subjects. In 1910, a rather more radical reform resulted in different organization and different nomenclature for the two levels: reverting to the original name, Escuelas de Artes y Oficios were charged with introductory studies, while the more simply named Escuelas Industriales (or Escuelas de Industrias) offered more advanced studies.[86] Financial support for these institutions came from different sources: some were state-funded, while others depended on the local town hall and provincial government, and others still on a combination of all three. In Madrid, the central Escuela de Artes y Oficios was located at calle de la Palma, 5, and the Escuela de Industrias at calle San Mateo, 5. Other branches of the Escuela de Artes y Oficios were dotted around the city. For instance, the "second section" was located at calle Marqués de Cubas, 13, and this was the school visited by a journalist in 1928 whose report furnishes a full accounting of the range of classes as well as four eloquent photographs of the interiors of different classrooms, complete with students.[87]

Between them, the Escuelas de Artes y Oficios and the Escuelas Industriales offered a remarkably wide-ranging variety of subjects for study.

These included various types of drawing and painting, anatomy for artists, modelling and decoration, embroidery, lacework, tailoring/dressmaking, embossing techniques, language, Castilian grammar and handwriting, stenography, typing, accounting, practical arithmetic and geometry, physics, chemistry, industrial geography, industrial economics, physical mechanics, and principles of building.

The Escuela del Hogar y Profesional de la Mujer (Household and Professional School for Women) was founded in 1911. After initially occupying temporary quarters in the city, it was installed at Paseo de la Castellana, 60. Its focus was more traditional and, as its name implies, more oriented toward the domestic sphere than was the Escuela de Artes y Oficios, though there was overlap in the subjects offered for study. Women were initially not allowed in the various Escuelas de Artes y Oficios, but by the 1920s many of these had classes for women students (*secciones femeninas*), while others simply allowed course enrollment for both sexes. Up until 1925, the subjects taught at the Escuelas del Hogar were divided into three areas: general, professional, and those specifically related to the home. Under the first category, we again find basic scholastic subjects;[88] the second covered several different and more specialized areas, and prepared students to enter jobs then thought "suitable" for the female sex;[89] and in the third topics oriented toward the maintenance of the household.[90] From 1916 on, one could also qualify there as a primary school teacher. However, reforms implemented in 1925 by the Primo de Rivera government removed almost all the subjects oriented toward professional preparation, the only ones remaining being stenography and typing.[]91

ARCHITECTURE AND DESIGN

Architecture was one of the subjects originally taught by the Real Academia de Bellas Artes de San Fernando. A major structural reorganization of the academy led to the creation in 1844 of a separate teaching unit, the Escuela de Nobles Artes (School of Noble Arts). The following year, the new school established a course referred to as "special studies" for trainee architects, but then, in 1848, an entirely separate institution was created, the Escuela Especial de Arquitectura (Special School of Architecture), which occupied space in the Reales Estudios de San Isidro on calle de Toledo and calle de los Estudios. In 1857, as part of the

Ley Moyano, the name was changed to Escuela Superior de Arquitectura, but more importantly the school was now linked to the Universidad Central, so that students of architecture could henceforth work toward a university degree.[92]

The Escuela Nacional de Artes Gráficas (National School of Graphic Arts) was founded in 1911. Its origins lay in the Calcografía Nacional (specializing in copper plate engraving), a unit of the Imprenta Real (Royal Press) that had survived after the press was closed in 1867. Located at calle de la Libertad, 15, it offered classes in engraving, colour engraving, photogravure, photoengraving, lithography, photography, decorative composition, and decorative drawing from nature.[93]

The Escuela de Cerámica de Madrid was also founded the same year. It grew indirectly out of a tradition dating back to the eighteenth century of state-sponsored china factories, whose last incarnation was the Fábrica y Escuela de Artes Cerámicas de La Moncloa (Factory and School of Ceramic Arts of Moncloa), opened in 1874 by the three Zuloaga brothers, Guillermo (1848–1893), Daniel (1852–1921), and Germán (1855–1886), but which was forced to close before the end of the century. When the new Escuela de Cerámica started, it occupied space in calle Fernando el Católico, 12, in buildings that had once formed part of the old Asilo de San Bernardino. Its director was the well-known art critic Francisco Alcántara. Eventually, it moved to more suitable premises, to an area nicknamed "La Tinaja," located beside the chapel of San Antonio de la Florida, which is where the Zuloaga establishment had previously been installed.[94]

COMMERCE, INDUSTRY, TECHNOLOGY, SCIENCE, AND MEDICINE

There were many other places of learning, but these specialized in areas at a greater remove from literature and the arts. In the official governmental records, the Anuario Estadístico for 1920–21, we find listings for numerous other schools,[95] and by 1930–31 several more had appeared.[96]

OTHER CENTRES AND MODES OF STUDY

Not all places of study depended financially on the state or local government, though this was indeed the case for most that operated at the tertiary level of education. The celebrated Institución Libre de Enseñanza (founded in 1876) was throughout its existence an independent institution that offered both primary and secondary education.[97] After operating in temporary headquarters at calle Esparteros and calle Infantas, it moved in 1884 to a large house, complete with garden, at Paseo del Obelisco, 8 (nowadays Paseo del General Martínez Campos, 14), which it acquired in 1887. The Instituto-Escuela (School Institute), established by the Junta para Ampliación de Estudios (JAE) in 1918, can in some ways be thought of as a government agency's attempt to emulate the Institución Libre and pursue similar progressive pedagogical practices (see chapter 4). As its name suggests, the International Institute for Girls in Spain was a private, US-based organization that again catered mainly to primary and secondary students, but which also became increasingly involved with the Residencia de Señoritas (another JAE creation) (again, see chapter 4).

It was a common practice for established artists to use their studios as teaching spaces for a select number of students, in a kind of evolution of the old apprenticeship model; these were commonly known as the *taller* (workshop) or *academia* (academy) of the artist in question.

Residences

As of 1920, there were eleven public universities in Spain, those of Barcelona, Granada, Madrid, Murcia, Oviedo, Salamanca, Santiago de Compostela, Sevilla, Valencia, Valladolid, and Zaragoza, plus two private ones, the Universidad de Deusto in Bilbao and the Universidad Pontificia in Comillas (Madrid). At this time, students going to college tended to enroll in the one nearest to where they lived, and they tended to live at home. This was the traditional arrangement, partly for economic reasons, and partly because what few other options for accommodation that were available were often less attractive. Evidently, not everyone at university lived in a university town, and so other arrangements needed to be made. Where possible, many families opted for the student to live with relatives or close friends who did reside in one of the aforementioned cities. Otherwise, the main alternative was the traditional *pensión* or *casa de huéspedes*, that is, a room in a house with a landlady where the student could sleep and take some or all of their meals.[98] Ramón Carande evokes the contrast between "typical" student life of the time and that led by the fortunate few housed in the first Residencia de Estudiantes on Madrid's calle Fortuny:

Students of that time, even those of us who lived in the bosom of our family, know a good deal about the appearance and the vicissitudes of the innumerable boarding houses occupied by the students who, coming from the provinces, arrived in the capital and installed themselves in the streets in the immediate vicinity of the building of the old University (Hita, Estrella, Horno de la Mata, Abada, Tudescos, Jacometrezo and so many others that today have disappeared, totally or partially) ... [In the Residencia] the hours for study had an appropriate framework and those for leisure a different tone. After-dinner conversation in the Residencia itself replaced the *tertulia* in any old café; visits to museums and attendance at concerts replaced the dances in the Bombilla park and the late-night fourth session of a *zarzuela* performance at the Apolo or Romea theatres.[99]

Rafael Méndez is more succinct but makes essentially the same point: "To be transported from a boarding house to the Residencia de Estudiantes was like entering a marvelous world."[100] The *pensión*, then, while it was a solution that was unavoidable for some, more often than not offered sub-standard board and lodging and provided an atmosphere that was not exactly conducive to serious study.

Besides the boarding house, the only other commercial alternative was a hotel, something that only very well-off families could contemplate using for any length of time, but which could serve as a stop-gap measure while searching for something more permanent or waiting for a room to open up. A few examples have been documented: in the early 1920s, prior to his premature death in 1924, the poet José de Ciria y Escalante lived with his wealthy parents in rooms at the Palace Hotel;[101] in March 1926 Lorca spent three nights at the Hotel Málaga on calle de Alcalá before managing to get into the Residencia de Estudiantes;[102] and when Concha Méndez returned to Spain in 1931, she lodged at the Hotel Dardé in Madrid, and soon discovered that her future husband, Manuel Altolaguirre, was also staying there.[103] Perhaps the most telling case, however, is that of José María Hinojosa. When he moved from Málaga to Madrid in the fall of 1923 to study at the Universidad Central, he wanted to live at the Residencia de Estudiantes, but his parents opposed this choice, suspicious of its liberal reputation and fearful that it might encourage his poetic leanings.[104] Instead, he lodged in *pensiones*, first at calle Imperial, 9 and 11, 3° izqda, then calle del Barco, 7, 3°, and then calle Lagasca, 50.[105] Later, in 1926, Hinojosa gives his address as the Hotel Majestic, in the Salamanca district, at the corner of calle de Velázquez, 49, and calle Ayala, 34.[106] And later still, when he was in Madrid he stayed at the Fundación del Amo.[107]

All these observations regarding accommodations for university students also apply, at least to some degree, to the other types of colleges mentioned in this chapter, though ones that also had branches outside Madrid would obviously have drawn fewer students from the provinces. These foregoing comments also serve to contextualize the importance that all historians and critics ascribe to the Residencia de Estudiantes, even though it could only cater, at its peak, to a few hundred students at a time. They also explain why members of the JAE thought it so important to create such a facility, and why it grew so rapidly from its very modest beginnings in 1910.[108] As has been well-documented, the Residencia was modelled on the residential colleges of Oxford and Cambridge and offered board and lodging and a range of other facilities that, as the two quotations above suggest, were much superior to those normally available to students living in *pensiones*.[109] As a cultural "melting pot" of this period, a place where young talents encountered each other and grew into gifted writers and artists, the Residencia has become a stereotypical example of the youthful effervescence of Madrid at that time, even something of a cliché, readily to hand whenever a journalist needs to evoke the two decades before the Civil War. It is precisely because the Residencia has already attracted so much attention and commentary that I decided not to use it as a case study in this book, even though it surely offers the most numerous examples of the kinds of intersections that concern me here. In the wake of the Residencia de Estudiantes, another residence was created by the JAE for women students in 1915, the Residencia de Señoritas (see chapter 4), which has more recently begun to attract a certain amount of critical attention.

Alongside the Residencia de Señoritas, we need to mention the Residencia Teresiana de Madrid (Saint Teresa Residence of Madrid). In 1911, the priest Pedro Poveda Castroverde and a group of supporters had started to set up in several provincial towns a series of Academias

Teresianas (a kind of boarding school), which would help women prepare for entry into the Escuelas Normales de Maestras, Institutos de Segunda Enseñanza (secondary schools), and other forms of secondary education. As an offshoot of this progressive Catholic initiative, the same organization opened in 1914 the Residencia Teresiana in Madrid at calle Goya, 46, 4°, for the purpose of housing women students enrolled at the Escuela de Estudios Superiores de Magisterio and at other similar schools or university faculties. In its first year of operation, ten of the twelve residents were pursuing studies in teacher training; in later years, though, the ratio of students at different faculties of the Universidad Central grew steadily. Because of rapid expansion, the Residencia moved later in 1914 to Cuesta de Santo Domingo, 20, where it could house twenty residents, and this pattern repeated several times over subsequent years until it found more permanent headquarters at calle Alameda, 7, with a large four-storey house and garden. By 1935, there were almost two hundred residents spread between this and two additional addresses, at Cuesta de Santo Domingo, 3, and calle Mendizábal, 15. The Residencia also eventually offered some language classes, lecture series, and educational excursions.[110]

The Residencia Fundación del Amo (Amo Foundation Residence) was, as its name suggests, a private initiative supported by the eponymous foundation based in California and whose goal was to foster exchange and understanding between that US state and Spain. The physician and businessman Gregorio del Amo (1858–1941) initially authorized funds in 1928 for the construction of a residence hall for students at the Universidad Central, but the project really got under way in 1929 when, at the same time, the Fundación was legally established. The Residencia was built over 1929–30 in a modern style and a large H pattern on the grounds of the new campus, the Ciudad Universitaria in Moncloa, which was only just beginning to be developed, and became the first building to be completed and start functioning on that site. Unfortunately, because the Moncloa area became part of the front line during much of the Civil War, and especially the Siege of Madrid, the building was completely destroyed.[111]

CHAPTER 2

RAFAEL BARRADAS AND THE CAFÉ DE ORIENTE

ATOCHA

The Uruguayan painter Rafael Barradas (1890–1929) spent the years from 1918 to 1925 in Madrid, and over that time formed a *tertulia* at the Café de Oriente, located close to the Glorieta de Atocha, a large square and (nowadays) roundabout flanked on its southern border by the Atocha railway station. The origin of the name Atocha is disputed, with a variety of possible derivations, but it has served as a Madrid toponym since 1200.[1] It is associated with a city gate, the Puerta de Atocha, in one of the medieval walls, though, confusingly, this structure was originally situated elsewhere, closer to the city centre. The station, the Estación Central de Madrid, opened in 1851 and was enlarged in 1860, but suffered a serious fire in 1864. After several delays, the new Estación del Mediodía was constructed between 1890 and 1892 employing the wrought-iron and glass techniques typical of the period, and in a major expansion between 1985 and 1992 it was split into the Estación de Puerta de Atocha and the Estación de Atocha-Cercanías, with the distinctive architectural features that we know today.

A very large, irregularly shaped space opens in front of the station and is the point where several important city streets and boulevards converge: Paseo del Prado, calle de Atocha, Ronda de Atocha, Paseo de Santa María de la Cabeza, Paseo de las Delicias, calle de Méndez Álvaro, Avenida de la Ciudad de Barcelona, and Paseo de la Infanta Isabel (in earlier decades called the Paseo de Atocha). This square, whose official name is Plaza del Emperador Carlos V, was known until 1941 as the Plaza de Atocha or the Glorieta de Atocha.[2]

On the northwestern edge of this square, the corner plot of land bordered by the south side of the end of calle de Atocha and the Glorieta itself was for several centuries occupied by a variety of hospital buildings, starting from just before 1600. The evolving ground plan involved a large rectangular structure set on the very corner, and then a second rectangle beside it, and hence set back further from the calle de Atocha.[3] Several phases of demolition and major reconstruction followed. The eighteenth-century building occupying the second rectangle (also referred to in period documents as the Patio Grande) continued to function as a hospital until 1965, when it was finally decommissioned. After extensive refurbishment, this opened as the Museo Nacional Centro de Arte Reina Sofía in 1990, while at the same time another wing of the hospital complex became the home of the Real Conservatorio Superior de Música.[4]

THE CAFÉ DE ORIENTE

Much of the land actually fronting the calle de Atocha was sold off in 1861 by the hospital to the Municipality of Madrid.[5] On this plot were built several modest apartment blocks and behind them the Plaza de Sánchez Bustillo (now renamed Plaza de Juan Goytisolo). Two narrow streets, perpendicular to the calle de Atocha, border this lot, the calle del Dr Drumen and the calle Dr Mata, so named because of the area's historical connections with medicine.

The Café de Oriente was installed on the ground floor of the building located at calle de Atocha, 118, at the corner of calle del Dr Drumen.[6] The earliest municipal records for this address date back to 1887, which is also the date of the café's inception, suggesting that the building was newly constructed.[7] The café was opened on 22 June of that year, as a joint venture between José Rodríguez Fernández, already the owner of the Hotel de Oriente (hence the name, though the hotel was located elsewhere, at calle del Arenal, 4), and Manuel Zapatero y García, a lawyer and politician.[8] Its interior was described as "capacious, elegant, extremely spacious and ... decorated with real opulence. The attractive marble counter, the magnificent mirrors that cover the walls, the ornaments and the paintings on the ceiling are the equal of those in the most central and best decorated cafés in Madrid."[9] The café quickly became a favoured meeting place for Federal and so-called Posibilista politicians, those who continued to

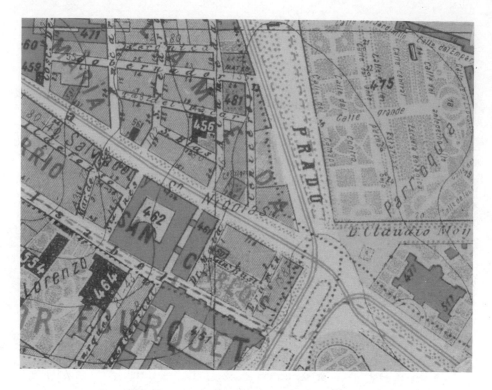

2.1. Detail from Madrid city plan of Facundo Cañada López (1902).

support the idea of a federalist, republican Spain after the restoration of the monarchy at the beginning of 1875. Newspapers report political gatherings there, with speeches and meals, over the ensuing years.[10]

At some point, ownership was ceded exclusively to José Rodríguez,[11] and on his demise in 1906 it passed to his widow, María Maciá, and family.[12] Before 1915, it was sold to a new proprietor, José Llanos, who was based in Gijón, where he ran the Hotel Française, "La Iberia," and the Restaurant "La Terraza," but who is also listed as the owner of the Café-Restaurante de Oriente in Madrid.[13] In 1919, a newspaper article noted the café's convenient proximity to the Cuesta de Moyano and the second-hand bookstalls there, and in particular the patronage of Ramón Gómez de la Serna, who would carry back his haul for the day, which "he then examines lovingly in the neighboring Café de Oriente."[14] Altogether less salubrious is a report from August 1928 on the inhabitants of the short stretch of calle Drumen between calle de Atocha and Plaza de Sánchez Bustillo, who were unable to open their windows and enjoy a little relief from the summer heat because "beside the wooden fence of the aforementioned site, thoughtless people passing by there urinate and defecate."[15]

The Café de Oriente remained open till the end of the 1960s. Thereafter, it was significantly remodelled into the Bar-Restaurante Dorna, but as of 2001, Brihuega could still write that, "although completely transformed by the trappings of a 'typical inn,' the premises of what was the Gran Café de Oriente are still preserved ... Inside, the twin columns of cast iron are still perfectly recognizable."[16] As this book goes to press, the exterior of the original five-floor building remains intact on the corner of Atocha and Drumen and its ground floor houses a branch of Kentucky Fried Chicken;[17] the "ten openings" in the structure where full-length windows or doors were to be installed are still clearly visible, as are the original iron columns inside.[18]

The variants of the café's name, Café Social de Oriente and Gran Café Social de Oriente, may be the inventions of those of its patrons who wrote about the place, as they never appear in the press or advertisements.[19] Several modern critics refer to it, almost generically, as the Café de Atocha, because of its location, but this is incorrect and misleading because another café actually called the Café de Atocha was located directly across on the northern side of the street, at calle de Atocha, 161, on the corner that meets the southern tip of the Paseo del Prado. The Café de Atocha was for a number of years a *café cantante*. It disappeared in 1924 during the construction of the Hotel Nacional, which opened in 1925 and occupied that entire corner lot. In its basement area, the Hotel Nacional itself had a café or cafeteria that with time became another popular meeting place for *tertulias*.[20] Various period photographs of the Glorieta de Atocha and the Hotel Nacional are available on different websites.[21] Unfortunately, no close-up images of the Café de Oriente premises appear to have survived. The upper stories of the building at calle de Atocha, 118, that housed the café can be made out in the distance in a number of the panoramic shots, but the ground floor is always obscured, either by trees or dark shadow.

RAFAEL BARRADAS (RAFAEL PÉREZ GIMÉNEZ BARRADAS), 1890-1918

The salient features of Barradas's biography have been well-documented: his birth and childhood in Uruguay, his departure from Montevideo in August 1913 and arrival in Genoa, a short stay in Milan, travel through Switzerland, then several months spent in Paris (where we can place him on Christmas Day 1913),[22] a very brief return to Milan, and then his trip over to Barcelona, where he likely arrived in May 1914. He stayed there for several months, but toward the end of the year, and running short of money, he decided to set out on foot for Madrid. Thus begins of one of the most frequently recounted episodes of the painter's life: his trip with an itinerant knife sharpener and the route they took through the province of Teruel to an area close to Lechago and Calamocha. There, Barradas's health broke down and he was taken in and looked after by a local girl named Simona Láinez and her family of shepherds. Transported to Zaragoza, he convalesced in the Hospital de Nuestra Señora de Gracia over Christmas 1914. Once recovered, he decided to stay in Zaragoza, romance thereafter blossoming between him and Simona, whom he always called Pilar; they married on 14 April 1915.[23] In Zaragoza, Barradas was soon contributing to various magazines and newspapers, briefly set up a design and advertising business, and held at least two exhibitions of his work. In October 1915, he was joined in Spain by his mother, his sister Carmen (1888–1963), and his brother Antonio (1893–1963) (who published writings and artwork under the name Antonio de Ignacios). But restlessness got the better of Barradas again, and in early 1916 he and his family abruptly left Zaragoza and returned to Barcelona, where they remained for over two years.

During this second stay, which coincided with the flowering of the Catalan avant-garde, several contacts and new friends would come to play an important role in Barradas's life and career: the artist Celso Lagar (1891–1966) and his companion the sculptor Hortense Bégué (1890–1956), the Uruguayan artist Joaquín Torres-García (1874–1949), the gallery owner Josep Dalmau (1867–1937), the poet Joan Salvat-Papasseit (1894–1924), and the writers Juan Gutiérrez Gili (1894–1939) and Huberto Pérez de la Ossa (1897–1983). Besides continuing to paint, Barradas also found work as a book illustrator and contributed to magazines, both popular and avant-garde. Over 1917–18, he was also able to hold a number of exhibitions: in 1917, he participated in three collective shows (one in Madrid), and an important joint show with Torres-García at the Dalmau gallery; in 1918, there was one collective show and a solo exhibition at the Laietanes gallery.[24]

BARRADAS IN MADRID, 1918-1919

Barradas and his family moved from Barcelona back to Madrid in August 1918, again principally in the hope of achieving greater economic stability.[25] Their first apartment was on calle León, 8, 2° dcha, quite close to the Plaza de Santa Ana and in the middle of the Barrio de las Letras, in one of the older parts of the city. Barradas's first publication in Madrid was a drawing in a newspaper for a commemorative number celebrating Uruguayan independence, and it was soon followed by others.[26] He and his family also continued designing and making dolls and providing illustrations for the Pagés company, and likewise Barradas sent back to Barcelona illustrations for children's books produced by Editorial Muntañola.[27]

One of the first contacts that Barradas may have made – or rather, re-established – upon his move to Madrid was with Guillermo de Torre (1900–1971). The adolescent Torre had contributed eight texts to the Zaragoza magazine *Paraninfo* over 1915–16, and *Paraninfo* was the publication with which Barradas was most closely associated during his Zaragoza period, when he designed a number of covers and became its art director.[28] At that time, Torre was living with his family in Fonz, Huesca, just over a hundred kilometres from Zaragoza, and it seems that they met in the latter city. From the fall of 1916 onward, Torre attended the Universidad Central, but he spent the quite lengthy holidays back home. Torre had also discovered Joaquín Torres-García and his book *El descubrimiento de sí mismo* (Gerona: Tipografía de Masó, 1917), and he was impressed by it, describing it as Futurist.[29] In the first extant letter exchanged between Barradas and Torres-García, dating from 28 August 1918,[30] the latter writes, "I received a very enthusiastic letter from Guillermo de Torre. We can count on him. He's completely with us."[31]

Later in the fall, another friend from Barcelona, Celso Lagar, was in Madrid. While it was likely Salvat-Papasseit who had introduced Barradas to Torres-García, in the summer of 1917, it was in all probability Lagar who had previously introduced Barradas to Salvat-Papasseit.[32] Lagar and

Bégué were in Madrid for an exhibition of their works that opened at the Ateneo on 21 November 1918 and ran into December. The invitation to the show lists thirty-two paintings by Lagar under the heading of "Planismo,"[33] together with four animal sculptures by Bégué.[34] One of Josep Maria Junoy's calligrammes is reproduced on the facing page of the invitation; it takes as its subject the two artists.[35] But a week earlier, Barradas and Lagar had already sent a brief postcard of greetings to Torres-García, mentioning the upcoming exhibition and noting that they were writing it sitting in the Café Colonial.[36] And as is well-known, the Colonial was the meeting place of the *tertulia* of young poets who surrounded Cansinos Assens; within a matter weeks from the date of the postcard, this same group would launch the *ultraísta* movement.[37]

Not the only positive review of the show, but the most extensive, was published in *El Fígaro*. The whole page was given over to its coverage: the text by López Martín accompanied by three drawings.[38] Top left was a *Dibujo planista* by Lagar, a complex drawing by Barradas sprawled from bottom left to top right and depicted five floors of an apartment block,[39] while in the bottom right another, smaller drawing by Barradas entitled *Celso Lagar* appears to have been inspired by the Junoy "calligramme" mentioned above. A few days after the exhibition closed, Xavier Bóveda wrote an article about his visit with Lagar.[40] Bóveda was a member of the Colonial *tertulia*, and it would be his interview with Cansinos Assens, published on 27 November, that would be cited in the first *ultraísta* manifesto that came out in early 1919.[41] Rather than an interview, the article ends up being much more about Bóveda himself, and his alignment with Lagar's style in art (that he describes as Futurist) and with that of the *ultraístas* in poetry.

At the same time as Barradas was reconnecting with Torre and Lagar, he was also expanding his network and seeking more possibilities for remunerative employment. In this context, a key figure was the influential art critic José Francés (1883–1964), who often published under the pen name Silvio Lago and was one of the handful of Spanish commentators of his time open to, and indeed enthusiastic about, modern trends in art.[42] Francés was also the force behind the yearly exhibition known as the Salón de Humoristas, which started in 1915. It is not known when Barradas and Francés first met in person, but Barradas (while still living in Barcelona) exhibited in the III Salón that opened in January 1917 (at Madrid's Galería General de Arte), and he would do so again in the V Salón of March 1919 (at the Círculo de Bellas Artes). That Barradas and Francés were in contact is demonstrated by various references in the correspondence with Torres-García. On 13 September 1918, Torres-García commented on "the good reception that José Francés has given us."[43] And later in November, Barradas wrote to his friend about plans for a possible exhibition and the need to coordinate "with our great friend Francés."[44] In another letter, Barradas must have urged him to send Francés a copy of his book *El descubrimiento de sí mismo*, and Torres-García responded positively to both letters on 13 December.[45]

It seems reasonable to assume that once Barradas was established in Madrid, an in-person meeting with Francés would have followed fairly shortly thereafter. Francés often wrote for the magazine *La Esfera* (1914–31), which together with *Mundo Gráfico* (1913–38) was part of the Prensa Gráfica publishing group (1913–39); the magazine *Nuevo Mundo* (1894–1933) joined Prensa Gráfica in 1915. Antonio de Ignacios recounts that the meeting occurred at the Prensa Gráfica offices, and that a little later, through the connection with Francés, Barradas was able to start contributing to *Nuevo Mundo*.[46] A series of children's cartoon strips about a character called Panchulo started appearing there in November 1919 and continued sporadically through to April 1920.

Francés was also instrumental in another very important way. Barradas's brother details that it was Francés who brought the artist to the attention of a friend of his, Gregorio Martínez Sierra (1881–1947). Martínez Sierra was a prolific writer, dramatist, poet, theatrical impresario, and publisher who, in perhaps his most important endeavours, created and ran two publishing houses, Editorial Renacimiento (1910–15), and Editorial Estrella (1917–26), as well as the forward-looking Teatro de Arte, based at the Teatro Eslava (corner of calle Arenal and the Pasadizo de San Ginés), which operated from September 1916 to October 1930.[47] This event likely occurred in late 1918 or early 1919. As mentioned, Barradas continued contributing illustrations to the children's stories published by Editorial Muntañola, and one day when taking a packet to the mail he bumped into Francés, who asked to borrow them so that he could look at them more carefully. Francés's "day job" was an administrative position at the main post office.[48] He in turn, on his way home, encountered Martínez Sierra and enthusiastically showed him the drawings. Martínez Sierra, recognizing Barradas's talent, asked Francés to have Barradas visit him. At their meeting, he proposed "a contract with the 'Biblioteca Estrella' ... to illustrate Martínez Sierra's own books and those by other writers; and furthermore, since his style was so interesting and modern, [he suggested] that together they could bring about many innovations at the 'Teatro Eslava,' in set designs, posters, costumes, and thus transform the artistic trends then current in Madrid."[49] Barradas's first commissions, then, were to illustrate books from the Biblioteca Estrella series.[50]

Barradas's other important contact from the world of art criticism was Manuel Abril (1884–1943). Abril was also a dramatist, poet (close to the *ultraístas*), novelist, translator, and journalist; in his art criticism he was, like Francés, one of that minority favourably disposed toward the various tendencies of modern art. Over these months Barradas was also thinking about his own painting and career path, and in the correspondence with Torres-García we can observe, in a state of considerable flux, various proposals for solo or joint exhibitions. Torres-García wrote on 13 September 1918 that "our friend who is going to facilitate our entry into the Ateneo is spending this summer in Terrassa; I have not been able to see him yet, but I will see him before he returns to Madrid."[51] This "friend" was Abril, who at the time was secretary of the Fine Arts Section of the Madrid Ateneo.[52] He wrote again on 5 November, "I have spoken here with that friend who is going to get us into the Ateneo and everything is arranged."[53] Shortly thereafter, in the wake of the Lagar exhibition at the Ateneo, Barradas wrote Torres-García – over-optimistically – that "around December I'm exhibiting at the Ateneo";[54] in the event, things played out rather differently, with the Ateneo show not happening until another fifteen months later, in March 1920.

In 1919, Barradas did participate, as already noted, in the V Salón de Humoristas (March), and then had his first solo Madrid show in the Salón de la Librería Mateu, a bookstore that had opened at the beginning of 1918 (at calle Marqués de Cubas, 3, located just round the corner from the Parliament building). The initial plan was to mount an exhibition of works for children, as Barradas had discussed more than once with

Torres-García, but things changed once José Francés got involved.[55] Ignacios also describes another moment in the history of the evolving project, when Barradas invited Francés to his studio to see the group of works he intended for Mateu: the critic commented on them while at the same time the painter explained how he conceived of them.[56] The show ran from 5 to 20 April and included thirty-seven pieces.[57] Press coverage was patchy. The longest article in a mainstream publication appears to have been Francisco Alcántara's in *El Sol* (9 April); Francés's own was laudatory and sought to defend him from largely negative responses;[58] Torre's came out in the first and only number of a minor avant-garde journal, *Perseo*.[59] Torre enthused rhapsodically over Barradas's painting, claiming that while the lethargy of the dominant, early twentieth-century style in literature had now been broken by "our *ultraísta* cry," only Barradas, together with a small group of young painters based in Cataluña, was doing the equivalent in art.

During the rest of the year, Barradas continued on with his various commissions and his own painting. In October, the family moved to a new apartment, on Paseo de Atocha, 29, 2° izqda, about which Barradas commented that "now I'm in a much better situation to be able to work."[60] A visitor from Montevideo offers a description of the new residence, saying that Barradas

> was able to permit himself the luxury of having his small apartment on a famous avenue, the Paseo de Atocha, in an outer and sought-after district of the city. From its windows one could make out the Estación del Mediodía, also called "del Pacífico," with its great metallic roof, curved and dark, the streets swarming with people … And further off the red sheet of the Castilian plain packed with historical memories … The apartment was small but sufficient. At the front there were two rooms, one of which served as Barradas's studio, while in the other pride of place was given to a piano on which his sister Carmen, an artist of fine sensibility and already with a prestigious reputation, created her musical compositions, complementing them with the manufacture of highly original dolls that were in high demand.[61]

Very shortly after the move, Barradas invited Manuel Abril to come and see him and spend the afternoon.[62] And as the painter's brother Antonio remembers, given Abril's enduring enthusiasm for Barradas's work, he "tried to get details from the painter himself, chatting with him in the café and in his own studio, where they would frequently meet to talk about art."[63] As for the room in the apartment that Barradas had taken over: "from that date forward his studio located at Paseo de Atocha 29 was filled with colours, as on enormous canvases that he stretched out on the walls he experimented with a new style for scenography: set designs that later were used in the 'Teatro Eslava' with great success."[64] Later, Barradas would end up painting directly on all four walls of the room that served as his studio.[65]

BARRADAS IN MADRID AND BARCELONA, 1920

At the end of 1919, Barradas's work with Martínez Sierra began to diversify and intensify. For the Christmas and New Year season of 1919–20, the impresario wanted to create some new theatrical entertainments, which eventually took the form of two shows: *Eslava-Concert*, described as a "caricature of a variety show" and attributed to Antonio Asenjo and Ángel Torres del Álamo (premiered 28 December 1919, running through 21 February 1920), and *Kursaal*, another miscellaneous show in three parts each with various numbers (premiered 23 February 1920, running through 29 April). But even before these two spectacles took shape, Barradas had been developing various ideas and pitching them to Martínez Sierra. As he wrote to Torres-García on 21 December:

> This month I've worked a lot preparing the first visual spectacle that I'm bringing to the theatre.
>
> You will remember those things that I wanted to do with Médici;[66] well, from 25 December through 6 January the first work of what I consider "my theatre" will be performed in the Teatro Eslava.
>
> It's a children's story. The actors are drawings that can move, which will work well; and, if this pleases the public, we already have plans made up with Martínez Sierra to do some *very daring* things.[67]

Evidently, this project was postponed and then shelved, perhaps in favour of *Eslava-Concert* and, subsequently, *Kursaal*, because as of 19 January 1920, Barradas was still cautiously optimistic about the possibilities for staging his work:

> Possibly in February my visual spectacle will go on in the Teatro Eslava.
>
> It's ready to go and marvelous (we're already rehearsed it), and if it still hasn't been performed, it's because my great friend Martínez Sierra wants it to be staged the same day as another work that he is preparing right now, which has a great visual appeal. A play in three acts performed by actors ... but, basically, with the same visual impact ...
>
> In one of the scenes – that is, inside a children's bedroom – the music is a lullaby, quite fabulous; then a march, as the Three Wise Men pass across the stage. Then a little music of the stars, which has something to it of crystal, frogs, and dry leaves. They are all very beautiful.[68]

What Barradas seems to have had in mind was a puppet play primarily for children, using two-dimensional, cut-out figures with articulated limbs not too dissimilar to a paper doll that he had also designed.[69] At some later date (the incomplete letter is headed 27 August but lacks the year), Barradas returned to the idea of, in his words, a "flat puppet show."[70]

Over the years, Martínez Sierra employed a considerable number of set designers, costume designers, and illustrators for his publicity material: in the first category, the principal figures were Manuel Fontanals and Sigfrido Burmann, and in the second Rafael de Penagos, José Zamora, and Fernando Mignoni. With time, Barradas would join the ranks of both. There is no firm evidence of his involvement in *Eslava-Concert*, but it is possible. A Charlie Chaplin-esque figure appeared in both *Eslava-Concert* and in *Kursaal*, and one of the backdrops used in *Kursaal* was directly based on a design by Barradas that also features a "Charlot."[71] He contributed what are described as "caricatures" (perhaps grotesque

costumes) to another number in *Kursaal*, "Arte de amar."[72] Barradas
provides fascinating insight into the different responses to its premiere:

> Last night we premiered in the Teatro Eslava a work based on
> my Expressionist painting. They didn't understand it ... Martínez
> Sierra, the author of the script, is very happy; La Argentinita, the
> main performer, also. And I am, *of course.*
>
> I hope that, with my formula, I will convince them. When? I don't
> know, but one day it will come. My formula is very simple given my
> ability to be humorous; first I make them laugh, then the other stuff
> *will sneak in.*
>
> This spectacle with clowns that we've created has a caricature-
> like appearance, but deep down ... *that*: what I *make them swallow*;
> that plasticity, which remains ours even when it wears the mask of
> humorousness ... *is caustic.*
>
> Last night, at the premiere, at first it went well; the people didn't
> dare to boo; however, for a moment I believed that the jam-packed
> theatre was going to fall apart. How much you really would like this
> work of mine!
>
> From the umbrella and the suitcase of the clowns to their
> characterization, and the costume designs, interpreted by Carmen's
> needle, everything, everything is fully mine, with a strange and new
> logic to its expression.
>
> This theatre of mine will open up a path. It will be like a painting
> in the theatre, where the characters are insignificant visual actors.
> Now, we are preparing another one even more ferocious.
>
> Martínez Sierra – who is the man in Madrid who has best
> understood me – tells me to do what I want, that he believes in
> my theatre. What things I will do, Torres! They'll carry me off
> to prison![73]

At the same time – opening on 20 February 1920 – a modest exhibition
of portraits of Catalina Bárcena done by Barradas was mounted in the
vestibule of the Teatro Eslava.[74] Bárcena was the leading actress of the
Eslava company and had been working with the "Teatro de arte" since
its inception (she was also Martínez Sierra's long-term mistress). She

starred in most of the productions and became a favourite subject for Barradas, who produced many dozens of portraits, sometimes for posters, handbills, or other publicity material.

The next project assigned to Barradas was set and costume design for García Lorca's first play, *El maleficio de la mariposa*, which was also highly unconventional since all its characters were various kinds of insects, principally cockroaches. In June 1919, Lorca had met Martínez Sierra and Bárcena in Madrid, introduced by the playwright Eduardo Marquina, and they saw each other again shortly thereafter in Granada, at an event honouring Fernando de los Ríos. A poem recited by Lorca impressed Martínez Sierra, and he commissioned the young poet to turn it into a play. This would be known as *La comedia ínfima* and *La estrella del prado* before receiving its definitive title. Barradas's costume designs were used, but at a late stage new decor by Mignoni was substituted.[75] Indications are that the actress/dancer Encarnación López Júlvez, otherwise known as La Argentinita, convinced Martínez Sierra to make the change; besides Bárcena, she was the other principal in the production and would also be a lifelong friend of Lorca's.[76] There were repeated delays at the beginning of the year as Lorca struggled to finish the text; indeed, parts of the production were already in motion before the final manuscript was received. The play premiered on 22 March 1920 and was a major flop, receiving at most four performances before being removed from the repertoire.

It is not clear whether Barradas and Lorca had met before they were brought together by preparations for the play's production, but henceforth they remained friends throughout Barradas's lifetime. Barradas was in Madrid from August 1918 onward; Lorca spent two spells in the city in 1919, staying in *pensiones* (from late April to early June, and again from late November to late December), and then was back again, now lodged at the Residencia de Estudiantes, in mid-February 1920.[77] It is possible therefore that in the spring or fall of 1919 friends already established in Madrid might have taken Lorca to the *tertulia* held at the Café del Prado that Barradas frequented.

March was a particularly busy month for Barradas. The VI Salón de Humoristas opened on 3 March, and once again Barradas was a participant. But uppermost in his mind was likely his second solo Madrid show, which ran from 1 to 15 March at the Ateneo.[78] Barradas exhibited twenty-nine works in oil, in a variety of styles and split into three sections: "Landscapes," "Portraits," and "City Scenes." What is clear is that he had moved on from the *vibracionista* style of the year before, and some canvases were now somewhat reminiscent of Cubism while others demonstrated the beginnings of a style that he would call *clownismo*.[79] Press coverage was again very patchy; mainstream critics found the works derivative of Futurism or Simultanism, but the *ultraísta* Evaristo Correa Calderón and Manuel Abril were, predictably, more enthusiastic.[80]

It seems as if Barradas did one more set design for Martínez Sierra that spring, for another of those special shows favoured by the impresario. Toward the end of their season in the Teatro Eslava, starting on 30 April, six short pieces were staged as part of what Martínez Sierra called *La revista de Eslava*: *Rosina es frágil* (by Martínez Sierra), *La multimillonaria* (by Antonio Asenjo and Ángel Torres del Álamo), and *Charivari*, *Inconsolable*, *El talismán del caudillo*, and *París-New York* (all by Catalina Bárcena). With other numbers added or removed, the entertainment ran through to 16 May.[81] One source affirms that Barradas did the set and/or costumes for *La multimillonaria*.[82] Meanwhile, Barradas's expanded collaboration with Martínez Sierra was formalized in a new contract dated 5 May 1920. The purview of his activities was increased, extending now to the illustration of books, the creation of posters, and set and costume design. For this he would receive a monthly retainer of four hundred pesetas, while undertaking to perform this kind of work exclusively for Martínez Sierra.[83]

Very shortly thereafter, the impresario and his company were to depart for an extended stay in Barcelona.[84] By April, Torres-García had made the decision to leave Barcelona and move to New York, and Barradas was looking forward to seeing him but at the same time also asked him about the possibility of showing his works from the recent Ateneo exhibition at the Dalmau gallery.[85] Barradas left Madrid a few days before the end of the Eslava season, arriving in Barcelona in time to attend the farewell dinner for Torres-García, held at the Restaurant de Parc on 13 May. In attendance were Salvat-Papasseit, J.V. Foix, and Josep Junoy, among a host of others from the worlds of arts and letters.[86] Performances ran at the Teatro Goya for over two months, with the company's debut there slated for 19 May and ending on 6 July. Consequently, also transferred to the vestibule of the Goya was Barradas's exhibition of portraits of Catalina Bárcena.[87]

Likewise, his plan to take advantage of the stay in Barcelona to transfer his Ateneo exhibition to Dalmau was successfully realized. Consisting of thirty oils, it opened on 22 May; there was an illustrated catalogue with a text by Guillermo de Torre and the reproduction of a portrait by Barradas of Isaac del Vando-Villar.[88] Reaction to the show was tepid.[89] After Martínez Sierra and his company moved to the north coast of Spain for the summer season, Barradas stayed on in Barcelona at least until the end of August. A letter to Salvat-Papasseit dated 10 September apologizes for not seeing him due to an unexpected departure, although, curiously, the letter is still ascribed to Barcelona,[90] and another to Torres-García dated 14 September opens with the phrase "Back in Madrid" and later refers to "the months that we spent there [Barcelona]."[91]

BARRADAS AND THE *ULTRAÍSTAS*

Despite Barradas's broadly avant-garde artistic orientation, during the first years that he spent in Madrid there was limited contact between him and the nascent group of *ultraístas*.[92] Torre's article in *Perseo* about the 1919 show has already been mentioned, and in that single number of the magazine there were drawings by Enrique Garrán, Antonio López Sancho, and Barradas. Barradas participated in the Pombo and Café del Prado *tertulias*, which were also attended by several *ultraístas*. But there is scarcely more than this. Notwithstanding Barradas's long-standing friendship with Torre – a prime mover among the *ultraístas* – it would really only be from the fall of 1920 onward, when Barradas was back in Madrid after his lengthy sojourn in Barcelona, that he grew close to the group.[93] Torre remembered that Barradas disappeared from Madrid for a while and on his return joined in the "period of maximum *ultraísta* effervescence."[94] Isaac del Vando-Villar had moved from Sevilla to Madrid in April 1920,[95] and given the date of Barradas's line portrait of him (mentioned above) he and Barradas must have met more or less immediately, almost certainly through Torre. Barradas also contributed a line portrait of Torre for his "Manifiesto ultraísta Vertical" that was inserted in the last number of Vando-Villar's magazine *Grecia*, number 50, from 1 November 1920. And at the very end of the year, Barradas was a major presence in the single number of

Reflector, an *ultraísta* magazine run by José de Ciria y Escalante and Torre. He designed the front cover and masthead (with stylistic influences from Futurism's expressive typography and Apollinaire's calligrammes) and published a drawing and two woodcut illustrations.

Barradas started contributing to the new *ultraísta* magazine *Vltra* with its second number, of 10 February 1921, and thereafter was a frequent presence, both on its cover and within its pages. Number 2 contained a text by Manuel Abril about Barradas and illustrated with a woodcut by Barradas of Catalina Bárcena. At almost the same time he was also in touch with Adriano del Valle; Valle had dedicated a poem, "Bristol Hotel," to him in the first number of *Vltra* (27 January 1921), and in a letter of early February Barradas thanks him and then continues: "Together with our great Isaac [del Vando-Villar] I count you two as my most admirable friends and artists."[96] In a letter home, from shortly after 12 April, García Lorca tells his parents of a little party he held in his room at the Residencia de Estudiantes: "People who attended: [Gabriel García] Maroto, Barradas, [Regino] Sáinz de la Maza, Tomás Borrás, Adolfo Salazar and two or three *ultraístas*, besides my friends from the Residencia."[97]

April was another busy month. On the twenty-eighth, the *ultraísta* group held a banquet in honour of the Polish painter and art critic Marjan Paszkiewicz at the Oro del Rhin restaurant.[98] Barradas was there, in the company of a full complement of *ultraístas*, Ciria y Escalante, César A. Comet, Jaime Ibarra, Rafael Lasso de la Vega, Ernesto López-Parra, Tomás Luque, Juan José Pérez Doménech, Eliodoro Puche, Humberto Rivas, José Rivas Panedas, and Torre, as well as other interested parties such as the artists Wladyslaw Jahl, Gabriel García Maroto, and Daniel Vázquez Díaz. Two days later, the *ultraísta* group held the second of their two *veladas*, modelled distantly on the Dadaist soirees. The first had been at the Parisiana (an establishment that was a mix of restaurant, club, casino, and pleasure garden), but this time it was at the intellectual centre of the Ateneo, and Barradas was a key participant. The press announced a special backdrop curtain by Barradas and posters by Jahl.[99] Barradas also delivered a brief talk on the topic of "'El anti-yo,' estudio teórico sobre el *clownismo* y dibujos en la pizarra" (The "anti-I," theoretical study on *clownism*, and drawings on the blackboard), the text of which is unfortunately not preserved (it may have been improvised).[100]

Two weeks later – on 14 May 1921 – there was another homage banquet, this time in honour of Daniel Vázquez Díaz and Eva Aggerholm for their recent exhibition in the Palacio de Bibliotecas y Museos. The dinner was at the Excelsior restaurant, the event was sponsored by the magazine *Vltra*, and Barradas was on the organizing committee, together with Robert Delaunay, Adolfo Salazar, Abril, Humberto Rivas, Torre, José Rivas Panedas, and Ciria, among others.[101] Other attendees included Comet, Ibarra, López-Parra, Pérez Doménech, Ramón Prieto y Romero, as well as Francés, the painters Salvador Bartolozzi, Sonia Delaunay, and Javier de Winthuysen, and the sculptors Juan Cristóbal and Ángel Ferrant.[102]

While living in Barcelona, Barradas had befriended the poet, dramatist, and journalist Juan Gili Gutiérrez. They likely met in 1916 via their work for the Barcelona-based magazine *Revista Popular* (1910, 1916–25), which had started up again in that year.[103] Around October 1921, Gili was sent to Madrid to serve as the literary correspondent for the Barcelona newspaper *Correo Catalán*.[104] Thanks to the pre-existing friendships between Barradas and Gili and between Barradas and Vando-Villar, within a month and a half of his arrival in Madrid Gili became the secretary of Vando's new *ultraísta* magazine, *Tableros*, and published texts in all four of its numbers (15 November 1921–8 February 1922).[105] Barradas also played a key role in *Tableros*: although not identified as such, he effectively served as its art director. A different woodcut appeared on each of the four covers, the repeated masthead was also his, and he included several of his drawings.[106] Vando published a laudatory article about Barradas's artwork in number 3. And over these selfsame months he was also still contributing covers and illustrations to *Tableros*'s fraternal rival, *Vltra*.

In the early months of 1922, both magazines, *Vltra* and *Tableros*, together with more or less the entire *ultraísta* group, collaborated on two somewhat unusual events. On 28 January, there was a banquet held at the Hotel Palace for the writer and politician Luis Araquistáin. He was not a member of the group; rather, its members came together to express their support in a dispute that Araquistáin had had, in print and in person, with José María Carretero Novillo, commonly known by his pen name El Caballero Audaz.[107] Barradas appeared in the long list of attendees. Then, in February, a different cause was taken up by the *ultraístas*, in this instance the famine afflicting Russia and in particular Russian children. Martínez Sierra was now also involved. On the twenty-fourth a special performance was held at the Teatro del Centro: sets were designed by Barradas and Jahl; a large variety of numbers were performed, including by the clowns Pippo and Seiffert, "with visual effects by Rafael Barradas," and piano pieces performed by Carmen Barradas.[108] Alongside the theatrical presentation, there was also an art show at the Círculo de Bellas Artes: all works would be sold or auctioned off with proceeds going to the fund. Here, the organizer was Luis Bagaría, in conjunction with Abril, Barradas, Francés, Jahl, Victorio Macho, and Javier de Winthuysen.[109] This exhibition opened on 1 March and ran through to the fifteenth of the month.

Gutiérrez Gili was an old friend of Barradas's, but an even older friend, dating back to childhood, was Julio J. Casal, a Uruguayan who had held consular appointments in La Rochelle (starting in 1909) and then La Coruña (1913–26).[110] The tone and content of the first extant letter, from April 1919, suggests that they may have just got back in contact, after Casal sent Barradas a copy of his book *Nuevos horizontes* (Madrid: J. Pueyo, 1916). Casal reproduced drawings by Barradas in four out of five numbers of an early magazine that he directed in La Coruña (numbers 2–5 of *Vida*, 1920–21), including one that may reflect the inside of the Café de Oriente, in number 4 (1921).[111] A little over a year later, when Casal assumed editorial control of the magazine *Revista de la Casa América-Galicia*,[112] Barradas began appearing there very regularly (from November 1922 onward, starting with a portrait of Francés). Likewise, when the magazine changed its name, to the definitive form *Alfar*, in September 1923, Barradas continued on as a staple of the publication. While *Alfar* cannot strictly be described as an "Ultraist magazine," because of its more diverse and eclectic contents, many of its contributors were *ultraístas* or close to the movement. Finally, Barradas also published a drawing in *Horizonte*, number 2 (30 November 1922), a short-lived magazine directed by Pedro Garfias and José Rivas Panedas and whose artistic director was Jahl.

There are two other indicators of Barradas's closeness to the *ultraísta* group. Over his career he produced a great many portraits (the highest number, evidently, being of Catalina Bárcena), and the subjects of a good number of them provide direct evidence: Buñuel, Cansinos Assens,

Ciria y Escalante, Correa Calderón, Garfias, César González-Ruano, Gutiérrez Gili, Eugenio Montes, Torre, and Vando-Villar, as well as others associated with the group, such as Abril, Francisco Luis Bernárdez, Casal, Dalí, Francés, García Lorca, García Maroto, Gómez de la Serna, Jarnés, Rafael Sánchez Ventura, or José María Ucelay.[113] Similarly, Barradas provided illustrations for books by Abril, Bernárdez, Casal, Gómez de la Serna, Gutiérrez Gili, Martínez Sierra, Salvat-Papasseit, Torre, and Vando-Villar.

BARRADAS AND THE TEATRO ESLAVA, 1921–EARLY 1922

Building on the success of the 1920 exhibits of Bárcena portraits in the theatres in Madrid and Barcelona, on 11 February 1921 Barradas opened an expanded show of these works at the Ateneo.[114] This was the immediate reason for the Abril article in *Vltra*, already mentioned; otherwise, as usual, press coverage was patchy, and generally – though only mildly – positive. As was his wont, he also sent some contributions to the VII Salón de Humoristas, which opened on 4 March in the Palacio de Bibliotecas y Museos.

After *El maleficio de la mariposa* (and then *La multimillonaria*), there was a lull in Barradas's theatrical activity until close to the end of the following year. A new Christmas-time entertainment, *Linterna mágica*, was conceived by Martínez Sierra and premiered on 16 December 1921. Again composed of a series of varying numbers, it was announced as utilizing music by María Rodrigo played by the Orquesta Filarmónica, with choreography, and no less than "fifteen new sets by Fontanals, Burmann and Barradas."[115] Although mainstream press reaction was positive, a long, combative article by Humberto Rivas denounced Martínez Sierra's overly commercialized efforts and lamented the prejudicial effect that they had on the work and reputation of Barradas, for whom Rivas had nothing but praise.[116]

This was soon followed by the launching of the long-postponed "Children's Theatre." Special performances began on 29 December of *Matemos al lobo*, by Luis de Tapia (a new version of the Little Red Riding Hood story), with three sets by Barradas, *Viaje al portal de Belén*, by Abril (a version of the Nativity story), music by Conrado del Campo, and five sets by Fontanals, Burmann, and Barradas, and certain numbers from

Linterna mágica, adapted for the purpose. The characters were drawn from children's stories and fairy tales, with the addition of Charlot (Charlie Chaplin).[117] On 4 February 1922, Martínez Sierra himself contributed a third piece to the repertoire, a "comedy with magic" entitled *Viaje a la isla de los animales*, featuring Pinocchio, with six new sets and costumes by Barradas, together with two additional short closing pieces, *Aladino, o la lámpara maravillosa* and *Charlot, viajero* (from *Linterna mágica*).[118]

OTHER *TERTULIAS*: THE CAFÉ DEL PRADO, CAFÉ DE PLATERÍAS, AND POMBO

As we saw, Barradas's first established residence in Madrid was at calle León, 8. In the acute angle formed by the merger of calle León and calle del Prado was situated the Café del Prado (opened in 1868 and closed in 1960), which had entrances giving on to both streets. A famous figure associated with this café was Santiago Ramón y Cajal (1852–1934), who was a regular visitor; his book, *Charlas de café: Pensamientos, anécdotas y confidencias* (Madrid: Juan Pueyo, 1922), is partially based on the time that he spent there.[119] At some moment – likely in 1918 or 1919 – a group of *ultraístas* and their friends (or proto-*ultraístas* if before 1919) established a *tertulia* there. It is not known how, exactly, this came about, and who might be identified as founding members. What we do have, though, is a series of memoirs and recollections evoking the meetings of that *tertulia*. González-Ruano remembers a gathering of "seven or eight bohemians, among them the poet Heliodoro Puche,"[120] while Buñuel refers more specifically to "a group of *ultraísta* poets, of which I formed part."[121] Juan Chabás is also mentioned as having frequented the gathering;[122] there is a copy of his book *Espejos. 1919 – Verso – 1920*, published in 1921 (Madrid: Pueyo), dedicated to Salvat-Papasseit and signed by both Chabás and Barradas (with a small drawing).[123]

Given the extreme proximity of Barradas's lodgings, it is very easy to imagine how he would have joined the group, and indeed, most descriptions of this *tertulia* name him as one of its members, if not its leader.[124] Casal calls him "an assiduous attendee."[125] One of the *ultraístas*, Evaristo Correa Calderón, commenting on a portrait of Francés, extravagantly claims that Barradas "turned his laboratory at the Café del Prado into another Eiffel tower, which irradiated thought-provoking ideas."[126] While evoking literary debates at the Ateneo, Forcada Cabanellas – who was close to the group – remembers that, "One afternoon, coming out of the Ateneo, I met up, in the café that was opposite, the famous Café del Prado, with Isaac del Vando-Villar, who at that time was publishing the magazine *Tableros*, replacing *Grecia*; with Guillermo de Torre, who was the director of *Reflector*, also a publication of the avant-garde; and with Rafael Barradas."[127] Barradas's brother Antonio likewise conjures up the many discussions held there about art and new artistic styles.[128]

It is unsurprising that Barradas and the Café del Prado figure most prominently in Torre's recollections. In his tribute of 1929, he recalls him as "the centre of a group, as the steadiest mainstay of a daily afternoon gathering made up of those of us who at that time were the leaders of 'Vltra.'"[129] He offered more details in the following reflection, from 1944:

> There was there an afternoon literary *tertulia*, presided over by the painter Barradas ... Barradas stood out because of his greater affinity with the literary avant-garde of those years, and came to be – as I wrote back then – the personification of constant Inquisitiveness, with a capital *I*. He talked, he theorized enthusiastically, he motivated people infectiously. Without ever achieving full verbal mastery, he nevertheless had the ability to throw out theories and to illuminate with pyrotechnical flares each and every artistic question. He lived in constant creative effervescence, and at the same time as he tirelessly expatiated and consumed coffee after coffee, he also filled the marble tabletop with drawings, caricatures, or sketches for paintings.[130]

And again, in a later reflection from 1970:

> A café with cats on the banquettes upholstered in maroon velvet, with dating couples from the neighbourhood in the corners, a piano that always remained silent, and sleep-walking waiters. Off in the distance, remote in all senses of the words, we used to point out to one another the figure of don Santiago Ramón y Cajal who, ignored by the regular customers of the café, came here to ruminate alone on his misanthropy. But our hub, the permanent centre of the *tertulia* was Barradas, an

inquisitive, innovative Uruguayan painter who had settled in Madrid, who drew the front covers of our *ultraísta* magazines.[131]

The *tertulia* at the Café del Prado was not the only one that Barradas attended. Another was held at the Café Platerías, located on calle Mayor, 38, and with another entrance, behind, from the Plaza de Herradores. In a letter dated to the middle of July 1925 from the painter Pancho Cossío to Francisco Bores, Cossío asked him to convey his regards "to the dear friends [Manuel] Abril, Barradas, [Guillermo de] Torres [*sic*], [Melchor Fernández] Almagro, in short, everybody from the old Platerías."[132] Buñuel likewise remembers Barradas at Platerías, along with other *ultraístas* as well as Eugeni d'Ors and Ángel Samblancat.[133] Other writers mention Pedro Garfias, Emilio V. Santolaria, and Rafael Sánchez Ventura.[134] Several more accounts, starting with that offered by César González-Ruano, do not mention Barradas, or, for that matter, most of the other names just listed. This suggests that the situation at Platerías may have been quite complicated, with more than one *tertulia*, perhaps overlapping *tertulias*, or a *tertulia* or *tertulias* whose membership varied significantly over time.[135]

The most famous *tertulia* of the period was that founded in 1915 and led by Ramón Gómez de la Serna at the Antiguo Café y Botillería de Pombo, on calle Carretas, just south of the Puerta del Sol.[136] Because of the rivalry between Gómez de la Serna and Cansinos Assens, and hence between the *tertulias* at Pombo and the Colonial, relatively few *ultraístas* were part of the Pombo group.[137] But one name that stands out as bridging both is that of Guillermo de Torre. In addition, one of the "core" members at Pombo was Manuel Abril, who is one of the nine figures to appear in Gutiérrez Solana's iconic painting of the *tertulia*, which was hung in the room of the café where they met. And Celso Lagar, during the periods he spent in Madrid, was also a visitor.[138] Thus it is easy to imagine that once established in Madrid, and once he had connected or reconnected with these friends, Barradas would have been taken along one Saturday evening and introduced to the group.

Logically, therefore, he is not mentioned in Gómez de la Serna's first volume, *Pombo*, from 1918, but he does make a number of appearances in the second volume, *La sagrada cripta de Pombo*, of 1924. In a detailed

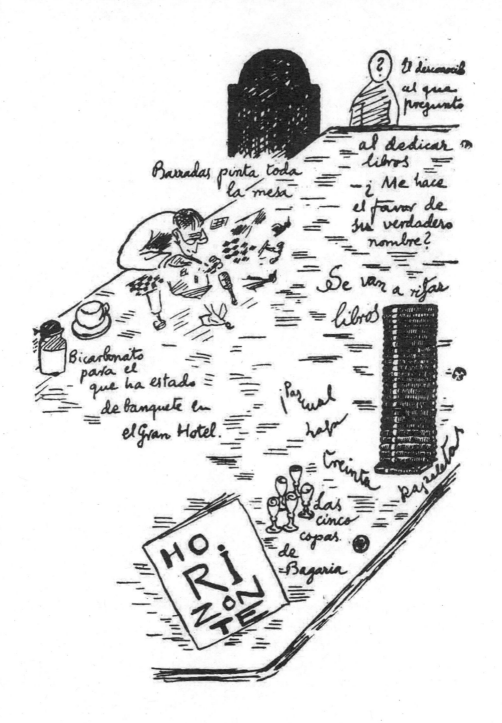

2.2. Barradas at the Pombo tertulia.

doodle made by Ramón depicting the main table around which the *tertulia* met, Barradas can be seen sketching, accompanied by the caption "Barradas paints the whole table."[139] Gómez de la Serna also inserts a series of sketches by Barradas of attendees at Pombo, as well as some of his own.[140] Barradas was present for the banquet at Pombo offered for Gutiérrez Solana on 5 January 1921, shortly after the hanging of the aforementioned painting.[141] Ciria y Escalante lists Barradas among the *pombianos* in an article of March 1921.[142] And some time also in 1921 Barradas created a sketch of Gómez de la Serna presiding over the room, with a curious short poem in the middle of it.[143] On 12 March 1923, Ramón was the honouree of a banquet at the Lhardy restaurant, and Barradas was on the organizing committee of the less expensive, alternative version, the so-called *edición económica*, held at El Oro del Rin the same evening.[144] Barradas also designed and executed a kind of scroll, with a drawing of Ramón, which all the attendees signed.[145]

On 15 October 1923, Barradas wrote to Casal about his plans for a series of "books for children,"[146] which came to fruition the following year, with texts authored by Gómez de la Serna, illustrated by Barradas: *En el bazar más suntuoso del mundo*, *El marquesito en el circo*, and *Por los tejados*, together with *El gorro de Andrés* by Abril (all Madrid: Calpe).

CAFÉ DE ORIENTE

At some point, Barradas started frequenting the Café de Oriente. The obvious reason would have been his move in October 1919 from calle León to the Paseo de Atocha, 29 (nowadays called Paseo de la Infanta Isabel). The new apartment was a good deal further out from the city centre, a little east of the Estación del Mediodía, and the direct route from it toward the Puerta del Sol would have taken him past the station, across the Glorieta and up calle de Atocha. Thus, Barradas would have passed by the Café de Oriente regularly.

The chronology and sequence of various developments over the 1919–22 period cannot be determined with any precision. It seems very likely that Barradas would have spent time on his own at the Café de Oriente, which served simply as his local café before it became the home of a *tertulia*. However, after October 1919 Barradas did not stop going to the

Café del Prado, though as time passed these visits probably became less frequent. During a visit from Alberto Lasplaces in fall 1920, his friend recounts that "together with Barradas I visited *tertulia* groups and outdoor restaurants – at that time his usual bolthole was in the Café del Prado … – and I met many prestigious artists and writers who felt much admiration and affection for him."[147] Also, his at least occasional presence at Pombo stretched well into the 1920s. It is plausible to speculate that some of the regulars from the Café del Prado *tertulia* might have started meeting with Barradas at the Café de Oriente. There, he would also have started gradually acquiring new friends. The most likely scenario, therefore, is that various overlapping changes occurred over a period of months if not years. Rather like the proverbial chicken and egg, some of the Café del Prado group may have followed Barradas and constituted the beginnings of the new *tertulia*, or a new *tertulia* with other attendees may have started forming around Barradas at the Café de Oriente, which then attracted some of the regulars from the Café del Prado. Whatever the case, the presence of some of the core members of the Café de Oriente *tertulia* cannot be confirmed there until 1922 or 1923.

From Barcelona, Barradas brought with him a well-established taste for coffee and an ingrained custom of spending hours in cafés, which is how we see him, in two undated photographs, sitting in a booth beside a window.[148] In this instance, he is working on paper, but he would also frequently sketch directly on the marble tabletops. Gómez de la Serna remarked on this proclivity at Pombo, as did Torre at the Café del Prado.[149] As he recounts philosophically to Torres-García in a letter of 15 March 1919,

> Yesterday … I made a drawing on the marble of a table in my café, on *my* marble. A drawing that had to be made precisely on that marble *of mine*, and a drawing that had to be precisely that one. And, then, I realized that *my* marble and *my* drawing are not two things that are foreign to one another; but rather for EVER, they have been one single thing *of mine*.
>
> Afterwards, the waiter wiped it with a soapy rag. I have returned to *my* marble, and my drawing has been erased by the soap.[150]

And nine months later – on 21 December 1919 – when he might have been ensconced in the Café de Oriente, he exclaimed, "I am more interested in this little drawing made five minutes ago on the marble of the table in my café, than in everything that I have painted up to this moment."[151] Barradas even sketched himself engaged in this compulsive habit, titling it "Últimos garabatos hechos en mi mesita de Oriente" (Latest scribblings done on my little table at the Oriente).[152] And this is how he is depicted, too, by César González-Ruano, who describes Barradas as "sitting afternoon, evening, and night in the Café Social de Oriente, where he filled the tabletops with his drawings."[153]

Luis Buñuel's membership of the Café del Prado *tertulia* has already been mentioned; Guillermo de Torre remembers that it was he – or perhaps one of the *ultraístas* – who first introduced Lorca to the group. As both Buñuel and Lorca were living at the Residencia de Estudiantes at this time, the suggestion is entirely plausible.[154] What cannot be established is whether this event pre- or postdates Lorca's getting to know Barradas via Martínez Sierra in the early spring of 1920, as the time frames are very close. Whatever the case, these friendships and meetings continued on, extending into the period of the Café de Oriente, as is demonstrated by a famous photograph (reproduced in figure 2.10 below), in which Barradas appears not only in the company of Buñuel and Lorca but also that of Jarnés and Pérez de la Ossa, who were never members of the Café del Prado *tertulia* but were key members of the later one at Oriente.

Buñuel preserved among his papers two pages of an album in which Barradas produced rapidly executed line portraits of various members of the group: Barradas himself (misidentified by Buñuel as depicting Lorca), Buñuel, Abril, Dalí, the *ultraístas* Pedro Garfias and Eugenio Montes, Buñuel's friend from the Residencia de Estudiantes Rafael Sánchez Ventura, and the painter José María Ucelay.[155] The length of Dalí's hair suggests that they may have been done during the fall of 1922.

As noted above, Gutiérrez Gili arrived in Madrid in the fall of 1921, and he, too, seems to have spanned the Café del Prado and Oriente. In an undated text entitled "Apuntes inéditos sobre Barradas," he writes, "In his life and in his work ... he has managed ... to make an opening in the Pyrenees, and to 'let the seed fall and move on ... ' – words of his. At the Café del Prado the seed has not fallen on barren ground; here we

2.3. Rafael Barradas, *Café de Oriente*, undated, pencil on paper, 27 x 20.5 cm.

are winding the golden skein that he put in our hands."[156] There is also a drawing by Barradas that he identified as "Café Oriente – del álbum *Figuras de Puerta Atocha*," dedicated "to my exquisite poet friend Juan Gutiérrez Gili." Also relevant in this context is a portrait by Barradas of García Lorca done in black pencil and watercolour, dedicated to José de Ciria y Escalante and, rather curiously, also signed by Gabriel García Maroto, Federico G. Lorca, and Juan Gutiérrez Gili.[157] A more finished double portrait, of Maroto and Lorca – this time done with oils on board – must date from a very similar time.[158] Barradas would also produce a portrait of Gutiérrez Gili for the invitation to a reading of poems from his book *Surco y estela* at the Ateneo on 31 March 1923.[159]

A significant landmark in the history of the Oriente *tertulia* was Barradas's meeting with the sculptor Alberto (Alberto Sánchez Pérez, 1895–1962). Alberto had returned to Madrid in 1920 after completing his military service, and was working in a bakery. Denied entry into the Escuela de Artes y Oficios, he developed his drawing and sculpture skills alone in his free time. And like Barradas, he had also been frequenting the Café de Oriente on his own, and indeed practised drawing there.[160] Evidence regarding the initial encounter between the two is limited. Valentín de Pedro provides the best account closest to the actual events. In his article from 1925, he traces Alberto's biography, noting the cramped conditions in which he lived, his first engagement with sculpture, and then a subsequent passion for drawing. Lacking space,

> He replaces his home, where the most basic amenities are lacking, with the café ... And there, leaning over the marble table, he continues giving life to the offspring of his mind.
>
> Chance brings to that same nook a painter who enjoys working on the marble of the café tables. Any reason is a good reason to strike up an acquaintance. Just by looking at each other they have recognized each other as brothers. That painter is the resilient and original Rafael Barradas. Alberto's sculptural drawings impress him deeply. As much as by his drawings he is impressed by his life. With generous enthusiasm, Barradas spreads the news of his discovery. Painters and critics file through the café. Alberto, a little self-consciously, shows them his drawings, his sculptures ... He talks to them about his art, his intentions, his plans.[161]

Decades later, Alberto would identify a period that he associated with the Puerta de Atocha – "1923, 24 and 25" – and date the encounter with Barradas to the last of those years.[162] However, in notes taken by Luis Lacasa based on conversations with Alberto, Lacasa offers an earlier date: "Toward 1922–23 (when he was 27–8 years old), in the Café de Oriente, by

2.4. Rafael Barradas, Alberto, and Enrique Garrán.

the Puerta de Atocha, he met the Uruguayan painter Barradas. Straight away they became firm friends. Alberto greatly respected Barradas because he realized that he knew a lot about art."[163] Indeed, 1922 is the date favoured by most modern critics.[164] For health reasons, in the summer of 1923 Barradas left Madrid to go and stay in the village of Luco de Jiloca, from which did not return until the fall.[165] In a letter to Jarnés from 11 September 1923, Barradas sends his best regards to Alberto,[166] so for the Alberto-Barradas friendship to be firmly established by this date, it would need to have begun by early 1923 at the latest. Alberto refers simply to "our café" without going into more detail, but he provides a painstaking description of Barradas's compositional process in producing a portrait of one of the café's regulars, a prosperous cattle rancher from Vallecas.[167]

Alberto (middle) can be seen in figure 2.4 above with Barradas (left) and Enrique Garrán (right), at a café table, likely at the Oriente. Through Barradas Alberto also came to know all of the other members of the *tertulia,* such as Lorca and Dalí.[168] Another photograph from around 1923 shows Alberto in the company of Dalí and Buñuel, as well as the poet José María Hinojosa.[169] Likewise through Barradas, Alberto connected with

2.5. Federico García Lorca, Alberto, and Salvador Dalí.

Casal and published in the *Revista de Casa América-Galicia* and *Alfar*.[170] Evidence of their closeness and likely mutual influence is provided by two drawings of similar café scenes, one done by Barradas (August 1923)[171] and another by Alberto (July 1924).[172]

Other key members of the *tertulia* were, like Alberto, neither part of the *ultraísta* group nor students lodging at the Residencia de Estudiantes. One of them, Benjamín Jarnés (1888–1949), was born in Zaragoza and trained at different seminaries. At age twenty-two, he changed course radically and joined the army. He received various postings, and later transferred to the Intendencia General Militar (the headquarters of the Quartermaster Corps) and moved to Madrid at the beginning of 1920.[173] The Parque de Intendencia, where he was posted as of October 1921,[174] was located on the calle Pacífico (nowadays known as the Avenida de la Ciudad de Barcelona), which leads away in a southeasterly direction from the Glorieta de Atocha and lies just north of the rail tracks leading to the Estación del Mediodía and its siding yards. Jarnés had found lodging at the Parador de Picazo (Ronda de Atocha, 7), located just yards away from the Glorieta, at the tip of the angle between the Ronda de Atocha and the Paseo de Santa María de la Cabeza.[175] Consequently, he lived even closer to the Café de Oriente than did Barradas. We do not know when Jarnés and Barradas first met, nor exactly how instrumental Jarnés was in forming the *tertulia*; what is clear, however, is that he was one of its key members. Furthermore, over the years 1923–25 Jarnés became increasingly connected within the literary scene, eventually visiting Pombo[176] and, later, also joining the exclusive *Revista de Occidente tertulia*.[177] Jarnés was close with Barradas and visited him during the convalescent period that he spent in Luco de Jiloca and recorded some of his impressions while there.[178]

A good deal less is known about the artist, illustrator, and caricaturist Enrique Garrán Herráez (1898–?), who sometimes used the pseudonym Adolfo Negro. His day job was at the Ministry of War. He published quite extensively in newspapers, humour magazines, and some of the little literary magazines. Gómez de la Serna included a caricature that he did of him in *La sagrada cripta de Pombo*.[179] And toward the end of the decade, Garrán illustrated several children's books written by Abril (*El domador de leones, El brujo estrujalímones, El cuento de ¡"No es verdad"!, Cuentos para niños, La nuez de Bartolo y el constipado del diablo*).

Jarnés and Garrán appear with Barradas (and Barradas's puppy) in several photos – two of them shown below in figures 2.6 and 2.7 – evidently taken on the same occasion; they are sitting at a table on a Madrid café terrace, quite possibly the Oriente.[180] Another less well-known shot of just Barradas and Garrán may be from the same day, though they have switched seats and Garrán has removed his jacket. The same group of three return in one out of a set of photographs perhaps dating from another moment; reproduced in figure 2.8, it shows them posing against a set of doors or large, full-height shutters with square-shaped inset panels.[181]

Another friend was Huberto Pérez de la Ossa (1897–1983), journalist, critic, novelist (a dozen works), short-story writer, poet (one volume in 1922), and translator. As a student in Barcelona, he published poems and

2.6. Enrique Garrán, Benjamín Jarnés, and Rafael Barradas.

2.7. Rafael Barradas and Enrique Garrán.

2.8. Benjamín Jarnés, Rafael Barradas, and Enrique Garrán.

articles in that city's *La Revista Quincenal* and also worked on translations. He attended gatherings at the offices of the *Revista Popular*, where various friends congregated, among them Salvat-Papasseit, Barradas, and Gutiérrez Gili.[182] Between 1919 and 1920, he was employed by the newspaper *El Correo Español*; one of his colleagues there was Gutiérrez Gili, and they both resigned at the same time.[183] After graduating university, he moved to Madrid, where we find him contributing to *El Imparcial* in 1923 and *Heraldo de Madrid* in 1924. He also published in the magazines *Nuevo Mundo, Hojas Selectas, España y América, El Consultador Bibliográfico,* and *Revista de Occidente*. His name appears frequently in the press as an attendee at homage events for a variety of writers, both those resident in

2.9. Rafael Barradas and a group of friends.

Madrid and those visiting from farther afield. A singular achievement was winning the Premio Nacional de Literatura for 1924 with the novel *La santa duquesa*, a prize that he shared with Claudio de la Torre.[184]

The web of friendships that existed between these *tertulia* members, and the strong correlation with the Café de Oriente, are well illustrated by three photographs, the last of which is much better known and was first published by Guillermo de Torre in 1929.[185] In the first (see figure 2.9), we can identify Jarnés and Luis Buñuel at the back, and Barradas, Casal, and Garrán in the very front, posing once more in the same spot, evidently a favourite location for taking photographs.

In the second (not reproduced here), Barradas and Jarnés are with two of the unidentified friends from the middle tier in the previous photo.[186] And in the third (see figure 2.10), Jarnés, Pérez de la Ossa, Buñuel, Barradas, and García Lorca are posing together in front of the window of a café. Torre identifies it simply as being "in Atocha," so the natural assumption is that they are outside the Café de Oriente. This photograph

2.10. Benjamín Jarnés, Huberto Pérez de la Ossa, Luis Buñuel, Rafael Barradas, and Federico García Lorca.

is normally reproduced with the left edge cropped, but here we can clearly see that the group is actually gathered in front of the same door or full-height shutters (with square panels) as in a number of the previous images, except here these are now open, allowing us to see the window behind.[187] Jarnés is wearing an overcoat, and Barradas has his hat. Also, the hat that Lorca is wearing, his tie, and his general appearance are worth comparing with the two Barradas portraits referenced above. Finally, another group photo, but this time of family members – Barradas, Pilar, Carmen, sister-in-law Antoñita, and cousin Juana – must date from the same occasion, as they are standing in front of the exact same window with the "REFRESCOS Y VINOS" sign.[188] Little doubt, then, that this is indeed the Café de Oriente.

Besides Alberto, Jarnés, Garrán, and Pérez de la Ossa, certain other lesser-known names are also mentioned in association with this *tertulia*. Among these, I would single out Alejandro Sánchez Felipe (1888/1893/

1895?–1971 – sources vary on Sánchez Felipe's birth year), though information on him and his career is scant. He was an artist and illustrator who had studied at the Escuela Especial. We find him first in 1921 exhibiting in the Exposición Nacional de Bellas Artes (May 1921), and then in a solo show of drawings and etchings at the Ateneo in December of that year.[189] Good examples of his work are reproduced in *Los Lunes de El Imparcial*.[190] He also illustrated the novels *La mocita del collar de cerezas*, by Fernando Mora, and *A la antigua española*, by Federico García Sanchiz (both published in 1922). Writing to Jarnés from Luco de Jiloca, Barradas sent "affectionate greetings" to Sánchez Felipe.[191] That same month – September 1923 – it was announced that he had been contracted by the newspaper *Diario de la Marina* in Havana to join the editorial staff as an illustrator.[192] In Cuba, he published a selection of his works under the title *Dibujos, pluma y lápiz. Rincones coloniales, retratos, composiciones*. And several years later, back in Spain, he brought out a second collection, *Dibujos: España, Francia, Venezuela, Colombia*, with an introduction by Jarnés.

THE MAGAZINE *CASCABELES*

In early 1923, the Café de Oriente group decided to produce their own little magazine. With a clear intent to be both risqué and humorous (via parody and satire), it was entitled *Cascabeles. Semanario Indispensable y Genial*, and its first and only number was dated 17 February 1923 (see figure 2.11 below). Costing thirty céntimos, its "Redacción y Administración" were listed as being located at Ronda de Atocha, 7 – Jarnés's home address. Cansinos Assens gives the following (somewhat reliable) account of its beginnings:

> The Oriente *tertulia* is beginning to become important – claimed Garrán. They are talking about it in the centre ... Ramón [Gómez de la Serna] is on alert ... We should do something so that they can really find out who the Atocha people are ...
>
> That something was the foundation of a magazine, to which we should all contribute and which he would illustrate with caricatures. Something youthful, frivolous, and irreverent ... We would call it *Cascabeles*, and for humorous purposes *Cascabeles* would pick on everybody.

2.11. *Cascabeles,* no. 1 (17 February 1923), front cover.

Jarnés was approving of the idea for a magazine, whose costs naturally he would have to defray, based on the double-dealings of the Quartermaster Corps; but he wanted to give it a more serious aspect, more like the style of the *Revista de Occidente*. But Garrán's idea prevailed and the first number of *Cascabeles* came out, a humour magazine directed by Benjamin Jarnés, and which – needless to say – did not get any further than the kiosks on the Glorieta [de Atocha], where its pages rapidly took on the look of yellowing old age, because of the effect of the sun ...

But when all was said and done, that tactic attracted to the *tertulia* some young writers, carrying their portfolios of work to glory.[193]

Opening with a brief, absurdist parody of the typical magazine manifesto – "Pautas" – other similar pieces follow (such as the one written from the perspective of a nihilist who argues for reducing the birthrate to zero but who himself has four children). We also find a drawing by Sánchez Felipe, drawings and caricatures by Garrán, an essay by Benjamín [Jarnés] on the caricaturist Bagaría, some quasi-*greguerías* entitled "Bengalas" by "Canuto," an erotic short story by one "Ofelia Blanco," a review of a non-existent novel, *Las virgencitas blancas*, by Corneja, and other similar material.

GABRIEL GARCÍA MAROTO

Maroto had moved back to Madrid in the fall of 1920, and Lorca had met him at least by the beginning of 1921, through Juan Ramón Jiménez;[194] whether Maroto met Barradas through Lorca or via other possible connections is unknown. The joint portrait done by Barradas of Lorca with Maroto, and Maroto's signature on Barradas's solo portrait of Lorca, have already been noted. Likewise, in the letter home from after 12 April 1921, among the guests at the party that he organized, Lorca lists both Maroto and Barradas.[195] Maroto was one of those who contributed to the art exhibition to benefit Russian children held in March 1922, and Barradas was a member of the organizing committee. Later that year, Maroto, Barradas, Javier de Winthuysen (another member of the committee), and Cristóbal Ruiz exhibited together at the Ateneo (4–20 December). All four knew each other from before: Maroto had exhibited with Ruiz at the Exposición Nacional de Bellas Artes (1920),[196] and Barradas and Ruiz are listed as attendees at a homage banquet for José Gutiérrez Solana at Pombo held on 5 January 1921.[197] In 1923, we find Barradas and Maroto mingling in the same social circles, at banquets for Gómez de la Serna, Jacinto Grau, and Luis Bagaría.[198] Each of the four artists exhibited between four and six works at the Ateneo, and although small, the joint show attracted much critical attention.[199] Seemingly as an adjunct to the exhibition, Carmen Barradas gave a piano recital of her own compositions at the Ateneo just after it closed, on 22 December 1922.[200]

SALVADOR DALÍ AND MARUJA MALLO

Dalí arrived in Madrid for the first time in September 1922, to study at the Escuela Especial, and while doing so lived at the Residencia de Estudiantes.[201] Maruja Mallo had moved to Madrid in 1921 in order to prepare for the entrance exam to the EEPEG, and also entered the school in the fall of 1922; she lived with her family in an apartment.[202] Dalí and Mallo, then, were classmates, and Mallo was the only female student granted entry in that particular year.[203] They became fast friends: "When I was a student, Dalí also came to the Academy to study. Those are the laws of chance ... One day I found him in class wearing a big black beret and he immediately wanted to be my friend. He started to talk to me about Picasso, because he was obsessed with Picasso."[204] Dalí frequently visited the Museo del Prado throughout the fall of 1922 and the winter of 1923, and he did so often in the company of Maruja Mallo.[205]

Meanwhile, Dalí had been very withdrawn during his first few weeks at the Residencia de Estudiantes, spending most of his time shut in his room working when not at meals or classes. The story of how he was "discovered" by Luis Buñuel, Pepín Bello, and other *residentes* has been told many times, and it was their influence and friendship that led him to "come out of his shell."[206] García Lorca was not in Madrid at this time; his father, frustrated at his lack of academic progress, kept him in Granada through all of 1922 and he did not return to Madrid until February 1923.[207]

Exactly when or how Dalí and Barradas first met is unknown, but given what information we do have of dates, people's movements, acquaintanceships, and membership of *tertulias*, it seems very plausible that it could have been Buñuel who took him along from the Residencia de Estudiantes to the Café de Oriente.[208] Barradas's sketches of Dalí in Buñuel's papers and in Gómez de la Serna's *La sagrada cripta de Pombo* have already been noted. Santos Torroella makes a strong case for Barradas having influenced the young Dalí (and also Lorca), seeing the impact of the style known as *clownismo* in a variety of the latter's works.[209] Dalí himself remembers a group of friends composed of Pepín Bello, Luis Buñuel, García Lorca, Pedro Garfias, Eugenio Montes, R. Barrades [*sic*], and others.[210]

Mallo did not get on as well with Buñuel, or, rather, Buñuel's misogynistic leanings made him less accepting of her, but this did not stop her from accompanying Dalí, Buñuel, and later, Lorca, for meetings and out-ings.[211] Dalí's ink and watercolour entitled *Sueños noctámbulos*,[212] which we can confidently date to the later fall of 1922 (or even over the holidays of 1922–23), depicts Dalí, Mallo, and Buñuel at a number of different mo-ments during a late-night walk around the city centre.[213] The group of three is easily discernible a little above and to the right of centre, and also in the extreme bottom left, but just to the right of bottom centre a much smaller cameo depicts four figures: a man in full-length coat and hat, the burly-shouldered Buñuel, Dalí still with his long locks, and the shorter Mallo with bobbed hair and a dress. The figure to the left is almost cer-tainly Barradas, making his farewells to the others (to go home to his family) before they continue their nocturnal perambulations.

If we can reasonably speculate that it was Buñuel who introduced Dalí to Barradas, then it is also probable that Dalí brought Mallo into the Café de Oriente *tertulia*. While Barradas does not figure prominently in Mallo's recollections of the period, she certainly thought it important to mention him, "whom the boys admired so much, especially Dalí."[214] Although it is not positively identified, it is likely that the café – with its small, round, marble table – represented in another contemporaneous Dalí work is the Café de Oriente, as is assumed by the title given to it: *Salvador Dalí y Maruja Mallo en el Café de Oriente*.[215] Harder to identify is the third person in the picture, because of his less distinctive facial features and hair. Some critics see Barradas, while others entertain the possibility that it might be Pepín Bello.[216] In 1923, Dalí also sketched line portraits of Barradas with his wife Pilar in the Oriente, as well as a more general scene of the café that may include Rafael, Pilar, brother Antonio, young sister-in-law Antoñita,[217] as well as, in the background, the building's fluted columns.[218]

Once Lorca was back in Madrid (February–June and November–December 1923; January–June and November–December 1924), he would have resumed his pre-existing friendship with Barradas, while Mallo would have been promptly introduced.[219] Finally, it should be noted that a much-reproduced portrait of Lorca by Dalí ascribed by the artist to "1924" and to "Madrid Café de Oriente" is in fact from the postwar period and hence the inscription is apocryphal; besides the clearly much later style of the work, it is done on the reverse of a sheet of writing paper through which the upside-down letterhead of "BEVERLY HILLS HOTEL" can faintly be read.

ALFAR AND THE *ALFAREROS*

Many modern critics claim that the members of the Café de Oriente *tertulia* were known as *los alfareros*,[220] because of their prominent presence in the pages of *Alfar*. The earliest mention of the nickname that I have found occurs in a brief biography of Casal from 1927, where we find him "closely connecting with the *ultraístas*, and bringing young writers together as *alfareros*, who contributed to the pages of that magazine [*Alfar*]."[221] Then, in 1929, Torre writes of "a café on the Glorieta de Atocha, the centre for the *alfareros*, or Madrid-based contributors to *Alfar*, and in constant contact – at the other end of the wire – with Julio Casal, located beside the Atlantic, in La Coruña."[222] Indeed, Barradas would have served as the chief conduit for these contributions, sent from Madrid out to Casal in Galicia. As mentioned, Casal's influence can be detected starting with the third number of the magazine under its new name *Revista de Casa América-Galicia* (number 23, November 1922), and continued on with its subsequent name change to *Alfar* in October 1923.

Barradas appeared in just about every number from November 1922 onward. His brother Antonio de Ignacios appeared there too, as did his sister Carmen.[223] Likewise his good friends the art critics Manuel Abril and José Francés. Core members of the *tertulia* were frequent contributors: Alberto, Jarnés, Garrán, and Pérez de la Ossa. Present, too, were the likes of Buñuel, Dalí, Maroto, Chabás, and Gutiérrez Gili. Madrid's first *vanguardista*, Gómez de la Serna, figured quite prominently, but Cansinos Assens's presence was minimal. Guillermo de Torre, Barradas's old friend and enthusiastic *ultraísta*, appeared with considerable regularity, as did – from Buenos Aires – his fiancée and her brother, Norah and Jorge Luis Borges. In listings of *ultraísta* magazines, *Alfar* is often named, and while the label is not strictly accurate, it is understandable, for the magazine published a lot of *ultraísta* writings and artwork. (See appendix 1 at the back of the book for a list of the poets in question [in section b], others close to but not in the movement [section c], and associated artists [section d].)

Casal rarely came to Madrid, and when he did it was for a brief visit. One such occasion was when he gave a reading of poems from his upcoming collection *Árbol* (1925) at the Residencia de Estudiantes, on 10 December 1923.[224] The newspaper article explains that the idea arose spontaneously to hold a dinner in his honour on 12 December. The organizers are listed as Manuel Machado, Gómez de la Serna, Abril, Barradas, Torre, Garfias, García Lorca, Jarnés, and Garrán.[225] Among the other attendees we find Pérez de la Ossa and Paszkiewicz, as well as well-known figures such as Eugeni d'Ors.[226] Almost exactly a year later, a journalist, Manuel Pedreira, celebrated *Alfar* in a long article in a Madrid newspaper in which he pointed out its many qualities, including longevity, quality, and vitality, which residents of La Coruña were barely aware of.[227] Furthermore, he stressed the blend of names to be found in its pages:

> Right now it represents the most perfect and admirable exponent of the new, avant-garde generation that was incubated by the *ultraísta* movement – carefully selected, their original shortcomings eliminated, and their aspirations and contributions directed into deeper and surer channels – alongside the purest and steadiest established figures, who in spite of their official recognition feel a noble longing for artistic renewal without abandoning their aesthetic ideals.

BARRADAS AT THE RESIDENCIA DE ESTUDIANTES

In describing these many encounters, friendships, and gatherings, I would not want to give the impression of a "one-way street," with all roads in Madrid leading down to Atocha and the Café de Oriente. Evidently, Barradas and his friends ventured into many other fora. García Lorca, Buñuel, and Dalí all lived at the Residencia de Estudiantes, and this is one of the places that we know Barradas visited. Already cited is Lorca's account of a get-together in his room that included Maroto, Barradas, [Regino] Sáinz de la Maza, Tomás Borrás, Adolfo Salazar, plus some other *ultraístas*, in addition to "my friends from the Residencia." And as Torre remarked, "there was, then, a human and literary link between García Lorca and the *ultraístas*, manifested in personal terms by the visits to the Residencia with which some of us repaid his attendance at the Café del Prado *tertulia*."[228]

The fourth member of the tight-knit Residencia group of Lorca, Buñuel, and Dalí was José "Pepín" Bello, and he, too, met and got to know Barradas, though perhaps less well than the other three. As he remembered, "Rafael

Barradas, the Uruguayan painter, was also a member of our group. I met him in a bar with Federico. He drew well, and for a time he was a major influence on Dalí. He did a pencil portrait of me ... Barradas was a completely bohemian man."[229] Santos Torroella documents two portraits of Bello done by Barradas, and also the influence of his thinking on Buñuel.[230]

EVOCATIONS OF THE *TERTULIA* AT THE CAFÉ DE ORIENTE

Over the years, several writers evoked the surroundings and atmosphere at the *tertulia* held in the Café de Oriente. Tomás Borrás was one of the earliest, and also the most succinct, picturing the members "grouped around Barradas. And Barradas, putting spectacles on them, with a different colour in each lens, so that they see everything and see nothing."[231] Around the time that Barradas left for Luco de Jiloca, Jarnés published an affectionate portrait:

> Here is the searching pilgrim of art who made a stop at the motley and polyphonic inn of this popular café ... At the door of the [Café del] Oriente is seated the anti-pope.
>
> Already a little tired ... Rafael Barradas came to rest up in a tall and thoughtful pontifical throne. Here he was taken by surprise by the vigorous pencil of the sculptor Alberto ... Before this, our profane ears had already caught him in a full torrent of encyclical demolishing Color and Light, the old gods of art ...
>
> His chair has as its back a mirror. Here is where Barradas's bubbling mind rests, that is to say, in itself. His table is that of an alchemist magician who possesses the secret of changing anecdote into category, an accident into substance ... His table is that of some ancient celebrant of the cult of two dimensions, who has now repudiated the rite, because his pencil makes furrows and his eyeglasses strip men and things naked of all superficial arabesques.
>
> Attempted *planismo*, just like the attempted *faquirismo*[232] is the product of this mind that is so *deep* and so vibrant! ... he has turned the café into a workshop and the marble into a laboratory vessel, and with all the living canvases that are renewed daily at [the Café del] Oriente ... And his pencil – a marvelous recreator of figures

and nuances – will capture and fix, permanently, the diverse and undulating soul of his motley and polyphonic inn where, on his return from the latest trenches, he installed his solemn pontifical chair.[233]

Somewhat later, Rafael Cansinos Assens also offered his characteristically sardonic vision of the café.[234] In his novelized memoirs, the episode is included just after an event that occurred in May 1924,[235] but the founding of *Cascabeles*, in February 1923, takes place several pages into the same section, so the chronology is, at best, approximate. In any event, many details point to this account being set *after* Cansinos became distanced from the *ultraísta* group, in the latter half of 1922. He commences hyperbolically by depicting the area of Atocha as "this sleeping suburb of the city,"[236] while it was Jarnés who revealed to him the existence of the *tertulia*:

Another poet of the suburb ... Benjamín Jarnés, a slim young man, with eyeglasses and a peevish and skeptical expression on his face, has revealed to me a whole *tertulia* of artists in that Café de Oriente, at the end of the calle de Atocha, in front of which I have passed so many times without suspecting that those lyrical swallows had slung their nest there.[237]

The presentation of Jarnés – "the man of limits" – is hardly flattering:

Jarnés's whole life took place within that limited perimeter, around the Glorieta de Atocha ... Only rarely did that intellectual ascend the Atocha hill, which leads to the centre, to the real city. He was always at the foot of that Olympus, not daring to scale it, but still wanting desperately to do so. How Jarnés envied the writers of the centre, what he would have given to be able to be a regular at the *tertulias* of the [Café] Colonial and of the Cripta de Pombo! ...

Jarnés shrugged his shoulders, in a gesture of contented apathy and leaned back on his banquette in the Café de Oriente, or in his wicker armchair on the terrace ... with a large beer in front of him.[238]

With dubious accuracy, Cansinos then makes Jarnés the central figure of the *tertulia*:

Jarnés was lavish in invitations and around him he had gathered artists of the suburb, residents of those recently constructed streets around the Glorieta de Atocha who acknowledged in him a certain leadership, because of his inclination to generous patronage. Not only did Jarnés invite them to have coffee, beer, and sandwiches, but he also took them to his home ... and organized in their honour feasts worthy of Pantagruel.[239]

Then he starts to enumerate the other members:

The most notable among those friends was a certain Garrán, a small and ugly young man who was employed in the Ministry of War and drew caricatures and figures of women with legs in the style of Demetrio López,[240] and hung around, with barely any luck, the editorial offices of *Buen Humor* and *La Hoja de Parra*.[241]

Cansinos also briefly mentions a minor journalist, José de Silva,[242] who contributed to *La Villa y Corte de España*, *Buen Humor*, and *La Risa*, as well as an article in *Cascabeles*.[243]

Once again bypassing Barradas, Cansinos finds that the most intriguing of the *tertulia*'s members was Alberto,

a big strong fellow with a brusque disposition, coarse, proletarian, iconoclastic, who did not acknowledge anybody's prestige and thought that visual arts started with him.

Alberto was a bakery worker ... who had unexpectedly revealed himself as a sculptor and who received a small grant from the Diputación Provincial de Toledo, to receive an artistic training in Madrid ...

Alberto was a case of heroic willpower, he fully believed that he would triumph, he was always drawing, at home, in the café: the basis of everything – he asserted – is drawing – and he modelled small figures in black stone, for he was enthusiastic about the latest thing that was African art.[244]

Cansinos paints a typical scene with Garrán and Alberto arguing violently, Jarnés trying to convince them that they were both right, and

Silva focusing on the *tapas*, while two young ladies employed by the café owner play music for the customers.[245]

We know that Pedro Garfias must have been at least an occasional visitor to the *tertulia*, but Cansinos distorts the situation, making it sound as if he had been tracked down there, and also as if Barradas were not a central figure:

> The worst was when the *ultraístas* discovered my whereabouts and came to seek me out in the distraction and isolation of Atocha, where I had taken refuge. One night unexpectedly Pedro Garfias appeared there, along with Barradas and a very young man of slight build, with a rosy, simpleton's face ... Antonio [Cleofé] Puertas de Raedo, a poet according to him aligned with the *ultraístas*.[246]

Cleofé Puertas de Raedo seems to have been an infrequent visitor;[247] he is usually identified as a "bohemian" poet and grouped with others like Armando Buscarini.[248] Another new arrival was Rafael Pizarro, whose main claim to fame was that he was the nephew of the "erotic novelist" Felipe Trigo.[249]

According to Cansinos, Garfias became a more regular visitor, supposedly "drawn there by my presence."[250] At the same time, Cansinos noticed changes in Jarnés: "he started to adopt more and more the attitude of a literary pontiff and treated his new friends with a tone of superiority."[251] As for Garfias:

> Jarnés receives him offhandedly, almost rudely, but then he realizes that he can be useful to him as a link with Pombo and becomes very friendly with him.
>
> Jarnés, who initially spoke scornfully of Ramón, now aspires to interact with him. Ramón has connections with the *Revista de Occidente* and in Pombo he offers translation commissions to his friends ...
>
> These suburb poets are burning with desire to climb the Atocha hill, just as I was to descend it.[252]

And thus it came to pass that it was Garfias who introduced Jarnés into the Pombo circle, where he was cheerfully welcomed by Ramón.[253] And from Pombo he soon moved on to the *Revista de Occidente*:

And so; father Jarnés, with his modest air and his accommodating words, managed first to get into Pombo, and then, through contacts that he made there, he even reached the *Revista de Occidente*, he was introduced to Ortega y Gasset, and he placed his first article in those pages hallowed by the prestige of the Philosopher.

Jarnés had triumphed. No longer was he a writer of the suburbs.[254]

As time passed, Cansinos tired of the same people, conversations, and attitudes:

The Glorieta de Atocha lost more and more of its attraction for me. I encountered among those poets of the suburb the same rivalries and jealousies as among those whom I had left behind in the cafés of the centre … and also a longing to climb up the greasy pole of notoriety, which was more intense the further they felt from the top.[255]

And so he gradually stopped going to the *tertulia*.[256] A letter from Cansinos to Jarnés alludes to his withdrawal – it is unclear whether temporary or permanent – from what seems to be the Oriente gathering. A reference to *Cascabeles* dates it to the spring of 1923; Cansinos announces "my withdrawal from that café banquette, which up to yesterday had been calm," motivated by "the impertinence of that young man" (who remains unidentified) and compounded by the fact that Jarnés stayed and did not leave with him.[257]

ARTWORKS OF ATOCHA AND THE CAFÉ

Barradas painted the Glorieta de Atocha several times, shortly after arriving in Madrid. There is a study and the final work of *Puerta de Atocha* (1919, graphite, coloured pencils, tempera, and oil)[258] and of *Atocha* (1919, oil on canvas).[259] Similarly, we have a study and resulting work rendering the perspective from close to where Jarnés worked looking toward the square: *De Pacífico a Puerta de Atocha* (1919, pencil, charcoal, and oil on canvas)[260] and *De Pacífico a Puerta de Atocha* (1919, oil on canvas).[261] Barradas also depicted blocks of apartments in the immediate vicinity of the station: *Estación del Mediodía* (1922, oil on canvas).[262]

Barradas's predilection for spending long hours in cafés was already firmly established during the time spent in Barcelona,[263] and a number

2.12. Rafael Barradas, *Gente en el café* (Estudio), 1919, watercolour and pencil on paper, 23 x 26 cm.

2.13. Rafael Barradas, *Escena en el Café de Oriente*, undated, ink on paper, 20.3 x 13 cm.

of depictions of the interiors of cafés and of customers date from this period. Notable here are *Café futurista* (1917, ink on paper);[264] *Hombre en la taberna* (1917, watercolour on cardboard);[265] *Escena de café* (n.d. [ca 1918], pencil and coloured pencils on paper);[266] *Interior de café* (1918, oil on cardboard);[267] another *Interior de café* (1918, oil on cardboard);[268] *Composición vibracionista* (1918, oil on cardboard);[269] *Café* (1918, oil on collage on cardboard);[270] and *Dama en el café* (1918, tempera on paper).[271]

He carried this fondness to Madrid, as can be appreciated in *Gente en el café (Estudio)*, shown in figure 2.12. The fluted iron columns of the Café de Oriente can be seen in *Escena en el Café de Oriente*, in figure 2.13. Barradas emblazons the name on another sketch that simultaneously combines various planes: *Recuerdo de la naturaleza muerta. Un café, por Barradas* (n.d., no details).[272] Barradas would sometimes ascribe the work specifically to the Café de Oriente, as in his *Retrato del pintor Bon* (1920, charcoal on paper).[273] Likewise, Barradas was also given to rendering regular café customers – for example, in *Hombre en la taberna* (1922, oil on canvas)[274] and *Home al café (Atocha)* (1923, oil on canvas).[275]

BARRADAS'S OTHER ACTIVITIES, 1922 ONWARD

Besides everything already documented for 1922 and 1923, Barradas also found time for other activities. Thus he participated in the VIII Salón de Humoristas held in June 1922. A critic commented that, "with his disconcerting drawings, which he calls *extraplanistas*, [Barradas] intends to give the sensation of tables with glasses and bottles, with Futurist ambivalences."[276] On 20 November 1922, much of literary and artistic Madrid turned out for the homage to the critic and poet Enrique Díez-Canedo held at Pombo, and Barradas was there.[277] He also illustrated two books by Francisco Luis Bernárdez, *Bazar* and *Orto* (both Madrid: Imp. Sucesores de Rivadeneyra, 1922) and one by Alfonso Vidal y Planas, *Los gorriones del Prado* (Madrid: Estrella, 1922), for which he then did the posters for its production at the Teatro Eslava in February 1923.

In 1923, he illustrated Torre's *ultraísta* collection *Hélices* (Madrid: Mundo Latino). That year also saw the normal round of banquets, such as the one held on 17 March in honour of Jacinto Grau for the premiere

of *El Señor de Pigmalión* in Paris; among the many other attendees were
Maroto, Bagaría, Winthuysen, Fontanals, Cristóbal Ruiz, García Lorca,
and Manuel Ángeles Ortiz.[278] During the summer months spent in Luco
de Jiloca, he published several drawings in *Color. Revista Quincenal*
(Barcelona), which helped to keep him economically afloat.[279] In the
fall, he sent three canvases to be included in the Salón de Primavera in
Montevideo.[280] He was also trying to arrange an exhibition of thirty or
forty of drawings, hoping that some sales would bring money for the
oil paints he needed, and in November there was a trip to Barcelona on
business for Martínez Sierra.[281]

In 1924, there is less visible activity, and Barradas's name appears much
less frequently in the daily press. The first four books in the "Cuentos para
niños" series were published by Calpe (referenced above), and Barradas
also illustrated Vando-Villar's *La sombrilla japonesa* (Madrid: Tableros).
In the fall, he was listed as one of the set designers for the new season
in the Teatro Eslava.[282] This was also the year in which he made contact
with Ortega y Gasset, recommended to him by Abril, and he went on to
contribute illustrations to the *Revista de Occidente*.[283]

LATER INCARNATIONS OF THE *TERTULIA*

Barradas was a significant participant in the epoch-making exhibition
in Madrid sponsored by the Sociedad de Artistas Ibéricos and running
May–July 1925; sharing two rooms with Alberto, he showed more
canvases there than anybody else.[284] But tensions with Martínez Sierra
were growing, and at the end of August there was a falling-out.[285] A friend
of Barradas in Barcelona judged the event harshly: "Martínez Sierra – in
a despicable gesture that we shall never be able to forget or forgive – got
rid of him, abandoned him."[286] Most critics propose that it was Barradas's
closeness, perhaps even devotion, to Catalina Bárcena, Martínez Sierra's
long-term mistress, that led to this crisis.[287] It was also during these
months – April through October – that Martínez Sierra exhibited the
work done by the Teatro Eslava at the major International Exhibition of
Modern Decorative and Industrial Arts in Paris (the exhibition that gave
us Art Deco).[288] The display featured four posters by Barradas; four set
designs each by Fontanals, Burmann, and Barradas; six puppet figures by
Barradas; four miniature theatres, unattributed (but likely by Barradas);

and the book *Un teatro de arte en España, 1917–1925*.[289] Ironically, Martínez Sierra would go on to win one of the top prizes, and Barradas both a "grand prix" and a "diplôme d'honneur."[290]

At the same time, Martínez Sierra decided not to renew his annual lease on the Teatro Eslava for the whole of the 1925–26 season. He staged productions there between October and January, with Burmann acting as the chief designer.[291] Already when visiting Paris in the fall of 1925 he was formulating his plans to try his luck abroad.[292] Meanwhile, with their ties severed, Barradas left Madrid for Barcelona around the end of September, and originally he planned to travel on to Paris shortly after.[293] Although he was on the brink of making the trip, it likely never occurred.[294] Rather, Barradas spent time in Bordeaux, Biarritz, and St Jean de Luz around the end of the year and the beginning months of 1926.[295] From there, he returned to Barcelona, or more precisely Hospitalet, where he stayed until his eventual return to Montevideo.

A *tertulia* is not a static entity; some people attend more or less regularly, others just sporadically; new members start coming, older ones drift away or leave town. The later life of the Café de Oriente *tertulia* is beyond the scope of this chapter, but it certainly continued on even after Barradas's departure. When the aspiring young artist Francisco "Pancho" Lasso arrived in Madrid from the Canary Islands on 17 September 1926, he headed almost straight away to the Café de Oriente, where he found, and was immediately impressed by, Alberto.[296] As he recounts,

> before going to drawing class I used to go to the *tertulia* of "artists" at the Café de Oriente … This *tertulia* was not a leisure activity or frivolity, it was a class on how to enter the world of art as an artist. There was talk of critics' writings, exhibition, styles, techniques employed, individual secrets … But without all these pieces of knowledge I would not have known how to go through a museum, or tour a studio. At that time I had no idea how to give my opinion … but I listened … because we were artists and there was originality and inventiveness there.

The Café de Oriente and its *tertulia* finally received more extensive newspaper coverage in the fall of 1929. In his series on the *peñas literarias* of Madrid, Santiago de la Cruz reported on both its present configuration and its past history.[297] Various things stand out here, including the photograph of "Barradas's table," demonstrating that the artist's memory was still vivid. The names cited by De la Cruz are a mix of the familiar and the less familiar. Among the founders he identifies Jarnés, Barradas, and Garrán, but also Alejandro Sánchez Felipe and Rafael Pizarro. Among visitors he cites Lorca, Dalí, Garfias ("director of the magazine *Horizonte*, whose last two numbers took shape in this café"), Montes, Pérez de la Ossa, Abril, Valentín de Pedro, Maroto, Cansinos Assens, Torre, Casal, but also the Peruvian poet César Cáceres Santillana, the Polish painter Marjan Paskiewicz, and the Argentinian writer Jorge Luis Borges (who visited the capital only briefly). The rest of the article is concerned with the large number of people attending the *tertulia* as of 1929, which reveals that while the regular gathering continued on, the membership had almost completely changed.

CONCLUSION

Barradas moved in a number of distinct but overlapping circles: the artistic and literary friends that he had made in Barcelona; Martínez Sierra, the Teatro Eslava, and the other designers, actors, and playwrights who worked with the company; the *tertulia* of the Café del Prado and the wider world of the Ultraísta movement; the Pombo *tertulia*; the group of people who were residents or friends of residents at the Residencia de Estudiantes; the tentative avant-garde art world of Madrid in the 1920s; humour magazines; children's literature; the publishing and journalistic worlds; and last but not least, his own *tertulia* at the Café de Oriente. Given that all these circles had Barradas in common, he served as a potential nexus point to bring many members of different groups into contact, and when individuals were already in touch via other connections, he reinforced pre-existing relationships. It is in these ways that he is exemplary of the extraordinarily rich and complex interconnectivity of the literary and artistic worlds of Madrid of the period.

CHAPTER 3

THE PASAJE DE LA ALHAMBRA TIMES TWO

Manuel Ángeles Ortiz's Studio and Julio Moisés's Academy

The Pasaje de la Alhambra

The Pasaje de la Alhambra was located in the Chueca neighbourhood of central Madrid, inside the city block bordered on the north side by the calle del Arco de Santa María (nowadays known as Augusto Figueroa), on the south by the calle de San Marcos, on the east by the calle del Barquillo, and on the west by the calle de la Libertad. A mix between an alley, a mews, a patio, and a square, the Pasaje was constructed by the well-known architect and contractor José Purkiss Zubiría between 1887 and 1888.[1] Its name came from the grounds where it was built, which previously had been the site of the pleasure gardens attached to the Teatro de la Alhambra,[2] a building erected in 1870 on the corner of calle de la Libertad and calle de San Marcos.[3]

The Pasaje was oriented more or less on a north–south axis, and thereby connected the calle de Colmenares (to the south) with the calle Válgame Dios (to the north). Two matching archways, at the T junctions of Colmenares with San Marcos and Arco de Santa María with Válgame Dios, afforded access, through a tunnel-like passageway, to the inner courtyard that opened out into a broader open space.[4] On the map shown in figure 3.1 below, it appears as a regular cross street ("P. Alhambra"), but

3.1. The vicinity of the Pasaje de la Alhambra in Madrid.

the narrow passages at the north and south ends (see figure 3.2 below) served as somewhat restricted access points.

From 1892 onward – for many years thereafter, in fact – the Imprenta de San Francisco de Sales was installed in Pasaje de la Alhambra, 1, and the press of the newspaper *La Correspondencia Militar* and of the publishing company El Progreso Editorial was also to be found in the same building.[5] Likewise, the Imprenta Helénica was based in Pasaje de la Alhambra, 3, and this print shop continued in operation until the 1930s. After a long series of lawsuits and much legal wrangling between the residents and tenants of the Pasaje de la Alhambra and development companies, the Pasaje was eventually approved for demolition in 1970, and in its place a new complex of buildings, again with an inner courtyard, was constructed.[6]

3.2. One of the entrances to the Pasaje de la Alhambra.

The top level of the Pasaje de la Alhambra, 3, was purpose-built as an artist's studio, and immediately upon the completion of the new development, in the spring of 1888, the well-known painter Casto Plasencia Maestro (1846–1890) began occupying the space.[7] The press offered several descriptions, with the following being one of the most detailed:

His new studio on the Pasaje de la Alhambra makes you want to write a book. It is the foremost in Madrid; it has something of a museum and something of a temple about it, it seems borrowed from a tale in the *1001 Nights* ...

It is, overall, a large room, 16 metres by 9, lit from above, as painters say (zenith lighting) that can be modified by half curtains that have been skillfully installed. The four sections of wall are covered with a rich plush material in four different colours: dark maroon, bronze green, navy blue, and old gold; a large baseboard of Cordovan leather edges the walls, and this is intersected by a very richly embroidered frieze, in the style of the eighteenth century. The doors that lead to the inner rooms are covered with heavy, drooped curtains, in the Greco-Roman style, blue background, finished at the top with artistic embroidered valances.

In the room there are chests and wardrobes from the Renaissance, suits of armour and armchairs from the time of Charles V and Philip II, vases from Talavera, Roman amphora, earthenware cornucopias from the beginning of the century, statues, and characteristic weapons.[8]

By the fall, Plasencia had also started to use the ample studio to hold a kind of weekly salon, which on Fridays brought together painters, writers, musicians, and amateur enthusiasts of the fine arts.[9] The queen regent, María Cristina, visited him there on 19 June 1889, an event that gave rise to another round of press coverage.[10] Among these reports one stands out, which again provides a detailed description of the working space:

On entering one encounters a fairly spacious room, which is the true workshop of the numerous pupils of Plasencia. Next to this is the large room that is indeed amply proportioned; ... the *salón* being described here measures 16 metres long, 8.5 metres wide, and 5.5 metres high; it receives zenith light through a wide skylight that is 1 metre long and 6 metres wide.

The walls, covered in deep plush ... in different colours that are artistically combined, give the room an overall look of beauty together with sobriety that creates a most pleasant impression. Two columns in the Churrigueresque style, standing at the entrance to the room, each serve as pedestals for attractive and fanciful porcelain vases.

Decorating the sections of wall there are, placed in no particular order or flamboyant combination, various objects of value and a few artworks …

The studio, where in one of the corners there is a really lovely Rönisch piano, [provides] eloquent proof of the musical enthusiasms of the master of the house.[11]

Unfortunately, Plasencia Maestro was only able to enjoy his new studio for a couple of years, as he died in May 1890, at which point the interior was cleared out and the furniture and other miscellaneous objects sold in a liquidation auction.[12] At the beginning of 1892, the space was occupied by the painter José Jiménez Aranda (1837–1903). He had returned to Madrid in 1890 after having spent nine years in Paris,[13] and according to press reports from January 1892, Jiménez, "compelled on the one hand by his love for Spain, and on the other by the requests from his many pupils who seek instruction from the distinguished master," decided to establish himself "definitively" in Madrid in Plasencia's workshop.[14] However, it was not long before he changed his mind and left Madrid for Sevilla, his native city, and so in 1893 he transferred the Pasaje studio to his good friend Joaquín Sorolla (1863–1923). At the same time, he also passed on his pupils and various pieces of furniture.[15]

Sorolla would work in the space for a decade, until the end of 1903. We find him here, for example, in May 1897, receiving the visit of two noblewomen, the Duchesss of Denia accompanied by the Baroness of Bogel: "The splendid studio of the famous painter (in a house in the Pasaje de la Alhambra) is decorated with much taste, without overdoing the *atrezzo*. There are very good carvings, a Gothic seat of honour, a Louis XV console, and many other things of beauty."[16] In the long history of the space, this span of Sorolla's occupation is the best documented, and there are over twenty photographs, as well as various canvases, showing the interior of the studio.[17] There are photos of his workspace (for an example, see figure 3.3. below), the many trappings on the walls,[18] classes with a number of his private pupils,[19] and his own impressionistic renderings of works in progress and assorted furniture.[20] Importantly, we can also appreciate how the architectural design of the studio, strategically located

3.3. Sorolla's studio space, Pasaje de la Alhambra.

as it was on the uppermost floor, allowed for the unobstructed entry of a great deal of natural light.

Sorolla finally left the studio in 1904, when he moved to a house on calle Miguel Ángel that served as both residence and workspace.[21] Meanwhile, José Villegas Cordero (1844–1921), after a long stay in Rome, had returned in 1901 to Madrid, and when the studio became vacant he was its next occupant.[22] He worked there for a while, but late in 1908 he decided to transfer to a space inside the Museo de Prado, as he was at the time the museum's director, a position that required his continual presence.[23] When this article on the Pasaje by Francisco Alcántara appeared, Sorolla was in the United States, preparing an exhibition at the Hispanic Society of America held between 4 February and 8 March 1909. The article contains information about Sorolla's plans for the future:

When Sorolla returns from the United States, where currently he is organizing a major exhibition similar to those held in Paris, Berlin, and London, he will establish in it [the space recently vacated by Villegas] a Free School of decorative arts with the collaboration of artists and scholars. The house where the studio is located belongs to the Duke of Tovar, who is allowing it to be used, free of charge, for such a lofty purpose. Sorolla is proposing to solve with his Academy the problem of the introduction of our artistic youth to modern methods of teaching decorative art, and even if he only achieves a little in this direction, he will be doing a great good for our culture. The body of our teachers do not yet feel the need to return to the direct study of nature, in order to create a new art, or even to achieve a modern interpretation of the old one.[24]

Unfortunately, this ambitious project was not realized.[25] Also, it has not been possible to identify the tenants of the Pasaje de la Alhambra studio over the stretch between 1909 and 1919, although we might reasonably suppose that they, too, would have been painters, though probably largely forgotten ones, given the dearth of information available.

Manuel Ángeles Ortiz

Our narrative resumes on 19 November 1919, when Manuel Ángeles Ortiz (1895–1984)[26] married Paquita Alarcón in Granada. The couple had met some time before 1912 in the Granada studio of José de Larrocha (1850–1933), when Manuel Ángeles was studying with the painter and Paquita was working for him as a child model. Immediately after the ceremony, they took the train to Madrid to move into the Pasaje studio that Ortiz had just rented.[27] He knew the city well, as he had started studying there in the atelier of Cecilio Plá (1860–1934) in 1912, splitting his time for several years between the capital and Granada.

A few days later, their close friend Federico García Lorca travelled to Madrid and took lodgings in a *pensión* where their mutual friend Ángel Barrios, the guitarist and composer from Granada, was also staying.[28] Lorca was in Madrid from 23 or 24 November up until just before Christmas, when he returned to Granada. Around 7 January 1920, he was supposed to occupy his reserved room at the Residencia de Estudiantes, but he lingered in Granada for a considerable time and did not return to the capital until well into the month of February.[29] The date when Lorca again returned to Granada cannot be established precisely: he seems to have stayed in Madrid through Easter (in 1920 falling on 4 April), but then he attended a concert given by the guitarist Regino Sáinz de la Maza at the Hotel Alhambra Palace in Granada on 20 May 1920.[30]

During both of these periods in the capital – late November to late December 1919, and mid-February to April/May 1920 – Lorca spent a lot of time with the young couple at the Pasaje de la Alhambra studio. Over these months late in 1919 and early in 1920, he was working on the script of *El maleficio de la mariposa* for its upcoming performance at the Teatro Eslava, a premiere postponed several times but that finally took place on 22 March (see chapter 2). According to Ángeles Ortiz, "The poem, which later would be *El maleficio de la mariposa*, was written by Federico in Granada, but he recast it in great part in my studio in the Pasaje de la Alhambra. Paquita and I knew the play because Federico had read it to us, and as he read aloud so extraordinarily well, we believed that it was going to be a significant success."[31] Not only this, but the studio space became, with the arrival of Manuel Ángeles and Paquita and then Lorca, the base for the Madrid branch of the Granada *tertulia* called El Rinconcillo.[32] At that time, several of its members were living or studying in Madrid, including José Fernández-Montesinos, José Mora Guarnido, Melchor Fernández Almagro, Miguel Pizarro, and Juan de Dios Egea, among others.[33] Ángeles Ortiz picks up his narrative:

> Federico was the most assiduous visitor, because as he said he found that it was like being "at home." "Paquita and I ... started to get to know, by name and reputation, his new friends at the Residencia. Federico was always passionate about the new. His most recent friends always captured his attention, and he knew it ... "
>
> "My friends from the Rinconcillo were sure that [my baby] was going to be a girl. All of them had a part in choosing her name. One day Miguel Pizarro proposed: 'We need to call her Isabel Clara, thinking of the portrait by Titian, of the queen Isabel Clara, which is in the Prado.' And everybody was in agreement."

3.4. Manuel Ángeles Ortiz, *Retrato de José Fernández-Montesinos*, 1920.

"When I met up with Federico it was almost always in my studio, because he came to have lunch almost daily, and sometimes he brought along his companions from the Residencia."[34]

In one of his first letters to his family from 1920, Lorca commented, "You cannot imagine how well Manolo and Paquita treat me. Twice I have had to stay to eat with them, and they are nothing but kind and affectionate. Never in my life have I seen a happier or nicer married couple."[35] In another he told them, "Today I'm writing you from Manolo Ortiz's home, who's invited me to lunch."[36] And in a third, "Yesterday was Paquita's saint's day and I spent the whole day with them; I was very happy and a little muddle-headed because there were plentiful sweets and liqueurs. I had a wonderful time."[37]

During the summer of 1920, Lorca was back in Granada, but other members of the Rinconcillo remained in Madrid. A group of them sent Federico a collective letter, dated "Manolo's studio in Madrid. Pasaje de la Alhambra. 31 August 1920, night!!" Fernández-Montesinos ends his portion of the missive thus: "Manolo and Paquita, who aren't going to Paris just yet, are both marvelous and Pizarro is just lovely. Stopping now so they can add something."[38] Ángeles Ortiz continues:

Dear and amazing Federico:

As you will see we are still in Madrid where we will be until the beginning of December, that is if Paquita doesn't experience any complications of any kind. The cause of our having delayed our trip to Paris had been on account of my great patriotism which was rebelling against the prospect that a Spaniard of rugged mettle should have an *enfant poilu* [i.e., a French child].

Pizarro and Fernández Almagro then closed with brief but affectionate notes.

Lorca returned to Madrid and the Residencia de Estudiantes toward the beginning of October.[39] Later that month he informed his family that "Paquita is almost at full term but is feeling very good, and Manolo is excellent and painting very well. Yesterday they were with me having afternoon tea and Don Antonio was also there."[40] In November he let them know that "Paquita will give birth any day now ... and there is anticipation to know if it's going to be a boy or a girl."[41] Manuel and Paquita's daughter, Isabel Clara, was born on 18 November 1920, and Lorca asked his family, "what present are you going to give (mother to mother) to Manolo's little girl? I think that you should make some gesture of kindness, given the great friendship that we profess."[42] At the baptism, on 5 December, Lorca became the child's godfather.[43]

A few weeks after that, the young family left the Pasaje studio and headed to Paris, where they took lodgings in a *pension* in Montmartre. Ángeles Ortiz enrolled in drawing classes offered by the Académie de la Grande Chaumière.[44] They returned to Spain in the spring of the following year, passing through Madrid on their way back to Granada, where they would stay with family during the summer. Lorca was able to see them when they stopped off in the capital, and he give Manuel messages for his family.[45]

Back again in Madrid in September, the Ángeles Ortiz family now took up residence in a new apartment, an attic on Paseo General Martínez Campos (previously known as the Paseo del Obelisco).[46] Paquita had never fully recovered from the pregnancy and birth of Isabel Clara, and now her health was on the decline. That fall, Lorca did not return to Madrid, so it fell to Fernández Almagro to keep him apprised of developments. Hence, in a letter of 13 October, he reported that "Paquita is ill; it appears that [it is] serious enough to be worried about."[47] She passed away on 13 January 1922. Another friend from Granada and member of the Rinconcillo, the sculptor Juan Cristóbal, created a bronze funerary mask.[48]

Later, grieving deeply following his loss, Ángeles Ortiz travelled through several Andalusian cities. Lorca told Fernández Almagro that he had been in Granada: "Poor Manolo! Now he is calmer, but he went through a very bad patch, as everything was memories."[49] Later, he spent time in Algeciras, Ronda, and Málaga.[50] From Algeciras, he was in contact with Fernández Almagro, to whom he described his anguished state of mind.[51] He was in Ronda in March,[52] and from there took a train to Bobadilla: "And there I said to myself: I'm getting on the first train that comes along. And one arrived that was going to Málaga. I rented a room on La Caleta, near the Baños de Carmen."[53]

While he was staying in Málaga, he witnessed a severe fire on 26 April in the customs building beside the port, and it transpires that Emilio Prados was there too.[54] As Ángeles Ortiz would recount in 1970,

> Federico spoke about me to him so much and in such a way that I imagine that, because of that power of seraphic transmission that Federico had, Emilio was able to sense that I had to be the person who was close to him. It was the year of that fierce fire in the Customs House of Málaga. I was among the onlookers and Emilio who was also there saw me and wrote to Federico asking him if I was in Málaga and Federico sent him my address.[55]

Another version given to Antonina Rodrigo is only slightly different, in that they are there the day following the event; Prados's "innate shyness" stops him from approaching Ángeles Ortiz on the street, but as soon as he receives the address from Lorca, he comes to introduce himself.[56]

When he got back to Granada after his travels, Ángeles Ortiz and his young daughter returned to his mother's house on calle Zacatín and he set up a new studio on the Cuesta del Caidero.[57] He arrived in time to participate, with García Lorca and Manuel de Falla, in the final preparations for the Concurso del Cante Jondo, which would be held in the Plaza de los Aljibes in the Alhambra complex on the nights of 13 and

14 June 1922, coinciding with Corpus Christi week – a major event in Granada's calendar. During the previous summer, in discussions among members of the Rinconcillo *tertulia*, Ángeles Ortiz had contributed to the birth of the idea, and from Ronda, in March 1922, he wrote to Falla, congratulating him on the official approval that the Concurso had received from the Granada city council.[58] As he recalls, during the weeks immediately before the event, "Federico and I devoted our time to visiting neighbourhoods, taverns, villages, farms. We would ask for the old people of the place who knew how to 'stylize.' And we would head there."[59] Ángeles Ortiz also designed the main poster for the Concurso, using a modern, almost avant-garde, style for its execution. As a result, it was initially rejected by the Centro Artístico, Literario y Científico de Granada, the organization officially in charge, but when it received unconditional backing from Ignacio Zuloaga, the Centro reversed its decision and adopted it.[60]

In July, with the Concurso deemed an unqualified success, focus now turned to ideas for puppet performances that had been another subject of recent discussion. Mora Guarnido, in Granada, kept Fernández Almagro abreast of the Rinconcillo's plans:

> One of them is a trip to the Alpujarras to be undertaken by Federico, Falla, Ortiz, [Fernando] Vílchez, one or two others, plus me, taking a puppet theatre and some ballads to pay our way giving performances in the villages. Another is the foundation of the Spanish "illuminated" theatre.[61] Federico and Ortiz have had the idea of creating a theatre with flat [two-dimensional] puppets with backgrounds like those of the miniatures of ancient codices in order to perform reworkings of the ballad corpus and the Spanish classical theatre.[62]

From Asquerosa, Lorca wrote to Manuel de Falla during the second half of July: "I'm enthusiastic about the plan for a trip to the Alpujarras. You well know what a dream it is of mine to create some popular Andalusian puppet shows full of Andalusian emotion and exquisite popular feeling." He was counting on the collaboration of Falla, Ángeles Ortiz, and Mora Guarnido in such an endeavour.[63] In the end, however, despite the enthusiasm they engendered, these plans would not be realized, though Lorca did arrange and perform, using a similar technique, a puppet show in the drawing room of his family house in Granada, on the day of Epiphany – 6 January – 1923.[64]

Meanwhile, Isabel Clara, Ángeles Ortiz's daughter, was becoming accustomed to being looked after by her grandmother, and the painter started to feel again – as had happened at the end of 1920 – the irresistible attraction of Paris. In October 1922, he decided to move there, and set out accompanied by Emilio Prados and his brother Miguel. From Madrid, Ortiz wrote to Falla apologizing for not having made his farewells with him in person when he left Granada.[65] In Paris, the travellers were met at the station by Ismael González de la Serna, another painter from Granada and the Rinconcillo but now based there; Ismael was a childhood friend of Ángeles Ortiz and had encouraged him to relocate to the French capital.[66] Shortly after their arrival the three of them wrote a collective postcard to Lorca; the cancellation on the stamp appears to be from 18 October.[67] There is text by Ángeles Ortiz and Emilio Prados, a mix of comments and salutations, plus a series of small drawings, the most remarkable of which are caricatures of the heads of the three signatories. The Prados brothers set off again from Paris almost immediately afterwards; Emilio was going to the University of Freiburg, and Miguel to Munich.[68] Ángeles Ortiz initially lodged in various hotels in Montparnasse before finding a new studio located at 3 rue Vercingétorix, where he would remain for a long time, although with frequent visits to Madrid and Granada.[69] For Christmas and New Year 1922–23, he travelled to Germany, where it seems that he visited, in the company of Emilio and Miguel Prados and yet another mutual friend from Madrid circles and the Residencia de Estudiantes, José Antonio Rubio Sacristán, several cities, including Dresden, Berlin, Munich, Nüremberg, and Hinterzarten.[70] Thus began the long Parisian phase of his artistic career.

The Academia Libre of Julio Moisés

Ángeles Ortiz would not return to the Pasaje de la Alhambra after he left it in December 1920. New occupants arrived there at the beginning of 1921: another painter from Granada, Francisco Soria Aedo (1898–1965), and his friend the painter Pedro Antonio Martínez Expósita (1886–1965), from Almería, who jointly used the space until 1923.[71] Both of them worked in more traditional styles than Ortiz. When they in turn left, the new tenant would be Julio Moisés Fernández de Villasante (1888–1968), who had decided to follow a certain fashion of the time and omit his surnames, signing simply as Julio Moisés.[72] According to different sources, it was in 1920 or perhaps 1923 that Moisés moved to Madrid from Barcelona (where he had lived since 1912).[73] At this juncture, Moisés was in the middle of a successful career: during the 1920s, the press praised him almost unanimously every time that he participated in a collective exhibition or had an individual show, such as the one held at the Círculo de Bellas Artes at the end of 1921. He was not an avant-garde artist and was known above all for his portraits, particularly of girls and women, but neither was he totally reactionary in the way that a number of established painters were in 1920s Spain.

Although today his Academia Libre is mentioned with a certain frequency, relatively little is really known about it.[74] In the first place, his exact motivation for deciding to establish it is something of a mystery, since by far the most widespread practice of the time was for a successful painter to take a limited number of pupils, who sometimes also worked for him as apprentices. Clearly, in this regard we should remember the frustrated plans of Sorolla and the Duque de Tovar for the space, which may have served as inspiration. Most existing sources give its date of foundation as 1923, but the press indicates clearly that the doors of the Academia were not officially opened until the spring of 1924. Thus on 7 March readers were informed that, "Tomorrow, Saturday, the 8th of the month, at six in the evening, the Academia Libre de Madrid will be officially opened; it is located in the Pasaje de la Alhambra, number 3 (studio), and in it three daily classes of drawing and painting will be given; the afternoon session is exclusively for young ladies."[75] "Hesperia" records the event in a kind of newsletter on recent happenings in the world of art: "the Academia Libre de Madrid for drawing and painting has just been officially opened; it belongs to our friend Moisés, who with extreme skill has managed to realize his idea, giving it a form that is so attractive and practical that the atmosphere will surely be very favourable among the artists."[76]

In May of 1924, the painter Ramón José Izquierdo y Garrido (1873–1931) published an article about Julio Moisés. He began by reflecting in general terms on the professional formation of young artists in Spain, a process that he found deficient or, at the very least, incomplete: "Official teaching, however appropriate it may be, the workshop of a master, however much he may be worth, are not sufficient for the complete formation of an artist, because of their uniformity, of their way of seeing things from only one angle, which may be contrary to the temperament of the pupil."[77] Precisely because of this, he praised the fact that in Paris there existed important "free academies," where the training provided was very different:

> In that environment those free academies are what is missing, academies of absolute eclecticism that bring together artists of all tendencies, all orientations and backgrounds, as occurs in Paris in the famous academy on the rue du Dragon, the Académie Julian, and the Académie de la Grande Chaumière; there, in absolute freedom, artists find models with little outlay and masters free of charge among their own companions; the air of the world is breathed inside the confines of a workshop, because you can hear all different languages spoken and you can see all different concepts executed, and if this were the occasion and we had space, we would pause to spell out in detail the profound transformations that this kind of exchange of ideas has introduced into painting of the current time.

It was within this context that one could judge the value of Moisés's initiative: "A young painter, with a praiseworthy enthusiasm for the art of his country, has rounded out the newsworthy artistic events of this year, by establishing in Madrid one of those academies that we are talking about." At the first opportunity, the writer visited in person:

> We gave haste to see with our own eyes this important innovation, which if it takes shape will speed up the pace of artistic progress in Madrid, and so we headed to the Pasaje de la Alhambra, where after an "aerostatic ascent" we found ourselves in a large room with

zenith light and big windows, raised platforms for models, lecture seating, many easels and independent lighting systems, etc., etc.; in short, an academy in the modern style, with all its amenities.

On the large dais a model was posing, on the big easels sheets of paper awaited the hands of the artists, and in a corner, separate from that labyrinth, Juan Cristóbal, [Enrique Estévez] Ochoa, and the creator of the establishment "Julio Moisés" were in conversation.

The next – and the last – explicit mention of the Academia Libre that I have found occurs almost a year later, when the young artists who attended it offered a meal in Julio Moisés's honour, "as an expression of gratitude for the noble act entailed by the maintenance of said artistic centre."[78] It was held on 22 January 1925 in the Mesón del Segoviano, located in the Cava Baja. It seems that this celebration was not somehow connected with its possible impending closure, and that the academy was still functioning at least as of April of that year.

There is no complete list of the aspiring artists who made their way to the Academia, but those among them who later became well-known have left a range of first- or second-hand accounts. In this group we find Francisco Bores (1898–1972), Juan Cristóbal [González Quesada] (1897–1961), Salvador Dalí (1904–1989), Enrique Estévez Ochoa (1891–1978), Wifredo Lam (1902–1982), Maruja Mallo [Ana María Gómez González] (1902–1995), José Moreno Villa (1887–1955), Benjamín Palencia (1894–1980), Rafael de Penagos (1889–1954), Carlos Sáenz de Tejada (1897–1958), Francisco Santa Cruz [Francisco López Martínez] (1899–1957), and Eduardo Vicente (1909–1968).

Several of these individuals knew each other beforehand, and some of them started going to the Academia when introduced by a friend. Yet others would have met each other there. However, as it is impossible to establish the dates during which they attended classes, and the regularity with which they went, we cannot determine exactly which and how many first encounters can be ascribed to the Academia. Furthermore, information on some of the less celebrated figures listed above is lacking: there are few autobiographical accounts of their experiences and little detailed biographical documentation. Given these various limitations, the following paragraphs can only offer an incomplete image of the contacts that were established or reinforced thanks to the Academia Libre of Julio Moisés. But before broaching this subject, let us first sketch in as far as is possible the pre-existing links that had already been created at other points of convergence.

THE ESCUELA ESPECIAL DE PINTURA, ESCULTURA Y GRABADO AND THE RESIDENCIA DE ESTUDIANTES

More than half of the artists listed above also attended the Escuela Especial, but sometimes at very different moments. Thus Penagos and Cristóbal belong to different cohorts and entered and left without coinciding with others. Sáenz de Tejada officially finished his course of study at the Escuela quite early, in 1921, but still visited the building with some frequency and in addition attended the conservatory's El Paular summer program in 1922 and 1923, for which he was listed as an *agregado*, a kind of special invitee.[79] In this way he came to meet Dalí, and on the occasion of Dalí's first (temporary) expulsion from the Escuela Especial in the fall of 1923, the director of the conservatory, Miguel Blay, recruited Tejada to serve as an intermediary between the Escuela and the Dalí family.[80] Dalí and Mallo were strict contemporaries, as they started in the same year and consequently were already friends. Lam arrived one year later – 1923 – but during his first months in Madrid seems to have lived at somewhat of a distance from the majority of the other students. Eduardo Vicente enrolled in the Escuela Especial in the fall of 1924, by which time the Academia was already functioning. As for Dalí and Moreno Villa, they first met at the Residencia de Estudiantes, where both of them lived.

THE STUDIO ON TRAVESÍA DEL HORNO DE LA MATA AND THE CAFÉ SABOYA

Another important nexus was the artists' studio located on the fourth floor of a building that stood on the Travesía del Horno de la Mata, 7–9.[81] At the end of 1916, Sáenz de Tejada and Ismael Cuesta (Ismael Ricardo Cuesta de Juan, 1899–1982), who were already friends from the Escuela Especial, signed the rental contract and occupied it from the beginning of 1917 onward.[82] Cuesta, the son of a famous professional photographer, was from Madrid, and he entered the conservatory in the same year – 1915 – as did Tejada. A little later, other occupants were invited to share the studio and help with the communal expenses: Aristóbulo de

Juan, a cousin of Cuesta, Joaquín Valverde, a fellow art student at the Escuela, and Vicente Díez de Santos, a photographer and step-brother of Aristóbulo.[83] Another student at San Fernando and sometime visitor has described the space and activities as follows:

> It was composed of a large room with central light from the ceiling and a large set of windows facing west; beside the main room, in a small bedroom, a photographic workshop had been installed (belonging to Vicente Díez, an amateur photographer) ... Life there was extremely simple and merry ... There were carnivals, pantomimes, and merrymaking, and in the midst of everything people painted. They painted a lot. The canvases started to cover the walls of the studio, piling up on the floor ... In the winter they had installed there a heater that burnt sawdust and the flooring was wooden. Carlos's parents, from time to time, sent shipments of pieces of furniture or decorative items to the studio.[84] The exoticism of the things that they sent him filled everyone with joy. Chinese tunics, incense burners, etc., etc. To celebrate those shipments there were big parties.[85]

One of Madrid art critics left his own impression:

> We went up to the pigeon loft that, together with the painter Sáinz [sic] de Tejada, Cuesta occupies in the Travesía del Horno de la Mata, to surprise the artist, currently doing his military service, in his artistic work, which is productive and copious; and there we spent an agreeable morning, admiring the collection of very amusing pencil drawings, ink drawings, gouaches, and watercolours that Cuesta has hung on the walls of the studio and in large portfolio cases, original works that he is preparing as illustrations for newspapers and for new exhibitions, with a hopeful anticipation, an innocence, and a modesty that are all charming and put one in mind of a big child who has not yet experienced the sorrows of the calvary of art.[86]

There were many other visitors to the studio: besides Manaut Viglietti, there was Manuel Abril, Enrique Díez-Canedo, Julio Romero de Torres, Juan de la Encina, Salvador Bartolozzi, the caricaturist Bon, Antonio Marichalar, Ramón Estalella Pujolá, Timoteo Pérez Rubio (from the Escuela Especial), Francisco Santa Cruz, Ramón Gómez de la Serna (Sáenz de Tejada's cousin), Sonia Delaunay, Juan Esplandiú, Eduardo Santonja Rosales, Fausto López Romero (the last three from the Escuela), the North American Henry Strater, and Benjamín Jarnés.[87] In addition, through the Escuela Especial, his participation in a variety of exhibitions, and his attendance at a variety of café *tertulias*, Cuesta also got to know Barradas, Salvador Bartolozzi, Pancho Cossío, Estévez Ochoa, Ismael González de la Serna, Rafael de Penagos, Gregorio Prieto, and Guillermo de Torre, among others.[88]

Cuesta left for Paris at the end of 1922 or the beginning of 1923, at which point Tejada invited Francisco Bores to share the studio.[89] Sáenz de Tejada would likely have met Joaquín Peinado (1898–1975) in the fall of 1918, when Peinado entered the Escuela,[90] and there are photos of Tejada, Timoteo Pérez Rubio, and Peinado together at El Paular in the summer of 1921.[91] Pérez Segura speculates that Peinado may have been the original link between Tejada and Bores, since Peinado studied, from 1920, in the studio of Cecilio Plá, where Bores was also a pupil.[92] On the night of 20 January 1925, Bores was sleeping at the studio while Tejada was away, working in the studio of another friend, Esplandiú. A fire broke out, destroying much of the studio and most of the artworks there.[93]

Overlapping with the activities at the Travesía del Horno de la Mata was a small *tertulia* of four friends who met regularly at the Café Saboya, located in the same building as the original Teatro Apolo on calle de Alcalá. These were Sáenz de Tejada, Santa Cruz, Bores, and the only writer among them, Miguel Pérez Ferrero. As the latter recalls, "we used to meet, like other similar groups that were starting up, every day at the fall of evening in a café, which was our place for connecting and relaxation. The one chosen by us was called Saboya. The Apolo theatre was living out, perhaps without foreseeing it, its last days … In that same building, on one of its sides … was to be found our coterie."[94] As for their

sympathies and preoccupations, Pérez Ferrero wrote that "in content –
and in form – we followed the currents of a postwar less than ten years
old and we affiliated ourselves with tendencies that came together in ...
these words: modern – not *modernismo*, new, young, and in a term that,
like almost everything that suddenly becomes fashionable, was destined
to be discredited very soon: *avant-garde*."[95] Tejada contributed a line-
drawing portrait of Pérez Ferrero for his collection of poetry *Luces de
Bengala* (Madrid: Marineda, 1925).[96]

FRANCISCO BORES

Francisco Bores was born and grew up in Madrid. He did not attend the
Escuela Especial; rather, after abandoning first a university course in engineering and then, somewhat later, a course in law, he entered the private
art academy run by Cecilio Plá in Madrid,[97] where he studied between
1916 and 1921.[98] It was there that he met other younger painters, such as
Manuel Ángeles Ortiz, Pancho Cossío, and Joaquín Peinado.[99] In 1922, he
exhibited his work for the first time, in the Exposición Nacional de Bellas
Artes.[100] He soon entered some of the more forward-thinking literary and
artistic circles in Madrid. He was an early friend of Juan Chabás, who in
turn was acquainted with many of the then up-and-coming young writers.[101] Mangini also places Bores at the Café de Oriente *tertulia*,[102] while
Carmona notes that Bores frequented not only the Oriente but also the
Café de Platerías, with its own *tertulia* (see chapter 2).[103]

It is likely, therefore, that Bores already knew some of the other people
at the Academia Libre, and that this experience served as much to bolster
pre-existing relationships as to create new ones. Carmona proposes that
Bores and Palencia must have met around 1923, possibly not in a café
tertulia but rather through their contacts with the journal *España*, where
Palencia published in November 1923 and February 1924 and Bores in
January 1924.[104] Likewise, Carmona also conjectures that it could have
been Bores who encouraged Palencia to attend Moisés's classes.[105]
However, as just mentioned, Bores shared a studio with Sáenz de Tejada
from the beginning of 1923 onward, and we also know that the whole
group associated with the Café Saboya went along to the Academia (a
point to which I shall return below in the section dedicated to Tejada).[106]
At all events, Palencia, who like Bores never attended the Escuela Especial,

does remember him as a fellow student at the academy: "Bores, Dalí, and I ... did go to the Academia Libre, founded by Julio Moisés in the Pasaje de la Alhambra. I used to draw nudes ... to learn how to overcome the difficulties."[107] When Dalí and Lorca wrote a joint postcard to Palencia from Cadaqués, on 14 April 1925 (during Lorca's first trip there, to spend Easter with the Dalí family), the two of them addressed it to "(*Academia Libre*) / Pasaje de la Alhambra, no. 3," and also included at the end their "Regards to Bores."[108] When, in July 1925, shortly after the Sociedad de Artistas Ibéricos exhibition closed, Dalí wanted to enlist several friends (Barradas, Palencia, Moreno Villa, and others) in protesting the backward state of the Spanish art scene, he wrote to Bores in Madrid, asking him to coordinate the effort.[109]

Finally, it is worth noting that around 1924 or 1925, the brothers Eduardo and Esteban Vicente took a studio on the Paseo del Prado,[110] and that Bores, along with Pedro Flores García (1897–1967), Pedro Salinas, Manuel Abril, José Ortega y Gasset, Zenobia Camprubí, and Juan R. Jiménez, would drop by, forming another impromptu *tertulia* using the workshop space.[111]

JUAN CRISTÓBAL

Not a great deal of detailed biographical information is available about the sculptor. With his mother and siblings, he settled in Granada when he was ten years old, and came to consider himself an adoptive son of the city. He took classes in Granada at the Escuela Superior de Artes Industriales from 1906 to 1913, and it was there that he met, among other people, Ismael González de la Serna and Manuel Ángeles Ortiz. From 1908 onward, he also worked as a bellhop at the Centro Artístico y Literario, and thanks to what he saw there, he started to become interested in sculpture. Several members of the Centro gave him support, in particular the influential local politician Natalio Rivas. Between 1909 and 1913, he received classes in the studio of the Granada-based sculptor Nicolás Prados Benítez.[112] He moved from Granada to Madrid in 1914, and Rivas arranged for him to enter Mariano Benlliure's studio, with financial support from the Ayuntamiento and Diputación Provincial of Granada. But he only stayed with Benlliure for a few months, and soon pursued other artistic directions. Shortly afterwards, then, he established the first studio of his own in an attic on calle de Atocha, 151. As would happen later with Ortiz's workspace on the Pasaje, this also served as a meeting place for other friends from Granada who were in the capital (such as Ismael González de la Serna, Manuel Ángeles Ortiz, Miguel Pizarro, and José Fernández-Montesinos).[113] Likewise, during the periods when Cristóbal returned to Granada, he remained an active member of the *tertulia* of the Rinconcillo.

In Madrid, he enrolled around 1915 in the Escuela Especial, with grants from the Ayuntamiento, the Diputación Provincial, and the Centro Artístico y Literario of Granada. Like the majority of students at the conservatory, he also worked in the Museo del Prado and in the Museo de Reproducciones Artísticas, located in the Casón del Buen Retiro; in addition, he took night classes at the Círculo de Bellas Artes. Over February–March 1917, he held his first exhibition at the Ateneo de Madrid, jointly with Ismael González de la Serna.[114] A couple of months later he won a prize in the Exposición Nacional de Bellas Artes. In his Madrid studio he also created the marble bust of Ángel Ganivet that forms part of the monument erected in Granada in 1921, after a long campaign.[115]

Recio Aguado has identified Cristóbal as someone who attended or at least was sometimes present at the Academia Libre,[116] a claim that would seem to be confirmed by the mention of him in the newspaper report quoted above. Although his time at the Escuela Especial ended before the close of the 1910s, it is hard to imagine, as we move into the 1920s, that , with his multiple contacts in numerous artistic and literary circles, Cristóbal would not already have met some people like Salvador Dalí, Moreno Villa, or Maruja Mallo.

Two examples will illustrate the range of these contacts. On 25 March 1920, a farewell meal was held for the avant-garde Chilean writer Joaquín Edwards Bello, who was returning to his homeland. Among the great variety of attendees we find Ramón del Valle-Inclán, the Chilean Teresa Wilms Montt, Andrés González-Blanco, Julio Romero de Torres, Rafael de Penagos, Rafael Lasso de la Vega, Javier Winthuysen, and Juan Cristóbal.[117] One year later, on 14 May 1921, the magazine *Vltra* sponsored at the Excelsior restaurant a banquet in honour of Daniel Vázquez Díaz and Eva Aggerholm, to celebrate their recent exhibition (held over March and April in the Palacio de Bibliotecas y Museos). Members of the organizing committee included Robert and Sonia Delaunay, Francisco Iturrino, Rafael Barradas, José Sanz Arizmendi, Juan José Mantecón, Adolfo Salazar, Manuel Abril, Alfonso Reyes, Humberto Rivas, José Rivas Panedas, José de Ciria y Escalante, Guillermo de Torre, and Juan José Pérez Doménech. And among the numerous attendees were Ramiro de Maeztu, Juan de Nogales, Francisco Alcántara, Enrique Díez-Canedo, Ángel Vegue y Goldoni, Margarita Nelken, José Francés, Manuel de Falla, Eugenio Hermoso, Ángel Ferrant, Gregorio Prieto, Salvador Bartolozzi, Enrique Estévez Ochoa, and, once again, Juan Cristóbal.[118]

SALVADOR DALÍ

For those who arrived in Madrid closer to 1924, when Moisés's Academia opened, the situation may have been rather different. Salvador Dalí was in the capital during the academic year 1922–23, and for a few weeks during the fall of 1923, before his expulsion from the Escuela Especial for the rest of the year.[119] Little is known about his return to Madrid in the spring of 1924, but we can speculate that he (or his father) may not have wanted to "lose" the rest of the year and that this may account for why he arrived at the Academia Libre. Several contemporaries remember him there. Palencia does, in the quotation reproduced above, and José Moreno Villa recalls that "this started toward 1924. I attended the free classes of the painter Moisés, in the Pasaje de la Alhambra, which Dalí and Maruja Mayo [sic] also came along to, among others."[120] Santos Torroella states, without citing a source, that it was during this period that Dalí painted the well-known *Retrato de Luis Buñuel*.[121] The Academia opened officially on 8 March, and Dalí might have returned to Figueres to spend Holy Week with his family, which in that year fell on 13–20 April. Whether he did or not, he was definitely back in Cataluña by May, because on the twenty-first he was arrested and briefly imprisoned for reasons that are complex and remain rather murky.[122] We can conclude, therefore, that the time he spent at the academy must have been relatively short, at the very most ten weeks and quite possibly considerably less. Restored to classes at the Escuela Especial in the fall of 1924, nothing suggests that he returned to the Academia in 1924–25, although he was aware that as of April 1925 both Palencia and Bores had continued attending sessions there.

Summing up: Dalí coincided with Maruja Mallo at the Escuela Especial and with Moreno Villa at the Residencia de Estudiantes, and because of the prominent presence of both Bores and Cristóbal in artistic circles, it is probable that he would have met them during his first year in Madrid. As for the other students, the Academia Libre could indeed have been the site of Dalí's first encounter with them – if they coincided there chronologically. Palencia became a friend, but as far as is known there are no further traces of ongoing connections with other pupils of Moisés.

ENRIQUE ESTÉVEZ OCHOA

There is not a great deal of information about Estévez Ochoa and the Academia Libre. After a childhood and adolescence spent in the Philippines, Toledo, and Sevilla, he arrived in Madrid in 1914, where he lived and worked until the middle of the 1920s, when he moved to Barcelona. He distinguished himself as a commercial illustrator of magazines such as *Por esos Mundos*, *Blanco y Negro*, *La Esfera*, and *Nuevo Mundo*, as well as several books. He had many friends in the Madrid bohemian and avant-garde circles,[123] and knew Rafael de Penagos, who was also a student of the Academia. He contributed to the *ultraísta* magazine *Tobogán* (1924). According to Irene Falcón, around that time he gave some private art lessons to Maruja Mallo and Falcón herself.[124] The contemporary press article quoted earlier in this chapter places him in Moisés's studio.

WIFREDO LAM

The Cuban Wifredo Lam was born in Sagua la Grande and in 1916, at the age of fourteen, was sent to Havana to live with relatives and study law. However, in 1918 he also entered the Escuela Nacional de Bellas Artes "San Alejandro."[125] In 1923, he held an exhibition in Havana and another in his native town; thanks to this, he obtained from the local municipality a grant to go and study in Spain.[126] He arrived in Madrid toward the end of 1923 with a letter of recommendation for Fernando Álvarez de Sotomayor, the director of the Museo del Prado and member of the Real Academia de Bellas Artes. Sotomayor invited him to enroll in the Escuela Especial and also to attend his own studio.[127] As in the case of Dalí, Lam found the academicism then dominant in established artistic circles in Madrid very restrictive, and so he also struck out on his own, copying old masters in the Prado and going to Moisés's Academia Libre some afternoons.[128] Economic turmoil in Cuba in 1924 resulted in the suspension of Lam's stipend, and by mid-1925 – around the time the Academia Libre probably closed – Lam's increasing money problems obliged him to go and stay with the family of a student friend in Cuenca.

MARUJA MALLO

Maruja Mallo moved to Madrid in 1921 in order to spend a year preparing for the entrance exam for the Escuela Especial.[129] After passing the test – and as she remembered, she was the only woman to do so in her cohort[130] – she started to study there in the fall of 1922, and completed the full course of study over four consecutive years, from 1922 through 1926. According to Mangini, Mallo met Palencia through her brother Justo, while the Café de Oriente *tertulia* that she and Dalí sometimes attended also counted among its sometime members Gabriel García Maroto, Bores, and Palencia.[131] In 1924, she decided to supplement her official training with classes at the Academia Libre. Given her friendship with Dalí, it is easy to imagine that one of them may have encouraged the other to attend. Moreno Villa's account mentions her presence there, a fact that motivated a question posed to Mallo by Maria Lluïsa Borràs:

> Curiously, replying to my questions, Maruja Mallo confirmed to me that sometimes a very likeable Cuban came to the Escuela Libre. This was none other than Wifredo Lam, who, to recover from the boredom of Fernando de Sotomayor's workshop, where he worked in the mornings, "in the afternoon went to learn painting with a Catalan who had an academy near the *pension*."[132]

With Dalí back in Madrid to repeat his second year at the Escuela Especial (1924–25), their friendship would have resumed, and of the other attendees at the Academia she would likely have seen most of Palencia, a friend of both her and Alberti through the 1920s.[133]

JOSÉ MORENO VILLA

Born in 1887, José Moreno Villa was one year older than the founder of the Academia Libre. While he was working in the area of art history at the Centro de Estudios Históricos between 1910 and 1919,[134] he began his close association with the Residencia de Estudiantes in 1917.[135] During his youth he had shown an inclination to painting, and briefly had two art teachers:

> Painting makes an appearance in my life from when I am ten years old. When I was eleven I met my first drawing teacher, in the secondary school of El Palo, founded by the Jesuits in the outskirts of Málaga …
>
> My second teacher was called Fernández Alvarado. He had a big studio … With this man, who was short and plump, I did not make much progress …
>
> I don't believe that I went to his studio for more than three months. Neither of these two teachers interested me. I was hotheaded and wanted to cover the first stage as fast as possible. I wanted to paint. And I wanted to see painting. Fortunately, my father and my grandfather had old and modern works … My father and my grandfather had drawn when they were young. I wanted to outdo them. But without having teachers.[136]

Moreno Villa spent the 1921–22 academic year in Gijón, where he had been posted after passing the competitive examinations for a position in the Departmento de Archivos, Bibliotecas y Museos, and it seems that it was precisely during this period that he started to work seriously on his own art.[137] According to Pérez de Ayala, in Gijón "he enters into contact with the painters Nicanor Piñole and Evaristo Valle, spending time in their studios and starting to paint with pastels in Piñole's studio."[138] The following year he returned to Madrid and to the Residencia (with an official posting as librarian to the university's Facultad de Farmacia), and several of his canvases can be dated to 1923. In 1924, he attended classes at the Academia Libre, a phase in his development that receives only a brief comment from Carmona: "Some drawings that are technical studies have been preserved – we can be sure executed in Julio Moisés's studio around 1924 – that already speak to us of his well-grounded ability in drawing."[139]

In the context of this conjunction of people and events, Moreno Villa described his own experiences as follows:

> I encouraged in so far as I could that youthful movement in its most difficult phase, that of abstraction. And, to be totally sincere, I started to paint with genuine fanaticism. This started toward 1924. I attended the free classes given by the painter Moisés, in the Pasaje de la Alhambra ... There we drew nudes, but without guidance from anyone. After a month, I stopped going. But at home I made great efforts to create cubist paintings that I only knew through reproductions. My feeling for colour connected with Juan Gris's, with Braque's ... In my fanaticism I reached the point of not being able to look at a painting in the Museo del Prado.[140]

This autobiographical sketch of his artistic development can be filled out with material drawn from several articles published by Moreno Villa on allied themes, which document a remarkable evolution in his thinking. In 1919, he criticized severely what he called the "search for the unexpected" and the idea that "genius consists in the absurd and the disconcerting," which predominated in France at the time. He went on to refer to "that deceitful métier, whose pontiff is Picasso, a Catalanized native of Málaga who, from Paris, mocks art and people."[141] The following year, writing about an exhibition of Barradas's work, he explained what he understood by *simultaneísmo*, a pictorial style that, in its evocation of a real scene observed by the artist, tended to produce, in the opinion of Moreno Villa, a *barullo* – a hubbub, racket, mishmash, or general confusion. And he continued, "Now, we need to know if a mishmash can be the foundation of emotive art, and if, as these painters claim, visual art can manage to detach itself completely from representational form. I have the sense that it would be very difficult for a thing or a grouping to be evoked without its visual representation."[142] Reviewing an exhibition by Daniel Vázquez Díaz in 1921, he found that "his current paintings have, in part, that disconcerting element of revolutionary painting"; furthermore, "nowadays he is not concerned with themes. He allows himself to be intoxicated either by the expressive force of the light or by the expressive force of volume." And this led Moreno Villa to some more general reflections:

This path followed by modern art that condemns the theme – I just do not know where it will lead. Confronted by it, many artistic minds hesitate. Others, on the other hand, accept it as a matter of course and with all its consequences, because they prefer anything, absolutely anything, over lethargy and unchanging repetition. The state of mind of these latter is doubtless that favoured by art.[143]

From this position first of outright criticism and then of serious reservations, he moved over 1924 and 1925 to one of mild approval and then of complete enthusiasm. Thus, for example, he stated that "if we think about a Picasso or a Juan Gris, we will see that what is being pursued in them, the aesthetic goal, is accompanied – and helped – by a technique of their own, ideal and irreplaceable,"[144] and then, some months later, he dedicated a long essay to modern trends in which he concluded, "Among what most interests me today in the world of art are those movements: cubism and neoclassicism."[145]

Apart from Dalí and Mallo, whom Moreno Villa already knew, his experience in Moisés's studio seems to have put him in contact with other painters about whom, later, he would write essays and reviews, such as Bores, Palencia, or Eduardo Vicente.

BENJAMÍN PALENCIA

Benjamín Palencia, who was originally from Barrax (Albacete), arrived in Madrid around 1909, when he was fifteen years old. He came to live with his adoptive uncle, Rafael López Egóñez, and initially he was self-taught. Later, he took some art classes with Elías Tormo y Monzó (a personal friend of Egóñez and a researcher at the Centro de Estudios Históricos), who encouraged him to go and study the old masters in the Museo del Prado, but he never enrolled in the Escuela Especial.[146] After he exhibited at the Primer Salón de Otoño, he met Juan Ramón Jiménez in 1920, who visited him in his first studio located on calle Fernando el Santo, 7.[147] Since we know that Pancho Cossío (1894–1970) had set up in a studio in the same street in 1919, it is quite possible that the two used this same space years before they came to share, in later years, a studio in Paris.[148] Also relevant is the fact that both of them showed works in an exhibit held by the Círculo de Bellas Artes in 1919.[149] Over the following years, Palencia slowly developed his career, participating in more collective exhibitions, publishing in 1923 a *plaquette* of drawings entitled *Niños* in the series of books brought out by Jiménez's magazine *Índice,* and contributing drawings in November 1923 to *España* and *Revista de Occidente* and in February 1924 more to *España.*[150]

There are photographs showing Palencia together with Sáenz de Tejada at El Paular that can be dated to the summer of 1923.[151] In 1924, according to Palencia, "Bores, Dalí, and I used to go to the Academia Libre, founded by Julio Moisés, in the Pasaje de la Alhambra. I used to draw nudes ... in order to learn how to overcome the difficulties."[152] As already established, then, Palencia knew Bores and Sáenz de Tejada before he went to the Pasaje de la Alhambra, and quite possibly had also met Dalí, Mallo, and Santa Cruz.

RAFAEL DE PENAGOS

Rafael de Penagos is, alongside Moreno Villa, one of the oldest artists to have gone to the Academia Libre.[153] He had studied for four years at the Escuela Especial, from 1904 to 1909, and after travelling to Paris, Barcelona, and London, in 1915 he established himself in Madrid in a studio located at calle Alfonso XII, 36. In the summer of 1921, he was one of the students named for a residency at El Paular landscape school.[154] He occasionally worked as a set designer for Gregorio Martínez Sierra's Teatro Eslava,[155] but he achieved fame above all for the illustrations that he contributed to multiple magazines and newspapers, done in the then emergent "Art Deco" style.[156]

CARLOS SÁENZ DE TEJADA

Born in Tangiers, Tejada received his first art lessons from Daniel Cortés, in Orán, where he then lived with his family.[157] From 1910 onward, during the academic year he stayed with his uncle and aunt in Madrid and took more classes, first with the Sociedad Fomento de las Artes, and then in the private studio of José María López Mezquita (the direction of which was later taken over by Fernando Álvarez de Sotomayor).[158] Fellow students at the studio were the painter Ramón Estalella Pujolá and the future critic Antonio Marichalar.[159] He entered the Escuela Especial in the fall of 1915,[160] although he continued taking classes with López Mezquita until

1917. At the Escuela other first-year students were Ismael Cuesta, Joaquín Valverde, Timoteo Pérez Rubio, and Rosa Chacel. Sorolla, a professor at the conservatory from 1918, was a strong influence.[161] During Tejada's career there, he won a number of end-of-year prizes from the EEPEG and he exhibited his work several times in collective shows, between 1917 and 1921. In 1918, he participated in setting up a student organization at the Escuela Especial, and in 1919 he started contributing illustrations to the press (*La Libertad*).[162] Works that he showed at a national exhibition late in 1920 were highly praised.[163] When he left the school, from 1921 onward he continued to contribute heavily to newspapers and magazines, and at the same time made frequent trips exploring above all the landscape and villages of Castilla and meeting the people living there, and this subject matter is reflected in his work of the time.

Apart from the links already documented between him and Santa Cruz, Bores, and Dalí, Tejada also met Palencia; exactly when or under what circumstances is not known, but it was toward 1923, since there are photographs of them in El Paular during the summer of that year.[164] Over this time he also frequented several *tertulias*: occasionally that of his cousin Gómez de la Serna at Pombo, ones at the Café de Platerías and La Granja de El Henar, and, rather more regularly, that led by José Francés, the so-called *tertulia de los humoristas*, which met at the Lyon d'Or and then moved to the Café de Jorge Juan in November 1923.[165] After the fire described in a previous section of this chapter, Tejada did not produce many more new oil paintings, only a few that he made for the exhibition of the Sociedad de Artistas Ibéricos (1925).[166] This is the moment, then, at which he decided to focus exclusively on drawing, a vocation that he continued to pursue after moving to Paris in 1926.[167]

Miguel Pérez Ferrero left two evocations of meetings of the *tertulia* of the Café Saboya, one included in his book *Unos y otros* and another in an homage to Sáenz de Tejada. It was in the former work that he recounted his memories of the time:

That was, [though] we did not foresee it − because the news of its demolition to make way for a bank exploded that day like a bomb − the last period of the Apolo theatre, and in the building it occupied had also been installed a ill-appointed café, the Saboya ... Writers and artists fetched up there, as well as theatre personalities, and, in short, those "recognizable faces" that are always seen everywhere. Around seven o'clock every evening, four friends would turn up in one of its corners: Sáenz de Tejada, Francisco Santa Cruz ... Francisco Bores, and the writer of these memories ... The first three were painters, and topics connected with painting obviously absorbed almost all of our conversations. Some evenings we stayed only a very short time in the café, because we were going to a free academy of drawing that I was expelled from because they noticed immediately that I was not a member of the profession and the only thing I did was to get in the way and distract the other attendees.[168]

This "free academy" must be none other than Moisés's, and consequently we can deduce that not only Bores – who constituted a well-documented case – but also Sáenz de Tejada and Santa Cruz, and even Pérez Ferrero, frequented the studio for a certain period of time.

FRANCISCO SANTA CRUZ

Santa Cruz was born in Sigüenza and received his first art classes there from Benito Palacios. Having completed his high school education, in 1915 he moved to Madrid to start studying for a medical degree, which he never finished. On a trip to Paris accompanying his father, he fell under the influence of the Russian artist Boris Grigoriev. Somewhere around 1920 he decided to become a painter. We do not know how the first contact came about between him and Sáenz de Tejada (or indeed him and Ismael Cuesta or Joaquín Valverde), since Santa Cruz never entered the Escuela Especial; all that is documented is that he began to frequent the shared studio on the Travesía del Horno de la Mata at the beginning of the 1920s. In 1921, he participated for the first time in a collective exhibition, in Sigüenza. He contributed artwork to the *ultraísta* magazines *Vértices* and *Tobogán*. He took part in the IX Salón de Humoristas (1923) and in two collective exhibitions held in 1924 (Exposición Nacional de Bellas Artes and the Salón de Otoño). As in the case of Sáenz de Tejada, some of his canvases were destroyed in the studio fire, but, again like Tejada, he participated in the exhibition of the Sociedad de Artistas Ibéricos, sharing Sala X with Tejada, Dalí, and Moreno Villa.[169] As we have just seen, he formed part of the *tertulia* of the Café Saboya and, according to Pérez Ferrero, must have attended for a time Julio Moisés's Academia Libre.

EDUARDO VICENTE

A native of Madrid, the young Eduardo Vicente started his art studies in an informal fashion with his father, who was an amateur painter, and with his elder brother Esteban (1903–2001), also a painter. Eduardo abandoned his high school education at the Instituto de San Isidro before obtaining his diploma, preferring instead to enter the Escuela Especial in 1924.[170] There, he would meet Cristino Mallo, the younger brother of Maruja, with whom he would establish an enduring friendship. His elder brother Esteban left the Escuela Especial in 1922, without completing the coursework for the degree, and set up his own studio in the calle del Carmen, which he shared with his friend the American painter James I. Gilbert (b. 1899).[171] Not too long thereafter, in late 1924 or early 1925, they moved to another studio located at Paseo del Prado, 14, which was the old studio of, at different times, Federico de Madrazo and Juan Gris, and they shared this new space with Eduardo and with another mutual friend, the painter Juan Bonafé (1901–1969).[172] There, besides working, they established a *tertulia* that was attended by Francisco Bores, Pedro Flores, Cristóbal Hall, Ramón Gaya, Wladislaw Jahl, Frédéric Macé, Pedro Salinas, Dámaso Alonso, Jorge Guillén, Rafael Alberti, Manuel Abril, Ortega y Gasset, Zenobia Camprubí, and Juan R. Jiménez.[173] In 1925, Eduardo obtained work as an assistant painter in the workshop of the set designer Eduardo Amorós and then later in the workshop of Fernando Mignoni.[174]

Eduardo's attendance at the Academia Libre would therefore have coincided with his first classes at the Escuela Especial. Summarizing this phase of his life, Gerardo Diego later wrote,

> In short, one has to paint, and not with a decorator's brush but rather with a specific and sensitive artist's brush. And the apprentice alternates proletarian handicrafts in the theatre with the unsociable aristocracy of the easel. And thus he finds himself in life drawing, drawing with a model. For one peseta they allow one

to work in the Escuela Libre of the Pasaje de la Alhambra, presided over by Julio Moisés.[175]

Apart from contact with Bores, Vicente must have already met Maruja Mallo and Dalí, through the Escuela Especial and his friendship with Cristino Mallo, but in general Vicente seems to have remained at some distance from the groups that are most familiar and best documented. As the artist recounted, "For the first time I see all that painting that back then was called avant-garde and nowadays they call abstract, which my brother Esteban and Ladislao Jhall [*sic*: Wladislaw Jahl] espouse with true fanaticism. I give that experiment a try but I do not have a good time with it so I give up continuing with it."[176] Around this same moment – toward the end of his first year at the Escuela Especial – Vicente participated in an exhibition organized by the Liceo de la Juventud and held at the Salón de Arte Moderno (calle del Carmen), where the majority of the artists being shown were students of the Escuela Especial.[177] None of the other names of the young artists mentioned is immediately recognizable, and so perhaps it is no coincidence that the only one praised by Marquina was Vicente himself.

Conclusion

The artist's studio in the Pasaje de la Alhambra provides an excellent example of the way in which networks of friends and acquaintances can be traced radiating out from and around single hubs – in this case, Ángeles Ortiz and Moisés. At the same time, it is illustrative of how this pattern of hub plus network is overlaid on a specific location, a location that serves not only as a physical site of encounters and gatherings but whose existence and function are actually responsible for many of these taking place, serving in this instance as the Madrid home away from home of the Rinconcillo *tertulia* and as the venue for the classes of the Academia Libre.

CHAPTER 4

ARTS STUDENTS AND THE RESIDENCIA DE SEÑORITAS

The Residencia de Señoritas: History and Organization

The Residencia de Señoritas, founded in 1915, was one of the creations of the Junta para la Ampliación de Estudios e Investigaciones Científicas. The JAE itself was established in January 1907 as part of a push, backed by liberal politicians, to modernize education in Spain. Although it was a government agency under the umbrella of the Ministerio de Instrucción Pública y Bellas Artes (itself only created in 1900, as part of reform efforts after the 1898 "disaster"), its special status placed it outside the regular public system of primary and secondary schools, colleges, and universities. The JAE took up a number of educational principles and goals largely inherited from the independent (i.e., non-state) Institución Libre de Enseñanza (f. 1876) and the Museo Pedagógico (f. 1882), and was presided over by the Nobel-winning scientist Santiago Ramón y Cajal together with a board of distinguished academics.[1] Day-to-day operations were overseen by the permanent secretary, José Castillejo, who as a student had come under Francisco Giner de los Ríos's tutelage and was in many ways the single most influential individual within the new organization.[2] Sánchez Ron, in his essay on the subject, studies what he calls the "network of personal relations" both within the Institución Libre de Enseñanza (ILE) and the JAE, as well as the considerable overlap and connection between the two, which is to say, "the dense web of personal and institutional relations that was formed over the little more than three decades of the existence of the Junta, in which, undeniably, both direct and indirect members of the Institución Libre de Enseñanza figured prominently."[3]

For the first several years, the JAE's headquarters were located at calle Moreto, 1, but the day-to-day operations of the "Secretaría" were run out of very modest offices located at Plaza de Bilbao, 6, 2° dcha.[4] One of its first initiatives was to create a Junta de Pensiones responsible for the allocation of grants for travel and research, which started to function immediately in 1907. While it languished over the period when conservative prime minister Antonio Maura was in office (1907–09), under the subsequent liberal government of Segismundo Moret the JAE received in early 1910 an infusion of increased funding and was responsible for establishing the Instituto Nacional de Ciencias Físico-Naturales, the Centro de Estudios Históricos,[5] and the Residencia de Estudiantes, all in 1910, the Residencia de Señoritas in 1915, and the Instituto-Escuela in 1918, as well as a range of laboratories, libraries, and other facilities for both pre-existing and new research institutions.[6]

The desire and intent to create a residence in Madrid for young women pursuing various kinds of higher education predated the opening of the Residencia de Señoritas by several years. Castillejo from within the JAE and José Ortega y Gasset from without were heavily involved in promoting this initiative. When, in 1913, construction started on the purpose-built pavilions on calle Pinar that would house the much-expanded Residencia de Estudiantes, the JAE administrators immediately realized that there was an obvious opportunity to repurpose the calle Fortuny houses on the Residencia's original site,[7] and numbers 28 and 30 were chosen for this new but parallel role of a Residencia de Señoritas.[8] Meanwhile, a Grupo de Niños, for the education of boys aged ten to sixteen, had been created in 1914, as a subsidiary entity of the Residencia de Estudiantes (and located at the calle Pinar site).[9] Directed by Luis Álvarez Santullano and his wife, it housed boarders and "semi-boarders" (who returned home at the weekend) and also provided their education, in an organizational pattern reminiscent of the "house system" of English boarding schools, and in 1915 it moved into the other two newly vacant Fortuny properties (at calle Fortuny, 24 and 26).[10]

At this time in Spain, students attending university, professional schools, or colleges tended to live at home or with relatives who lived in a college town.[11] The other option for male students – and this was quite frequently taken up – was the boarding house, but because of the social proprieties of the day this was much less common for female students.[12] Hence the pressing need for a residence for young women who wished to pursue some course of higher education in Madrid but who were not resident there or had no family or other connections in the city.[13] As one of the residents later wrote, "Only those of us who passed through the Residencia can fully grasp its great educational work, which, in addition, frees from the vulgarity and dangers of the boarding houses those young people who come from the provinces with the modest aspiration to pursue a course of study that might assure them a future."[14]

As early as mid-1913, María de Maeztu (1881–1948) was named as the first, and in the event only, director of the Residencia de Señoritas, although it did not open until the 1915–16 school year. She was from a well-known family: the writer Ramiro de Maeztu was her older brother, and the artist Gustavo de Maeztu her younger brother. Her assistant was Rafaela Ortega y Gasset, the sister of José, and for many years Eulalia Lapresta served as secretary of the institution. María obtained a degree from her local Escuela Normal de Maestras (1898), and taught various kinds of classes at different schools for the next decade, over which time she gained a reputation as a progressive educator. She obtained a high school diploma from the Instituto de Vitoria in 1907, and was an early recipient of a travel grant to London from the JAE in 1908. She was enrolled throughout 1907–09 at the Universidad de Salamanca for a bachelor's degree, where she was influenced by Unamuno. Between 1909 and 1912, she pursued a further professional qualification at the newly created elite Escuela de Estudios Superiores de Magisterio, where she was a student of Ortega y Gasset. She travelled to Belgium, Switzerland, and Italy (1909–10), and later went to Germany, namely to Leipzig and then Marburg, where, at Ortega's suggestion, she studied philosophy during the 1912–13 academic year. Having transferred from Salamanca to Madrid in 1911, she received a BA in philosophy and letters from the Universidad Central in 1915. At the same time, she worked in the Departamento de Filosofía Contemporánea of the Centro de Estudios Históricos (1913–16) and from 1913 to 1915, she also gave classes on education at the Instituto Internacional.[15]

The growth of the Residencia de Señoritas over the latter half of the 1910s and the decade of the 1920s, together with its evolving close collaboration with the Instituto Internacional, present a complex history. In 1917, it expanded into all four of the original properties of the Residencia de Estudiantes, as the Grupo de Niños, under continual pressures of space, had moved back to the Pinar site and the newly constructed Quinto Pabellón in 1917 (where in 1918 it underwent more radical reorganization).[16] In 1916, the JAE had bought outright those four detached houses (normally referred to as *hoteles*) at calle Fortuny, 24, 26, 28, and 30, and it also acquired two contiguous houses on the cross street, calle Rafael Calvo, 1 and 3, which the Residencia was able to use from 1921, when the second Grupo de Niños moved out.[17]

Much earlier than all these developments, the Americans Alice Winfield Gordon and her husband William H. Gulick had visited Spain in 1872 as Protestant missionaries, settling in Santander and setting up a modest primary school.[18] After a move to San Sebastian in 1881, which allowed them gradually to expand their operations, their educational initiatives coalesced in what became known as the Colegio Norte-americano. In 1892, Alice established in Boston the International Institute for Girls in Spain, which then became the name for the Gulicks's school. By this stage it was offering the whole span of primary and secondary education, and in 1897 two students went on to study at the Universidad Central in Madrid and receive undergraduate degrees. Alice also forged contacts with Gumersindo de Azcárate, who was closely associated with the Institución Libre de Enseñanza.[19] The school moved to the outskirts of Biarritz in 1898 because of the Spanish-American War, and it remained at that location until 1903. Nonetheless, in 1901 the Instituto Internacional was able to buy its first building in Madrid, situated at calle Fortuny, 5 (subsequently renumbered 53); the plot around it fronted Paseo del General Martínez Campos (then called Paseo del Obelisco) and stretched from Fortuny to the next parallel north–south street, calle Miguel Ángel.[20] This location put it close to the seat of the ILE, situated a little further west on Martínez Campos.[21] The house was refurbished and ready to open for classes in 1903, the year of Alice Gulick's death.[22]

At the same time as this purchase, the Instituto Internacional also acquired a building site directly south of the western half of the

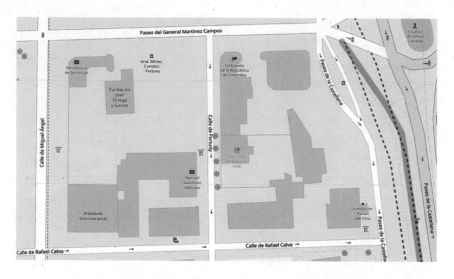

4.1. The area of the Residencia de Señoritas and the International Institute in Madrid.

previously described plot, occupying a large space on the corner of Miguel Ángel with calle Rafael Calvo.[23] An International Institute League was formed in 1903 with the chief purpose of fundraising.[24] After his wife's passing, William Gulick assumed the directorship, and further changes to the internal organization of the Instituto Internacional occurred in 1906.[25] Over the rest of this decade they were able to build Memorial Hall on the previously described lot, and it was completed in 1910 with the address of Miguel Ángel, 8.[26] More or less coinciding with this, the board hired a new director for the Instituto Internacional in Madrid, Susan Huntington, who had previously volunteered with Gulick.[27] After over ten years back in the United States and Puerto Rico studying and teaching, Huntington arrived in Madrid at the same time as the men's Residencia de Estudiantes was being inaugurated across the street on the even-numbered (eastern) side of Fortuny.

Huntington left her mark on the Instituto Internacional, severing most ties with its missionary beginnings and transforming it almost completely into an educational institution.[28] Over the period 1910–16, it became a highly prestigious private secondary school for girls as well as offering classes at other levels.[29] Subsequently, though, the First World War had an increasingly negative impact, leaving the Instituto Internacional struggling for funds and having difficulty recruiting teachers and students willing to cross the Atlantic. With the steady growth of the Residencia de Señoritas from 1915 onward and its continuing need for space for more classrooms and bedrooms, the proximity of the two institutions offered an obvious solution.[30] In practice, though, there were challenges, as some members of the Instituto Internacional's board were opposed. Lengthy negotiations resulted in Fortuny 53 and space in Miguel Ángel 8 being rented to the JAE for three years starting in 1917.[31]

Other aspects of the eventual arrangement – engineered by Castillejo, Maeztu, and Huntington – were for the Instituto Internacional's teachers to offer classes also in the Residencia de Señoritas, and for the establishment by the JAE in 1917 of a subsidiary Grupo de Niñas for the primary and secondary education of girls (mirroring the Grupo de Niños of the Residencia de Estudiantes, created in 1914).[32] Classes were held in Miguel Ángel 8 while the boarders moved into Fortuny 53.[33] The Grupo de Niñas was considerably larger than its counterpart, catering to girls aged six to sixteen, and in 1917–18 it reached 148 pupils (with 51 boarders or half-boarders and 97 day students). Because of its size, it was organized into three sections: preschoolers, primary, and secondary. In the fall of 1918, the opening of the JAE's Instituto-Escuela led to it taking over teaching responsibilities for a good number of the pupils, leading to significant drops in enrollment. Within a couple of years the Grupo ceased teaching and served basically as a boarding facility, principally catering to the Instituto-Escuela. In 1922, the living quarters were moved from Fortuny 53 to Rafael Calvo, with even fewer places, and then in 1923 to Miguel Ángel 8. The 1928–29 academic year was the Grupo's last year under the jurisdiction of the Residencia de Señoritas.[34]

These changes coincided with Huntington leaving the leadership of the Instituto Internacional because of her marriage, though she remained active in the organization; she was succeeded by a number of directors, who typically held the position for just one academic year. In 1920, the rental agreement was renewed for four years, and other modifications to the complex co-operative arrangement followed over the rest of the decade.[35]

Two categories of students were established at the Residencia de Señoritas: those pursuing university-level study – the Sección Especial

Universitaria, whose centre of operations was Miguel Ángel 8, and those preparing entrance exams to professional schools and colleges and those pursuing more general study – the Sección General, who were grouped in the houses at Fortuny 24–30.[36] One of Maeztu's basic aims remained that of increasing the proportion of university students within the entire population, a goal that the statistics show she largely accomplished.[37] Pérez-Villanueva Tovar points out that there were only thirty-one women registered at the Universidad Central in 1915;[38] the existence of the Residencia de Señoritas helped to increase that number significantly over the following decade, while at the same time that figure should also be borne in mind when considering the numbers of residents cited below.

Another JAE initiative, the Instituto-Escuela, was established in 1918 and installed in temporary quarters also in Miguel Ángel 8. It was an experimental primary and secondary school, initially coeducational;[39] Maeztu assumed the directorship of the primary section. The Instituto-Escuela also served as a training centre for future secondary-school teachers.[40] Its creation obviously had an impact on the teaching functions of the Grupo de Niños and the Grupo de Niñas. The Grupo de Niños was split into two, the "original" under Santullano, which was run down and closed in 1920, and a new branch, which catered to pupils of the Instituto-Escuela and who needed to be boarders or semi-boarders. The new branch was overseen by Gonzalo Jiménez de la Espada and initially installed in houses on calle Rafael Calvo, then moved in 1921 to the Quinto Pabellón (calle Pinar).[41] The Grupo de Niñas was administered under the joint auspices of the Residencia de Señoritas and the Instituto Internacional.[42] Organizationally, the Grupos remained part of the Residencia de Estudiantes until they were entirely absorbed by the Instituto-Escuela in 1928 (Niños) and 1929 (Niñas).[43] From a different perspective, one could say that the Grupo de Niños, and then the Grupo de Niñas, established under the oversight of the JAE,[44] were "dry runs" for the eventual creation of the Instituto-Escuela, an initiative that fulfilled one of the JAE's other progressive educational goals. The presence of boys in the Instituto Internacional building remained an irritant for the Boston board until the relocation in 1921 of those classes to the Residencia de Estudiantes campus, while the girls remained for the time being at Miguel Ángel 8.[45] The Instituto-Escuela completely vacated the Fortuny/ Miguel Ángel site in 1928.[46]

As the Residencia de Señoritas progressively occupied more space on Fortuny, Rafael Calvo, and Miguel Ángel, and was thus able to make more rooms available, residency rates also climbed. From a modest 30 in 1915, numbers had already risen to 65 in 1917, and 130 by 1921; by 1929, they had reached a maximum capacity of a little over 200.[47] Given this expansion, it became necessary to divide the buildings into four organizational groups, each with its own director: these were called Rafael Calvo (numbers 1 and 3, to which had been added 30 and the *piso nuevo* at 61), Fortuny 30 (subsuming numbers 24, 26, 28, and 30, together with the two purpose-built dormitories in the gardens), Fortuny 53, and Miguel Ángel 8.[48]

The history of the Residencia de Señoritas over the 1910s and '20s is one, therefore, of steady growth and of the equally frequent repurposing of buildings. The collaboration with the Instituto Internacional that started in 1917 contributed significantly to both of these features, with agreements for the use of given rooms in given properties being made and then changed almost on a year-to-year basis. This in turn reflects a complex juggling act, in respect to both internal politics and space, by which the organization's directors sought to satisfy various competing interests – the JAE, the Instituto Internacional, the Instituto-Escuela, and the Residencia de Señoritas itself – *and* at the same time cope with limited housing stock and yearly increasing demand for places as its reputation grew.

DAILY LIFE AND ORGANIZED SOCIABILITY AT THE RESIDENCIA

The Residencia de Señoritas appeared in several contemporary magazine and newspaper reports, and while these texts can offer pertinent information or useful insights, often the accompanying photographs are the most evocative elements. In 1923, an anonymous journalist touched on all the principal features of the Residencia's organization and operation, and presented photos of the common room (here called the "music and sewing room"), a rather luxurious student room, the dining room, and the library.[49] Five years on, the approach had barely changed, and much of the basic information had not varied either, save for the increase in numbers of buildings and enrollments.[50] Likewise, that report offered almost identical photos, of the library, the same bedroom (*la rotunda*), and the *salón de té*.

In 1929, Villaseca followed a similar path, though now in rather more detail.[51] His interview with María de Maeztu covered most of the salient aspects: the numbers of residents and the waiting list, the courses of study, the arrangements for oversight, the different buildings, etc. Seven photographs show Maeztu and Lapresta in the main office, a group of residents reading in the library, five residents taking tea in the *salón de té*, a group of students in the chemistry laboratory, two residents in one of the rooms, plus two exterior shots of large groups. Later that year, Juan del Sarto visited Miguel Ángel 8 to report on the new library established in a collaboration between the Instituto Internacional and the Residencia. Two shots show largely similar views of the main library room, plus there are photos of Eulalia Lapresta sitting at her desk across from Sarto, a large group of students posed on the main staircase, and an inset of María de Maeztu.[52] Later, the same journalist followed up with a more general piece, which was fairly short on text and long on illustrations: of a different sitting room, the chemistry laboratory, a group shot of residents in a garden, and a classroom.[53]

Finally, a very different perspective came from a student, Carmen de Munárriz, who claimed to provide the "inside scoop" on life at the Residencia.[54] Indeed, the piece focuses on a series of topics hitherto overlooked: boyfriends and fiancés, running short of money each month, the lending of clothes, competition for access to the one piano, late-night parties after the 11:00 p.m. lights out, studying for the end-of-year exams, and so on. The five photos only partly support this radically alternative viewpoint: one is of a studious library scene, and another of three residents standing looking at a book; after that, the obligatory taking tea shot, residents walking, talking, and reading in the garden, and, finally, eight residents chatting and laughing in a dorm room.[55]

In the course of their reports, both Iniesta and Sarto quoted from a pamphlet put out in 1926 by the JAE and entitled *Residencia de Estudiantes*: "This Residencia, by offering families the guarantee of a spiritual home, surrounded by beneficial influences, in which they [the students] can enjoy the advantages of group living, of a healthy moral atmosphere, and of all kinds of incentives and facilities for work, wants to help Spanish girls, guiding them in their studies so that their efforts produce maximum rewards."[56] Despite its generic title, the reference to *muchachas españolas* makes it clear that it was part of a specific "package" provided to interested parties visiting the Residencia de Señoritas.[57]

Similarly, in her interview with Villaseca, Maeztu called attention to the "triple oversight – material, intellectual, and moral – that we exercise over the residents," and pointed out with satisfaction that

> the virus of the artificial and the affected, which so much feminine intellectualism suffers from, does not thrive in the atmosphere of the Residencia. It is not a club for intellectuals, nor a group of suffragettes. Simply, a house of girls who apply themselves to their studies. There is no time for anything else from eight o'clock in the morning, when breakfast is served in the dining rooms, till eleven at night, when it's lights out.
> – Neither a convent, nor a North American university. The liberty afforded by a well-organized Spanish family. Diligent attention, meticulous vigilance, without it being felt and without ceremony. My dream is, in short, to make intellectual growth compatible with the maintenance of the moral virtues of the Spanish woman; her increase in culture [compatible] with her deep national feeling of honour and dignity, without which one cannot speak of true feminine spirituality ... Through the pleasant and agreeable surface that you have seen, it is not difficult to glimpse the persistent sacrifice and the intellectual effort that it covers.[58]

Indeed, Maeztu's goal was to achieve consistently high educational standards but also to maintain the regime of strict regulation, embodied in a lengthy and detailed set of rules much more restrictive than the corresponding norms of behaviour at the Residencia de Estudiantes.[59] This was the result of a combination of factors: the socially ordained standards of behaviour for young women that were much more limiting than those applied to men, the need to attract residents to the establishment and hence to reassure provincial bourgeois parents that their daughters would not "stray" in the big city, and in no small measure the attitude of María de Maeztu herself, who expected of her charges a high degree of rigor, discipline, application, seriousness, and moral probity.[60]

Consequently, social interactions were highly controlled, and again considerably less rich, free, or wide-ranging than for the students at the Residencia de Estudiantes. Such interactions that there were, were generally formal or semi-formal in nature, with their parameters clearly defined beforehand. Personal visitors were limited to four hours on Thursday and Sunday afternoons, with a sign-in book. All residents were to be home by 9:00 p.m. unless they had express authorization.[61]

Furthermore, the Residencia de Señoritas had adopted from the start the same model pioneered by the Residencia de Estudiantes (and emulating the arrangement found in Oxford and Cambridge) of having students living and working alongside older mentors. Because of a general sense of the gaps and shortfalls in the secondary education of women at the time, there was a concerted effort to offer more classes, in situ, complementary to the course of study that residents were pursuing for their formal education.[62] From the moment of the first agreement with the Instituto Internacional onward, some of these teachers and mentors also included professors and more advanced students from the United States.

There were also a large number of lectures, many with invited speakers, but others given by Maeztu herself or other members of her staff. Some of the lectures were open to the public, while others were private and exclusively for the residents; there were also poetry recitals, readings, concerts, and the like.[63] Saturday lectures were normally obligatory for the residents. There were organized excursions to places of interest, such as El Escorial, Alcalá de Henares, or Toledo, and sometimes farther afield.[64]

Another ingrained custom was afternoon tea, which Maeztu indirectly used to prepare the residents for social interactions in "polite society."[65] Quite often, besides the students, there would be several guests present, as J.B. Trend recalled when he visited.[66] There were a few formal parties each year, sometimes combined with the taking of tea to create a version of the *thé dansant*, held at the beginning of the school year, during Carnival, and at the end of the school year.[67]

The Art School of the Real Academia de Bellas Artes de San Fernando: A Brief History

The Real Academia de las Tres Nobles Artes de San Fernando was founded in 1752. It was dedicated to the pursuits of painting, sculpture, engraving, and architecture, and based on the main floor of the Real Casa de la Panadería (Plaza Mayor). Its growth led to the need for more space, and so it moved to the Palacio de Goyeneche, calle de Alcalá, 11 (now renumbered 13), purchased in 1773 and remodelled over the next couple of years, where it remains today, just steps away from the Puerta del Sol. The academy was set up essentially as a teaching establishment, with the number of students reported as three hundred in 1758 and over a thousand in 1800.[68] A major organizational change occurred in 1844, when it was divided into the academy proper, whose members were highly accomplished figures in the world of Spanish art, and the teaching arm, called at that point the Escuela de Nobles Artes. In 1845, a special section for architectural studies was set up; in 1848, the Estudio Especial de Arquitectura moved into separate quarters and in 1857 it became the Escuela Superior de Arquitectura and now a part of the Universidad Central. Nonetheless, new statutes enacted in 1864 defined the academy's goals as promoting "the study and cultivation of the three noble arts, painting, sculpture, and architecture, encouraging their practice and spreading good artistic taste through example and doctrine," and these were to be pursued through publications, exhibitions, art collections, the inspection of museums, the restoration of public monuments, etc.[69] Since then, its core mission has remained relatively unchanged. The current number of members has risen from thirty-six to fifty-six.

THE EEPEG, 1917–30

The Escuela de Nobles Artes came into being in 1844. The major educational reform act – Ley Moyano – of 1857 changed the name to Escuela de Bellas Artes Superior para los Estudios de Pintura, Escultura y Grabado, decreed that studies pursued there would be categorized as "higher education," and established the organizational and pedagogical bases that continued into the twentieth century.[70] Further name changes followed in 1861, to Escuela Superior de Pintura y Escultura, and in 1871, to Escuela Especial de Pintura, Escultura y Grabado (EEPEG).

Women were allowed to enroll in the school from 1873 onward, but their numbers were initially very low.[71] By the 1880s, there were always over 150 total students, but only an average of 6 women among them.[72] After the turn of the century, there was a modest increase, and by 1902 there were 17 among 167.[73] Because of the presence of naked male models, women were not given access to subjects involving life drawing.[74] They were in theory granted access to colouring and composition classes from 1887 onward, but extensive restrictions on entry requirements would have severely reduced their presence.[75] Female students were gradually allowed into pictorial anatomy during the 1890s.[76] Cabanillas and Serrano suggest that women were not allowed full access to all classes involving life drawing until the 1920–21 academic year.[77]

The overall enrollment figures for the EEPEG over the years that concern us are quite revealing. Writers on the subject do not agree on exact numbers, as can be seen in table 4.1 below, where each column represents a different source for the academic years 1917–18 through 1929–30 (women students/total number of students [where given]).

4.1. Student enrollment figures for the Escuela Especial de Pintura, Escultura y Grabado (Real Academia de Bellas Artes de San Fernando), 1917–1930.

1917–18:	11/136	12/133	9/
1918–19:	19/142	16/122	15/
1919–20:	12/108	11/108	11/
1920–21:	11/109	11/109	10/
1921–22:	11/95	11/95	11/
1922–23:	13/113	12/104	14/
1923–24:	15/139	15/139	13/
1924–25:	23/150	23/150	23/
1925–26:	27/143	28/144	27/
1926–27:	25/179	25/165	25/
1927–28:	28/165	23/141	23/
1928–29:	34/192	29/159	29/
1929–30:	27/179	34/162	34/[78]

Sources: *Anuarios Estadísticos*, Instituto Nacional de Estadística; Villarejo Hervás, "'Adorno' y profesionalización artística femenina," 80; Lomba Serrano, *Bajo el eclipse*, "Anexo 1," 260–2.

As can be seen, between 1917 and 1923, these figures remain in the low teens, whereas from 1924 onward there is a moderate uptick, with roughly double the number.

Estradé Gutiérrez's doctoral dissertation offers a comprehensive history of the conservatory from the reorganization brought about by the Ley Moyano through to the Civil War, while García-Luengo Manchado's article focuses on the experience of a group of students who entered in 1915.[79] Although 1857 was a key date, many other modifications to the rules and regulations and internal functioning of the school followed in subsequent years. Comparing the plan of study for students of painting as of 1916–17 with that which operated from 1922 onward, we can appreciate similarities as well as changes.[80] Both envisioned four years of coursework (the 1916–17 version then added two years of workshop-studio and specialities classes), and many of the subjects remained constant. However, 1922 saw a few topics suppressed and a few new ones added (theory of fine arts, preparatory studies for colouring, colouring and composition, and plein air painting). Subjects nominally attached to a certain year in the program could be delayed, and subjects failed needed to be taken again, so that the progress of a given student on their record sheet may diverge significantly from what was laid out in theoretical terms.

Each professor was in charge of one subject on the syllabus. Again, comparing the staff lists for 1916–17, 1918–19, and 1923–24, we can see that there was a significant core that remained constant, while at the same time, inevitably, others would come and go.[81] Such was the case of Ramón del Valle-Inclán, who gave courses on aesthetics in 1916–17 and 1917–18 and then left, or Joaquín Sorolla, appointed as chair of colouring, composition, and landscape in 1918 and who taught there until ill health forced his retirement in 1922. Student enrollment in individual classes varied between the high thirties and low eighties. A few classes met three times a week (either Monday, Wednesday, and Friday or Tuesday, Thursday, and Saturday), but most were daily. Depending on the subject matter, classes were of variable duration, mostly one or two hours. They could start as early as 8.00 a.m., or as late as 6:45 p.m., though most fell between those extremes. Ángel López-Obrero, who entered in the fall of 1925, described his experience as follows:

The classes were eminently practical ... and kept us occupied from nine in the morning till nine at night, with the natural intervals of two hours for lunch and a free hour here and there, between one class and the next, on alternating days in the afternoon. In the morning, we had the class Preparatory for Colouring and in subsequent years Painting with live models. That was three hours of intense work, from nine to twelve, without any rest other than the breaks that were given to the model. The timing was tight, because from twelve till one in the afternoon there was another class. And at three we were again in the Escuela with the theoretical classes on History of Art and Drawing, either of drapery or life drawing of the nude, until nine at night, as I have already said. This represented, overall, an approximate total of nine hours of work, an effort that was rather tiring and perhaps excessive; but in general we students did not complain as much about the timetable as we did about the professors ... [who] were officially personalities of acknowledged prestige in the field of art[82]

By the end of their time at the Escuela, students could, if they wished, aim for an official qualification as professor of drawing, which was considered equivalent to a BA degree; this title was needed in order to be employed in that position in any state-funded school or college. Once again, Estradé Gutiérrez details the various practical tests (paintings, drawings, sketches, designs), theoretical ones (two written exams), and oral exam that needed to be passed successfully in order to attain this qualification. Despite the organizational changes, in terms of methodology, teaching at the Escuela remained largely as it had always been and very traditional in nature. The body of professors repeatedly rebuffed ministerial efforts to induce them to espouse more modern or at least different pedagogical techniques.[83]

Reading Rosa Chacel's novel *Acrópolis*, one can gain, indirectly and in a piecemeal fashion, a perspective on the atmosphere of the Escuela Especial during the 1915–18 period.[84] For his part, Dalí offers a retrospective, and inevitably rather jaundiced, evocation of the overall feeling of the place, as of the spring of 1923:

One week beforehand there began a thoroughgoing house-cleaning of the Academy, which was transformed from a frightfully run-down state to one that was almost normal. A carefully planned organization was set up to change the aspect of the Royal Academy, and several clever ruses were implemented. In the course of the King's visit to the different classes the students were to run from one room to the next by some inner stairways and take their places before the King arrived, keeping their backs to the door, so that he would have the impression that there were many more students than there really were. At that time the school had a very small attendance, and the large rooms always had a deserted look. The authorities also changed the nude models in the life classes – young but very poor creatures, and not much to look at, who were paid starvation wages – for very lovely girls who, I am sure, habitually exercised much more voluptuous professions. They varnished the old paintings, they hung curtains, and decorated the place with many trimmings and green plants.[85]

A newspaper article from 1928, written by an EEPEG student, describes the facade of the building and the entryway into the main courtyard. It notes that the Academia occupied "the lower and main part of the building" and that there was an ongoing struggle for space between the Academia and the Escuela.[86] López-Obrero also outlines the strictly classical, "academic" training that the students received. The interior of some classrooms and some classes in session can be seen in a photographic report in *Crónica* from 1929.[87] These were mainly interior rooms on upper floors of the building.[88] There were six classrooms for painting, always crowded, and two for sculpture, much less so.[89] Students entered the Escuela through the main door of the Academia on calle de Alcalá, but in 1925 this practice was changed to the rear door situated on the calle de la Aduana, a modification that students protested to the authorities with a letter signed, among others, by José Rigol, Emilio Aladrén, Cristino Gómez González (Cristino Mallo), Alfonso Ponce de León, Maruja Mallo, Margarita Manso, and Carmen Ramos.[90]

Intersections

There are only two documented intersections between the men's Residencia de Estudiantes and the Escuela Especial over the period 1918–30. This is surprising, as students enrolled at a wide range of faculties in the Universidad Central and at various professional schools were residents there, studying law, architecture, medicine, pharmacology, sciences, engineering, humanities, etc. Paulino Vicente (1899–1990), no relation to the painter brothers Esteban and Eduardo Vicente, took the entrance exam in September 1919 and studied at the EEPEG during the 1919–20 academic year (while living at the Residencia de Estudiantes, thanks to a grant from the Diputación Provincial de Oviedo), and then again in 1923 through to 1927, over which years he is listed as residing at a range of other Madrid addresses.[91] None of the memoirs by individuals who lived at the Residencia mentions him, as is the case also with their correspondence, all of which suggests that for the single year during which he was associated with that establishment, he must have moved in other, less well-known circles.[92]

The situation is completely different in regard to the other art student and male resident, Salvador Dalí. Dalí famously took the entrance exam in September 1922 and was a *residente* and enrolled art student for 1922–23, briefly in the fall of 1923 before being suspended, and again in 1924–25, when he repeated the second year. For 1925–26, he registered as an *alumno libre* – a non-residential student preparing for the end-of-year examinations independently (in this case, mainly while living back at home with his family in Figueras), which led to the showdown with the EEPEG's examining tribunal in June 1926 and his definitive expulsion. While many biographers and critics have commented on this connection, which led to some of Dalí's classmates getting to know his friends among the other *residentes*, the stress has almost always been on access leading from the Escuela Especial to the Residencia, whereas in fact the flow in the other direction was equally important, with individual *residentes* becoming acquainted, via Dalí, with several art students (as varied as Emilio Aladrén and Margarita Manso).

A high percentage of women students attending the Escuela Especial were from Madrid, so in all those cases they would have lived at home.

There were a few from other cities around Spain, and they would normally have made alternative arrangements with relatives, close family friends, and so on.[93] Consequently, the number of aspiring women artists who also intersect with the Residencia de Señoritas is also low.[94] When we consider the years 1917–30, there are three primary candidates: Victorina Durán, Delhy Tejero, and Joaquina Zamora Sarrate.

Although records of students at the Residencia de Señoritas survived (the corresponding archives of the Residencia de Estudiantes were lost), they are incomplete and are sometimes not as forthcoming as one would like. Vázquez Ramil provides an extensive appendix with a listing of women residents and, when it is recorded, their course of study.[95] For the years 1917–30, this table identifies Tejero and Zamora, plus Dolores González Sánchez, listed for 1928–29 as studying painting and whose profession was given as "Dibujo Escuela Adultas de Oviedo."[96] Of course, the EEPEG was not the only school in Madrid at which to study art; there was, for instance, the Escuela de Artes y Oficios, on calle de la Palma. Pérez-Villanueva Tover offers a numerical table with a breakdown of the institutions where residents were enrolled or the type of study that they were pursuing; no students of painting are listed until 1926–27, with one, 1927–28, with three, and then one again for 1928–29 and 1929–30.[97] Murga Castro's study includes women artists who were students while living at the Residencia, as well as women who taught art and associated subjects in classes for the Residencia, but she is essentially working with the same available information.[98]

Not mentioned elsewhere but appearing in the database maintained by the modern Residencia de Estudiantes, we find several others; most of them were training to become teachers, but a few later made a name for themselves in the art world.[99] María Ángeles Torner Cervera (1905/7–1958), spent a couple of months, May and June 1928, at the Residencia de Señoritas pursuing a course of study described as painting, Vázquez Díaz, and museums;[100] she would go on to become a famous illustrator, known usually by her initials "a.t.c."[101] Dolores González Rodríguez (1890–1972, born in the Canary Islands, but at that time resident in Cuba) likewise had a two-month stint at the Residencia between October and December 1928 and was listed as studying painting.[102]

VICTORINA DURÁN

Victorina Durán (1899–1993) completed a whole course of study at the Real Conservatorio de Música y Declamación when she was still very young, between 1908 and 1917.[103] As she explains, she put up with her musical training, particularly the piano classes, in order to be able to enroll in the theatre courses, as her overriding ambition was to become an actress.[104] However, upon graduating, her family opposed her pursuing this career, so at the age of eighteen she re-channelled her energies and took art lessons over the summer of 1917 in order to prepare for the entrance exam to the Escuela Especial in the fall, which she passed.[105] In her autobiography, Durán mentions that her family moved around a lot, renting and then leaving a number of Madrid apartments; one of these is calle de Silva, 40–2, 1°,[106] the address that appears on all the records of the Escuela Especial. Consequently, it would appear that Durán was not living at the Residencia de Señoritas during her years at the art school.[107] However, there are some indications that she may temporarily have lodged there just before the fall of 1917.[108] Further, she would resume direct contact with the Residencia as of 1932–33, when she offered art classes.[109]

The detailed record (*Hoja de estudios*) kept in students' files from the Escuela Especial lists all the courses taken, the years in which they were taken, and the results (passed, prize given, failed, retaken, etc.). Unfortunately, Durán's is missing, but her career can be reconstructed from individual registration slips that have been preserved. Durán enrolled in a more or less full load of courses for 1917–18, 1918–19, and 1919–20; she also received various prizes and medals along the way. For 1920–21 and 1921–22, she only took one subject per year, suggesting that this was very much a part-time activity; in 1922–23, there are more subjects again, then back to one per year for 1923–24, 1924–25, and 1925–26.[110] As a result, her association with the conservatory lasted for a total of nine academic years. Durán includes different features of this experience in her memoirs, among them her ambiguous but close relationship with Rafael Doménech, who taught theory of fine arts,[111] and who subsequently recruited her to go and work and study, simultaneously, at the Museo Nacional de Artes Industriales (later Decorativas).[112] Durán also describes her closeness with Valle-Inclán, who taught aesthetics, as well as a friendship with Romero de Torres, who taught drapery.[113] These relationships led her to frequent the *tertulia* and the *saloncillo* of the Teatro Español and an impromptu *tertulia* at Romero de Torres's studio on the calle de Pelayo.[114] As for her classes with several other professors, she asserts that "all these teachers were extraordinary."[115]

Over these same years, 1917–26, Durán also engaged in a variety of other activities. She served as "unpaid drawing assistant" at the Escuela Normal de Maestras de Madrid, 1918–20;[116] she started to work at the Museo Nacional de Artes Industriales in 1918 or 1919; in 1920 she entered the Exposición Nacional de Bellas Artes, sección de Artes Decorativas, and received a prize; in that same year, she became "substitute professor of Arts Applied to Industry" at the Escuela del Hogar y Profesional de la Mujer;[117] she held an exhibition of her batik work at the Ateneo de Madrid in 1921; she sent works to the fundraising exhibition for Russian children (1922); she participated in the biannual Exposiciones Nacionales de Bellas Artes for 1922, 1924, and 1926, again receiving more prizes;[118] she won second prize in a Concurso Nacional de Pintura for Artes Industriales in 1923; she showed examples of her work at the major International Exhibition of Modern Decorative and Industrial Arts held in Paris 1925, where she won a silver medal; she received a travel grant from the Junta para Ampliación de Estudios to visit the exhibition and to study interior design in Paris in the fall of 1925;[119] she became a tenured professor of arts applied to industry at the Escuela del Hogar y Profesional de la Mujer in 1926 and secretary of that school in 1927;[120] and she exhibited at the III Exposición Internacional de Artes Decorativas in Monza, Italy, in 1927.[121]

At the end of 1928, she won the competitive examinations to become the chair in Costume of the Real Conservatorio de Música y Declamación, where she had been a student just eleven years previously. A banquet was held at the Hotel Nacional on 4 February 1929 to celebrate this remarkable achievement, and the list of sponsors and invitees indicates the range and diversity of Durán's connectedness: Fernando Álvarez de Sotomayor, Mariano Benlliure, Victoria Kent, Ángel Vegue y Goldoni, Margarita Nelken, Pilar Vega, María de Maeztu, Antonio Fernández Bordas, José Moreno Carbonero, Miguel Martínez de la Riva, Fernando José de Larra, José Carreño España, José Garnelo, Rafael Doménech, and Pilar Fernández de la Mora.[122]

Victorina made friends with a number of fellow women students at the conservatory. One of the first whom she mentions is Rosa Chacel (1898–1994), who was already there.[123] Chacel tells us that she entered the Escuela Especial in 1915 to study sculpture, and most sources indicate that she stayed for three academic sessions, her last therefore coinciding with Durán's first.[124] The partial records preserved only cover 1917–18 and 1918–19, but here Chacel appears enrolled in a number of typical first- and second-year courses.[125] Having become firm companions, they would go to the Ateneo together, to attend various cultural events, and Durán also recounts how much influence Chacel had on her aesthetic judgments at the time.[126]

The career of María Luisa Pérez Herrero (1898–1934) at the EEPEG parallels that of Durán at several points. Pérez Herrero's family lived in Madrid and she completed her secondary education at the Colegio San Luis de los Franceses. She failed the entrance exam in the fall of 1916, but entered the art school successfully in the fall of 1917, and was registered there for the years 1917–23 and again 1925–29. Over this long period of study, she attained a number of honours and participated in several exhibitions. She was appointed as assistant teacher of drawing at the Escuela Normal de Maestras de Madrid (which Durán had recently left), and in 1923–24 received a grant from the Junta para Ampliación de Estudios to study artistic techniques in France for three months.[127] Durán mentions her as a "companion," noting that she was in her studies of landscape technique a pupil of Antonio Muñoz Degrain, and that she was later able to go and study in Paris.[128] In 1927, she received a second grant from the JAE to study in Italy.[129]

Márgara Villegas – Margarita Fernández Villegas Niño (1899–1983) – received her education at the Instituto-Escuela, and coincided with Rosa Chacel and Victorina Durán at the Escuela Especial. Records show her taking the entrance exam in December 1917, and she subsequently enrolled in 1918–19, though the surviving paperwork only shows her there for that one year. Like Chacel, she was interested in sculpture, though it seems as if, again like Chacel, literature may have been her true calling.[130] She did not complete the coursework at the Escuela Especial and never pursued an artistic career, and is remembered today as the translator of John Dos Passos and as the wife of José Robles (a writer, academic, and political activist). Durán includes her in the same paragraph with Pérez Herrero and Chacel, writing of her in these terms: "the daughter of the writer who signed as *Zeda*, she was very entertaining, with a fine sense of humour, but her studies were not of any use to her, for she married and went off with her husband to the United States."[131]

Chronologically, Durán did also coincide with Maruja Mallo (1902–1995), who was at the Escuela Especial 1922–26. However, it is clear that, while aware of each other, they moved largely in different circles; as Durán laconically notes, "I was still in the Escuela when Maruja Mallo entered, whom years later I encountered in Buenos Aires."[132] Further, records of the courses taken while at the conservatory show that they must only have shared one class, general instruction in modelling, in 1922–23.[133]

In contradistinction, among these women students who were her contemporaries, Durán was closest to Matilde Calvo Rodero (1899–1982), and it is not surprising that their careers have a number of parallels. Not only were they classmates for several years at the Escuela Especial (Calvo had started in 1915, the same year as Chacel, but had had to take 1917–18 off because of ill health),[134] but Calvo also went on to work and study, simultaneously, at the Museo Nacional de Artes Industriales (later Decorativas), likewise recruited by Rafael Doménech.[135] She participated in various exhibitions and won several prizes. She received a grant from the Junta para Amplicación de Estudios to spend two months in Paris in the fall of 1925, and in 1927 was appointed to a post as adjunct teacher of handiworks (working with Durán) at the Escuela del Hogar y Profesional de la Mujer. In 1930, she received a grant from the Junta para Ampliación de Estudios to go and study leatherwork and bookbinding for two months in Paris. Her specialities were etching and various aspects of decorative design, including batik, ceramics, leatherwork, and bookbinding. She also served as a teacher of drawing and a primary school teacher at the Instituto-Escuela (starting at a date that is not recorded).

In her autobiography, Durán mentions Calvo frequently. She introduces her coming back from the year off for illness, and highlights her generosity with her family's money, which gets her the nickname of "the Dollar Princess."[136] Calvo is there with her at the Museo Nacional de Artes Industriales,[137] and in the sparsely attended supplementary classes toward the end of their careers at the school.[138] Durán spent a number of summers with the Calvo Rodero family, usually holidaying in Cantabria, Galicia, or Portugal,[139] and from 1925 onward Durán and Calvo had annual month-long stays in Paris during the summer.[140] At some point Calvo's father built an art studio for her on the roof terrace of the building at calle Ventura de la Vega, 1, right on the corner with the Carrera de San Jerónimo.[141] Calvo shared the studio with Durán and Juanita Cortadellas;[142] having furnished it to their own taste, it became a meeting point for other artists and their friends, whom, unfortunately, Durán does not identify by name.[143]

Rosa Chacel's autobiographical writings coincide largely with Durán's. Besides Durán herself, she mentions Margarita Villegas and another art student, Paz González.[144] In the course of commenting on Chacel's novel *Acrópolis*, Carretón Cano describes González as "extremely well-read, an example of Institución Libre de Enseñanza education."[145] Later, Chacel dedicated a sonnet to her, "En un corsé de cálidas entrañas," in *Caballo Verde para la Poesía*, number 4 (1936).[146]

Durán also identifies (as does Chacel) a number of male contemporaries at the Escuela Especial with whom she interacted. Most of the named individuals would go on to become well-known artists: Gregorio Prieto (1897–1992), Timoteo Pérez Rubio (1896–1977) (who married Chacel in 1921), José Frau (1898–1976), Joaquín Valverde (1896–1982), Carlos Sáenz de Tejada (1897–1958), Manuel Castro Gil (1891–1961), Marcial Muñiz (1892–1955), and Andrés Fernández Cuervo y Sierra (1897–1990).[147] Durán does not appear to have been particularly close with any of them (with the exception of Pérez Rubio),[148] but they were certainly companions with whom she shared classes. The same can be said for one other male student whom she singles out for more extensive treatment – Salvador Dalí.

Durán recalls Dalí's arrival at the Escuela Especial, which was nothing less than sensational:

One day Salvador Dalí appeared, as if he had arrived from Mars. He came with all the stylings of a painter: a rather tight suit, a floppy tie in a big bow, uncut hair, and enormous sideburns, long and wide, which framed his face and made it look even more gaunt. But most unusual of all was that he carried a walking stick.

– What's that? – someone asked.

– Who is that? – we were all asking ourselves.

And somebody said:

– He's a Catalan – as if this were a definitive explanation of that individual.[149]

Likewise, once installed there, he continued to cause trouble:

His conduct in the Escuela was even more outlandish than his person. He refused to copy the models. I remember that when faced with a bas-relief of an Italian Renaissance Madonna he got up to his usual mischief: a personal interpretation of it based on triangles, which cost him passing the course.

– They've failed me – and I cannot forget his sad eyes, his childlike face filled with tenderness and sorrow for that injustice, according to how he saw things.[150]

Perhaps the most interesting episode involves Dalí trying to interest Durán in Braque. Durán at that time had espoused an aesthetic that was a mixture of late symbolist, Art Nouveau, *fin de siècle*, and decadent. Consequently,

Because of this, the day when Salvador Dalí confronted me with Braque's painting, I rejected it roundly; that was the moment when I had a great admiration for the decadent friend of Wilde, the sickly and perverse Beardsley who, like his compatriot Oscar, transformed the worst of the soul into something beautiful and turned simple or vulgar things in life into a caricature or a joke.[151]

This matches up exactly with a recollection in Dalí's autobiography: "One day I brought to school a little monograph on Georges Braque. No one had ever seen any cubist paintings, and not a single one of my classmates envisaged the possibility of taking that kind of painting seriously."[152] In this regard also Carretón Cano reproduces a group photo (shown in figure 4.2) taken in the Escuela Especial, in which he identifies Gregorio

4.2. Victorina Durán, Salvador Dalí, and a group of other students
at the Escuela Especial.

Prieto, Pérez Rubio, Durán, and Salvador Dalí. Durán is the only woman
in the photo, sitting on a chair in the middle of the group; Dalí, still with
long hair and exaggerated sideburns (which places us in the fall of 1922),
is clad in an artist's smock coat.[153]

DELHY TEJERO

Tejero grew up in Toro (Zamora), where she received her first art classes
from a cousin who painted and a private teacher.[154] She may also have
had some instruction in drawing at the Fundación González Allende in
Toro.[155] As a teenager she showed talent, and around 1924 was able to place
some drawings in local newspapers, *La Independencia*, *El Noticiero*, and
El Popular.[156] In early January 1925, weeks before her twenty-first birthday,
Delhy – Adela-Petra Tejero Bedate (1904–1968) – was accompanied by her
father to Madrid to take a test for entrance into the private art academy of
the artist and art critic José Blanco Coris.[157] This introduction may have
come about through the writer and journalist Manuel de Castro Tiedra,
a family friend. She passed, and was admitted on January 10.[158] At the
same time, her father enrolled her in the private religious college of San

Luis de los Franceses, on calle Tres Cruces (near the Red de San Luis) to round off her education in a conventional middle-class fashion (including classes in general culture, French, and dressmaking).[159] Accommodation was arranged at the Residencia Hermanas Angélicas on calle Princesa.[160]

However, Delhy was only interested in the first of these educational opportunities:

> And tomorrow to Madrid. And the day after I'm taking the test in the art academy of that Mr. Coris. I believe that I'll pass it and be able to prepare myself in order to enter the Escuela. That's the only reason I'm going! The rest doesn't interest me at all: learning French and making patterns for dressmaking doesn't interest me. May father forgive me, but that's how it is. The only thing I want to do is paint. I want someone to teach me to paint. It's the only language that interests me, the one for which I was born.[161]

And she would also recollect, "Later I arrived in Madrid, 'to study languages and shorthand.' Many times I managed to leave these classes, in order to go and draw in the Escuela de Artes y Oficios."[162] Through the winter and spring of 1925, then, she prepared for the entrance exam for the Escuela de Artes y Oficios, where Blanco Coris was one of the professors, and passed it successfully in May.[163]

She was enrolled there for two academic years, 1925–26 and 1926–27. Sources place her at the Escuela de Artes y Oficios during this period, and then at the Escuela Especial, overlapping, starting in 1926–27.[164] However, the situation is actually more complex. Her record from the art conservatory (pictured in figure 4.3) shows that she took the entrance exam there during the 1924–25 academic year – that is, in the summer or early fall of 1925 – but failed on this first try.[165] She passed on a second attempt at the beginning of the 1925–26 academic year, and immediately registered as an *alumno libre* – one not attending the classes but able to take the end-of-year examinations, all five of which she passed.[166] She would have prepared for the exams while simultaneously attending the Escuela de Artes y Oficios. This also goes to explain why Delhy appears in a group photo of the banquet for the new director of the Escuela Especial, Rafael Doménech, which was held at the Restaurante Spiedum on 17 March 1926.[167]

HOJA DE ESTUDIOS del Alumno *Tejero Bedate*
D.ª *Adela* natural de *Toro* provincia de *Zamora*
justificada con los documentos contenidos en su expediente.

Asignaturas	Curso.	Escuela de B. A. donde estudió.	NÚMERO DE LA INSCRIPCIÓN DE MATRÍCULA		CALIFICACIÓN DE LOS EXÁMENES		Escuela de B. A. donde se examinó.	OBSERVACIONES
			OFICIAL	LIBRE	ORDINARIOS	EXTRAORDINARIOS		
Examen de ingreso.	24-25 / 25-26		"	"				
Perspectiva	"	"		"	Aprdo.			
Anatomía	"	"		"	Aprdo.			
Enseñanza general del modelado	"	"		"	Aprdo.			
Hist.ª del Arte en las Edades Antigua y Media	"	"		"	Aprdo.			
Dibujo de estatuas	"	"		"	Aprdo.			
Estudios preparatorios de colorido	26-27	"	"		S. de M.			
Hist.ª del Arte en las Eds. Moderna y Contemp.ª	"	"	"		Aprdo.			
Dibujo del natural en reposo	"	"	"		Aprdo.			
Colorido y composición	27-28	"	"		S. de M.			
Teoría de las Bellas Artes	"	"	"		Aprdo.			
Estudio de las formas arquitectónicas	"	"	"		Aprdo.			
Dibujo del natural en movimiento	"	"	"		S. de M.			
Pintura decorativa	28-29	"	"	"	N. de M.			
Pintura de paisaje y al aire libre	"	"	"		Aprdo.			
Dibujo de ropajes de estatuas y del natural	"	"	"		Aprdo.			
Modelado de estatuas 1.º								
Modelado del natural y de estatuas								
Modelado del natural								
Composición escultórica								
Est. práct. de materiales y proced. escultóricos								
Grabado de reproducción								
Grabado original								
Grabado y estampación								
Copia de medallas en modelado								
Modelado del natural aplicado a las medallas								
Composición de medallas								
Prácticas en la ejecución de medallas								
Dibujo científico	27-28	"	"		Aprdo.			
Estudios prácticos de ornamentación	28-29	"	"		Aprdo.			
Ent. de los métodos y proced. de enseñanza del Dibujo y del Arte en los Centros de enseñanza primaria y secundaria del Extranjero	"	"	"		Aprdo.			
Asignaturas repetidas.								
Col. y comp.ª	29-30	"	"					

4.3. Delhy Tejero's academic record at the Escuela Especial.

Her record also shows her, now as an *alumno oficial* at the EEPEG, taking three more courses in 1926–27 (this was, simultaneously, her second and last year at the Escuela de Artes y Oficios, where she received a grade of *sobresaliente*),[168] five in 1927–28, five in 1928–29,[169] and one in 1929–30 (that she was not able to complete). She participated in the group exhibition Exposición de Arte Pro-Cuba, organized to help with the relief of Cuba after it was struck by a major hurricane. This opened at the Museo de Arte Moderno on 4 December 1926; a striking period photo shows the participants – sixteen women and a crowd of men behind them.[170] According to one source, Tejero's painting was acquired by the Embajada de Cuba.[171] Interviewed in 1928 by fellow student and friend Ángel López-Obrero, she waxed philosophical:

> Adela Tejero, to our question as to whether new art concerns her, replies thus:
> – Art always concerns everyone who has something of an artist in their soul. But I believe that in art, whatever it may be, there cannot be old and new art; all there is, is art.
> For now, this young lady approaches the question intuitively. For her there is nothing else than the "essence" of everything that might signify art.[172]

After spending 1925–27 living at the Residencia Hermanas Angélicas, Tejero was able to move to the Residencia de Señoritas, where she stayed for the next three academic years, from 1927 to 1930, and where her course of study was naturally listed as painting and then painting: third year.[173] As she remarked, this enabled her to "live in the environment of the Institución Libre de Enseñanza ... and thereby save herself, little by little, from a more retrograde education."[174]

In the summer of 1927, she had received a state scholarship, and this was renewed in early 1929.[175] However, in the fall it was revoked, a victim of the growing political instability that led to the fall of Primo de Rivera at the end of January 1930.[176] At this point, Tejero faced the alternatives of returning to Toro or finding another way to support herself in order to continue living in Madrid: "It was necessary to earn my own way before completing the degree, because the alternative was to go home."[177] A very early entry in her journal attests to her arriving back in Madrid in October 1929, staying initially with the Castro family, and then fending for herself financially for the rest of the academic year.[178] To this end, she turned to her art, and started selling her drawings and illustrations. First to companions at the Residencia de Señoritas (the students from the United States favoured images of regional dress), and then to the children's magazine *Macaco (El Periódico de los Niños)* directed by K-Hito.[179] From there, she managed to place drawings in *El Perro, el Ratón y el Gato (Semanario de las niñas, los chicos, los bichos y las muñecas)*, the children's supplement to the magazine *Cosmópolis* directed by Antoniorribles. She was soon contributing to the publication conglomerate Prensa Gráfica (the magazines *La Esfera*,[180] *Nuevo Mundo*, and *Crónica*), as well as *Estampa, Blanco y Negro*, and, eventually, ABC.[181] The interview with her that dates from mid-March 1930 presents her as an artist and illustrator fully launched on her career, indicating that she had made major strides over the preceding six months.[182] It also includes two moody self-portraits, and an early example of her drawings of elves or goblins that she called *brujitas*. In addition, in the fall of 1929, she offered a drawing class internally within the Residencia, in all likelihood to supplement her income.[183] Ironically, given what she had to say about her first customers, several period photos of Tejero show her dressed in traditional regional costume, alone and with a companion; she can also be seen in street clothes with three others sitting on the steps of one of the Residencia de Señoritas buildings.[184] Capping off the 1929–30 year, she participated in two shows: one in May at the Unión de Dibujantes Españoles, at their new permanent home at Avenida Pi y Margall, 9,[185] and the Exposición Nacional de Bellas Artes, held May–June 1930,[186] where she received a *premio de aprecio*.[187]

Marina Romero Serrano (1908–2001) was born in Madrid and studied first at the International Institute and then at the Instituto-Escuela, and for some time lived at the Residencia de Señoritas; she would go on to become a writer. She coincided with Tejero there and they became close:

> The "greens," which were at the bottom of the garden, were famous because they were very rudimentary and had no heating. I seem to remember that four or six students slept there, among them my dear friend Delhy Tejero, a great painter, with whom every night of the bitterly cold winters, as they can be in Madrid, I used to go to the kitchen to get the glass bottles filled with hot water for the bed. And we returned with this treasure singing and hopping along, like little girls, because Delhy above all, and I, often lived closer to the world of children than to the other one that usually is not as welcoming.[188]

The "greens" refers to two buildings of student living quarters erected in the gardens of the original houses, or *hoteles*.[189] A period photo shows Tejero on holiday in Gijón with Marina Romero and other friends.[190] Romero's first book was *Poemas .A.* (Madrid: Asociación de Alumnos de la Residencia de Estudiantes, 1935), for which Tejero designed the vignettes.

Another friend at the Residencia was Josefina Carabias (1908–1980), who was there from 1928 to 1930 and who would become one of Spain's first professional women journalists.[191] Like Tejero, Carabias had struggled to leave the small town where she was born and grew up, and, again like Tejero, when she first arrived in Madrid she was obliged by her family to live for a year and a half in a women's residence run by nuns on the calle de Fuencarral.[192] Her time in the Residencia coincided with the second and third years of the law degree that she was pursuing, and María de Maeztu also helped her find additional employment to cover her costs.

Tejero also, like Durán, got to know the Valle-Inclán family, including the writer's daughter Mariquiña (1919–2003).[193] At the end of the 1920s, during times when protests against the dictatorship of Primo de Rivera were on the rise, residents of the Residencia would sometimes be sent to live with families in their homes, and Tejero went to Valle-Inclán's.[194]

At the Escuela Especial, Tejero coincided with a number of other women students. Durán and Calvo Rodero were just leaving when she arrived, and by birth date and entry into the school she and her nearest companions belonged to a younger cohort. These included Maruja Mallo, Carmen Ramos, Margarita Manso, Remedios Varo, and Francisca Bartolozzi.[195] Mallo (1902–1995), by a few years the senior member of this group, was at the conservatory for the four years 1922–26, thus only overlapping with Tejero's first.[196] Nonetheless, as Bartolozzi subsequently recalled, "another good friend was Maruja Mallo … one year ahead of me, but we were very close because there were so few of us."[197] Tejero remembered things rather differently: "At the Escuela I encountered Maruja Mallo, who was very interested in me, but she scared me with her swearing … For my whole life the Escuela de San Fernando was against me with its outdated cadre of professors, and as Maruja Mallo had had some victories there, I ought to have joined with her."[198] Summing up this ambivalence, she concluded that the relationship had not, overall, been a fruitful one.[199]

Carmen Ramos Fontecha (?–?) is mentioned by Mallo as a friend in her group: reminiscing about Dalí, she recalled that "he had a lot of fun playing with Margarita Manso, Carmen Ramos, and me in the courtyard of San Fernando. We held hands and spun around as fast as we could until we fell over."[200] Ramos entered the school for the 1924–25 academic year, took courses there steadily through 1927–28, and then repeated one or two courses each year through to 1930–31. In 1929, the then secretary of the Escuela, Manuel Menéndez, mentioned her in an interview: "The most notable women students, worthy of praise and encouragement, are: ... Carmen Ramos, the prizewinner in Colouring and Composition."[201] Although she coincided with Tejero for half a decade, her name does not come up in the existing literature, and she does not appear to have later made a mark in the art world.

A direct contemporary of Ramos, Margarita Manso (1908–1960) presents a different profile.[202] Her records show her taking classes at the Escuela Especial for three years, 1924–27 (she took only one class during her final academic year), and she did not complete the program. Although Manso was six years Mallo's junior and two years behind her in coursework, they became particularly close friends. She and Mallo formed a small group with Dalí and Lorca, some of whose adventures Mallo has recounted.[203]

Despite being younger than Tejero, thanks to her residence in Madrid and a progressively-minded father, Remedios Varo (1908–1963) had studied at the Escuela de Artes y Oficios for two years, 1922–23 and 1923–24, leaving there several months before Tejero arrived.[204] Varo successfully entered the EEPEG in the fall of 1924, completed substantial coursework from 1924 through to 1928, and repeated one class in 1929–30. Consequently, she coincided with Tejero over four academic years. Again as Bartolozzi recalls, "we always used to go around together, Delhy, Remedios, and me."[205]

Francisca Bartolozzi (1908–2004), also known as Francis, Piti, or Pitti, is a little more forthcoming on the subject of Tejero. Bartolozzi – daughter of the famous painter, illustrator, stage designer, children's writer, and puppeteer Salvador Bartolozzi – received her secondary education at the Instituto-Escuela from 1921 to 1925 and then attended the Escuela Especial from 1925 through to 1930.[206] As she later noted of her classmates, "There were very few of us girls whose parents allowed us to study, and it was even rarer when the course of study was something like Fine Arts. That was not viewed favourably."[207] Things had not changed very much. Of her time at the conservatory a decade earlier, Chacel wrote,

> The girls' freedom was regulated, in theory, by the old customs; in practice, by different degrees of modernization. Clearly, the progress made by the ideas of the century was general, but over and above what was happening deep down – morals, religion, tradition – it was social attitudes that decided things among the well-off classes, where girls still had chaperones. In the working classes and in those where the parents were employed in the so-called liberal professions, they followed the need for a contribution to be made to family income, or the parents' beliefs or ideologies, or the degree of confidence in their maturity and personal rectitude that each young woman managed to attain in her home. This third case applied to me and to my friends, except the Villegas girls, who had been educated at the Institución Libre de Enseñanza, and hence were sure of the model that they represented.[208]

At all events, because of the closeness in which they worked and studied, Bartolozzi recalls that friendships and romantic relationships were not infrequent:

> We had very diverse friends ... including José Luis Florit, Gerardo Lizárraga, whom Remedios married some years later, Pedro Lozano, who became my husband ... Delhy Tejero would turn up daily with a black hat and cloak, she was very entertaining. Delhy, Remedios, and I always used to go around together.[209]

Specifically in regard to Tejero, Bartolozzi evoked her thus:

> Delhy, who was an attractive woman, was a little extravagant; she was the one who most drew attention for her outfits, which she made

herself, she painted her fingernails black, she wore a black cloak, which in combination with her black hair gave her a mysterious air, she smoked using long cigarette holders and changed her signature from Adela to Delhy, influenced by a certain exoticism of the times and wanting thereby to leave behind a traditional past that smothered her.[210]

Interviewed alongside Tejero by their fellow student Ángel López-Obrero, Bartolozzi's answers were quite flippant:

And so there are some people – it seems – who take things jokingly, but without them losing any of their sincerity or verve.

Here we have, for example, a blond young lady, really attractive, who has just said something witty. It's Piti Bartolozzi.

– My aesthetic concerns – she says – consist of putting my beret on just right, for although it seems an unimportant thing, it's a big problem ...

– And in regard to the Escuela? By saying that it's even pleasant climbing the more than a hundred steps to go to class, nothing else needs to be said!

Piti Bartolozzi has told us with great wit that "she is a modernist from the very tip of her beret to the bottom-most point of her high heels. So much so that Josephine Baker, Matisse, and Gómez de la Serna seem like [ancient] Greeks to her"[211]

Bartolozzi also appears in a group photo of 1928 with Tejero and others, taken on the rooftop of the Academia de San Fernando.[212] Other larger group photos, on the roof (figure 4.5 below) and also inside (figure 4.4), show Bartolozzi, Mallo, and Tejero, among others.

It goes without saying that a number of significant male artists attended the Escuela Especial during the time that Tejero was there, and some of them have already been mentioned in passing. But it is worthwhile recalling these names with their dates of attendance: Salvador Dalí, 1922–25, with some interruptions (as mentioned above), José Rigol, 1922–27, Emilio Aladrén, 1923–29, Cristino Mallo (Maruja's younger brother), 1923–27, and Alfonso Ponce de León, 1923–28.

4.4. Delhy Tejero and Pitti Bartolozzi, with other students at the Escuela Especial. Cabanillas Casafranca and Serrano de Haro.

4.5. Delhy Tejero, Rosario de Velasco, Pitti Bartolozzi, and Maruja Mallo on the rooftop of the Real Academia de San Fernando.

JOAQUINA ZAMORA SARRATE

Joaquina Zamora (1899–1999) is less well-known today but was a successful artist and art teacher over her long career in Spain. She was born and grew up in Zaragoza, where she received her first art lessons from Antonio de Gregorio Rocasolano.[213] There are works by her that can be dated back to 1916–17. She first exhibited in 1919, in an Exposición de Artistas Noveles e Independientes, organized by the local Ateneo in the rooms of the Centro Mercantil, Industrial y Agrícola of Zaragoza, and then in the Exposición Nacional de Bellas Artes in Madrid in 1922.[214] After several frustrated efforts to move to Madrid and study at the EEPEG, she achieved this goal in the fall of 1924, when she received a fellowship from the Diputación Provincial de Zaragoza.[215] This was subsequently renewed at the request of the professors there. She spent four academic years at the Escuela Especial, from 1924 through to 1928.[216] During that time, her most influential professor was Manuel Benedito, who had been appointed to replace Sorolla and teach the course on colouring and composition.[217]

Attending the EEPEG from 1924–28 and completing a conventional course of study, Zamora overlapped with Tejero for three of those academic years. Zamora is notable because she is also listed in the register as living at the Residencia de Señoritas from 1926 to 1928, during which time she was studied painting, sculpture, and engraving, echoing the name of the conservatory.[218] During these years, Zamora also exhibited quite extensively. In Madrid, she was at the Salón de Otoño in 1925; the Exposición Nacional de Bellas Artes in 1926; and the Exposición de Arte Pro-Cuba in 1926;[219] these were followed by the Exposición Benéfica in Huesca in 1927 and the Exposición Girondo-Aragonesa in Bordeaux in 1928.[220] After her years in Madrid, Zamora returned to Zaragoza, where she embarked on a career in art that for economic reasons she needed to combine with teaching. She was appointed as an art teacher in March 1931, and continued exhibiting in 1929, 1932, and thereafter.[221]

Conclusion and Coda: The González Rodríguez Sisters

The experience of living (and/or teaching) at the Residencia de Señoritas and studying simultaneously at the Escuela Especial was, evidently, not a common one, but it must have been extraordinary. While today we have a very considerable amount of information concerning the parallel conjunction of Salvador Dalí at the EEPEG and the Residencia de Estudiantes, the same unfortunately cannot be said of Durán, Tejero, and Zamora. More work remains to be done on this and related topics. Most of the women artists mentioned in this chapter are currently under-researched, and we need monographic biographies and studies of each of them. Where autobiographical writings do not exist, all surviving correspondence needs to be recuperated and edited, for the unique insight that it can provide into the lived experience of the period, many details of which are still lacking.

The Residencia de Señoritas is a locus of other allied and equally interesting kinds of artistic and biographical intersections. Two other residents who lived there were the sisters Ernestina (1899–1976) and María Luisa (1900–1998) González Rodríguez, from Medina de Pomar (Burgos). They both enrolled at the University of Salamanca in philosophy and letters, where – like María de Maeztu before them – Unamuno was one of their professors and became close with María Luisa.[222] Ernestina started in Salamanca in 1915 and finished her studies in Madrid in 1921,[223] while María Luisa, a year younger, followed a similar course, starting in 1918. Vázquez Ramil lists Ernestina as living in the Residencia de Señoritas over from 1920 to 1924, and puts María Luisa there during the 1921–22 academic year.[224] Gállego Rubio indicates that María Luisa went to the Instituto Internacional in 1921, while Salaberria Lazarazu states that she went first to the Residencia in 1921, and then to the Instituto Internacional, where she was till 1926.[225] Montes López and Gallego Morón clarify that as the Residencia de Señoritas closed in the summer, María Luisa was obliged to find alternative accommodation for those first months in another residence close by.[226] In the interview, she refers to a certain "Estrada" who was likely Jiménez de la Espada, director of the Grupo de Niños allied with the Instituto-Escuela and in summer 1921 on the brink of leaving the houses on calle Rafael Calvo.[227] Once in Madrid, both sisters prepared for the competitive exams to enter the Cuerpo Facultativo de Archiveros, Bibliotecarios y Arqueólogos. Ernestina joined in 1921 and worked as a librarian until 1927; María Luisa joined in 1922 but took periods of time off from 1923 onward.

In 1919–20, Ernestina worked at the Centro de Estudios Históricos with Father Zacarías García Villada, and in the fall of 1920 in office administration for the Instituto-Escuela; in August 1924, she received a grant from the JAE to carry out six months' research in the archives in Paris, and at that time was listed as resident at calle Blasco de Garay, 9, 3°.[228] María Luisa became romantically involved with the student Juan Vicens de la Llave (1895–1959), who had lived at the Residencia de Estudiantes, and they married in 1925.[229] They spent time in Mallorca, then briefly experimented with running a windmill.[230] Vicens joined forces with the Madrid bookseller León Sánchez Cuesta and invested in his plan to open a branch in Paris, the Librería Española (10 rue Gay-Lussac). Sánchez Cuesta set it up in 1927 in conjunction with Gabriel Escribano, while Vicens and Sánchez Cuesta's brother Luis took care of the Madrid establishment. After Sánchez Cuesta returned to Madrid, Vicens and María Luisa moved to Paris and took over management of the store in 1928; shortly after, Vicens bought it outright from Sánchez Cuesta.[231] For a number of years it became an obligatory stop for anyone in their circle visiting Paris, and a gathering place for Spanish writers and artists living in the French capital.

The other point of intersection that concerns us here is the Residencia de Estudiantes, and more specifically the informal group that Luis Buñuel, then a resident, created and baptized the Orden de Toledo. The aforementioned temporary summer accommodation run by the Instituto-Escuela was offered to students who were staying in Madrid, either because they had no real home to return to (the case of the two sisters, who were orphans), or because they had failed end-of-year exams and needed to prepare for the re-sits that were held just before the start of the following academic year. It was there that María Luisa encountered Luis Buñuel, seemingly in the summer of 1921, though because she was studying hard for the exams to become a librarian-archivist, the friendship did not blossom until 1922.[232] Vicens entered the Residencia some time in the early 1920s; later, he was with Buñuel in Paris in 1925. Quoted in one source, María Luisa explained that her husband had "arrived at the Residencia a little later than we did, when our group was already formed. He immediately joined this group and many times came with us on excursions." In another, she explained that "we used to go on excursions on Saturdays and Sundays with the boys ... We used to go to Toledo, to the mountains, or to the Museo del Prado."[233] Buñuel dates his first visits to Toledo to 1921, and specifies the date of the founding of the Orden de Toledo as 19 March 1923.[234] Further, Buñuel identifies Ernestina González Rodríguez, along with Lorca, Francisco García Lorca (Federico's younger brother), Rafael Sánchez Ventura, Pedro Garfias, Augusto Centeno, and José Uzelai, as one of the founding members.[235] This matches with the chronology of the two sisters' arrival in Madrid and with María Luisa's encounter with Buñuel having occurred prior to her meeting Vicens. It is worth pointing out also that José Moreno Villa, who lived at the Residencia, was a member of the Orden, and also joined the Cuerpo Facultativo de Archiveros in 1921.[236] Buñuel identifies Ernestina as a founding member, but it is María Luisa who preserved a series of photos of herself with the group at the Venta de Aires, while Moreno Villa remembers both sisters sometimes participating in these excursions.[237] The Orden de Toledo, its members, and the visits to Toledo during which they roamed the streets of the old city at night have been much written about, to the point of mythologization, and it is not my intent to repeat that material here.[238] Rather, I simply wish to point out that to the conjunction of the Residencia de Estudiantes and the Orden, we need to add a further vector, namely, that of the Residencia de Señoritas and indeed the International Institute and the Instituto-Escuela.

CHAPTER 5

THE UBIQUITOUS GABRIEL GARCÍA MAROTO

Gabriel García Maroto, born in 1889, is older than the other primary figures treated in this book. His long career can be divided into several distinct stages, and the one that interests us most here – because of the activities he pursued and the people he met – started in 1919 and ended in 1927. No one can doubt that Maroto was a fascinating, multi-faceted individual: painter, draughtsman, woodcut maker, engraver, designer, illustrator, typographer, printer, publisher, magazine director, writer, poet, art critic, essayist, travel writer, lecturer, activist. Given the broad scope of his diverse enterprises, he came into contact with an extraordinary cross-section of the contemporary cultural scene. "Ubiquitous" is, to be sure, something of a hyperbole, but he appears in a wide range of contexts, interacting with a correspondingly wide range of people.[1]

One of Maroto's most memorable aspects was his personal manner or temperament. By far the most frequent adjective used to characterize him was *inquieto* – uneasy, restless, questioning, inquisitive, searching, and dissatisfied with the status quo. Indeed, in the contemporary sources that I consulted, this term is applied to him more than forty times. Juan de la Encina, while he avoids that particular cliché, nonetheless communicates a sense of why it was so commonly used: "Painter, lithographer, etcher, writer. A turbulent and active man: he speechifies tirelessly, he attacks ceaselessly ... [and] he defends from time to time. Just and unjust, like everyone else. Romantic for his fervour. Classical for his aspiration. He is not content with anything or with anyone. He is, finally, an early riser and keen on hunting. And he reads the great Frederick."[2]

Looking back, Maroto divided his career into various stages: his early engagement with art and literature, a period of doubt and then of nearly complete self-isolation, and then a more radical turn (in both the aesthetic and socio-political senses) that we can situate around 1919. A brief autobiographical note of 1927 summarizes the first stages of this evolution: "As a necessity ancillary to his work as a painter, he writes. He contributes to different publications. He publishes some books, which today he detests. He draws and paints for years, years distanced from exhibitions. He creates a culture for himself following his impassioned reasoning."[3] A little later, in a newspaper interview, he expanded on this version of events:

> I had such a strong feeling of the falseness of what I was doing back then that the expressions of praise nauseated me, and for six years I went without drawing a single line or painting a single stroke. Then I started working again, and I found that my hand was terribly clumsy, but a lot more sincere. "You've gone astray," they said to me; "you've got lost; you don't have any of your good qualities anymore." I knew, in spite of everything, that I was making truth – my truth – in my works ... Back then, I used to frequent some of the literary and artistic *tertulias*. I met writers, painters, and I saw that they were talking about fairly interesting things. But within a year I got tired of them, and retired to a farm in the Picos de Europa, where I did not see anyone for three years.[4]

Maroto was both right and wrong about his trajectory. While his career undoubtedly entered a new and important phase in the 1920s, what came before actually laid the groundwork for many of his pursuits and viewpoints. It is impossible to understand and appreciate fully his later activities without some familiarity with the range of experiences that led him to them.

EARLY YEARS: LA SOLANA AND MADRID, 1889–1913

Maroto was born and grew up in La Solana, a small village in La Mancha. His family was poor and he left school at age nine or ten to start working.[5] As a teenager, he had an inclination toward reading and writing, but also demonstrated a clear artistic vocation.[6] He received some art lessons locally,[7] and then during sporadic trips to Madrid he took night-school classes.[8] He passed the entrance exam for the Escuela Especial at the third attempt (in September 1909), enrolled for 1909–10, and started to live the student life in Madrid, supplementing meagre support from home with part-time employment.[9] By late spring 1910, this proved economically unworkable and he returned to La Solana, missing the end-of-year exams. When he was not granted a local government scholarship, he did not return to the Madrid conservatory.[10]

Over the next decade he bounced between Madrid, La Solana, Salamanca, Barcelona, and Frama, and wrote art criticism for newspapers, published books, and painted. His contributions to *El País*, the newspaper of the Partido Republicano Progresista edited by Roberto Castrovido, span from fall 1910 through – sporadically – to the end of 1914 (see appendix 2 for a full list of Maroto's publications, including his articles for *El País*).[11] One episode illustrates his attitude at this time. The Exposición Nacional de Bellas Artes for 1910 was delayed that year, and finally held 4–15 October. In a series of four pieces, Maroto was severely critical of the composition of the juries that accepted works and then, afterwards, awarded the prizes.[12] He would later describe these and subsequent articles in *El País* as "aggressive critiques and chronicles of a wannabee."[13] He followed up on 4 November with a lecture ("El arte. Los vencidos") delivered in the Palacio de Cristal – one of the exhibition halls – in which, with inflammatory rhetoric, he directed virulent criticism at the old fashioned, closed-minded, and generally second-rate jury members and also called for the burning of three-quarters of the contents of the Museo de Arte Moderno.[14]

His first book, *Del jardín del arte* (October 1911), based on a trip through Italy, France, Belgium, and Holland in the spring of 1911, is part travelogue, part art commentary.[15] When visiting La Solana, he made contact with the magazine *Vida Manchega* (Ciudad Real), where he would publish a number of articles. Back in Madrid, he listed his friends at the time as the writers and journalists Federico García Sanchiz and Tomás Borrás, the painter Federico Beltrán Masses, and the caricaturist Luis Bagaría.[16] From October 1912 is *La caravana pasa*, printed by a local La Solana press. It is a curious miscellany, with reproductions of drawings, poems, short prose pieces, dramatic dialogues, and fictive correspondence, demonstrating the wide range of his output as well as how he already straddled literature and art.

He later described his state of mind in "the Madrid of 1912 and 1913": "I am not comfortable in that Madrid that I recognize with love, but from which I demand ... a rejuvenating restlessness that I can espouse and to which I can dedicate myself ... At the time that I am referring to, I was suffering from tedium, helplessness, aspirations that find no path that leads them to fruition."[17] In February 1913, then, he enthusiastically participated in a promising new venture – the launching of an artistic society to be called "Los Independientes."[18] The initial call was signed by D.J. García de Alcañiz, Maroto, Manuel Góngora Echenique, Juan González Olmedilla, Alberto Insúa, Federico de Iribarne, and Segovia.[19] They described themselves as "full ... of hopes and dreams and ... with an abundance of rebelliousness," and appealing to artists of all stripes, from poets to architects, they proclaimed their lofty aims:

> To bring together brothers in art, those who, repulsed by the petrified and unhealthy atmosphere of other circles that call themselves artistic, in a battle against enervating cretinism, spurred on by the rebelliousness and independence of their souls, are seeking companions, not mentors; those who want brothers, not masters ...
>
> To facilitate spiritual exchange among youth seeking renewal, without a limit, an established canon, or an accepted formula being able to put any restrictions on the idea.

An initial meeting was held on 7 February, and another on the twentieth,[20] but nothing more appears to have come of it.

After visiting Paris and Ignacio Zuloaga's studio in the spring of 1913,[21] *El año artístico. Relación de sucesos acaecidos al arte español en el año mil novecientos doce* appeared in May. Anticipating a model practised by José Francés from 1915 onward, the book surveyed exhibitions held throughout the year; nearly half of it was dedicated to the Exposición Nacional and other shows around Spain. A tiny, privately printed pamphlet, *Pro-arte. El prestigio de un cuadro*, dealt with a recently identified painting by Rafael de Urbino.

SALAMANCA TO BARCELONA, 1913–18

By fall 1913, Maroto had grown tired of life in Madrid and he realized that he needed a change.[22] Equipped with a letter of introduction from Azorín, Maroto went to Salamanca to talk with Miguel de Unamuno.[23] Establishing himself in a very small village, Aldeaseca de Armuña, just north of the city, he started to write and paint. In his autobiographical writings, Maroto intimates that the interaction with Unamuno had a profound effect on him, as he found in him a model and mentor; indeed, he judged his "Unamuno-esque stay in Golden Salamanca, [and] in bare Armuña right beside it," as being "of extraordinary importance, formative to an extreme degree, deeply suited to my immediate needs," and he acknowledged gratefully "this time spent together, whose values still beat today in my depths, and the body of culture, which I acquired back then in my youth," concluding that "I consider my experiences during that year as decisive."[24] Maroto divided his time between Aldeaseca and Salamanca itself,[25] where he participated in events organized by the Ateneo and held at the university.[26]

Intensifying his activity in 1914, in January Maroto founded a journal called simply *Salamanca* and subtitled *Revista de Bellas Artes, Literatura y Ciencias*. It only lasted for two numbers; on the covers he reproduced two recent paintings, and in number 2 he printed part of his November lecture, "El naturalismo, el regionalismo y la decadencia en el arte." Around the same time, he brought out the full text as a pamphlet that he self-distributed.[27] His main arguments revolved around the stultification and careerism that he claimed characterized the art world in the big cities, and the need to return to pure emotion, sincerity, and inspiration, which were to be found in smaller towns, villages, and the countryside. On Unamuno's recommendation, he spent twenty days in a retreat at the monastery of Santo Domingo de Silos, 29 June–19 July 1914,[28] and in an article he commented that "intimate meditation has the power to console a soul longing for divinity, thirsty for the infinite."[29] Much of his poetry written at this time is collected in *La canción interior*, which he had printed by the sole press operating in La Solana, the Imprenta de Rogelio de la O.

Also produced by that press was a more substantial volume, *Teoría de las artes nobles. Elementos de filosofía e historia del arte español.* Vol. 1, *La pintura en España*. As its title suggests, this was addressed to art educators and offered a compendious coverage, with definitions and general ideas, as well as comments on the Spanish masters and their connections with those whom Maroto considered the best modern painters. The book was an outlet for the more academic work that Maroto undertook in La Solana, as he contemplated trying to gain employment as an art teacher.[30]

Back in Madrid in 1915 – a year that saw several significant events – Maroto started to put into practice the "lessons" learned from Unamuno.[31] He also shifted his art criticism from *El País* to *La Tribuna*. That year, the Exposición Nacional de Bellas Artes opened on 8 May, and the big scandal was the jury's veto on Federico Beltrán's canvas *La maja marquesa*. Beltrán was a close friend, and Maroto jumped to his defence, first with a newspaper article ("El reinado de la mediocridad"), and then a whole book that he compiled, *Federico Beltrán y la Exposición Nacional de Bellas Artes de MCMXV*. In the latter work, he gathered opinions on the painting from José Francés, Cecilio Plá, Rafael Marquina, Manuel Abril, Rafael Cansinos Assens, and a dozen other authors, framed by Maroto's own forceful comments on Beltrán and the work.

Beltrán was married to Irene Narezo Dragoné (1891–1970), an established painter in her own right,[32] and one of only three women included in the landmark exhibition of the Sociedad de Artistas Ibéricos (1925) (discussed later in this chapter and again in chapter 6). It was through Beltrán that Maroto met his future wife, Irene's younger sister Amelia (b. 1895), whose family was based in Barcelona.[33] Judging by the brief introductory note,[34] the material for *El libro de todos los días* (1915) was written while Gabriel and Amelia were courting and/or engaged, and, tellingly, it was printed in Barcelona. They were married in November and established their first residence in Barcelona.[35]

Maroto spent most of 1916 and 1917 there, where he met some members of the Catalan art scene, such as Anglada Camarasa and Santiago

Rusiñol, but not its most avant-garde elements.[36] He also befriended the novelist Gabriel Miró, who lived for a while in the same apartment house on Paseo de la Bonanova.[37] Unamuno met up with him, returning via Barcelona from Mallorca, and emulating the Santo Domingo de Silos experience, Maroto also spent a little time at the Real Monasterio de Santa María de Poblet.[38] That year – 1916 – he also brought out another poetry collection (his last), *Los senderos*, published under the imprint of the Biblioteca Dragonné.[39] In addition, his first child, Gabriel, was born; a daughter, Sara, followed in 1918.

In 1917, Maroto completely disappeared from public view: nothing was published, there were no mentions in the press, and no artworks were exhibited. Somewhat later, fortified by the Catalan experience, marriage, and fatherhood,[40] he returned to Madrid, but other things did not change that much: "I begin to live out a stage in my goals and abilities that, like all the others, does not register achievements, successes, discernible conquests that figure, to a lesser or greater degree, in the public history and chronicle of my Spanish life and times."[41] In 1918, he launched another new project, a publication that was supposed to be a journal but which, in the event, had only a single issue. *España y la Guerra. Revista Mensual* appeared in Madrid in January 1918 and was a compilation of strongly pro-ally texts by leading intellectuals, featuring Unamuno, Azorín, d'Ors, Rusiñol, Moreno Villa, and a number of others.[42] Unamuno's prominence may be indicative of his inspiration, as Maroto returned to Salamanca in the spring.[43] But he did not stay more than a few months, for by the summer he and his family were on the move again.

FRAMA (VALLE DE LIÉBANA), 1918-20

In the summer of 1918, the Maroto household moved to a tiny village located in the middle of the Picos de Europa, putting into practice the stance of *menosprecio de corte y alabanza de aldea* (scorn for the court and praise for the village) that he had proclaimed years previously. Amelia Narezo's grandfather was from Frama, located in the Valle de Liébana; one of his sons, Pablo, had gone to Mexico, where he married Sara Dragoné, and two of their children were Irene (Beltrán's wife) and Amelia. After decades spent in Mexico, Pablo Narezo had decided to return to his roots, but died in Barcelona while still in transit. His wife,

Sara, stayed on there, while also spending part of most of her summers in her father-in-law's ancestral home.[44] It was at his mother-in-law's invitation, or perhaps near insistence, that Maroto and his family went for the summer, but once installed they decided to prolong their stay, since they were "living a salutary, invigorating life, abundant in human, geographical, anthropological, and artistic discoveries."[45]

Besides seeking an agreeable setting in which to live, Maroto had also been grappling with an ongoing tension over where to direct his energies: To the world of letters or that of art?[46] Beyond 1917, he more or less abandoned the genre of poetry (his verse was very conventional and, frankly, rather uninspired),[47] but at the beginning of August 1918 Maroto started contributing to the magazine *La Voz de Liébana. Decenario Regional de Intereses Generales*, based in Potes, a larger village than Frama and capital of the *comarca* (district).

His first publication was a short novel, *Campanas bautismales. Glosario de la vida humilde*, described as a *folletín* (serialized novel) and printed back to back on pages 3–4, so that the text could be later cut out and bound. Further installments continued in almost every number through to January 1919.[48] In its opening pages, it was dated to "Frama, día de Santiago del año 1918" (i.e., 25 July) and dedicated to Santos Narezo (the grandfather). A transparently autobiographical though novelized account of the recent experiences of Gabriel and Amelia, in the text the married couple is called Manuel and Lina. They and their two children go to the Valle de Liébana, and Lina's childhood memories of the landscape lead the couple to believe that it will be a better environment for the young children to grow up in.[49] Maroto never essayed long-form narrative again, and instead would specialize in short, vignette-like stories with many *costumbrista* (relating to local colour and customs) details.

Maroto had not neglected his art during these months in the country, because April 1919 brought another watershed moment, his first individual show, held at the Ateneo in Madrid. It ran ten days, 11–20 April, with thirty-two paintings and drawings on exhibit. Critics quoted from Maroto's text in the catalogue, where he anticipated public and critical indifference, if not outright hostility, and alluded to the stylistic change in his painting: it was now "of a very simple design" and he explained that "in my thirtieth year I have felt the need to draw and to paint.

Nothing remains in my work of my old and odious facility. The blind covetousness of bygone times has been followed by a calm ambition seeking to express the ineffable with a light, allusive language."[50] Indeed, Maroto had turned thirty in January 1919, perhaps prompting him to take stock. Critics struggled to label the new style – Was it symbolist? Modernist? – and one identified as points of reference the strange combination of Cézanne, Marinetti, Picasso, and Amiel.[51] Maroto also participated in the competition held by *Nuevo Mundo* for magazine covers. Over two hundred designs were entered and exhibited, in the Círculo de Bellas Artes, and the jury found five of those submitted by Maroto to be "meritorious."[52] Over August and September, he also showed works in exhibitions in Santander (21 August–15 September) and Bilbao (31 August–beginning October).[53]

Maroto maintained a similar range of activity through 1920. He won third prize in a poster contest organized by the Círculo de Bellas Artes,[54] and he entered a second cover design contest arranged by *Nuevo Mundo*.[55] Between 12 and 22 March, Daniel Vázquez Díaz held an individual show at the Majestic Hall in Bilbao; Maroto and Margarita Nelken both contributed texts for the catalogue, and Maroto likely attended. The Exposición Nacional de Bellas Artes for 1920 ran in Madrid 1 June–15 July, and just before it opened Evaristo Correa Calderón published a long, important article fiercely critical of its organization, echoing virtually point by point objections raised by Maroto years earlier.[56] Ironically, Maroto was admitted to the show, but as Correa Calderón commented, he was consigned to the so-called "hall of crime" with two other art critics, Ceferino Palencia and Francisco Pompey.[57]

Meanwhile, Amelia's mother, who split her time between Barcelona and Paris, was in declining health and passed away at the end of May. Maroto and his family had travelled to Paris to be with her, and they spent most of the summer with Federico Beltrán and Irene, who lived there permanently. Maroto visited and wrote articles about the Théâtre du Vieux-Colombier and the sculptor Antoine Bourdelle, who had been a strong influence on the young Vázquez Díaz.[58] The family also consulted specialists on the recently discovered deafness of their daughter Sara.[59] They were back in Frama by the end of August, where Amelia gave birth.[60] At the end of September 1920, Maroto made a trip to Madrid, likely to prepare for their relocation, and exactly a month later his whole family left to establish their residence there. It seems that Maroto was now ready to tackle big-city life once again.[61]

MADRID: EDITORIAL CALPE (1920–21), IMPRENTA MAROTO (1921–28), *ÍNDICE* (1921), AND GARCÍA LORCA (1921)

Toward the end of 1920, Maroto arrived at an agreement with Editorial Calpe to provide the ornamentation for a new series of *Libros de aventuras* featuring authors like Fenimore Cooper, Robert Louis Stevenson, and Jules Verne. Six of these came out at the very end of 1920, and another four in 1921.[62] The books were also illustrated, but by another – and always different – artist. Maroto also restarted publishing in the periodical press (*La Esfera*), basing his writing initially on his experiences in Frama and then subsequently on his travels to many other villages in different parts of Spain.[63]

During the preliminary stay in Madrid in October 1920, Maroto was in touch with Juan Ramón Jiménez, with whom he had already exchanged a few letters.[64] A passing reference suggests that plans for a press were already crystallized, as Jiménez mentions the title of a small collection that he had prepared but eventually never published – *En la rama del verde limón* – that it seems he planned to have Maroto print: "I'm sending you this!, as a model for the size for *En la rama del verde limón*; and another four songs. I'm going to dedicate the book to your daughter."[65] On 12 October, Jiménez reported to Ortega y Gasset that Maroto was a candidate for the position of artistic director at Calpe and had asked him to put in a good word for him, and, indeed, Jiménez gave Ortega a glowing recommendation.[66] Maroto may already have had a modest contract with Calpe and was aspiring to more, or the interview may just have resulted in the ornamentations commission.

At all events, having brought his family to Madrid at the end of October 1920, Maroto worked rapidly to set up a printing press workshop, the Imprenta Maroto (located at calle Alcántara, 9–11), as well as a small office in the centre of the city (calle Caballero de Gracia, 60 [Edificio La Unión y el Fénix]).[67] What motivated Maroto to take this remarkable step is not entirely clear, as his own comments on the subject are not particularly illuminating:

It is in 1921 that I manage to fulfill a desire that I had been privately nurturing over a long period of much effort and of many reasonable longings: to join the arts, the letters, and the political obligations to which a man of my characteristics ought actively to devote himself, with an artisanal work that was full of possibilities, a desire for which I had been preparing myself, and likewise my brother Santiago, the youngest of the family, since my Catalan period.[68]

Evidently, he had become increasingly interested in decorative arts and book design, but this was a further step that very few artists (or writers) tend to take. It is possible that Maroto may have inherited some money from his mother-in-law that could have funded the venture. Contact with the Mexican writer Alfonso Reyes might also have provided a spark. Reyes was in Spain from 1914 onward, and was one of Jiménez's closer helpers with *Índice*. In 1930, he wrote of

> my fantasizing in Madrid, back then around 1915, when I wanted to have a printing press in my house to make books the way I wanted ... And when also in Madrid, I assisted JRJ [Juan Ramón Jiménez] with the publication of *Índice* ... how much we yearned to eliminate somehow that error of translation that always occurs between the will of the poet who conceives of his books and the run-of-the-mill, insipid realization of them by the tradesman who prints them.[69]

This was a goal shared by Reyes and Jiménez, who closely oversaw the printing of his volumes of poetry.

The only known description of Maroto's enterprise was offered by Francisco Alcántara, the art critic for *El Sol*. With distant echoes of an arts and crafts studio, and referring to the interior of the Imprenta, he offered the following scene:

> In it, the tools of the trade are mixed in with pieces of period furniture. The cretonnes, the colour of the walls, the straight or arching lines, filleted in blue or gold, the canvases and drawings of different schools and periods, all form part of an ensemble in which, without excessive amounts of space and without any sort of

luxurious touches, there beats the energetic sensation of a fervent mysticism, in which are fused together love for the work, aesthetic emphasis, and the verve that in the struggle for existence this fanatic of idealism is now displaying.[70]

On a day-to-day basis, the press was run by Maroto assisted by his younger brother, Santiago, who had moved from La Solana; in March 1921, they advertised a job for a boy to help out with errands.[71]

One of the first commissions was from Jiménez: *Obras de Rabindranath Tagore. La hermana mayor (y otros cuentos)*, a selection of Rabindranath Tagore's work translated by Jiménez's wife Zenobia Camprubí, which Maroto was working on typesetting in January 1921.[72] During this first year, at least nine other books by different authors and in a variety of genres followed, ranging from poetry by García Lorca and Luis de la Jara to works with a political bent by Ramón Turró and Alfonso Paquet.

Meanwhile, after exploring a couple of ideas for literary magazines to be entitled *Dinamismo* and *La Espiga*, Jiménez had firmed up the project for *Índice* toward the end of April 1921.[73] In May, he stated forthrightly that "Maroto and I are going to create a monthly magazine: *Índice*."[74] Letterhead with the title *Índice* bore the address of Imprenta Maroto.[75] Advertisements for the press appeared in numbers 1–3 of the magazine: "Those in charge of this press wish to encourage in Spain love for a beautiful printed work, a delight for refined minds. With that goal in mind, they request from you, as a reader of ÍNDICE, any kind of work related to the discipline in which they aspire to become masters." Services offered included "artistic editions," "illustrated advertising," "commercial printing jobs," and "books and pamphlets."[76] A poster or large flyer for the establishment likewise read, "MAROTO | PRINTER | Artistic Editions | Commercial | Printing Jobs | Illustrated Advertising | ALCÁNTARA 9 y 11 | T. 1790 S."[77]

One of these other jobs undertaken by Maroto was the catalogue for Vázquez Díaz's Madrid exhibition, held 26 March–25 April 1921, which included a prologue by Jiménez. Maroto's sole publication in *Índice* (number 1) was a commentary on this exhibition and on Darío Regoyos's show, also held in the Palacio de Bibliotecas y Museos.[78] He was full of praise for Vázquez Díaz and complained about the lack of attention –

perhaps willful indifference – that he received, whereas he was critical of Regoyos, whose artistic qualities he thought fell short.

Initially, the closing date for contributions to *Índice* number 1 was 20 May; by 11 June, Jiménez was soliciting texts for number 2, with a closing date of 20 or 22 June, though number 1 had not yet been published.[79] It eventually came out somewhere in the middle of July.[80] The colophon in Lorca's *Libro de poemas* is dated 15 June, so the typesetting and printing of this quite extensive volume may partly have caused these setbacks. Number 2 was similarly pushed back, from an original date of June all the way to September.[81] As the delays mounted, Jiménez became more impatient and irritated with his partner and his excellent opinion of him faded. On 18 August he complained that

> number 2 of *Índice* is dragging along at the pace of an army in disorganized retreat. There are not enough font letters for the complete number – 24 pages; ... and above all, the normal slowness and disorder with which you are already familiar, are now increased by the fact that the "topic" no longer matters to Maroto! – The issue with Maroto has been resolved. He will cease being an editor, and will only contribute the odd drawing. It could not be otherwise.[82]

In the same letter, besides Maroto's "demotion," Jiménez announced that he had engaged the services of another printer. On 3 September, the news was that "*Índice* is making progress, although not as I would have wished. In order to eliminate the delay, two numbers are being produced at the same time: one at Maroto's! and the other at the new press with which I am very pleased."[83] Maroto, therefore, printed number 2 (which *did* come out in September), while number 3 was already in the hands of José Maíz and the Talleres Poligráficos (calle de Ferraz, 72). While number 3 (which, despite Jiménez's efforts, did not appear until December) maintained the look and the format of numbers 1 and 2, Maroto's only contribution to it was a small coloured drawing. For his part, Maroto felt that Jiménez had overreacted:

> Customers? There were a lot, and always complicated ones, demanding the impossible, as in the case of Juan Ramón Jiménez,

otherwise such a good friend of mine, but capable of breaking off friendships for the most trivial reasons, but, above all, on account of anything related to the more or less accomplished printing of a card, a leaflet, a book, or a literary magazine of the quality that *Índice* had.[84]

Juan Guerrero Ruiz captured a moment during this transitional phase:

Yesterday evening from six till eight I was at Juan Ramón's home, talking about the magazine *Índice*, whose number 3 will be coming out very soon. The press cannot work for us from Thursday through Monday, and that completely disrupts our plans. Yesterday, the number 3 for the front cover that Maroto had drawn was so ugly that Juan Ramón said that it was a blot on the cover and he himself started to draw another one so that today the photoengraving could be made. We want to publish number 4 at the end of the month.[85]

Here "the press" must be the new printers rather than Maroto (both now cause delays), while his other comment indicates that the issue number on the front cover was hand drawn and that material originally prepared for number 3 by Maroto was later handed off to the Talleres Poligráficos. What is problematic is the date ascribed by Guerrero to this conversation: 6 February 1922, which must be in error; press reports tell us that *Índice* number 3 appeared toward the end of December 1921.[86]

It was Jiménez who first introduced Maroto to Lorca,[87] and thereafter he visited the Residencia de Estudiantes with some frequency, where he also met other students such as Emilio Prados and Luis Buñuel, as well as some of the mentors, including José Moreno Villa and Ricardo Orueta.[88] Maroto was an attendee at the party that Lorca held in his room on 5 April 1921, along with Barradas and various other guests (see chapter 2).[89] A first joint project emerged as early as January 1921, as Lorca announced: "It also seems that the magnificent magazine that we had planned will become a reality, because there are people who will give the money for it and we also have a magnificent press at our disposal."[90] In February, he was enthusiastically looking to the future: "Maroto has already opened his press where there are so many projects that we need to undertake."[91]

By mid-May, his scheme had taken shape: "We are going to produce two magazines; ... in the other one, the one for the young crowd, I will be the founder and director, because the ideas for it have been mine. In this second magazine of *advanced* ideas Manolito [Ángeles Ortiz], [José Fernández-] Montesinos, and Melchorito [Fernández Almagro] will contribute alongside me and other worthy young people."[92]

However, in the spring of 1921 focus shifted, temporarily, from the ongoing magazine project to the printing of Lorca's *Libro de poemas*.[93] Maroto seems to have taken the initiative in proposing the publication of the collection, which he presents, in part, as an act taken in order to preserve Lorca's output.[94] In a small suitcase or large briefcase, Lorca brought him a mass of manuscripts in a disorganized state, leaving his friend to sort through them, transcribe them, and turn them into a book: "I will never forget that youthful and poetic chaos, which was dropped into my hands as if crying out to be put into order."[95] Maroto hyperbolically describes "thousands of manuscript pages, loose, scrambled, battered, stained, and without any internal organization by means of numbering, pins, or turned-over corners."[96] Maroto also obliged him to compose a brief text presenting the collection.[97] Because of his work for *Índice*, Juan Guerrero Ruiz would sometimes drop by, and he described how he once found Lorca there: "In the spring of 1921 I encountered one day working on the boxes of letters a dark young man, cheerful, always smiling, his face and hands stained by the printing press ink. It was Federico García Lorca, who liked to go there, where his *Libro de poemas* was being typeset, and which was published that year."[98] In situ at the press, Lorca also corrected a set of first proofs, as he recounted to his parents on Imprenta Maroto letterhead in the middle of May.[99] In addition, Maroto commissioned from Lorca "some musical editions of children's songs ... to which I have added some very thought-provoking prologues," another project that came to nought.[100]

At exactly the same time as Lorca and Maroto were working on the *Libro de poemas*, plans were under way at the Residencia de Estudiantes for a production of Rabindranath Tagore's play *Sacrificio*, translated by Zenobia Camprubí in 1919. The play, in which Lorca and Buñuel had roles, and for which Maroto designed costumes and/or sets, was being prepared to coincide with a visit from the author.[101] Tagore had undertaken a year-long tour of Europe and the United States from mid-1920 to mid-1921, and on the last leg, in the spring of 1921, he was supposed to come to Spain around April or May. However, the visit never materialized, and instead he travelled from England to France, Switzerland, and Germany.[102] Consequently, the performance was never given.[103]

From this same period there is a fine photograph of the youthful Maroto dedicated to Lorca: "A Federico. Gabriel. Hoy 6 de junio de 1921."[104] *Libro de poemas* came out in the second half of that month.[105] In early July, Maroto wrote to Lorca (now back in Granada) about the dire state of his finances. On the one hand, he felt that it would be "madness to let go an attractive business and a noble undertaking because of fear of the difficulties right now," and that "above all it was Juan Ramón, who with abundant arguments has made me see that there is no reason for such a foolish decision. I did my sums ... and onward."[106] On the other hand, he recognized his present predicament: "in my press I have invested, of my own money, between forty and forty-five thousand pesetas," and he needed funds in order to "get out of this temporary bind."[107] He asked Lorca to intercede with his father, to see if he might lend him four thousand pesetas, with appropriate interest, as well as pay him the seventeen hundred owed for the book. Lorca's parents had not yet paid the bill for the printing of *Libro de poemas*, which they did shortly afterwards, but the additional loan was not forthcoming. Lorca lamented the situation on 2 August: "I have not received *Índice* and I am very sad and anxious about what is going on with Gabriel; you cannot imagine how much I like him, because he deserves it, as he is so good and so passionate."[108]

More or less simultaneously, on 1 August, Melchor Fernández Almagro had written to Lorca about the magazine project: "my hopes and dreams for *our* magazine survive intact. My enthusiasm, my excitement ... Whereas G. Maroto seems totally discouraged. When you get here, we will rekindle his enthusiasm. And if not, we will look for another collaborator."[109] In the fall, Maroto had recovered and he, too, was now eager to continue on with Almagro and Lorca. Almagro reports that he "sought out Maroto: we agreed to meet one night, and we talked about a magazine that he had conceived of. That can be *our* magazine. How he imagines it strikes me as very good. We left it that we would talk again."[110]

To which Lorca replied, "the plan for the magazine seems quite admirable to me, but I would appreciate it if you could reply right away with details of my very dear friend Gabriel's plans and all the rest."[111] Although Lorca planned to return to Madrid in the spring of 1922, he never did, which may be what finally sank the idea.[112]

Toward the end of 1921, Maroto launched another unusual initiative, using the space of the Imprenta to host what he called the Primera Exposición de Pintura, with works by him and others, among them Barradas. In the invitation/catalogue, whose physical description was ironically described by Alcántara,[113] Maroto explained himself:

> As an indication of my constant desires, I have gathered together in my press workshop a number of drawings and paintings by different artists, which I offer to the curiosity of a certain group of exceptional people.
>
> It will clearly be noticed that the primary intention of this gesture of mine, more than exhibiting my latest paintings and displaying some others, hitherto unknown, by others, consists rather in bringing forward the opportunity, which was getting postponed, to show off – while taking pride in it – the humble little workshop that in a clean and out-of-the-way location I have set up with exemplary aims.

Predictably, the show received almost no press coverage (Alcántara's article came well past the closing date), and very few details concerning it have been preserved. Beyond the definite presence of works by Barradas, there is very little documentation; Maroto included a couple of portrait line drawings done by Unamuno[114] and some probably also by Lorca, a supposition that seems to be borne out by a letter sent to him by Maroto announcing the exhibition.[115]

For 1922, I have only found three volumes printed by Maroto, one by Gobineau for Alberto Jiménez Fraud's publishing enterprise, a volume of poetry by Oscar Vladislas de Lubicz Milosz, and a textbook on shorthand. Beyond this, there are no records at all for 1923 or 1924, and just three for 1925: José María Hinojosa's collection *Poema del campo*, and two works by Maroto himself. Serrano de la Cruz Peinado states that the Imprenta Maroto functioned from 1921 through 1927,[116] so there may have been more books and other items printed there without explicit bibliographical indications of their material origin. She also mentions that over these years Gabriel and Santiago organized touristic trips through off-the-beaten-track parts of Spain to supplement their income.

Maroto continued to contribute to worthy causes, such as the campaign for hungry children in Russia, donating a painting, and making free posters.[117] According to one report, he attended the famous Concurso de Cante Jondo held in Granada 13–14 June 1922, in whose organization Lorca had played a major role.[118] Toward the end of the year, Maroto participated with Barradas, Cristóbal Ruiz, and Winthuysen in a joint show at the Ateneo, with approximately five works each. Most of the critics singled out Maroto and Barradas as being the more modern or progressive, and hence the more interesting, with Maroto's canvases *Día perlado* and *Día plomizo* receiving much comment, most of it very positive.[119]

The exhibition ran 4–20 December, and right around this time Maroto undertook a trip to Berlin. He merely identifies the year, 1922, but what we know of his two companions would suggest that the travel took place around the turn of the year 1922–23: "In search of better information on the subject of typography, visual arts, global culture, and the postwar mood of Germany, the losing and devalued side, I spend in Berlin, in 1922, a productive period of time, in the enjoyable company of two esteemed friends – Fernando de los Ríos and Julio Álvarez del Vayo."[120] The journalist, writer, and later politician Julio Álvarez del Vayo lived in Berlin for some time, working as a correspondent for the newspaper *El Sol.* The law professor and Socialist politician Fernando de los Ríos, however, was based in Spain, but a series of letters to his wife, Gloria Giner, place him in Berlin between 6 and 22 January.[121] In the first letter, Ríos refers to an evening spent in the company of Álvarez del Vayo and his wife; Maroto is not mentioned.

ORIGINS OF THE SOCIEDAD DE ARTISTAS ESPAÑOLES (1923) AND MALLORCA (1923–24)

Over the years, Maroto tried his hand, with varying success, at just about every literary genre, and theatre was no exception. A surviving typescript, entitled *Obra II. Mundo, demonio y carne. Farsa dramática en cuatro actos*, dated to 1923, suggests a prior *Obra I.* Maroto passed the text to Lorca, perhaps for him to read and comment on.[122] The play harks back to the Golden Age *comedia*, and is set in Valladolid in the sixteenth century around a troupe of theatrical players.[123]

However, what most preoccupied Maroto over the first three months of 1923 was a movement to reform the organization of the art world in Madrid in order to give younger, more progressive painters greater exposure. Maroto was not the only artist or critic to believe that such changes were long overdue. José Francés, in his review of the December 1922 Ateneo exhibition, threw out the comment that it "anticipates in miniature what can be the future Exhibitions of Independents."[124] Simultaneously, Juan de la Encina (pseudonym of Ricardo Gutiérrez Abascal) was having similar thoughts. In a general article about "La nueva generación artística," in which he criticized the "industry" that conventional art had become, he nonetheless saw promising signs of a possible renewal in some of the younger artists of the day, those who were open to the innovations arriving from outside Spain. Rather like Francés, he explained that "a modest exhibition of paintings in the small room of the Ateneo moves us to write these lines," though what prompted him was Pancho Cossío's show, which had followed that of the group of four.[125] Next, Encina took notice of an exhibition and competition organized by the industrialist and collector Luis Plandiura y Pou of recent Catalan art, wherein all tendencies were represented, a feature that Encina found particularly praiseworthy, as Plandiura had achieved something that was sorely lacking in Madrid.[126]

Meanwhile, an exhibition of works by Juan de Echevarría opened in the Salones de la Sociedad de Amigos del Arte (Palacio de Bibliotecas y Museos) on 1 February, and three weeks later the usual congratulatory banquet was organized in his honour.[127] The next day, Maroto wrote to Encina, enclosing the text of a hypothetical speech "that I would have delivered at the banquet for Juan de Echevarría ... had I thought of it in time."[128] Inspired by Francés and Encina, and endorsed by the latter,[129] Maroto returned to the topics of the stagnating art scene, the indifference (or worse) toward artists attempting to be true to themselves and to do something different, and the consequent need for change. But this time, instead of calling for reform of the Exposición Nacional and other state-sponsored exhibitions, Maroto proposed the creation of a Salón de

Primavera that would welcome precisely those artists generally excluded from the Exposición Nacional – a sort of Salon des Refusés.[130] Plandiura took notice and offered his support and participation, recommending that they start work immediately. Maroto had suggested for the organizing committee Juan de la Encina, Juan de Echevarría, Eugenio d'Ors, Javier Nogués, Juan Ramón Jiménez, and Manuel Abril, to which list Plandiura added Bagaría and the Marqués de Montesa, while Encina asked to be excused.[131] From this point preparatory activity went, as it were, underground, in the sense that there were no more press reports. But three meetings were held, one each in April, May, and June 1923, at which the members gradually came to disagree on the goals of the undertaking before finally dispersing.[132] However, a manifesto was drafted and d'Ors reproduces it.[133] The text ends with the bold proclamation that "today is established in Madrid a Sociedad de Artistas Españoles, the organizing body for a Fall Salon." From this document it is clear that the dissent must have arisen from the clash between d'Ors's more classicizing inclination and other members' greater propensity for the avant-garde. Unfortunately, d'Ors does not list those present, but Maroto was probably not there, because he had likely already left Madrid.

Maroto attended the banquet for Jacinto Grau held on 17 March at the Hotel Sudamericano,[134] and on 22 March the opening of an art show of works by Manuel Fernández Peña at the Salón Arte Moderno.[135] After this last, he disappears from the Madrid press for the rest of 1924 and 1925, save for one article about the Paris premiere of Grau's *El Señor de Pigmalión*.[136]

Maroto was on the move again, and he left for Palma de Mallorca at the end of March or beginning of April, followed a little later by his family after his exploratory trip.[137] Commenting later on this decision, the art critic Vegue y Goldoni explained it thus: "Here we have an artist in the grip of noble concerns, who, having performed an examination of his conscience, decided to move away from Madrid in order to work in Mallorca," while Encina simply described him as "having taken refuge … on the island of Mallorca."[138] Maroto explains that he was invited by his friends the doctors Virgilio and Vicente García Peñaranda, their sister Herminia, and her husband, the playwright Jacinto Grau. The two doctors had just established a clinic in the area of Can Bleda.[139] Can Bleda is on the road that leads to the idyllic coastal village of Deià,[140] which is where the Marotos settled:

> we rent a little house, and then soon after we buy another one up where there were olive groves, adapting this one to serve as a studio, where I complete a vast number of works, many drawings and paintings ... in the unforgettable, seaside Deyá, our little fishing village standing on the edge of Valldemosa, looking out on the sea of deep blue, among olive trees with phantasmagorical trunks and silvery branches.[141]

These nearly two years that Maroto spent on Mallorca saw an upsurge in his artistic creativity, and there are many landscapes from this period, mostly done in a style reminiscent of Impressionism and Cézanne.[142] In the middle of their stay, Maroto organized a major retrospective of his work at the Salón de la Veda in Palma de Mallorca in November 1923. The published catalogue, *Catálogo de la exposición de pinturas y dibujos de Maroto*, listed the works' titles but did not contain any reproductions. In the introductory "Palabras al viento" Maroto identified his ideal audience: anybody sleepless at night "longing to increase the extent of his knowledge and emotion, dreaming of delving with sincere conviction into the sanctuary of his fellow man"; any women attuned "to our spiritual dialogues and with whom we would have wished to entwine our purest expressions"; and children contemplating "the world of men as a marvelous spectacle." Thus, "[I] launch [my paintings] into the current of the world, wishing only that on the beach where they end up, whoever finds them might, through them, have an intuition of our soul."[143]

1925: EXHIBITIONS, THE SOCIEDAD DE ARTISTAS IBÉRICOS, TRAVELS

Maroto returned to Madrid and the art scene there with a splash, mounting an exhibition of sixty paintings and sketches that opened at the Museo de Arte Moderno on 2 February 1925.[144] It collected his work from the previous four years, evidently with a stress on the production from Mallorca,[145] and while it was running Maroto offered, in the same location, a lecture on "El arte contemporáneo en España."[146] Many artists had been inspired by the Balearic scenery, but both Encina and Alcántara found Maroto's work different and original. They were joined by Vegue in inscribing Maroto in traditions deriving from Impressionism, Cézanne, and Gauguin.[147] A selection of work from this show transferred to the Galerías Dalmau during the first half of April.[148] The relatively brief reviews published in Barcelona were generally mixed and in some cases quite negative.[149]

With Maroto now back in Madrid, meetings of that Sociedad de Artistas Españoles founded in 1923 reconvened.[150] Brihuega speculates that the spark might have come from encounters or discussions that occurred at an homage banquet for Joaquín Sunyer held on 6 February (at the Molinero restaurant) to celebrate his recent exhibition (at the Salón de los Amigos del Arte, 17 January–4 February, overlapping with the start of Maroto's show).[151] Although a long list of recognizable names from the worlds of letters and art appear in the newspaper reports concerning the event for Sunyer, strangely Maroto is not among them.[152] Manuel Abril picks up the story from here. In March, an organizing committee met at the café Lyon d'Or composed of Abril, Victorio Macho, Daniel Vázquez Díaz, Juan de Echevarría, Maroto, and Cristóbal Ruiz.[153] By 1 April, they had composed a new manifesto (superseding the one from 1923), though initially the grouping was still called the Sociedad de Artistas Españoles.[154] It was signed by all of the original six, plus several more, and widely reproduced in the Madrid press.[155] They argued that Madrid, unlike Barcelona or Bilbao, was lacking in the kind of exhibitions that would permit familiarity with the various tendencies in modern art, and so they had set out to remedy this situation, with broad principles of selection that would encompass all styles of art regularly excluded from shows. Remarkably, by 28 May they managed to put these ideas and plans into practice,[156] opening a major exhibition in Madrid.[157]

Meanwhile, Juan de la Encina was embroiled in a polemic with the painter Ricardo Baroja over a less-than-flattering review of an exhibition of Baroja's works at the Círculo de Bellas Artes.[158] The exchanges became quite heated, and Baroja soon extended his complaints to several other commentators on art, saying that he was pleased that Encina's articles were not signed by José Francés, Francisco Pompey, Ángel Vegue ... or Maroto.[159] This provocation pulled all those cited into the fray, and Maroto first retorted in a letter of 1 April – ironically, the same day as the first publication of the Sociedad de Artistas Españoles manifesto.[160] Besides sending letters to the press, Baroja also gave two inflammatory lectures, on 28 March and 3 April. This proved too much for Maroto, who responded in two lengthy articles.[161] He defended Impressionism against Baroja's attacks, and returned to his criticism of the "official" art scene, with its pecking order and its closed-ranks system of state-sponsored shows, juries, and prizes. Here the two issues came together – the Encina/Baroja polemic and the Sociedad de Artistas Españoles's contemporaneous manifesto, which Baroja had apparently also criticized in his lecture. Luis Araquistáin and Manuel Abril now entered the debate;[162] Baroja replied to both these new entrants, in what seems to have been an end to the often acrimonious exchanges in the press.[163]

The exhibition held by the Sociedad de Artistas Ibéricos (a change of names was made in the interim) opened in the Palacio de Exposiciones (i.e., the Palacio de Velázquez) in the Parque del Buen Retiro on 28 May, running through 5 July. It constitutes a landmark in the history of modern art in Spain, and more specifically in Madrid. There was large-scale press coverage, and it has received considerable critical attention in the decades since, focused particularly in the catalogue of the commemorative exhibition of 1995.[164] Maroto showed five landscapes and several drawings, in the room that he shared with Gutiérrez Solana, Valentín and Ramón Zubiaurre, and Nicanor Piñole.[165] Besides the artworks, there were also five lectures programmed, between 6 June and 4 July, offered on diverse subjects by Juan de la Encina, Marjan Paszkiewicz, Manuel Abril, Maroto, and Roberto Fernández Balbuena.[166] Maroto spoke on 25 June on the subject of "Elogio del impresionismo y otros temas," and put forth a spirited case for the enduring importance of Impressionism over and above other more recent isms such as Cubism.[167]

In reaction, Benjamín Palencia wrote to Lorca at the end of June:

You cannot imagine the scandal that there has been over these last few days at the exhibition, since Maroto attacked us moderns in a lecture that he gave, calling us "young gentlemen who pick up the magazine L'Esprit Nouveau and copy everything," because he says that it is impossible to create new art without leaving Madrid.[168]

Dalí also reacted badly, though in a more generalized way. In July, he wrote to Francisco Bores care of the *Revista de Occidente*:

> Motivated by the delicious inanities of *Nuevo Mundo* etc.,[169] I believe that it is necessary for the youngest of us to stand up for ourselves. I propose that you, Barradas, Palencia, Moreno Villa, etc. should sign these lines that I am sending you for the *newspapers*. I suppose that *some people* will be in agreement with this.[170]

The enclosed text was a hybrid between an open letter and a manifesto, and contained a number of *boutades* typical of Dalí. He also took a very indirect swipe at Maroto in the proposition that "those who are irreverent toward the classical, would seem to be precisely the people from the Academia de San Fernando, since now they are beginning to marvel as they discover the beginnings of French Impressionism."[171]

Ever tireless, once the exhibition was over Maroto embarked on a new project in the summer of 1925: an attempt to capture the spirit of different Spanish cities in a series of drawings, the first places to be covered being Madrid and then Toledo, which he visited in July.[172] An initial installment was offered in the *Revista de Occidente* in August,[173] focusing exclusively, as the title suggests, on the famous viaduct in Madrid that carries the calle de Bailén over the calle de Segovia. This was followed by the publication of two books of "perspectives" (*escorzos*) by the editorial arm of that same magazine and printed by the Imprenta Maroto: *Madrid visto por un pintor* and *Toledo visto por un pintor*.[174] These formed numbers 1 and 2 in a new series, Life Around and About (La vida en torno), which Maroto ambitiously hoped to expand eventually to twenty volumes.[175] None of these materialized, but many of the drawings that he made as part of the project later found their way into *La España mágica* (1927).

As a tie-in with the twin publications, Maroto arranged an exhibition at the Salón Nancy (Carrera de San Jerónimo, 40) of a selection of twenty-four drawings of Madrid and Toledo, which opened on 26 October and was extensively reviewed. Vegue remarked on "the two volumes with the reproductions of the work that Gabriel García Maroto is producing in

order to shape his sensibility throughout Spain," and later quoted from
a text, almost certainly from the invitation-catalogue, that Maroto had
written to frame the exhibition:

> Not a guide, nor even an overview, of the visual beauties that Ma-
> drid contains; only some perspectives free of all possibility of the
> picturesque, or in which the picturesque operates with noble values,
> through having been subjected to the principle of re-elaboration
> that sets art beyond the humble category of strict representation.[176]

A little over two years later, in December 1927, Maroto referred to a
"loose leaf listing of works of a distant, individual exhibition of drawings
and paintings" that took place "some two years ago," and then quoted
extensively from that catalogue:

> After having asserted, by my example, the many excellent things
> to be achieved by the voluntary limitation of visual themes; after
> having proposed as the maximum area for our aesthetic forays that
> space which is circumscribed by the walls of our small workroom;
> after the long endeavour of the close handling of everyday scenes
> and things; we are [now] starting the daring adventure of traversing
> Spain with the purpose of collecting from it artistic themes of varied
> rank and essence.
>
> The same work as in other days, the same appetite for unity, for
> revitalizing recreation, for the struggle, for the assertion – both friend
> and enemy of life around and about – of personal visual emotion.
>
> Now that the expressive mediums have been somewhat mastered,
> and with my will tempered, we are going to try to discover a new
> Spain in the depths of our sensibility ...
>
> Yes. That is what we are attempting; that is what we are to attempt
> in the future. And to that end we shall have to travel down many
> Spanish roads, we shall have to spend the night in the many inns
> that still wait patiently at the side of the road; we shall have to get
> up many days with the dawn, eager to capture the simple, innocent
> desertedness of the small villages of Spain.

As a painter, principally in search of emotion born of the visual, to double our pleasure we shall attempt to fix also, with written words, as an exacting complement to our initial intention, the diffuse, complex warp and weft of our sensations ...

No one that we are aware of attempted to gather into a tight sheaf, bound together by an aesthetic principle, this varied, surprising, and lively panorama that puts on its finery and comes out to meet the passionate observer ...

Province by province we will go discovering Spain. From Andalusia, first, along routes suited to our goal, we will start gathering what is essential to our purpose ...

From each Spanish region will be brought forth a group of drawings of varied themes, of diverse aspects, drawings whose value is to be found more in their visual force than in their descriptive quality, and which born of the surrounding reality, but rapidly set free and liberated from it, will live their true life in a world of formal laws, only minimally dependent on their original source. Life around and about will give them their initial impulse, but then they will become calm, grow, and achieve a state of plenitude in the world of aesthetic unity.[177]

Given the chronological markers and the general content of the passage, the unidentified exhibition that Maroto was referring to must be this one, held in October and November 1925.

For his part, Encina commented that "this painter is a nonconformist" and found that "in these fine and deft sketches of urban landscapes ... one perceives a vague and tremulous bloom of sensibility – the accent or lingering impact of Impressionism."[178] Another notable article was by the distinguished pedagogue and politician Luis de Zulueta: calling Maroto "this good friend of mine," he even-handedly assessed the drawings and used them to lobby for an open-minded attitude to modern art.[179] Just a week or two before, in the middle of October, Maroto had also shown a fairly substantial corpus of paintings and drawings in an exhibition held at the Asociación de Artistas Vascos in Bilbao that was well-received by local critics.[180]

1926: EXHIBITIONS AND LITHOGRAPHY

Relatively speaking, 1926 was a calmer year between the twin peaks of 1925 and 1927. As announced, in the spring Maroto undertook a major trip through Andalucía, sketching along the way, which would provide material for many artworks that were shown or published in 1927.[181] His itinerary is shown on a map included in *Andalucía vista por el pintor Maroto*; it included Úbeda, Baeza, Jaén, Córdoba, Sevilla, Cabra, Priego, Alcalá la Real, Granada, Lanjarón, Orjiva, Motril, Almuñécar, and Málaga.[182]

In his review of the Madrid and Toledo drawings show, José Francés had commented that

> these perspectives done by Maroto the painter have been conceived by Maroto the writer, then handed over to Maroto the printmaker and to Maroto the printer, so that at the end of the process Maroto the painter can gather them together again and then split out – from the collection that has already been sewn, glued, and put on sale in the bookshops – the landscapes that seem to him most eloquent for exhibition in the Salón Nancy.[183]

His newfound interest in another artistic medium, printmaking, seems to have evolved from there. A Primera Exposición de Litografía Artística was held at the exhibition space (the Salón Permanente) of the Círculo de Bellas Artes (Plaza de las Cortes, 4) from 26 April through 10 May, showing work principally by students from the Escuela Nacional de Artes Gráficas but joined by Juan Espina y Capo, César Fernández Ardavín, "Kari-Kato," and Maroto. Once again, Juan de la Encina provided the most extensive commentary, noting that "Maroto, I believe, has been doing lithography for only a few months" but that "we shall soon have a lithographer of the first order."[184]

As persistent as ever, Maroto submitted a number of works to the Exposición Nacional (19 May–11 July 1926), and one oil, *Bodegón de la botella negra*, two etchings, two lithographs, and two drawings were accepted.[185] The single oil attracted a good deal of positive critical attention, and there was praise also for the other pieces,[186] but Maroto received no official recognition. Consequently, he published an open letter in *La Voz* (Encina's regular newspaper) directed to the exhibition's jurors. There he claimed to be relieved *not* to have received a medal, because that would have indicated that his works were sufficiently mediocre to have appealed to the judging panel; hence, their non-award actually legitimized his endeavours. In closing, he reiterated his criticism of the ways in which artists could, and did, receive official recognition. Immediately beneath, the newspaper noted that friends of Maroto were planning a banquet for him as a kind of "compensatory gesture."[187] A second letter from him followed, this one more combative than ironic:

> there was a request made, according to what we read in the press, we seem to remember by Rafael Marquina,[188] for artists to offer initiatives for the reform and improvement of the national exhibitions, which have fallen into such disrepute. And we wrote a letter, shortly after the jury for prizes had been constituted, with the absolute knowledge that by doing so we were losing any remote possibility of receiving a prize, and directly seeking this breach, a letter in which we spoke of "foreign intervention," that is to say, judges from outside Spain to judge Spanish art admitted to the official exhibitions ...
>
> And the critics of the Madrid newspapers have a copy of that letter, and our friends know about it.
>
> And that letter has become topical again, and in an expanded form we intend to publish it. Because the atmosphere in which official artistic competitions are set up, held, and die needs to be clarified.[189]

The debate over the jury's decisions, and protests from different quarters, continued on in the daily press for several weeks,[190] but Maroto did not intervene further, having already functioned as one of the original catalysts.[191] The Sociedad de Artistas Ibéricos exhibition in 1925 had more than made its point, but it had not been enough to bring about wholesale change in the official system.

In June, Maroto also showed a selection of lithographs and etchings, plus one painting of Segovia, in the Salón de Exposiciones at the Calpe bookshop, but this received minimal press coverage.[192] In his review, Encina also told of Maroto's plans to start travelling around all of Spain, "from region to region, from province to province, from village to village ...

And anywhere that there is a visual detail – and in Spain they are every-where – to make a stop until he has captured it."[193] Such intentions were not new;[194] Maroto certainly did travel a lot, but exactly how much of this ambitious itinerary he accomplished is impossible to determine.

In late May the Sociedad de Amigos de Arte had staged a retrospective exhibition of the work of Alejandro Ferrant, the father of Maroto's sculptor friend Ángel, and Maroto later reviewed the show. He opened with a long excursus on the holdings of the Museo de Arte Moderno, most of which he found deficient. Back in 1910, he had advocated for substantial purging of this establishment's contents, but it was also precisely the place where his major show of February 1925 had been held. Now, he expressed his preference for painters from the late nineteenth century – including Ferrant – rather than the more recent ones of the 1910 and '20s.[195]

While Maroto undertook his principal tour of Andalucía in the spring of 1926, it is harder to pinpoint when he was travelling around Castilla. Judging by the dates of publications concerning towns in that region, he seems to have made at least two trips, one in the summer of 1926 and then another in the spring of 1927. Among the places visited he remembered Ávila, Segovia, Illescas, Ocaña, Pastrana, Cuéllar, Sepúlveda, Riaza, and Turégano, all the while "drawing, jotting down rapidly or with more nuance specific observations and overall syntheses."[196] During one of his short stays in Segovia, he met and befriended Antonio Machado, who worked as a French teacher in the secondary school there. Maroto describes the long talks that they had and the significant impact that Machado left on him.[197] Also evoked, more briefly, are Riaza and Sepúlveda.[198]

Meanwhile, in July 1926, we find the first mention of Maroto by someone who, in 1927, would become very important in his life. In one of his quirky articles in *El Sol*, Ernesto Giménez Caballero evoked Maroto – "an Aissagua from La Mancha, with an Iberian mop of hair" – and described his recent *Escorzos* dedicated to Madrid: "His drawings have the grey of flint, and they look as if they had been scratched with a scraper or a chisel from the Quaternary period."[199]

Over these months, then, and extending into 1927, Maroto pressed ahead with the ambitious travel project, as demonstrated by the publication of different series of drawings in *La Esfera* and *Revista de las Españas.*[200] Maroto's entrée into this latter magazine, which was only recently launched, was doubtless facilitated by Giménez Caballero, a major, permanent presence there. Rounding out Maroto's work in this vein for the year, he assembled another collection, *El plástico. Madrid. Esbozos*, again brought out by the publishing arm of the *Revista de Occidente* and quite possibly printed by his press. It received much less attention than the earlier volumes dedicated to Madrid and Toledo.

ESCUELAS DE PINTURA AL AIRE LIBRE, 1926-27

An exhibition of artworks produced by Mexican children attending the Escuelas de Pintura al Aire Libre opened in Madrid's Palacio de Bibliotecas y Museos on 18 December 1926. It had previously visited Berlin and Paris. José Francés gave a short speech contextualizing the works.[201] A few days later, on 22 December, Maroto offered a lecture on "La revolución artística mejicana." He found points of comparison between the children's paintings and some of the directions of modern European art. He also contrasted this example of progressive art education sponsored by the Mexican government, which now – thanks to the revolution – had revitalized priorities, with the deficient state of Spain's stagnating institutions (art schools, museums, etc.).[202] He also took another swipe at the contemporary art scene: "Madrid is not an environment in which someone who takes pleasure in art can find with any frequency an opportunity for genuine rejoicing, for pleasurable, unalloyed joy. Tedious boredom usually dominates artistic life with a lamentable persistence, blinding it, spoiling it for years and years."[203] The lecture was immediately self-published by Maroto as *La revolución artística mexicana: Una lección*, though, curiously, it was printed by Giménez Caballero's father's press, Imprenta E. Giménez, rather than Maroto's own.

Juan de la Encina was also intrigued by these examples of youthful art; he did everything he could to publicize the event, including writing a series of articles.[204] In the first piece, from 16 December, he – like Maroto – expressed his severe disappointment with official Spanish exhibitions, and drew a strong contrast with the present show: "I am horribly bored by the national exhibitions, the center, shelter, and defense for artistic bad taste, but I am moved by these modest works by beginning artists, almost all of them children, some of them already adolescents, the majority of them sons and daughters of Indians and Mexican *mestizos*. They are admirable!" He also read Maroto's lecture, and this led him to devote much of another article to the artist himself. Encina described Maroto as a "spiritual whirlwind" and an "exotic personality in our environment and at the same time very authentically Spanish." Citing Giménez Caballero's brief sketch in *El Sol* and the key features – Moroccan and European – identified there, he found that

> Some of his writings have that – so to say – African tone, and they are the ones that interest me least. In others, the African element injects ardour and impetuousness, and the European element, sensibility, analysis, ideas, and the restraint of moderation, and those are the ones that I like. And when I say writings, I also include in that words and actions, engravings and paintings.[205]

Encina went on to gloss the lecture in a generally approving tone. Not everyone was so impressed, though, as evidenced by Ballesteros de Martos's review.[206] Meanwhile, Maroto followed up with a more expository article, complete with illustrations; intended for a general audience, it rehearsed his main arguments in less combative terms.[207] Finally, Francisco Alcántara acquired a Mexican journal, *Forma. Revista de Artes Plásticas*, whose first number (October 1926) was dedicated to the topic, and transcribed an article by Salvador Novo on "Las escuelas al aire libre."

LA GACETA LITERARIA

Ernesto Giménez Caballero and Guillermo de Torre launched *La Gaceta Literaria* at the beginning of 1927. Giménez Caballero's relationship with Maroto must have evolved over 1926. Although he was initially listed among a group of "illustrators" that included Vázquez Díaz, Barradas, Bores, Bagaría, Salvador Bartolozzi, Sáenz de Tejada, T. Salazar, and Bon, Maroto became the house artist "at the urgent invitation, both fraternal and imperious – such is his character, such is his technique in relationships and such also his technique for success – issued by Ernesto Giménez Caballero, who was embarking on the publication of his *Gaceta*

Literaria, I participate from the beginning in giving the magazine an attractive and unique typographical appearance."[208] Maroto designed the masthead for the journal, its advertising poster – which also served, in miniature, as a kind of logo – as well as all of those section headings that featured a small masthead rather than regular typeface (e.g., "Postales ibéricas"). Two of his drawings (of Pío Baroja) appeared in number 2, one of Giménez Caballero accompanied a review of Caballero's *Carteles*,[209] two illustrated a review of one of his own exhibitions,[210] and one of Falla was included in number 22. *La Gaceta Literaria* celebrated the first anniversary of its founding with line portraits of its leading contributors: Giménez Caballero, "director," Guillermo de Torre, "secretary," Jarnés, Espina, Fernández Almagro, Chabás, Buñuel, Arconada, Ayala, Lafuente, all "editors," and just two "illustrators," Maroto, drawn by Barradas, and José de Almada Negreiros.[211]

The first issue of the journal included another article on the Mexican schools, likely inserted at Maroto's behest,[212] as well as a note on his 22 December lecture: "Maroto: inflamed, audacious, and full of fervour"; "Maroto, eyes of flint. Head of hair of an African. Sensibility of a European," clearly penned by Giménez Caballero.[213] There was also a large advertisement for the first volumes issued by Ediciones Biblos.

In the course of 1927, Maroto contributed three important texts to *La Gaceta Literaria*. Number 2 contained his essay on "El arte de hoy. La dominante óptica."[214] He argued that certain notable artists – namely, Léger, Picasso, Braque, and Gleizes – had responded to the machine age, but had been wrong to do so, and were taking art in a false direction, in conflict with its essential function and nature. Looking back, he again praised Impressionism, and illustrated the evolution of art, with three of his own sketches, through Bonnard and Ozenfant and finally – no false modesty here – himself.

On 15 April, the infamous polemic with *Martín Fierro* on the question of "Madrid meridiano intelectual de Hispanoamérica" erupted.[215] In the 1 September issue of *La Gaceta*, Giménez Caballero invited a range of Spanish intellectuals to weigh in. Maroto was one of them; initially, he adopted an even-handed stance that found excesses committed on both sides.[216] Pondering the literal meaning of *meridiano*, his line of thinking led back to the insufficiency of Madrid's contemporary art scene: "Can we sincerely assert that Madrid has sufficient aesthetic density to enrich the eagerness of the alert and keen minds of our America? Does there exist in Madrid the possibility of a life-enhancing discovery ... ?" On the other hand, he was also critical of the corresponding situation in Buenos Aires, "where one was not going to find, in regard to the visual arts, anything other than blandness, echoes of echoes, vain boasts, decadence, and snobbery." He eventually called the debate a kind of negative draw, in which both capital cities were "so little welcoming to the impulse of expressive modern art."

As we have seen, out of the handful of progressive art critics in Madrid in the 1920s, Juan de la Encina was the one who took a particular interest in Maroto. Toward the end of the year (15 November 1927, to be precise), and thinking back perhaps to the Baroja/Encina polemic and many other similar skirmishes, Maroto opened his extensive essay about Encina by evoking the resentment of many artists toward him, as the critic never minced his words and always spoke his mind.[217] For Maroto, Encina was the person who "has elevated to the level of criticism the old art column that a dozen years ago was close to expiring here in Madrid, amid babbling admiration and confused praise." This led into a long section on Encina's beginnings and career, based on an interview with him or written statements. Thereafter Maroto again turned to the lamentable state of art criticism in Spain, using Encina as a foil, and recalled – implicitly – some of the campaigns of 1923 and 1925 in which he had been involved: "Negative criticism? Without any doubt, to this critic has fallen the task of helping to defeat a terrible hour in the history of our art, of provoking a serious crisis, which still continues on and perhaps will extend through our whole lifetime." However, Maroto pointed out that Encina was also trying to steer people toward positive examples of modern art, and, in closing, he looked forward to the books that Encina was now preparing, which would allow him to engage in a kind of criticism not possible in the daily press.[218]

LA NUEVA ESPAÑA. 1930

La nueva España. 1930 is, in a sense, the book that Maroto had been preparing to write, on and off, since 1910, as it was inspired by his disillusion with the contemporary art scene and the many deficiencies and abuses in its structure and the various official organizations.[219] It was the example of the exhibition of the Escuelas de Pintura al Aire Libre that provided the final push to its composition: the demonstrable fact that things could be different, and the results that were so encouraging – particularly the children's artworks – filled in the last pieces of the puzzle, balancing the negativity of his criticism with the positivity of this new model. Maroto shut himself away and in six weeks produced the whole text.[220] The book was announced in the pamphlet version of Maroto's 22 December lecture, and in an article of 5 January 1927, Juan de la Encina alluded to his familiarity with part of it, "a book, written with a utopian vision."[221] Giménez Caballero also saw an early copy: "*1930* is the title of the book that Maroto is going to publish very shortly ... Maroto, with his elements from the past, has brought about an art that is close to proletarian, looking to the future, [with] a series of profoundly socialist themes: Socialism? Perhaps, 1930."[222] It was published in late March or early April, just three months after the Mexican exhibition had opened.[223]

The book was presented throughout as if it had been written at the end of 1930, as a summary of the achievements made over the last three years in the world of art.[224] There was also a clear political dimension here, corresponding to "ordering and specifying in me the embryonic conception that I had of art as a social function."[225] Nineteen twenty-seven was the middle year of the Primo de Rivera dictatorship, and from the (imagined) perspective of 1930, Maroto referred to "the recent conquests of Spanish democracy," "the essential transformation that the whole of life in Spain deserved and achieved," and "the new political and social Spanish state,"[226] as if a major upheaval had taken place during those intervening years. In the book's various chapters, he described in concrete detail this new system, its organisms and administrative positions, and his suggestions for the people who should fill them. The changes were radical: all existing institutions were to be swept away, replaced with ministries, exhibitions, professional schools, and museums organized along very different lines, with many new initiatives driven by the goal of outreach to under-served sectors of the population. As he later remembered,

> With passionate devotion laden with justice, prompted by the desire
> to serve that would never leave him, Máximo López [i.e., Maroto]

brings together in this book the principles of what the nation was in need of in regard to the visual arts, and summarizes them with stimulating and committed vigour. Borne along by the desire to create, by a proselytizing desire, he draws in to his purpose many men known to be capable, and hence obliged to agree and decide to do something. He puts others and himself at risk, "offering" each one a different task, but all coinciding in the same understood desire: to renew Spanish artistic life in accordance with all-embracing plans, in which the whole of Spain can fit; to ensure that culture has an active future integrated in the common people.[227]

The volume was extensively illustrated with black-and-white reproductions of artworks by contemporary Spanish and foreign artists, including Togores, Ucelay, Dalí, Picasso, Vázquez Díaz, Ferrant, Bores, Sunyer, Palencia, Barradas, all from Spain, and from elsewhere in Europe, Metzinger, Matisse, Derain, Braque, Vlaminck, and Modigliani. Never shy, Maroto reproduced eighteen of his own artworks – far more than anyone else – as well as incorporating various sketches that illustrated the text.

Critical reaction to the book was extensive. Encina was the first to mention it, and he promised a full review (which has yet to be located, if indeed it appeared).[228] Giménez Caballero painted him as a prophet in his own land.[229] Progressive critics generally gave it a warm welcome, while pointing out some of the limitations of its wildly utopian vision. Four of them related the contentiousness and fervour of the writing to Maroto's own character or temperament, which they described in more or less flattering terms.[230] For fellow radical José Díaz Fernández,

Maroto is the person who occupies with greatest perseverance and valour the most dangerous position, the furthest advanced of the shock troops. He has ... a combative temperament, human passion, and social concern. Maroto creates, argues, evangelizes, travels "on foot and without any money," and discharges the two barrels of his eyes against stupidity and privilege, against mediocrity that has been rewarded and group conventionalism.[231]

Twenty-five years later, Gaya Nuño looked back nostalgically to Maroto's impossibly utopic, and often utterly impractical, vision, and evoked his character as "abrupt and direct" and his art as "the art of a hard, self-confident man, somewhat pained that life should give him drubbings."[232] Still, it is very likely that the itinerant "Barracas del arte"[233] that Maroto described served, at least in part, as inspiration for Lorca's travelling theatre, La Barraca, *and* for the portable art exhibitions included in the outreach programs pioneered by the Misiones Pedagógicas during the first half of the 1930s under the Second Republic.

Although we are lacking specific details, there was reaction, too, from the Primo de Rivera regime: "After the publication of the book ... whose tone was undoubtedly subversive, Máximo López [i.e., Maroto] suffered, as was only natural, surveillance and threats on the part of agents in the devoted service of the ruling dictatorship."[234]

EXHIBITIONS AND ART CRITICISM

Despite many new activities in 1927, Maroto did not abandon journalistic art criticism. For *Nuevo Mundo* he reviewed the Concurso Nacional de Escultura (singling out the entry by Ángel Ferrant), an exhibition by Ignacio Zuloaga (about which he wrote two articles, where he now harshly judged the painter as behind the times and clinging to an outmoded style), the Exposición de Artistas Andaluces (put together by Rafael Marquina, another show that he found very lacking), and the Exposición de los Pintores Pensionados en Granada.[235] This last he used as a foil to extoll, once again, the superiority of the work produced by the Mexican children, and in the second half of the article he called on the corps of newspaper art critics to become much more proactive in their approach to the contemporary scene.

An Exposición de Litografías Artísticas, organized by Juan Espina, opened at the Museo de Arte Moderno on 6 March 1927. Maroto participated with some etchings, accompanied by Vázquez Díaz and a large number of other artists.[236] In April, Maroto contributed some designs for tiles (*azulejos*) to an exhibit of ceramics by Fernando Arranz.[237]

An important solo exhibition of Maroto's work was held at the Unión Iberoamericana and ran from 28 June until mid-July 1927. The Unión

Iberoamericana (calle de Recoletos, 10) was the entity behind the journal *Revista de las Españas*. The show gathered together drawings, etchings, and lithographs that Maroto had already brought out, or would shortly bring out, in one or other of the books and albums that he published through the course of 1927. There were ten drawings corresponding to *Andalucía*, fifteen for *Castilla*, fifteen for *Pueblo de Mallorca*, fifteen for *La Ría de Bilbao*, five for *Verbena de Madrid*, five for *Manuel de Falla*, and four for *Los de abajo*. In addition, there were three etchings of the Ría de Bilbao, three of Madrid, and three of Castilla, plus three lithographs of Madrid. A few other sundry items completed the catalogue.[238]

Francisco Alcántara's review gave a fairly jaundiced view of the proceedings. First, of the arrangement of the artworks, he complained that Maroto "is not exhibiting them, he has thrown them [on the wall] haphazardly," and he lamented the fact that "the misguided way in which Maroto is treating his recently created works is so harsh."[239] On the day of the opening, he reported that he was the sole visitor, and likewise on a return visit. Alcántara did, however, express his grudging admiration for what Maroto had done:

> with the violence of his character, he has positioned himself, with the audacious leap of a madman, directly in opposition to all the principles that governed, up to a short time ago, the field of book illustration. Against realism, naturalism, preciosity, the dull delight in description, sentimentality, and even the noble severity of the fully representational, all notes in which the immense vulgar public takes so much pleasure, Maroto has gone toward the most sober, violent, and even severe schematicism, a style in which he will eventually create admirable works along the same lines as some of those that he is now exhibiting.[240]

Antonio Espina's interesting and provocative review is too long and complex to summarize, but he sees in Maroto a cool stylist, and advocates a turn (or perhaps return) to a more "human" treatment of the subjects without losing any of the advancements achieved by the recent avant-garde movements.[241] Once again, Espina's text found its way back to an evocation of Maroto the man:

And here is a strange thing: when the whole work is viewed overall, we have the impression that it is that much more tranquil when Maroto is personally restless. Because Maroto is one of the most restless men in the world. An indefatigable man, with the mettle of a fighter, who travels, paints, writes, wanders, argues, plans, comes and goes, holding exhibitions, publishing books, ever ready for the assaults of art and debate.

DRAWINGS, "CARPETAS," AND *LA ESPAÑA MÁGICA*

Over these months (January–November 1927) Maroto continued to publish small groups of drawings, accompanied by a varying amount of text, in *La Esfera, Revista de las Españas,* and then *Heraldo de Madrid* and *Nuevo Mundo.*[242] This trend culminated in a piece in *La Gaceta Literaria,* a magazine in which Maroto typically placed other types of illustration and writing. Entitled "Un pueblo de Castilla," the article described not one of the dozens of villages that he had visited, but rather none other than his hometown of La Solana; echoing previous evocations of La Mancha, Maroto concentrated on the continuing cultural and educational impoverishment, providing an overall bleak view of the place.[243]

However, simultaneously he was also busy creating portfolios or albums of sets of works that appeared in book form. The smaller *carpetas* were published by *La Gaceta Literaria* and, in one instance, by *Litoral/* Imprenta Sur, Manuel Altolaguirre and Emilio Prados's press in Málaga that was, in some senses at least, a direct descendant from the Imprenta Maroto.[244] *La Gaceta Literaria* produced *Manuel de Falla. 5 dibujos de Maroto. 5 autógrafos musicales del maestro,*[245] *Verbena de Madrid: 15 dibujos de Maroto,*[246] and *La ría de Bilbao,* while *Litoral/*Imprenta Sur printed a portfolio of *25 dibujos de temas andaluces.*

The larger publishing company, Biblos, brought out two more substantial volumes. The first, *65 dibujos, grabados y pinturas,* gathered together – as the title indicates – a first compilation of oil paintings, pen and ink drawings, etchings, lithographic prints, as well as posters and book and magazine illustrations; these featured a diverse range of subjects, but mainly consisted of portraits, urban scenes, and landscapes. The second work, *Andalucía vista por el pintor Maroto. 105 dibujos y 25 glosas,* was based on the trip from the spring of 1926.[247] It included pen and ink and pencil drawings, and again offered images of individuals, street scenes, and the countryside. The twenty-five sections, corresponding to the textual "glosses" – what he described as "annotations on the road joyfully travelled"[248] – were organized thematically by subject matter, covering roads, villages, castles, farms, and so on. Encina offered a perceptive review of the latter collection: he preferred the prose *glosas* over the drawings,[249] and ended with yet another sketch of Maroto's character: "Coarse, wiry-haired, aggressive, trampled and trampling, the son of a labourer from La Mancha, in no way lenient with the works of others, he bears in the heart of such an uncouth brusqueness a deep spring of lyrical effusions, of Franciscan tenderness."[250] Giménez Caballero gave it an enthusiastic endorsement, calling it the best book by "that maniacal and steely animal tamer that is Maroto."[251] Marquina praised the work's combination of the artistic and the literary,[252] a feature of which Espina, for his part, disapproved.[253] But Espina appreciated Maroto's avoidance of the typical representations of Andalucía involving a lot of local colour, though he still felt that instead of absorbing the region's essence, Maroto had rather imposed his own vision upon it. Fernández Almagro was quite impressed, noting "the elemental rendering of Andalusian themes, thereby rid of trivial picturesqueness," and finding that the drawings and prose were well balanced and complementary: "these two versions of Andalusia – both with their own meaning – come together in a shared emotion: that which transmits everything that the feverish soul of Maroto conceives of and accomplishes."[254]

Finally, Maroto's own newly founded publishing enterprise, Biblioteca de Acción, produced three volumes on his own press: *Un pueblo de Mallorca, Castilla*,[255] and *La España mágica*. While *Un pueblo de Mallorca* and *Castilla* were relatively small compilations, *La España mágica*, its colophon bearing the date 27 December 1927, was significantly different. Like *Andalucía vista por el pintor Maroto* before it, but now with a much wider geographical focus (Madrid, Toledo, Galicia, Andalucía), it brought together, in a larger format, ninety-nine artworks and forty-six prose pieces. The art component, black-and-white engravings, coloured engravings, and pencil drawings, offered, as usual, urban and country scenes and images of inhabitants of the places visited. In an introductory prologue in the form of a letter, "Para Ángel Ferrant, en Viena," Maroto called it "the more or less felicitous crystallization of my travels and adventures over the roads of Spain." *La España mágica*, then, was a compendious selection of previous, more slender collections, bringing together elements from several trips. But it was also a capstone, and an implicit recognition of the fact that the promised twenty volumes would not materialize:

> Faithful to our plan, after *Andalucía*, from which some glosses and drawings are included in these pages, we offer this *España mágica*, the provisional summing-up of our wanderings through different Spanish regions, and which, by being restored, revitalized, expanded, and well arranged in this book, surpasses our initial intention: to exalt life as a function of everybody, and by seeking everyone out, to fulfill a social goal.[256]

In the letter to Ferrant, Maroto laid out carefully what he hoped to achieve with this project:

> Do not imagine that because it is the fruit of random travels this work is nothing more than an account, information, posturing, and an unoriginal report. No. If I sometimes journeyed hurriedly, I also rested and savoured. If I captured the direct beating of life, I was also able to slow it down, decant it, reshape it according to personal, differentiating principles.

His aim, he explained, was to express "my individualism and my essence," rather than

> the diverse natural world in which my eyes looked at themselves; I am content to reflect, stripped of superfluous elements, certain states in which life around and about me took shape in its fine intention to serve my alert sensibility ...
>
> Every day my intention of creating the great paintings that I dreamt of in my youth gets further away, and I attach myself more resolutely to the book, fulfilling in this way my great hope of effective

involvement in society, the well-meaning dream of reaching people eager for insightful and lively expression.[257]

Clearly a labour of love, Giménez Caballero called it "one of the most splendidly printed and published books in our country,"[258] and in a later, more expansive review developed the antimonies that he saw in Maroto.[259] Thus, the painter versus the writer, his static books versus the person always in movement, his modest, socially concerned stance versus these beautiful, luxurious editions, his dwelling on the local versus his animosity for the concrete, the mystical versus the secular – all of which he found reflected in the pages of *La España mágica*.

EDICIONES BIBLOS, 1927–28

The Biblos publishing house (based at Avenida Pi y Margall, 7) was founded at the beginning of 1927 by Ángel Pumarega García and Tomás Rodríguez Bachiller. The administration was handled by Pedro Pellicena Camacho, at offices located at calle de Alcalá, 17, and Maroto was a key contributor and a member of the editorial board.[260] Pumarega had a significant history of activism in various militant left-wing organizations: he had co-edited an anarchist magazine, co-founded the Spanish Communist Party, attended the 3rd World Congress of the Comintern, been expelled from the party, founded the Unión Cultural Proletaria and its associated newspaper, *Comunismo*, rejoined the Spanish Communist Party as part of its Sección Española de la Internacional Comunista, and co-edited the magazine *El Estudiante* (Salamanca). He was imprisoned on more than one occasion. He worked as a translator and proofreader for the *Revista de Occidente*.[261] When Biblos closed, some of its titles were picked up by Editorial Jasón, another Communist Party–sponsored enterprise.

Maroto's association with Biblos brings into sharp relief another facet of his evolving thinking. Given his own humble beginnings and the struggle to make his way in the world, from his early writings onward he reflected on the lack of educational possibilities and cultural engagement that affected many Spaniards, particularly those who lived in small agricultural communities such as his own La Solana.[262] One aspect of his repeated criticisms of the Exposiciones Nacionales was their elitism and exclusiveness, and an important feature of *La nueva España. 1930* were his many proposals for democratizing access to art and art education. The impact on him of the Escuelas de Pintura al Aire Libre exhibition led him directly to the many social reforms being instituted by the post-revolutionary Mexican government in the 1920s, reforms that he vaunted in contrast to the stagnating scene in Spain. By joining forces with Biblos, then, he was reacting to his vision of Spain as "suffering and incapable of finding the paths to true justice," a country where "those who have power ... appear to me to use that power as a function of stupid interests, of mean-spirited standards," and at the same time seeking a way "to fight effectively against a Spain with which I cannot get along, neither overall nor in the specific."[263]

Maroto published three of his own works with Biblos: *La nueva España. 1930, 65 dibujos grabados y pinturas*, and *Andalucía vista por el pintor Maroto*. He was also in charge of four series: Imagen, Clásicos Modernos, Idea, and Mosaico, and he provided illustrations and decorations for a large number of these. Over 1927–28, Biblos issued some twenty books; their offerings included several Russian novels (by Constantin Fedin, Isaac Babel, Dostoevsky, Ivan Byarne, and Lebedinsky),[264] the first Spanish edition of Mariano Azuela's *Los de abajo*, a volume by Trotsky, and progressive books on politics, religion, sex, and other topics.[265] Later, Maroto would reflect back on the beginnings of Biblos:

> A young publishing house, oriented toward the popular, proposes to undertake a task with resonances that are in a certain way subversive. As it is not possible to accuse directly the actions, somewhere between puerile and vandalistic, of the regime that Spain is enduring, Editorial Biblos plans a series of volumes as parts of a collection that *anticipates* certain cultural transformations that will only be achievable after the fall of the oligarchic system that since 1923 has been holding on to control.[266]

To what extent the publishing house's eventual offerings fulfilled this plan is difficult to say – at most, it was achieved more indirectly than directly – but the description does square with Maroto's own *La nueva España. 1930*.

Most of the catalogue was translated, by a number of different hands, but all the graphic work (ornamentation, illustrations in some of the volumes) was handled by Maroto. Biblos's principal commercial tactic was to price its products – at 3.75 pesetas a volume – well below what other publishing houses would have asked for a comparable book of equal size and quality. This did not go unnoticed. Thus, for Giménez Caballero the tomes were revolutionary not only in content, but even more so – and hence dangerous – for their price, undercutting others by approximately 50 per cent.[267]

There were distinct synergies between the different ventures in which Maroto was involved. Thus, in the first issue of *La Gaceta Literaria* (1 January 1927), there was a large announcement for Biblos's first three volumes, by Fedin, Trotsky, and Kreglinger, with Maroto's illustrations and decorations in all three advertised along with the contributions of the others involved. The advert itself was clearly designed and drawn by Maroto. Further publicity in Maroto's distinctive style, with his hand-drawn lettering font, followed in subsequent numbers, adding newly appeared tomes and finally refashioning the whole announcement as the list of publications grew.[268] In September, Giménez Caballero wrote a long and encomiastic introduction for an excerpt of Azuela's *Los de abajo* that appeared in *La Gaceta Literaria*.[269]

But Biblos also aroused hostility. In April, the conservative newspaper *La Nación* printed an article on the dissemination of "Bolshevik propaganda," which they now found not only in the periodical press but also in books, and cited the specific case of the first four Biblos volumes (the aforementioned three plus Azuela's).[270] The directors of Biblos responded with a letter, which *La Nación* commented upon and then reproduced in part.[271] Biblos contended that they were a purely industrial undertaking, that the start-up capital came from reputable sources (i.e., not the Communist Party), and that two of the first three books were far from being "Bolshevist." They concluded their letter as follows:

The Sociedad Biblos has set a uniform price of 3.75 pesetas for its volumes, but without any negative impact on the quality of the printing, because they believe that an attempt ought to be made to lower the price of Spanish books, which would be one of the solutions, in their opinion, to be applied to the crisis that exists in this Spanish industry. No one other than the Empresa Biblos will suffer

the consequences of their commercial error, if indeed it is an error —
and, furthermore, an anti-patriotic one — of offering good products
at a reduced price as a way to improve the workings of an industry.

Evidently, these statements were quite disingenuous and intended solely
as a smokescreen for their true purpose and strategies.

POST-GUERRA (1927–28), MAROTO, AND BIBLOS

The magazine *Post-Guerra* produced thirteen numbers between 25 June
1927 and 1 September 1928.[272] It was directed by Rafael Giménez Siles
and José Antonio Balbontín, with offices at calle Marqués de Cubas, 8.
It was an early example of an activist political magazine with strong
leftist tendencies, a type that would become much more common in
the 1930s.[273] However, unlike many of those other journals and some
publishing houses, it was not financed by a political party. Maroto was a
major contributor, essentially functioning as the magazine's art director.
He created the cover art and also provided the masthead design. The
cover illustration remained the same for numbers 1 through 4, and
then was replaced by another one for all the remaining issues (save for
the "extraordinary" number 10 for May Day 1928). Despite its general
orientation toward politically related subjects, *Post-Guerra* also printed
a review of Maroto's *Andalucía*, though the critic did find in it a clear
political undertone, with its depiction of "the people who feel and suffer,
who toil hour after hour, day after day in order to support themselves with
the efforts that their reduced situation demands of them. With suffering,
and with a rebellious sensation when in private; with resignation and
contentment when facing outward."[274]

From number 1 (25 June) onward, the magazine ran a large advert for
the "Biblioteca Post-Guerra"; typically, it occupied the inside of the back
cover, though occasionally it covered two pages. (An equally large advert
for Ediciones Biblos usually occupied the outside of the back cover, though
again, there was some variation.) As one of the major initiatives of *Post-
Guerra*, the "Biblioteca" was an attempt to get a variety of stripes of leftist
literature into the hands of more readers. A new and key feature was
the establishment of a mail-order business supplying many volumes at
15 per cent off bookshop prices.[275] Most of the titles came from the

Antorcha publishing house (which *was* sponsored by the Spanish Communist Party) and from Biblos, with which they obviously had very close contacts. Biblos actually produced two editions of popular titles, one sold at Biblos's standard price, and another "economy" version that was regularly sold at one peseta; with the discount offered by the "Biblioteca," these came in at just ninety céntimos. The demise of *Post-Guerra* and Biblos around the same time in the spring of 1928 demonstrates that, although appealing to the principals involved, for the way in which it made these books readily accessible to a public of scarce economic means, this was not a viable business model to sustain over the long term.

BIBLIOTECA DE ACCIÓN

At the same time as Biblos was getting under way, Maroto also launched his own publishing enterprise, called Biblioteca de Acción (the name is telling), whose titles were printed by his own press. Under this imprint, Maroto in 1927 brought out three of his own books of drawings, already mentioned above. Other volumes were the rather idiosyncratic *Jesús entre nosotros. Con 33 dibujos en color de Maroto. Textos del Evangelio según la versión del Padre Petit*, and the important *Almanaque de las artes y las letras para 1928*. When Maroto left for Mexico, his younger brother Santiago stayed on in charge, and oversaw at least one more publication by Maroto himself, *Veinte dibujos mexicanos* (1928).[276]

ALMANAQUE DE LAS ARTES Y LAS LETRAS PARA 1928

One of the last books that Maroto prepared before his departure to Mexico was the *Almanaque de las artes y las letras para 1928*, published at the end of 1927.[277] As he later recalled,

> Prompted by the sporting dynamic that characterizes the artistic and literary circles that are more or less subversive and reformist and to which I consider myself affiliated, and fulfilling an old desire that had been fostered ... by my vocation to disseminate reason, culture, and visual arts by means of publications ... with a systematic intent to be both informative and formative, I publish, under the trade name of a publishing house that I call Acción, ... an *Almanaque de las artes y de las letras*.[278]

It is an anthological work, with a highly miscellaneous feel to it. A large variety of authors and artists from several countries are represented. There are short prose pieces or fragments, a number of poems, excerpts of plays, photographs of paintings and sculptures, reproductions of ink drawings, pencil drawings, and etchings, even some fragments of musical scores in facsimile. Often the "illustrations" are keyed to the text, but sometimes the juxtapositions seem random.

In a brief editorial note, Maroto touched on a related aspect of the book's structure: "For the internal organization of this first volume ... I only followed my taste, with minimal attention, filtered and tentative, for the events offered by the passing of the days."[279] Giménez Caballero contributed a kind of introduction, "Folklor. El regreso al Almanaque," where he argued that this reinvented concept of the almanac was a genre of mass literature, and hence: "Almanac: a communist genre. Literature and science within the reach of all fortunes, all abilities."[280] Consequently Maroto's work corresponded to the *almanac spirit* that is borne by the Nunist[281] world, of the present day and of the future,"[282] and the miscellaneous and random qualities noted above were essential characteristics of this spirit: "The almanac spirit lives today on planes that are mutually heterovalent and difficult to reconcile. It is necessary to seek the *Almanac of the present day* a little bit everywhere, to surprise it and savor it in the windings and turnings and in the corners of the new, multidimensional life of the world."[283]

Vestiges of the almanac's traditional function are to be found in four of Maroto's own line drawings, headed "Invierno," "Primavera," "Verano," and "Otoño,"[284] and in pages headed with the twelve months of the year and offering a complete list of saints' days for each month.[285] However, these divisions by month are entirely irregular – the sections range from six to forty-two pages – and there is nothing else here related to the calendar. Rather, interspersed throughout the book are a number of blocks of related materials connected by region or country. The first of these is focused on the Soviet Union: images of the Kremlin, "Kalínin y su familia," and "El director de escena ruso, Meyerhold," are combined with texts on "Rusia. Las riquezas artísticas" (Georges Duhamel), "De *El sueño de un hombre ridículo*" (Dostoevsky), and "Periodistas a millares" (Julio Álvarez del Vayo).[286] Broadly similar blocks are subsequently dedicated to Andalucía, Mexico, Portugal, Chile, Cuba, Cataluña, and Argentina.

The original front cover of the *Almanaque* was designed and executed by Maroto, using hand-drawn block lettering and a design aesthetic highly reminiscent of the graphic work in *La Gaceta Literaria*. At bottom, a book lies open, with two maps headed "AMÉRICA" and "ESPAÑA."[287] Everything here points to a confluence between Maroto's own interests in regions, such as Andalucía, and countries, such as Mexico, with Giménez Caballero's own particular brand of pan-Iberianism.[288]

Maroto's most prolific collaborator was Francisco Ayala. He contributed all the installments of a series entitled "Las tertulias literarias" that offered thumbnail sketches of some of the most influential gatherings at magazines and cafés: the *Revista de Occidente*, *La Gaceta Literaria*, Pombo, La Granja (El Henar), Atocha (Hotel Nacional), and El Regina. For another running feature called "Lo que ha dado 1927. Y lo que se espera de 1928," Ayala interviewed five different individuals with expertise in their respective fields: for "Literatura española," he consulted with Giménez Caballero, for "Artes plásticas," Antonio Espina, for "Literatura extranjera," Antonio Marichalar, for "Teatro," Melchor Fernández Almagro, and for "Música," César M. Arconada.

For the rest, contributions tended to be limited to one or two pieces. Among well-known Spanish poets we find Alberti, Ramón de Basterra, Rogelio Buendía, Gerardo Diego, García Lorca, Juan Ramón Jiménez, Antonio Machado, Moreno Villa, Prados, Francisco Vighi, and Fernando Villalón. Drama is limited to Manuel Abril and Jacinto Grau. Prose writers, including essayists and journalists, are the most numerous, including Álvarez del Vayo, Araquistáin, Azorín, Corpus Barga, García Maroto, Giménez Caballero, Gómez de la Serna, Jarnés, Marichalar, Moreno Villa, d'Ors, Emiliano Ramírez Ángel, Ángel Sánchez Rivero, Guillermo de Torre, Adriano del Valle, and Julián Zugazagoitia. Writers in Catalan and Portuguese, and writers from other Spanish-speaking countries, appeared in the above-mentioned geographical blocks, including such luminaries as José de Almada Negreiros, Borges, Josep Carner, Norah Lange, Juan Marinello, Neruda, Salvador Novo, Fernando Pessoa, Carles Riba, Mario de Sá-Carneiro, Sebastià Sánchez-Juan, and Josep Maria de Sucre. The contingent of writers from other foreign countries who are translated into Spanish includes fewer prominent names, but some important figures here are Georges Duhamel, Gide, Charles-Louis Philippe, Rilke, Lidiya Seifullina, André Suarès, and Valéry.

As regards the illustrations, Maroto appears much more frequently than any other artist, though many pieces are unattributed, identifiable only by his characteristic style. Some may have been done specifically for this book, but many are evidently repeated from elsewhere. Other artists – painters and sculptors – are represented by photographs of their work or photogravure reproductions: José de Almada Negreiros,[289] Barradas, André Dignimont, Ángel Ferrant, Pablo Gargallo, Goya, Juan Gris, Cristóbal Hall, Karl Hofer, Metzinger, Diego Rivera, Renée Sintenis, and Joaquín Sunyer. Photographs and, to a lesser extent, line drawings offer portraits of many individuals either included or referenced: from Spain, Araquistáin, Pío Baroja, Luis Bello, Pablo Casals, Américo Castro, Falla, García Lorca, Góngora, Gabriel Miró, Ramón Pérez de Ayala, and Luis de Zulueta; and from elsewhere, D'Annunzio, Josephine Baker, Elisabeth Bergner, Antoine Bourdelle, Cocteau, Debussy, Anatole France, Greta Garbo, Gide, Mikhail Kalinin, Meyerhold, Mussolini, Anna Pavlova, Raymond Radiguet, and Ravel. More intriguing are a few other photographs whose presence – anywhere – in the book is harder to explain, and probably can be attributed to Maroto's caprice. These include "Jefe de tribu en Wobanganar" (at page 15), "Templo budista en Ceylón" (29), "Religioso tibetiano" (45), an "Ex-libris" for one Friedrich Katz (woodcut, 76), and "Fábricas en Alemania" (125).

Responses to the volume were largely restricted to Maroto's immediate circle. Jarnés offered a thoughtful review, noting that "an almanac has something of the anthology. And something of the newspaper column. And something of the examination committee," and also that "in this *Almanque* is collected together scrupulously the beat of all that is usually called 'literary life,' rather weak and finicky in Spain, but from time to time varied, rich at least in gestures, and intriguing."[290] In conclusion, then, "the *Almanaque*, as a whole, is attractive, thought-provoking, opportune." Predictably, Giménez Caballero praised the endeavour: "Once more Maroto is to be congratulated for his audacity and effort. Typographically presented with great care, and delightful in the information provided and the portraits."[291] A third contributor,

Guillermo de Torre, was in agreement, and singled out what was perhaps its most obvious quality as a miscellany:

> Such an almanac as this perfectly fulfills the condition of heterogeneity that is distinctive to the genre and [yet] it possesses a look of its own, without following any foreign model.
>
> It is not a simple memorandum of the artistic and literary year … nor is it a detailed list of events that have happened. It is, rather, a select anthology, prose and verse by current authors, intercalated with portraits and drawings.[292]

ARRIVAL IN MEXICO

The exhibition of Mexican children's artwork really galvanized Maroto and led him to take a particular interest in the cultural policies of the post-revolutionary Mexican government. Indeed, he gives us to understand that he wanted to research at first-hand the Escuelas de Pintura al Aire Libre, and may even have been invited to collaborate with the project.[293] Furthermore, both the paternal and maternal lines of Amelia Narezo's family had roots in Mexico, so Maroto would have heard a lot about the country from his wife and her relatives.[294] A rather strange review from September 1927 deals with a collection of photographs of *Iglesias de México. Cúpulas*.[295] Maroto imagines a scene in which a man and a woman are looking through it; the man exclaims in wonder at the photographs and the woman replies, "Mexico! You promised me that some day, some far-off day, that together we would get to know, before our dotage, Mexico, my homeland. You promised me that one day, without my asking you to, simply because back then you were more attentive and attuned than you are nowadays to where my mind was going." It is hard to avoid the conclusion that this is a more or less transparently autobiographical scene. The supposition is largely borne out by a later comment that Maroto made in which he recalled that "my wife is keen on a return to her Mexico, of which she retains vague memories that she would like to confirm."[296] Furthermore, also in September, commenting on the "intellectual meridian," he confided the following:

I intend to go to America some day ... If I were to go to America, it would have to be Mexico, which is where an artistic movement of surprising power has been created and forcefully channelled toward certain goals. Mexico, where one can say will soon be found the artistic meridian of America, a meridian that, in its true values, I do not know if the violent young men of *Martín Fierro* heed or esteem.

If I go to America, it will have to be in order to learn, at the same time as to teach, to debate, to refine myself, to seek a means of training that I can join and in which I can intermingle, but not to practise any tutelage nor accept any servitude.[297]

These intentions rapidly crystallized into action. In his texts of 1945 and 1958, Maroto suggests several other motivations, including the stifling intellectual and cultural atmosphere under Primo de Rivera, the reluctance, refusal, or inability of the majority of artists to respond to Maroto's calls for radical change ("dictatorship and submission, out of exhaustion, out of convenience, out of mediocrity in feeling and disinclination toward doing"),[298] and the siren song of Mexico, where vigorous new art was emerging.[299] At the same time, he alludes cryptically to the fact that "both accurate details and claims of doubtful veracity played an equal role in what prompted Máximo López [i.e., Maroto] to set off for Mexican lands," and summarizes the reasons for his decision as "a recommendation from the Madrid police, and repeated disappointment in regard to the potential that the Spanish people displayed to collaborate effectively in their common obligation of making a better homeland."[300]

There were at least two farewell dinners, one on 14 December, organized by a group of friends,[301] and another on the twentieth, held by *La Gaceta Literaria*.[302] In Madrid in December, Maroto was interviewed at length by the Cuban journalist Rafael Suárez Solís, who reported that he was travelling on the liner *Cristóbal Colón* and that it would stop for forty-eight hours in Havana on its way to Veracruz.[303] The ship docked in the Cuban capital around 30 December, and Maroto was able to spend some time with a group of writers, artists, and intellectuals, many associated with the *Revista de Avance*.[304] He arrived in Veracruz on 3 January.[305] From there, he continued on to Mexico City, arriving there by at least the eighth,[306] and a few weeks later was joined by the rest of this family.[307] In the middle of January, he gave a substantial interview to Alejo Carpentier.[308] In it, Maroto offered a summary of his life history, and described himself in the following terms:

> I cannot work in rooms full of fillets and gilded mouldings. I go to bed at nine o'clock at night; I rise with the day; I do not drink, I am almost vegetarian. And when some waiter calls me "sir," I ask him: "Are you – talking to me?," because it seems implausible to me that he should address me thus.

After Carpentier added that Maroto "boasts of living in third class," Maroto explained that

> I have a lot of influential friends in Mexico; when I announced my trip to them, they offered me positions, subsidies. But I rejected them all. I want to retain my absolute independence of mind. I travel on my own means, and thus I will have the freedom to join the movement that most interests me ... if I end up joining any ...
>
> In spite of having a letter of recommendation from a government minister for the captain of the ship, I started my crossing in third class ... Only in the last days, weakened by seasickness, did I identify myself. Thus, at least, I have spent several days among sincere people who are not *poseurs*.

Maroto's activities upon arriving in Mexico City, and especially his involvement with the group associated with the magazine *Contemporáneos*, constitute yet another chapter in his long and varied career, and they go beyond the scope of the present discussion.[309] Overall, though, it seems as if Maroto did not find all that he had expected,[310] which may be the reason why at the beginning of 1929 he left for the United States.

CONCLUSION

Maroto was always something of an anti-establishment figure, or at least a person who frequently went against the grain. We can observe this in his repeated rejection of Madrid in favour of village life and the countryside, in his sustained critique of the official art world, and in his increasingly leftist leanings as the 1920s progressed. He rarely minced words, and his disapproval could be expressed in harsh terms, a feature of his personality that disconcerted many and repelled more than a few. This emerges in his rejection of the "conventional" dynamic of the typical *tertulia* and his pride in his own independent thinking. Of one of his early periods in Madrid, he writes, "I detest the *tertulias* drowning in vain words and poisonous clouds of smoke, and truly I am much pained by both old-fashioned Spanish and cosmopolitan frivolity – two extremes of a common affliction."[311] Returning to the capital after time away, he stands apart:

> I return, therefore, to live there but not with the Madrid of the café, sometimes closed-minded and loud-mouthed, an eloquent and smoky chaos, often irresponsible, overbearing, and encouraging of puerile vanities ... ; I do not live with those who are found in the *tertulia* ... a watering hole for their intellectual formation.[312]

By the mid-1920s, his attitude had not changed:

> I form a part, often only tangentially, of *tertulias* and of so-called avant-garde artistic and literary movements – for I never felt connected or in solidarity with principles that my intuition revealed to me to be in many cases transitory and insubstantial, but this did not stop me from studying them and ... incorporating them into my current cultural stock.[313]

At the same time, it is remarkable how many worlds he moved through: art, art criticism, literature, journalism, magazines, publishing, printing, political activism. He was also driven by various passions, some would say compulsions. Projects and pursuits emerge, disappear, morph, and reappear. And as a result of all this, he was often on the move, psychically and physically, and he was associated for different lengths of time with a large variety of locations and organizations. In the first category we find La Solana, Madrid, various cities in Italy, France, Belgium, and Holland, Paris, Salamanca (Aldeaseca de Armuña), Astorga, Santo

Domingo de Silos, Barcelona, Monasterio de Poblet, Frama (Valle de Liébana), Santander, Bilbao, Palma de Mallorca, Deiá, Toledo, villages in various parts of Spain, including Castilla la Vieja, La Mancha, Galicia, and Andalucía, and then Mexico, New York, and beyond. And in the second category, there is the Escuela Especial de Pintura, Escultura y Grabado, the Exposición Nacional de Bellas Artes, the Ateneo de Madrid, the Círculo de Bellas Artes, the Residencia de Estudiantes, the Sociedad de Artistas Españoles/Ibéricos, the Museo de Arte Moderno, and various newspapers, numerous magazines, publishing houses, and print shops.

It is impossible to list all the people whom Maroto knew and interacted with. Among them number many of the luminaries of the period, including Unamuno, Azorín, Machado, Ortega y Gasset, Juan Ramón Jiménez, Alberto Jiménez Fraud, Luis de Zulueta, Enrique Díez-Canedo, José Moreno Villa, Federico García Lorca, Rafael Barradas, Ernesto Giménez Caballero, Juan de la Encina, José Francés, Manuel Abril, Ángel Vegue y Goldoni, Francisco Alcántara, Roberto Castrovido, Alfonso Reyes, and countless others.

Looking back on these years, Maroto was perhaps his own harshest critic. In *Acción plástica popular* (1945), he introduces Máximo López, a personage who is quite transparently Maroto himself.[314] He then quotes (from an unidentified source) a kind of quasi-confessional statement whose date of composition is hard to establish. The newspaper articles that he footnotes are from 1925, at the end he says that what he describes occurred around 1926, and the books footnoted are mainly from 1927, yet there is also a reference to "at forty-five years."[315] If this were his age, it would place us in 1934, but it may instead be a nod to the date of publication of *Acción plástica popular* – 1945. The text opens thus:

> I wanted to become a painter, a creative painter with the clear ability to stimulate to a greater or lesser degree the aesthetic milieu of my time in my native Spain. At forty-five years, after much and varied effort, trying to live with profundity, responding to and serving in a way that I consider generous what life asked of me, I recognize that I did nothing that defines me or qualifies me as an authentic visual artist.

If it was a lack of talent, or if it was the diverse and apparently contradictory demands on me from everyday life that I had to deal with, that blinded my expressive wellspring, is something that I have not determined, and perhaps will never clarify. I was not the painter that I dreamt of being. I almost did not become any kind of painter, despite the laudatory opinions that indulgent or ignorant critics expressed about my artistic labours.

I have written some books, without achieving the good work that my intentions were seeking. Nor do I seek excuses blaming "life" for what may be lacking in my innate abilities.[316]

A stern and unjust summation, to be sure, but it was judgments such as these that, in subsequent years, steered him increasingly toward educational projects, particularly those involving some form of artistic expression.

CHAPTER 6

MARUJA MALLO AND RAFAEL ALBERTI

Their Circumstances and Relationship

The artist Maruja Mallo (1902–1995) and the writer Rafael Alberti (1902–1999) were in an intimate relationship from 1925 to 1930, yet for many decades thereafter this fact was not known outside the circle of their close friends. While modern biographers and critics have in recent years provided much in the way of interesting context, there remain many details to be determined and others to be corrected, episodes to be fleshed out, and different moments in the complex dynamic between the two to be explored and clarified, as Alberti and Mallo have yet to receive anything like the kind of close attention devoted to contemporary figures such as Lorca, Dalí, or Buñuel. Indeed, as Laurenson-Shakibi writes, their "complex relationship ... is perhaps one of the least documented artistic associations of 1920s Madrid, an era in which a vigorous dialogue between cultural discourses and artistic practices was conducted by several (and varied) couples."[1]

Mallo: Biographical Details, 1921–30

In the town of Avilés, where she lived with her family as an adolescent, Maruja Mallo (née Ana María Gómez González) received private art lessons and studied at the local Escuela de Artes y Oficios.[2] In the fall of 1921, she went to Madrid to prepare for the entrance exam for the EEPEG, and stayed at a *pensión* with her brother Justo, a year younger than her but already a pharmacy student in the capital.[3] She took the exam on

6.1. Maruja Mallo, another art student, and Salvador Dalí.

24 May 1922.[4] Back home in the summer of 1922, she participated in the collective show II Exposición de Artistas Avilesinos (21 August–4 September), sending fourteen works that received laudatory notices in the local press.[5] A review by José Francés reproduced a fine *Retrato de mi hermana* by "María Gómez Mallo," and contained some words of high praise from the critic.[6] Also that summer, her father, don Justo (Justo Gómez Mallo), a customs official, was transferred to Madrid, and the whole family moved there in September, to a large apartment on the calle del Reloj (9, principal), just south of the Plaza de España.[7]

Mallo started at the Escuela Especial in October. Like others, she made multiple visits to the Museo del Prado, using Eugenio d'Ors's recently published handbook, *Tres horas en el Museo del Prado* (Madrid: Rafael Caro Raggio), as a guide.[8] Another member of her first-year cohort was Salvador Dalí, who was equally enamoured of the Prado, and the two also coincided in all five classes taken.[9]

Dalí's China ink wash *Sueños noctámbulos*, from late 1922,[10] shows that Mallo was by then already spending time with him, Buñuel, and Barradas.[11] She would have met Lorca shortly after his return to Madrid and the Residencia de Estudiantes in the middle of February 1923.[12] In another Dalí work in the same medium, *Salvador Dalí y Maruja Mallo en el Café de Oriente*, they appear seated at a table with a third, unidentified individual.[13]

Also around this time, Mallo and her young friend Irene Falcón[14] took private classes with Enrique Estévez Ochoa.[15] Falcón went with Mallo in the break after lunch and before afternoon work starting at 5:00 p.m.; they bartered with Ochoa to receive art instruction in exchange for classes in French and other subjects.[16] According to Meléndez Táboas, these private lessons were specifically intended to help with her skills in life drawing.[17] Falcón remembers Mallo as someone who "talked very loudly, had a strong character, and was a very likeable girl," and strolling on the Paseo de la Castellana together commenting on "the young women with *mantillas* who were out in search of a husband."[18] In the summer of 1923, Mallo sent just three works to the Exposición de Arte Gallego held in Santiago de Compostela (Casino de Santiago, July) and La Coruña (Palacio Municipal, August–September).[19]

Emilio Aladrén became a friend after he started at the Escuela Especial in the fall of 1923,[20] and when Margarita Manso entered in the fall of 1924 she became another close companion of Mallo and also a new but integral member of the Lorca-Dalí-Mallo group.[21] Through her brother Justo, Mallo met various other writers and artists, including José Bergamín and Benjamín Palencia.[22] Around 1924, she supplemented her formal studies (again with a view to improving her life drawing) by also enrolling in the Julio Moisés's Academia Libre, also attended for periods of time by Dalí, José Moreno Villa, Francisco Bores, and Palencia, among others.[23]

From 1925 onward, Mallo developed another close friendship, this time with Concha Méndez, who has recounted a number of their exploits.[24] When Mallo's father was named to a new position in Tenerife in the middle of 1925, the family maintained their Madrid apartment. Mallo, her mother, Pilar (María del Pilar González Lorenzo), and some of her sisters (there were fourteen siblings in all) spent the summer in Tenerife; while in Santa Cruz, Maruja toured the island, painted, and wrote a number of letters to Méndez.[25] After then going to visit relatives in Galicia, the family returned to Madrid in time for Maruja to start the new academic year at San Fernando.[26] Pilar and one daughter subsequently went back to Tenerife, leaving most of the other children living together in the Madrid apartment. Some members of the family, including Maruja, may have spent time in Avilés (Asturias) during the summer of 1926, where they lodged at the Hotel Ferrera.[27] Pilar died at the end of December 1926, and don Justo returned to Madrid for January and February 1927, but then reassumed his position in Tenerife until the end of 1928.[28] Meanwhile, in Madrid, in October 1926, the family had moved to a new apartment on calle Ventura Rodríguez, 3, 1° (today 24), near the Plaza de España.[29]

Mallo studied at the Escuela Especial for a total of four academic years, 1922 through 1926, passing all the yearly exams in June and receiving several "diplomas of merit."[30] After graduating, she continued taking private lessons with one of her professors, José Moreno Carbonero.[31] In May 1926, Mallo, with the support of several prominent painters and critics – Fernando Álvarez de Sotomayor, Francisco Llorens, Francisco Alcántara, José Francés, and Julio Camba among them – successfully petitioned the Diputación Provincial de Lugo for continuing financial support, considering her "exceptional talents for pictorial art."[32] The grant – a *bolsa de estudios* – was initially for one year (1926–27), but after satisfactory progress it was renewed for a further two years (1927–29). Over August–September 1929, Mallo made a special request for a further extension (1929–30), in order to continue studying with Moreno Carbonero and Álvaro Alcalá de Galiano, both of whom supported her application, and it was subsequently approved.[33]

In the summer of 1926, shortly after leaving the EEPEG, Mallo exhibited nine works at the Exposición de Arte Gallego held in Santiago de Compostela (Colegio de San Clemente, 21 July–8 September), but attracted no more than a modicum of critical attention.[34] However, it was around that same time that she really began to develop her first modern and unmistakable style, captured initially in such canvases as *El mago*, *La mujer de la cabra* (first known as *La isleña*), and *Ciclista*, and then in the series of *Verbenas* and various sets of *Estampas*, which she produced between mid-1926 and mid-1928.[35] Her new works – twenty in number – were exhibited at the Feria de Muestras in Gijón (10–25 August 1927), where they caused quite a stir.[36] José Díaz Fernández writes of her throwing off "the academic corset of San Fernando," and tells of his having been among "many young people dedicated to intellectual pursuits who have passed through her home in Madrid, where those paintings awaited the public exposure of an exhibition."[37] He also forecasts that "this town of painters [Gijón] will be fastened to the history of this singular artist." At exactly the same time, she caught the attention of the young Madrid-based critic Luis García de Valdeavellano, who also wrote of a visit to her house to view her new paintings, which likely occurred just prior to her departure for Gijón.[38] A month later, in a broad review of "Spanish painting done by young artists," she was the first of the many whom he named.[39] Her talent was even recognized in Tenerife, with Ernesto Pestana Nóbrega dedicating two articles to what he saw as her breakthrough style.[40]

Another turning point can perhaps be dated to later that fall, on 5 December 1927. Jorge Guillén tells of a visit to Mallo's home made by a group composed of him, Melchor Fernández Almagro, Pedro Salinas, and Manuel Abril: "We go to the home – all of us, less Moreno [Villa] – of a nineteen-year-old painter: miss Mallo. Painting in the style of prints, Pehushka [sic], *bariolage*, large-scale miniaturism, Ramonismo,[41] fantasy, and who knows what else!"[42] Then, on 2 April 1928, Fernández Almagro wrote to his friend in Granada, Antonio Gallego Burín: "Maruja Mallo continues on here going from triumph to triumph, inspiring admiration in everyone who sees her works. It has almost become fashionable to visit her and then talk about her. This discovery owes something to me, and my vanity as a 'promoter' has been satisfied."[43] These "home visits" to Mallo's studio were clearly all the rage, and Gómez de la Serna was another who dropped by, seeing "that room of hers that gave on to the patio."[44] Growing enthusiasm was simultaneously stoked by an article authored by Pérez Ferrero in February 1928,[45] with reproductions of two of the *Estampas*, a piece by Giménez Caballero in March, with reproductions of three works from the *Verbenas* series,[46] and a thoughtful essay by Quiroga Pla in April, with two more *Estampas*.[47]

It was Almagro who, by all accounts, drew Mallo to the attention of Ortega y Gasset. In one version of events, he took a sample of her drawings to Ortega, who responded very positively,[48] and in another it was Almagro who arranged for her to meet Ortega, who then visited her home to see her work.[49] Ortega arranged for her first Madrid exhibition to be held – quite exceptionally – in the fourth-floor rooms of the *Revista de Occidente*, Gran Vía (Avenida Pi y Margall), 7, opening on 26 May 1928.[50] There were ten paintings (including the four *Verbenas*) and thirty drawings (*Estampas*) done with coloured pencils and charcoal.[51] They received almost universal acclaim, and the exhibition was reviewed in a host of publications.[52]

In 1928, shortly after this exhibition, Mallo drew this first original phase of her work to a close. Thereafter she embarked on something stylistically quite different, the series of sixteen *Cloacas y campanarios*,[53] which may have been partly inspired by excursions to the area of Vallecas. Starting at a date that remains difficult to pin down – perhaps some time in 1928, but certainly by 1929 – she regularly joined the sculptor Alberto, Benjamín Palencia, and possibly others on their rambles through the countryside outside Madrid, at a moment when the concept of the so-called Escuela de Vallecas was only just coming into existence.[54] As she commented, the works represented a

visual style that has arisen from the poorer suburbs and the outskirts of Madrid.

At this time I was very struck by nature eliminating garbage. The earth burnt and covered in puddles. The sewers pushed by the winds. The belfries toppled by the winds. The world of things that are transitory. This tangible vision of things that are transformed, which I often encountered at the outer railway stations ringing Madrid, is the fundamental basis of the content of my work at that time …

These were necrological panoramas that I found in the centre and at the dumping sites in the surrounding areas of the capital, 1929–1931.[55]

In the fall, she attended the openings of shows given by Palencia (18 October)[56] and José de Togores (27 November).[57] Mallo designed the sets and costumes for a performance of Concha Méndez's *El ángel cartero*, at the Lyceum Club Femenino on 7 January 1929.[58] Some of Mallo's *Verbenas* featured in Giménez Caballero's film *Esencia de verbena* (1930). Besides the continuing *Cloacas y campanarios* series, over 1929–30 Mallo also embarked on two other projects: various stage designs – for Méndez, for an upcoming play by Ignacio Sánchez Mejías (never staged), and characters and costumes for two series that she called *Figuras de guiñol* and *Colorín colorete*,[59] and then also, but rather differently, a sequence of drawings related to stars of American silent film, grouped as *Los cómicos del cine*.[60] She also made for the Diputación Provincial de Lugo a special painting entitled *Guía postal de Lugo*, which was reproduced alongside an encomiastic essay about her in a 1929 volume celebrating *Lugo y su provincia*.[61] At the Casa de los Tiros in Granada, an Exposición Regional de Arte Moderno was held over November–December 1929; Mallo participated alongside Picasso, Gris, Vázquez Díaz, Moreno Villa, Ángeles Ortiz, Peinado, Dalí, and Lorca.[62] In the summer of 1930, she made another request for a further extension of the grant that supported her studies, but this time no funds were available.[63] Some of her paintings were included in an Exposición de Arquitectura y Pintura Modernas held by the Ateneo Guipuzcoano at the Gran Casino in San Sebastián in September 1930,[64] and in the annual International Exhibition of Paintings at the Carnegie Institute in Pittsburgh (16 October–7 December 1930).[65]

Alberti: Biographical Details, 1917–30

Alberti's family moved to Madrid in May 1917, taking an apartment initially on the calle de Atocha and then moving to calle Lagasca, 101, where he would live until 1931. While he, too, aspired to be a painter, he never attended art school and only took some private lessons with teachers employed by his family. Through one of his first new friends in Madrid, Manuel Gil Cala, he was introduced to Daniel Vázquez Díaz, who lived close by at Lagasca, 119; Vázquez Díaz had recently returned from France, in the fall of 1918, and would be a major personal and artistic influence.[66] Alberti seems to have met Gregorio Prieto (1897–1992) (a former student of the EEPEG) by as early as 1919; a drawing dated San Rafael, "XII Sept. MCMXIX" is dedicated "To my good friend Georg."[67] In February 1920 Alberti accompanied his father down to Málaga, to stay with relatives and take advantage of the mild winter climate.[68] The visit cannot have lasted very long, for they were back in Madrid when Alberti's father died in March 1920. He tells us that he wrote his first poem that same night.[69] Certainly by this time he had been reading poetry extensively, with his early friends Gil Cala and Celestino Espinosa.[70] Hernanz Angulo's discovery of a notebook containing Alberti's earliest verse confirms that he started writing in the spring of 1920, but the floodgates seem to have opened in July of that year, the date of a considerable number of compositions in the notebook.[71]

During the summer of 1921, Prieto visited him during another of his stays at the sanatorium in San Rafael de Guadarrama and gifted him Lorca's *Libro de poemas*, whose colophon is dated to 15 June.[72] Alberti returned to Madrid at the end of August, and later in 1921 he likely got to know both Juan Chabás and Dámaso Alonso.[73] Chabás gifted him a copy of his collection *Espejos* (from the fall of 1921; reviewed in the press in November and December); Alberti situates their initial meeting at a Salón de Otoño art exhibition, which in 1921 opened on 1 October. Alberti showed works at both this one and the previous (October 1920); in 1921, his paintings, along with those by Palencia and Vázquez Díaz, were the subjects of mocking caricatures.[74]

According to Alberti, a week or so after Chabás's first visit to his house, Chabás returned with Alonso, who brought a copy of his *Poemas puros. Poemillas de la ciudad* (also from 1921), and Alberti locates the encounter on "a winter afternoon in 1921."[75] Alonso, however, remembers their first encounter differently: he recounts that he was a classmate of Juan Antonio Espinosa, that he also knew his younger brother, Celestino Espinosa, and that it was through him that the two poets met.[76] But Alonso also situates this in 1921, shortly after the publication of *Poemas puros*.

In his memoirs, Alberti mistakenly links these early contacts with an exhibition of his paintings and drawings at the Ateneo, which actually opened later, on 20 March 1923.[77] Alberti credits Chabás with organizing this show. It drew very little critical attention. Also through Chabás, Alberti met Pedro Garfias, likely in 1922, who included three of his short poems in *Horizonte*, number 3.[78] Vicente Aleixandre claims to have been introduced to him at the aforementioned Ateneo exhibition;[79] still, Alberti disputes this, believing their first meeting was considerably earlier, though he cannot remember the circumstances.[80] Chabás and Alonso also seem to have been instrumental in Alberti meeting Buñuel, at a date that is difficult to determine with precision, but plausibly in late 1922 or 1923.[81] Meanwhile, Alberti's health remained a concern; over the summers of

1922–24, he continued his long stays in the Sierra de Guadarrama,[82] and in April 1923 one of his doctors decreed a period of an enhanced diet and no conversation with friends, as this excited him too much.[83]

Alberti visited the Residencia de Estudiantes and met Lorca most probably in the late spring of 1924, with the initial introduction being made by Prieto.[84] The exact date has been the subject of some confusion: in Max Aub's *Conversaciones con Buñuel*, Alberti gives it as "toward the end of '23," and in *La arboleda perdida I y II*, he specifies it as "an afternoon at the beginning of fall" during which Lorca recited his "Romance sonámbulo" (a poem dated on the original manuscript to 2 August 1924).[85] However, in a letter from Alberti to Prieto dated Madrid, May 1924, he states that "I had lunch with Federico, the extraordinary Federico," the tone of the adjective employed suggesting that their first encounter may still be very recent.[86] Also in May, three poems of his were published in *Alfar*.[87] At the Residencia he also met Pepín Bello and José Moreno Villa.[88] It was Lorca who introduced Alberti to José María Chacón y Calvo,[89] and in the same manner, in the fall of 1924, Alberti met Dalí (back in Madrid to repeat his second year at the Escuela Especial).[90] Although José María Hinojosa and José Bergamín were never residents, they were frequent visitors to the Residencia, so Alberti would also have come into contact with them around this same time.[91] In July, Dámaso Alonso and Chabás also introduced Alberti to Enrique Díez-Canedo at the La Granja El Henar café.[92]

With one of his sisters, Milagros, Alberti attended the opening of an exhibition of the recent artwork of Gregorio Prieto at the Círculo de Bellas Artes on 3 January 1925.[93] Immediately thereafter, he left for an extended stay with another sister, María, in the village of Rute, arriving on the sixth.[94] During his time there, he finished *Mar y tierra (algas)*, the collection that became *Marinero en tierra*, and sent it to Chacón to enter in the national literature competition.[95] He remained in Rute for a little over three months, where he received a visit from Hinojosa, who had travelled up from Málaga to see him.[96]

The first letter that Alberti wrote to Prieto after his return to Madrid was begun on 12 May and then continued two weeks later on 26 May; in that second part he stated that he had now been back in Madrid for a month and a half and that he was looking forward to the exhibition of the

Sociedad de Artistas Ibéricos in the Retiro's Palacio de Exposiciones that was to open "the day after tomorrow" – 28 May.[97] Alberti is unsure when he met the sculptor Alberto, but wonders if it could have been around this time;[98] he seems to have been in contact with Alberto's friend Palencia at least by the summer of 1925.[99] At the end of May – the thirtieth, to be precise – Alberti and José María Hinojosa visited Juan Ramón Jiménez, bringing him a copy of the manuscript of *Marinero en tierra*;[100] Hinojosa likely took samples of his *Poema del campo*, published days later, on 10 June (by Imprenta Maroto).[101] Alberti and Gerardo Diego both won prizes in the national literature competition: the official document recording the jury's decision was signed on 6 June, and two days later the information appeared in a newspaper.[102] On 17 June, Manuel Altolaguirre wrote to Diego, pleased by the successes enjoyed by Diego and Alberti, "the two good friends of mine." He went on to elaborate on the evolving plans for founding *Litoral*, initially to be directed by him, Prados, Hinojosa, and Alberti;[103] Hinojosa may have acted as the liaison between Málaga and Alberti.[104] In July, the sole number of Jiménez's *Sí. Boletín Bello Español* included an ample selection of fifteen poems from *Marinero en tierra*.

Some time well into the summer of 1925, Alberti undertook a lengthy car trip with his brother Agustín through Old Castile, Cantabria, and the Basque Country, all the while working on his next book of poetry, *La amante*, which he claimed was inspired by a "beautiful lady friend far away – from my days of rest in the Guadarrama," who was "more dreamt than real."[105] On his return, he found the proofs of *Marinero en tierra*, which was published in November.[106] At the end of that month, he left for a second stay in Rute, taking with him the completed manuscript of *La amante* and the unfinished one of *Cales negras*, which would become *El alba del alhelí*.[107] At the end of January 1926, Alberti travelled from Rute to Málaga to visit Prados and Altolaguirre, and gave them the manuscript of *La amante* to be published by *Litoral*'s Imprenta Sur.[108] He continued on to Almería, to stay with another of his sisters, Pepita, during February and March.[109] There, he finished *El alba del alhelí* and briefly fell in love with "an attractive girl from the Philippines" also staying with his sister, who advised him that it was time for him to return to Madrid.[110]

Once back in the capital, he remained there for the rest of the year. He started work on *Pasión y forma*, which was to become *Cal y canto*, and also participated in the first preparatory meetings for the Góngora celebrations, of which he was named secretary.[111] On 17 April 1926, he and Gerardo Diego finally met in person.[112] Although Gómez de Tudanca speculates that Alberti and José María de Cossío may have come into contact in 1924, Alberti places their encounter in the spring of 1926, and indeed the first preserved letter is from July of that year.[113] In the summer and fall he was working hard on *La pájara pinta*.[114] *La amante* was printed over October and November, with a colophon of 27 November.[115] Meanwhile, Alberti stayed on in Madrid through to the spring of 1927.[116] In the chronology outlined by *La arboleda perdida*, his next trips outside the capital were not until Sevilla and the Puerto de Santa María in May 1927,[117] and then briefly to Pontevedra in July.[118] Of course, Alberti participated in the famous Góngora event held in Sevilla in December 1927: the group left Madrid on the fifteenth and stayed for several days.[119]

The account of Alberti's movements in 1928 offered by *La arboleda perdida* is of dubious accuracy. What we know is this: after Sevilla, he returned to Madrid,[120] but he soon left again for the Puerto de Santa María, where he spent most of January 1928. Alberti was supposed to travel to Barcelona for the opening of Giménez Caballero's exhibition at the Dalmau gallery on 8 January, but the lack of press confirmation indicates that he, like Lorca, bowed out. In El Puerto, he wrote a long poem on the history of the Casa Domecq.[121] After spending February and March back in Madrid, he headed to Tudanca for an extended stay over the months of April, May, and June.

Alberti dates the onset of the severe depression that he links with the composition of the poems collected in *Sobre los ángeles* to just after the completion of his "Tercera soledad (paráfrasis incompleta)," published in *La Gaceta Literaria* on 1 June 1927.[122] After December in Sevilla, things had become worse,[123] leading to the much-quoted lengthy description in *La arboleda perdida* of his state of mind during early 1928.[124] It was at this juncture that he took up Cossío's invitation to go and stay in Tudanca. Alberti attended the premiere of Ignacio Sánchez Mejías' play, *Sinrazón*, in Madrid on 24 March.[125] Cossío was in Valladolid in late March, and at the opening of an exhibition of artwork by his brother, Mariano, in Madrid on 3 April; Alberti was also there.[126] Cossío planned to go to Tudanca during "the first fortnight of April," and it is even possible that

Alberti accompanied him there from Madrid.[127] He stayed with Cossío until 30 June, at which point he returned to Madrid.[128]

Alberti describes the small village of Tudanca during that spring, his daily work reading and writing in the house's "orchard of flowers and fruit trees," and a mild flirtation with a maid, Carlota.[129] During these nearly three months, he wrote many of the poems in *Sobre los ángeles*.[130] He and Cossío also engaged in a variety of other activities. On 30 April, in Torrelavega, Alberti gave a reading of his poetry, presented by Cossío, sponsored by that town's Biblioteca Popular,[131] and the following day, in Santander, at the Ateneo, Cossío spoke on the subject of "contemporary Spanish poetry," followed by another reading by Alberti.[132] In May, Diego and Luis Á. Piñer visited Tudanca, where they heard a first reading of some of the poems of *Sobre los ángeles*,[133] and Cossío and Alberti reciprocally visited Diego in Gijón.[134] On 20 and 22 May, Cossío and Alberti, accompanied by Carlos Gardel, were at the Estadio El Sardinero in Santander for the first two of three championship soccer matches; this is when Alberti composed the ode to "Platko," published in *La Voz de Cantabria* on 27 May.[135] Immediately thereafter, they visited Palencia.[136] On one of these occasions, or on yet other trips, Alberti also remembers visits to Santillana del Mar, Oviedo, and the caves of Altamira.[137] In May or June, Altolaguirre wrote to them jointly; he had the manuscript of *Cal y canto*, sent to him by Alberti, but it was progressing very slowly, and he closed with the exclamation "How lovely the book of the angels is going to be!!!," indicating that he, like Diego, was fully up to date on Alberti's projects.[138] At the very end of his stay, Cossío and Alberti again went to Torrelavega and Santander 28 and 29 June, met up with Diego, and attended the third and final soccer match. The next day, the thirtieth, Alberti took the train back to Madrid, perhaps accompanied by Diego, who was setting out on the first leg of his trip to Argentina.[139] All in all, the picture that emerges is hardly one of Alberti moping around the cold corridors of the large stone house in the isolated village of Tudanca.[140]

In his memoirs, Alberti says that he simply passed through Madrid on his way to the Puerto de Santa María,[141] but that visit to the South had actually occurred in January, so it is very likely that he stayed on in the capital. During the summer he would have witnessed the tremendous success of Lorca's *Romancero gitano*. Also around this time he would have visited his unmarried sister Milagros, who had needed to enter the psychiatric hospital Sanatorio Esquerdo.[142] In the fall, Alberti continued on in Madrid, seeing to the publication of *Cal y canto* with the *Revista de Occidente* (switched from his original choice of the Imprenta Sur)[143] and finishing up *Sobre los ángeles*. He gave readings of the latter on 24 October,[144] at the art exhibition by Benjamín Palencia being held in the Salón of the Palacio de Bibliotecas y Museos,[145] and then on 20 December, at the Residencia de Estudiantes, with a presentation by Pedro Salinas.[146]

Nineteen twenty-nine brought the publication, around March, of *Cal y canto*[147] and the delayed distribution of *El alba del alhelí*. Meanwhile, Alberti had been publishing poems from *Sobre los ángeles* since March 1928, in the magazines *Carmen*, *Papel de Aleluyas*, *Revista de Occidente*, *La Gaceta Literaria*, *Filosofía y Letras*, and *Meseta*, and the collection came out in May or June 1929.[148] A second edition of *La amante* was produced in July.[149] Overlapping with these publications, a series of poems from *Yo era un tonto y lo que he visto me ha hecho dos tontos* appeared in *La Gaceta Literaria*, May through September; on 4 May, in the interval during the Sixth Session of the Madrid Cineclub, Alberti recited several of these *Yo era un tonto* poems.[150] It is in the spring of 1929 that Carlos Morla Lynch situates the start of Alberti's frequent visits to his house.[151] Around this time, he also began work on poems for *Sermones y moradas* and on *El hombre deshabitado*.[152] Once again in somewhat precarious health, he spent the summer in the Guadarrama.[153] On 29 October, Alberti gave a reading, including poetry and *La pájara pinta* and *El colorín colorete*, to the Asociación de Estudiantes de Filosofía y Letras.[154] He delivered his notorious lecture "Palomita y galápago (¡No más artríticos!)" at the Lyceum Club Femenino in Madrid on 10 November.[155] Around November, he gave a reading of Fernando Villalón's verse play *Don Fermín de Plateros* to a small group assembled in the Teatro Español, with a view to its production by Ricardo Calvo,[156] and he attended the Madrid premiere of Buñuel's and Dalí's *Un Chien andalou* on 8 December.[157]

Alberti symbolically dates the composition of his poem "Con los zapatos puestos tengo que morir. Elegía cívica" to 1 January 1930.[158] On

7 January, a newspaper reported that two film critics, Juan Piqueras and
Luis Gómez Mesa, were launching a series of biographies – "Figuras
del cinema" – about movie personalities, and one of the volumes would
be written by Alberti.[159] On the eighth, at a banquet offered by Ramón
Gómez de la Serna for Ernesto Giménez Caballero and held in the Pombo
café, Alberti distributed an irreverent, satirical skit, *Auto de fe. (Dividido
en un gargajo y cuatro cazcarrias)*, directed against Ortega y Gasset and
the editorial team at the *Revista de Occidente*.[160] On the ninth, he gave
a reading of his poetry on Unión Radio.[161] Before the twenty-eighth, he
took part, with Santiago Ontañón and Eugenio Montes, in a violent street
protest against Primo de Rivera.[162] Also during January, we find the first
mentions in the press of *El hombre deshabitado*.[163] On 20 March, Madrid's Orquesta Sinfónica with the singer Laura Nieto performed a new
composition by Óscar Esplá, five "Canciones playeras," settings of texts
from *El alba del alhelí*.[164] On 2 April, Alberti read his play *Santa Casilda*
to the Josefina Díaz/Santiago Artigas company,[165] who were about to em-
bark on a long tour abroad. Later that day, he offered "a humorous talk
entitled 'Visibly moved'" to round off the special performance of a play
Una muchacha de vanguardia, by Ángel Custodio and Javier de Burgos,
for the Alumnos de Arqueología de la Universidad Central.[166] On 3 May,
he gave a lecture and a reading of *La pájara pinta* at the Residencia de
Señoritas entitled "Poesías y comentarios."[167] And on the seventh, he attended a luncheon given at Giménez Caballero's home for the visiting
Count Keyserling.[168]

After further health problems, he spent the summer in Cercedilla,
staying at the Hotel Frontón,[169] and was back in Madrid by 20 September.[170]
Through the fall, he was still hoping to arrange the production of his play
Santa Casilda with the Díaz/Artigas company,[171] and continued working
on the poems for *Sermones y moradas* and *El hombre deshabitado*.[172]
On 15 November, Juan Ramón Jiménez published in *La Gaceta Literaria*
an article in which he offered portraits of Lorca, Dámaso Alonso, and
Alberti, all three very far from flattering.[173] Indeed, throughout November
and December Alberti is reported to have been working on a "satirical
portrait" of Jiménez,[174] while – strangely out of character – at the end of
December he published seasonal poems in *Blanco y Negro* and *ABC*.[175]

The Sociedad de Artistas Ibéricos Exhibition of 1925 at the Palacio de Exposiciones (Palacio de Velázquez)

As an art student in her third year of study, and as a friend of a number of young artists, some of whom were exhibiting there, Mallo was doubtless an enthusiastic and frequent visitor to this landmark show. Likewise, Alberti, the artist turned poet and dramatist and also with numerous artist friends, was, as noted above, especially looking forward to it. But as the day of its opening approached, neither of them could have foreseen the role it would come to play in their lives.

The exhibition was, arguably, the most important one held in Madrid in the 1920s. In chapter 2, we saw that Barradas and Alberto were there, sharing two rooms; more works by Barradas were shown than from any other contributor. As noted in chapter 3, several of the artists who passed through Julio Moisés's Academia Libre sent works. A section of chapter 5 traced the prehistory of the exhibition, from 1923 through 1925, and the key role that Maroto played in its genesis, planning, and realization. Maroto also showed a number of his own works and gave one of the "outreach" lectures that were programmed to accompany the show.

The exhibition ran from 28 May through 5 July at the Palacio de Exposiciones (a.k.a. Palacio de Velázquez) situated in the middle of the Parque del Buen Retiro, south of the large rectangular boating lake and north of the perhaps better known Palacio de Cristal.[176] A total of forty-seven artists were invited and participated, among them Alberto, Bagaría, Barradas, Bores, Norah Borges, Dalí, Maroto, Pancho Cossío, Moreno Villa, Palencia, Peinado, Sáenz de Tejada, and Santa Cruz, and somewhere in the region of five hundred works were shown. Contemporary press coverage was very extensive. The show and its broad historical significance have been the object of considerable study, notably in the commemorative exhibition of 1995 and a later, multi-volume doctoral dissertation.[177]

Mallo's and Alberti's Relationship, 1925–30[178]

It is really quite remarkable that Mallo's and Alberti's paths did not cross until 1925, as for several years prior they had been moving in similar and to some degree overlapping circles. The extended period that Alberti spent in Rute may have contributed to delaying his and Mallo's first encounter until the early summer of 1925, and Mallo's subsequent absence in Tenerife would have prevented the development of the relationship until the fall of that year.

The precise circumstances of their first meeting remain unclear. There are three sources, provided by the two principals plus Concha Méndez, but their accounts contain certain inaccuracies and do not coincide completely. In January 1925, Buñuel had left for Paris, effectively bringing to an end a long, formal relationship with Concha Méndez, and that spring Méndez met and became friends with Lorca.[179] This brings us to the crucial passage in Méndez's memoirs:

> In the Palacio de Cristal in the Retiro park there was held, a while ago, an exhibition of Ibero-American painting, at whose official opening Federico offered a poetry reading ... Federico recited expressing himself with his hands; it was not only from his voice that poetry emanated, but rather from his whole body ... "I can do that as well" – I said to myself ... And it was that night, after I returned home, when, in silence, because of my joy, I wrote my first poems.
>
> At the Palacio de Cristal I had met, among other artists, Rafael Alberti ...
>
> The night of the discovery that I made in the Palacio de Cristal I had met the painter Maruja Mallo and I started to go out with her around Madrid.[180]

Méndez's exhibition of "Ibero-American painting" is without doubt that of the Sociedad de Artistas Ibéricos. Likewise, the "Palacio de Cristal" would actually be the nearby but considerably larger Palacio de Exposiciones (the Palacio de Velázquez). Lorca and Dalí certainly attended the inauguration on 28 May,[181] but Lorca did not give a recital then; rather, it took place on 15 June.[182] Pérez Ferrero remembers the event as follows: "Once the exhibition had been set up ... Federico García Lorca offered a recital of the first fruits of the compositions for *Romancero gitano*."[183] And in a later evocation, he locates it precisely in the Palacio de Cristal: "one afternoon in front of a less than numerous audience Federico García Lorca read poems from his *Romancero gitano*."[184]

Although Mallo's account does not really match up, it seems possible to blend it with Méndez's:

> On one occasion Dalí, Federico, and I were in the Retiro. Some
> young men passed close by and greeted us like this with their arm.
> I asked: "Who are they?" and Lorca replied to me: "One of them
> is a very good poet and the other is a very bad poet." They were
> Alberti and Hinojosa ... Alberti liked painting and we used to see
> each other in the Prado, and so by the third day we got labelled, but
> I don't want to talk about love affairs.[185]

In light of Alberti's and Hinojosa's joint visit to Jiménez on 30 May,
the Retiro setting, and the presence of Lorca and Dalí, it would not
be far-fetched to ascribe the scene just described to the period of the
Sociedad de Artistas Ibéricos exhibition, and most likely to 15 June.[186]
However, we also know that Mallo's father and other family members
arrived in Tenerife by steamer on 18 June,[187] so we must conclude either
that the episode occurred earlier than 15 June or that she joined her
family somewhat later on another ship. Either way, given the time frame
involved, her description of the evolution of the relationship must surely
apply to the *fall* of 1925: "we used to see each other in the Prado, and so
by the third day we got labelled."[188]

These two versions contrast with that offered by Alberti, where
he seems to be engaging in some creative rewriting of history. Most
significantly, he claims to have still been in Rute, and to have forgotten
about his submission, when news unexpectedly arrived of his having won
the Premio Nacional de Literatura for 1924.[189] However, Alberti had in
fact been back in Madrid for half of April and all of May, and was fretting
about whether he would win.[190] This provides the relevant background to
Alberti's later assertion that "I had met that painter a little while after I
received the National Prize for Literature for my *Marinero en tierra* ...
Her name was Maruja Mallo, she was Galician, and I believe recently
graduated from the Academia de Bellas Artes in Madrid."[191] If Alberti and
Mallo did indeed meet on 15 June (or during the week immediately prior),
then the chronological indication with respect to the announcement of
the prize would be correct.

What happened next is not entirely clear. Méndez narrates the
immediate result of her meeting Alberti:

I met up with him the following morning and I showed him my things. "But when did you start to write?" – he asked me. "It was last night, after I returned home." He was amazed; but my amazement was even greater because poems were coming out of me involuntarily. Rafael and I started to arrange to meet, to read our things, on the bench of a park. He explained to me what a metaphor was, what an image was.[192]

And in answers to Aub's questions, she recalled:

– When were you in a relationship with Alberti?
– With Alberti it was just a few days, you could say.
– I see. When, in what year?
– Well, it was after I broke it off with Buñuel. I met Alberti's group at an exhibition of Ibero-American painting, where Federico García Lorca gave a lecture. That's where I met him. I didn't realize at the time because ...
– Who did you meet, Rafael or ...?
– That's where I met everyone ... And when I heard Federico recite, I said to myself: "I can do that as well." Then I started writing, and Alberti, who was the one who was advising me, said: "The influence of Juan Ramón is noticeable."[193]

Just over two weeks after Lorca's recital, Méndez left Madrid to spend the summer with her family in San Sebastián, arriving there 4 July, and she wrote to him the following day: "Do you remember that thing that you said to me one day, that I would still find a source of calm and sweet affection? Well, even though this may seem incredible to you, a few days after you left Madrid,[194] I found there that affection that I was in real need of."[195] And when Buñuel turned up in San Sebastián to see her, "I started out by telling him that I was in love with someone else."[196] In her second letter to Lorca, from 20 July, she writes, "I have been remembering you all and in particular *Rafael Alberti*," and "my new object of affection exists. In addition 'he' is good. And I love him."[197] For his part, Alberti wrote to Chacón on 6 July that "I have been distracted by affairs of the heart. But the turmoil has already passed. I am back to being free and content, as always."[198] Given the absence from Madrid of both Méndez and Mallo from early July onward, and given the lack of other details, it is impossible to identify the person to whom Alberti refers, though it might well have been one of them.[199]

Méndez and Mallo, and Méndez and Alberti, remained close friends. Méndez wrote to Lorca in November 1925: "Speaking of letters: did you receive one that I sent to you together with another one from Maruja Mallo?"[200] Champourcin commented to Conde on 27 August 1928 that "She [Mallo] and Concha Méndez are very close friends, they are inseparable."[201] Mallo also painted a portrait of Méndez, and used her as a model in some of her other canvases.[202] As for Alberti, Méndez recounts that "he wrote me some charming letters, and … he wanted to dedicate a group of poems in one of his books to me."[203] In April 1927, he was still spending time with Méndez, as is reflected in a letter of his to Prieto, where he teases the painter about Méndez being in love with him.[204] And all three of them went out together, as Méndez remembers: "One day, when I was at the San Isidro fair with Maruja Mallo, Rafael [Alberti], and the son of the painter Regoyos, we witnessed an encounter straight out of a painting."[205]

However, some time in the second half of 1925, there began what was by all accounts a consuming and tempestuous love affair between Mallo and Alberti, which lasted, with more than one interruption, until the very end of 1930. For one thing, while Mallo was mostly in Madrid, just spending parts of some summers in Asturias and Galicia visiting family and attending her exhibitions (1926, 1927), Alberti was absent on multiple occasions. The first of these came at the end of November 1925, when he left for Rute; after subsequent stays in Málaga and Almería, he was not back in Madrid until April 1926. It may have been during the remainder of this year that their relationship really flourished, coinciding with the time when Mallo was living at the Madrid family apartment with several of her numerous siblings but with little or no parental supervision. There were visits to the Prado and, later, excursions together to Vallecas, with Alberto and Palencia.[206] While Alberti may have started work on *La pájara pinta* in 1925, 1926 was the year of greatest effort devoted to it,[207] involving a close collaboration with Mallo: "María Mallo would create the costume designs and the sets … The prints that Maruja drew, in full colour, were

6.2. Maruja Mallo and Rafael Alberti at the gates of the Parque del Retiro.

something rather more than just costume designs."[208] Originating in the same year, another similar project was Alberti's *El colorín colorete*, which Mallo illustrated rather later.[209] This is probably also the period of the episodes recounted by Alberti, of a very active social life, frequent cinema-going, and illicit lovemaking at night in the Retiro.[210]

According to Ferris, it was Alberti who brought Mallo's paintings to the attention of Fernández Almagro;[211] Nuevo Cal and Ínsua López state that Almagro was a close friend of Maruja's brother Justo;[212] Francisco Ayala identifies Concha Méndez and Mallo as members of Almagro's *tertulia* at La Granja del Henar as of 1927;[213] while Escoriza Escoriza points to María de la O Lejárraga as the initial link.[214] Clearly, then, there were multiple points of contact, and the significance of Alberti's role in bringing about Mallo's *Revista de Occidente* exhibition is impossible to gauge.

A further complication is that around this same time Alberti became enamoured of another young woman, Victoria Amado. Alberti's friend José Bergamín was engaged to Rosario Arniches (the couple wed in the summer of 1928); Rosario's father, the famous playwright Carlos Arniches, owned a property in Hortaleza, then a village just outside Madrid, called the "Huerta de Mena," and Arniches had been a member of the judging panel that awarded Alberti the Premio Nacional de Literatura.[215] In October 1927, Alberti wrote to José Bello: "The only person whom I see is Pepe Bergamín, who remembers you and sends his regards. At the home of his fiancée, Arniches's daughter, he made me recount exploits of yours, ours."[216] Whether this refers specifically to Arniches's Madrid apartment or the rural property is unclear. At all events, Arniches's nephew and niece, José María and Victoria Amado, used to frequent the Huerta, as did Bergamín and Alberti, and it was there, and on outings to the cinema, that Alberti courted Victoria, forming a relationship that never progressed very far and which can be characterized as romantic, almost sentimental, and certainly platonic, in contrast to the much more intimate relationship with Mallo.[217] José María Amado referred to it as "that half-engagement with Victoria,"[218] and she has been described by García Montero as "a young lady who was more than a little pretentious, someone just learning to paint, who had very little comparable with the figure of Maruja Mallo."[219] For a while Alberti may have dated both women simultaneously.

The principal evidence regarding Victoria is an album, made by Alberti and dedicated on the opening page "To Victorita Amado. Rafael Alberti. Madrid. 1928. March."[220] Here we find collages, drawings, hand-copied texts of love poems from various centuries, and a mixed-media celebration of her house in Madrid, at calle Sagasta, 24, that included several tram tickets from the line (to Argüelles) that passed by her building.[221] A closing poem, "FIN," by Alberti himself, is dedicated "to Victorita. 1927."[222] This turns out to be the fourth section of "El cuerpo deshabitado," from *Sobre los ángeles*. The first line reads, "You. Me. Moon. To the pond," and as Victoria's brother explains:

> To the left of the large avenue lined with stout trees that led from the wrought-iron gates up to the house, lay the pond of *Sobre los ángeles* …

The pond, with ducks that dove in the water, was opposite the caretaker's little house and there, at its edge, I remember you sitting with my sister Victoria.[223]

The dating of the poem "FIN" in the album; the indication on the autograph manuscript of the collection preserved by Cossío of "(1927–1928)";[224] Alberti's separation from Mallo "halfway through *Sobre los ángeles*";[225] and the publication of "Los dos ángeles" in March 1928,[226] all demonstrate that the composition of the first poems collected in *Sobre los ángeles* started well before Alberti decamped to Tudanca.[227] It may well be significant that the aforementioned album was presented to Victoria in March 1928, and Alberti may have made the snap decision to withdraw to the countryside in early April motivated at least in part by a desire to gain some respite from recent emotional turmoil.[228] What cannot be determined is the precise or immediate cause of his distress: frustration with or rejection by Amado, and/or a breakup with Mallo or with both women, and/or his inability to choose between them.[229] In an interview from the early 1970s, Alberti rather surprisingly brought up a contemporaneous play rather than *Sobre los ángeles*:

During the period of *El hombre deshabitado* undoubtedly I was experiencing a great crisis of youth … that work posed … a problem revolving around love that in a certain way concerned me, although I have never explained it well, that issue of temptation that appeared in opposition to another pure woman.[230]

José Corredor-Matheos for his part glosses some statements and directly quotes others made to him in 1979:

In *Sobre los ángeles* there is: the breakup with a pre-existing love, the appearance of that girl to whom Vivanco refers – "a love affair that one might describe as difficult, completely romantic," "that was not anything, almost all of it was breakup," the disappearance of that girl and the recovery of the previous love. "It is all in *Sobre los ángeles*." And in different poems of this book he alludes to those relationships that never managed to coalesce into anything solid.[231]

In 1985 Alberti offered this version of events:

> Some angel, as the spirit of inconstancy and evil, led me to fly toward
> another person, to whom I became very attached, and in spite of her
> name – she was called Victoria – she led me, from what I thought
> was the ascent up to the stars, into the most dizzying fall into hell.[232]

However, one of the most explicit statements (relatively speaking) had
come years earlier, in 1979, where, with respect to *Sobre los ángeles*,
Alberti said,

> Undoubtedly I was involved with two people who came together to
> create that book. One person whom in a certain sense I was leaving,
> and another person who was there but with whom, as it turned
> out, I did not have any relationship like the ones that pleased me at
> that time.
>   Part of the drama of *Sobre los ángeles* is her; ... I separated from
> her halfway through *Sobre los ángeles*, and then I fell in love with
> another girl, but that did not turn out well.[233]

The first person is clearly Mallo and the other Amado. In a 1984 interview,
Alberti referred to her as "Victoria Bárcena ... , a lovely, marvellous girl ...
but who was practically unattainable, and who was not very clear-headed,
unreflecting, without anything really [and] there were even insults."[234]

He spent most of April and all of May and June 1928 in Tudanca; this
is the period when he wrote the bulk of the collection: "there, amidst
those winds, mists, and mountains, I continued *Sobre los ángeles*. There
the solitude and the sonorous silence were intense."[235] His general state of
mind is described in a much-quoted passage from his memoirs,[236] from
which I would highlight the following phrases:

> How many real things, in chiaroscuro, had been pushing me until I
> fell, like a crackling lightning bolt, into that deep abyss! Impossible
> love, love wounded and betrayed in the best hours of intimacy and
> trust; the most furious jealousy, capable of plotting during the
> sleepless hours of night a cold and calculated crime.[237]

It is impossible to untangle the real-life referents ("How many real things"); "impossible love" could refer to Victoria, but "hours of intimacy and trust" sound rather more like Maruja; the jealousy, too, could be attributed to Victoria's coolness or, equally, suspicions that she or Maruja was interested in someone else.[238] What is striking, though, is the contrast between this evocation of his state of mind and what we know of his daily life and activities during those nearly three months in Tudanca. Thus, to Pedro Lorenzo he wrote on 5 May that "we have fond memories of the days we spent in Torrelavega. Me, showing off in front of the girls ... I remember those girls who were so very pretty and who, sitting right there in front of me, listened to my songs of sea and land. Oh what wonderful girls! I miss all of them so much." And again on 1 June, "What's going on in Torrelavega? And what about all my *darling girls*?"[239] One curious detail involves a request he makes of Lorenzo: "Could you do me a favour? If it is no trouble, go to the station that is indicated, present this consignment ticket, and pick up this package – a painting without any artistic value – that a good female friend has dispatched to me, and then send it over here, to Tudanca."[240] Who else could this "good female friend" be but Mallo? But if the painting is one of hers not included in the just-opened exhibition, why is it "without any artistic value"?

The very next phrase following the quotation given above refers to "the sad shadow of the friend who committed suicide, like a silent bell-clapper pounding in my forehead."[241] This haunting memory was connected to a car accident that occurred in Madrid while Alberti was in Tudanca. But, curiously, what actually happened and the related chronology have not been scrutinized carefully. Mallo's Madrid exhibition opened on 26 May, and while there is no closing date recorded, it is a safe assumption that this would have been on 8, 9, or 10 June. In all the May and June correspondence that we have, both to and from Alberti, there are no references to Mallo or the exhibition (save, possibly, for the "good female friend" just mentioned). The automobile accident occurred on Tuesday, 12 June, and we know that Alberti stayed in Tudanca until the thirtieth. This hardly squares with what Alberti wrote in 1985: "And one day, on opening a newspaper that had arrived from Madrid, I read, truly terrified: 'The painter Maruja Mallo has an automobile accident, and Mauricio Roeset [*sic*], believing that he has killed her, commits suicide.' (The fable of Pyramus and Thisbe was being repeated.) I went down to Madrid immediately."[242] Even allowing for the delay in newspapers being received,[243] through the second half of June Alberti stayed on in Tudanca, attended the third and final leg of the hotly contested soccer championship in Santander on the twenty-ninth, and arranged to travel down to Madrid the following day by train in the company of Gerardo Diego.

Meanwhile in Madrid, early on the morning of 12 June, Mauricio Roësset Velasco, Carmen Manso Robledo, and Maruja Mallo had gone out for a drive in Mauricio's father's car, on the road from Chamartín toward Alcobendas. Mauricio (1899–1928) was the younger brother of the painter Marisa Roësset Velasco (1904–1976),[244] the nephew of the painter María Roësset Mosquera, or "MaRo" (1882–1921), and the first cousin of the sculptor Marga Gil Roësset (1908–1932). Carmen (1907–?) was the elder sister of Margarita Manso (1908–1960), Maruja's close friend and fellow student at the Escuela Especial, and the three in the car were all friends.[245] While taking a corner, the car skidded and overturned, causing them all injuries described as "bruises on different parts of the body, light scratches and scrapes and injuries of little significance."[246] By the time the Guardia Civil arrived on the scene, another passing car had already transported them back to Madrid, and in a first-aid post in Buenavista they received treatment and made a statement, after which they all returned to their respective homes.

Alberti gives us to understand that Mauricio – also a friend of his – was Maruja's new love interest ("she had a new friend");[247] the belief may have been the cause of his jealousy, though there is no independent source to confirm that the two were anything but friends. What *is* certain is that a narrative originated by Alberti concerning the specifics of the accident and later widely repeated is entirely incorrect. According to Alberti, "that person [Maruja Mallo] lost consciousness, and her friend thought that she had been killed. He committed suicide, later, a day afterwards, surely believing that that person ... but no, that person is still alive today."[248]

This version of events is directly contradicted by the report on the injuries given by the "physicians on call" at the first-aid post and by all the newspaper articles concerned with what drove Mauricio to this act. It turns out that Mauricio was forbidden to take out the family car without supervision, as he was still a novice driver, and so on returning home with visible injuries he fabricated a story about a taxi that he had hired to take the three on a drive and which had suffered the rollover.[249] Hours later, when the police traced the damaged car's registration to its owner, the truth emerged. After being confronted by his family, Mauricio withdrew to his room, wrote two letters, one to his mother and one to the investigating judge, and then shot himself, dying from his head wound several hours later.[250] In the second letter, Mauricio stated that he had been planning to commit suicide for some time and that his involvement in the accident was what finally prompted his action.

Details regarding the summer months of 1928, once Alberti was back in Madrid, are few and far between. Despite the serious discrepancies just noted, it is obvious that he, Mallo, and their other friends would have been much affected by Mauricio's suicide. Alberti describes the return to Madrid as "entering again the regions under the earth."[251] That "the sad shadow of the friend who committed suicide"[252] hung over him seems to be reflected in a letter of July to Cossío: "I am not well. I am not in the mood to write you an entertaining letter,"[253] though this was the moment, too, when his sister was in the psychiatric clinic. Connell records Alberti's statement that the suicide "had a big influence on me," that the poem "Novela" contains a brief but direct reference to Mauricio, and that in regard to the anecdotal element in that poem, "the atmosphere of that storyline lingered on in me."[254]

As for Mallo, García Montero asserts, without citing any sources, that "the breakup of the love affair [with Alberti] had caused a psychological imbalance in Maruja Mallo,"[255] which, as Mangini rightly points out, would only have been aggravated by the accident, the suicide, her injuries, and the overall trauma.[256] Hence, as reported by her brother Emilio, Maruja "was depressed for a long time."[257] Furthermore, these events coincided more or less exactly with the radical change in her style, from the bright, colourful, and animated cheerfulness of the *Verbenas*, to the dark, almost monochromatic gloominess of the *Cloacas*, and it is hard not to suspect some sort of causality involving not only the visits to Vallecas and environs, but also the vicissitudes of her love life, the car accident, and the death of her young friend. Laurenson-Shakibi does,[258] and finds confirmation in the rather cryptic comments that Gómez de la Serna made about Mallo:

Something serious has happened. The man has not found a way of consoling her, he has disappointed her, he has not measured up to her expectations, and the painter has eaten away at Don Juan, she has put him in graves where garbage is buried, and she has dressed him in his slashed suit of bone[259] ...

Perhaps this is the most fanciful moment of her life, but soon she remains alone, confronting winter, that whole landscape that is always wintry, more wintry than ever.

She has gone through her tragedies alone, courageous ...

She lives a tormented life.[260]

That Alberti would have been concerned is indisputable, but exactly how, when, and where he reconnected with Mallo is uncertain. Mangini states, without providing a source, that "after the accident ... she and Alberti got together again ... and he spent many hours at the head of her bed in the Marqués de Salamanca apartment,"[261] but we know that Mallo's physical injuries were in fact relatively minor. A letter from Alberti of 15 August reflects a complex mixture of sentiments. Reacting badly to the – later reversed – rejection by the *Revista de Occidente* of poems from *Sobre los ángeles*, he wrote, "I am working a good deal, again. I swear to you: poetry is the only thing that binds me to this world ... But now I am a very sad poet."[262] He also alluded to his sister's mental health: "My sister is slowly getting better."[263] However, the same letter opens with a long paragraph invoking two archetypal models of sexual libertinage, Aretino and Sardanapalus:

Here you have me, in the greatest destitution. But, I do not know why – out of Aretinism, doubtlessly – happy and going all over the place. And the thing is that I have now lost the little moral sense and the scarce sense of shame that I still had. A misfortune. Perhaps a stroke of luck. The issue is that I am now given over to all the vices. Why hide it any longer? I am, right now in the middle of 1928, the true reincarnation of the immoral and depraved Sardanapalus. That is how it is. Does that grieve you? Not me, not a jot.[264]

If he was really indulging in this kind of behaviour and not just posturing, one wonders whether it was with Mallo or possibly with some other, briefer and unidentified love interest.

At all events, at least by fall 1928 he and Maruja were back together as a couple. Guillén reported to his wife on 18 October about the "official opening of the Benjamín Palencia exhibition. Alberti and Maruja Mallo, lovey-dovey. For God's sake, I do wish that Maruja Mallo – the painter – would save the young Apollo! *Il s'agirait d'un véritable redressement moral, ah, oui, très moral!*"[265] Champourcin attended the first session of Giménez Caballero's Cineclub at the Callao cinema on 23 December, and reported to Conde the following day: "All the representatives of the young literary set were there. Among them, the inseparable pair of Maruja Mallo-Rafael Alberti. They are only friends; in the afternoon I saw them also together at the Lyceum Club. She is pretty keen on him, but he ... they say that he is of the sort who do not fall in love."[266] Days later, on 9 January, she wrote again: "This girl is very original and interesting. What a pity that her success has made her a bit conceited! She and Alberti are beginning to 'turn into fools.'"[267]

Nineteen twenty-nine was the year of Alberti's and Mallo's closest and most prolific collaboration. Mallo's drawings of the *Figuras de guiñol* and *Colorín colorete* series were directly connected with several of Alberti's never-completed dramatic projects, including *La pájara pinta*, *El colorín colorete*, and *Lepe, Lepijo y su hijo*. Only one illustration related to *La pájara pinta* has survived: titled *El arzobispo de Constantinopla*,[268] it depicts a line of nine characters in which the archbishop, with the Pájara Pinta directly above his head, occupies the central position.[269] Likewise, in regard to *El colorín colorete* only one example survives; untitled, it depicts a figure surrounded by flowers, letters, and other shapes.[270] Both drawings are elaborate, full-colour works, and both are signed "Maruja Mallo 1935," indicating that they are later versions. The *Colorín* image is also inscribed "Editorial Plutarco, Madrid." The *Almanaque literario* published by Plutarco in 1935 reproduced four line drawings by Mallo that resemble the figures in the two colour drawings,[271] suggesting that both may have been made for publication there but were not included.

On 1 July, *La Gaceta Literaria* presented Alberti's poem about/to Mallo, "La primera ascensión de Maruja Mallo al subsuelo," illustrated with two small reproductions from her *Cloacas* series, *Huella* and *Cloaca*.[272] Alberti started publishing poems from *Yo era un tonto y lo que he visto me ha hecho dos tontos* in *La Gaceta Literaria* on 15 May, and two of the subsequent installments, on 1 and 15 September, were accompanied by drawings by Mallo: *Wallace Beery, Detective, Charles Bower, Inventor, Las bodas de Ben Turpin, Farina y los fantasmas*, all part of the *Los cómicos del cine* series.

Alberti had spent the summer of 1929 back in the Sierra de Guadarrama, apparently again for health reasons.[273] He lodged in the village of Collado Mediano, close at hand to Mallo's family, who regularly summered in Cercedilla:

When I was writing *Sermones y moradas*, a little after *Sobre los ángeles*, my state of confusion was even greater. I was spending some days of summer with Maruja Mallo, who lived in Cercedilla, and every night I would go to Collado Mediano, closing my eyes while I made my way from the station to my house, jotting down with a pencil in a small notebook the poems that occurred to me, over a little more than half a kilometre that I had to cover. Then, the next day, I corrected the poem and made a fair copy.[274]

Besides his own new book of poetry, Mallo and Alberti were able to work on their joint projects:

Alberti, besides being a true poet, is a cheerful young man. This summer I saw him walking from Guadarrama to Cercedilla decked out in a pearl-grey pullover and a beret adorned with a star, for which, as well as a good mood, one needs a certain intrepidness ... He has composed, in collaboration with María Mallo, a book.[275]

Champourcin confirms the details and supplies a little more information: "Alberti is summering in Cercedilla, which is where Maruja Mallo is too. They are collaborating together on a book about *excrement* and he goes strolling around with a star embroidered on his beret softly singing shepherds' folk songs."[276] The volume in question was possibly a plan to combine poems from *Sermones y moradas* with images from the *Cloacas* series. This was also the summer during which Alberti and Mallo met the young poets José Herrera Petere and, most likely, Luis Felipe Vivanco (Petere and Vivanco had themselves met in Cercedilla the previous year).[277] In his article on *Sobre los ángeles*, Vivanco alludes to his friendship with Alberti at this time: "in the first poems of the book there is a great tragedy to do with love. I personally knew Alberti, and I have accompanied him through the streets of Madrid and the meadows of Cercedilla and I became his friend when this tragedy was causing him pain."[278]

Back in Madrid in the fall, Mallo was in the audience for Alberti's "scandalous" lecture at the Lyceum Club Femenino (10 November), "Palomita y galápago (¡No mas artríticos!)," and was one of the very few women who remained in the auditorium after the majority had left in protest.[279] She was also there in a small group when Alberti read Fernando Villalón's play *Don Fermín de Plateros* to Ricardo Calvo, with a view to its staging (21 November).[280]

One other aspect of Alberti's public appearances over these months should be noted. At the sixth session of the Cineclub, held on 4 May 1929, when Alberti read a number of his *Yo era un tonto* poems, he also included "a special set of gestures synchronized with sounds, whistles, and revolver shots."[281] Then, at a reading of his work to students on 29 October, "Rafael Alberti committed suicide with a pistol that had previously been checked over by the official representative. This inspection, and the fact that he had already committed suicide previously, from what they tell, in one of the sessions of the Cineclub, are sufficient to reassure the ranks of his admirers."[282] Furthermore, during the past summer spent in the Sierra, he had also "practised" the same disruptive act: "and he even had time to rehearse on the platform of the station up in the mountains, to the astonishment and then the rapid dispersal of members of the summer colony, the shot that he would then repeat in front of the students."[283] At the end of his November lecture at the Lyceum Club, "he released the dove and shot at it three times with a toy pistol."[284] Alberti writes that, after returning to the building the following day, and finding that the dove had been killed, "I fled, weeping, from the house of crime, and out in the streets I wrote this elegy." He reproduces the poem from *Yo era un tonto* that originally bore the title "¿Tuviste tú acaso la culpa de que las balas de un revólver no te hirieran y de que en cambio comprobaras que una hoja de otoño no vale ya ni para sepultar dos alas difuntas?"[285] While this string of provocations might seem reminiscent of Breton's famous dictum that "L'acte surréaliste le plus simple consiste, revolvers aux poings, à descendre dans la rue et à tirer au hasard, tant qu'on peut, dans la foule," the Second Surrealist Manifesto from which it comes did not appear until *December* 1929. Hence, we must attribute them to Alberti's own attitudes and state of mind at the time and, very likely, the lingering impact of Mauricio's suicide with a pistol.

The relative scarcity of press reports over 1930 suggests that the couple may have engaged in less public activity over this year. Salinas commented laconically to Guillén on 11 April that "Alberti's a little reclusive."[286] Still, in January they attended together a "conversation" at Giménez Caballero's house with the visiting Anton Giulio Bragaglia,[287] and Carlos Morla Lynch records a visit to his house in May:

> A few days ago [Alberti] turned up accompanied by a young female friend of his, a talented artist – painter: Maruja Mallo, modern without going to the extreme. And the poet read to us his somewhat mystical play, *Santa Casilda*, which we listened to religiously ...
>
> Maruja Mallo is the inspired creator of the sets for that theatrical work that has the character of a gospel, and, as Rafael goes along with his reading with a soft and musical voice full of lulling rhythms, she spreads out on the floor, on the carpet – with silent gestures – the sketches that illustrate the different scenes, which are all done in light shades, pink and sky-blue, pale and virginal.[288]

In the summer, Alberti was unwell again. Morla Lynch noted his concern: "But Rafael Alberti is ill; during the month of June we find that he looks pale and, as he is dear to us, we take care of him: it is the beginning of an ulcer that is causing him suffering."[289] Alberti's own diagnosis was different; he told Cossío on 16 August that "I was very ill with my liver. I had a serious attack at the banquet for Azorín. Now I am better."[290] As before, Alberti summered outside Madrid, but now staying in Cercedilla itself, at the Hotel Frontón. Writing to Cossío on 16 August, he signed off as "Rafael alias Pietro Aretino"; a couple of weeks later, he complained that "I am doing very badly as far as money is concerned and yet I need, for my health, to be in the mountains until the month of October."[291] However, he was actually back in Madrid by 20 September, when he, Diego, Salinas, Guillén, Lorca, Cernuda, Dámaso Alonso, and Juan Guerrero all had lunch together.[292] This is the summer when Maruja's brother Justo took a number of photos of her, posing with a large animal skull and a variety of other disparate objects as props, sometimes on railway tracks.[293] It is also the moment when she received notification that the *bolsa de estudios* from the Diputación Provincial de Lugo could not be renewed again.[294] *La Gaceta Literaria* reported of the couple briefly: "RAFAEL ALBERTI. – With Maruja Mallo, in Cercedilla. Both angel hunters, be they spiritual or corporeal, take on in summer the look of kids from the mountains. Up there they are out in the sun, in the open air, and afterwards they return looking like Bedouins."[295]

In the fall, Mallo showed three paintings at the Exposición de Arquitectura y Pintura Modernas held at the Gran Casino in San Sebastián. Moreno Villa gave a lecture there on 9 September about "the new schools of painting," followed by the projection of *Un perro andaluz* and *Esencia de verbena* in the Ateneo Guipuzcoano. A few days later, a poetry recital was given by Alberti.[296] Their last public collaborative act seems to have been a drawing Mallo made to accompany three of Alberti's "light" poems on bullfighting themes, published on 9 November.[297] Also in November, Alberti was introduced by Rodolfo Halffter to his fiancée, Emilia Salas; weeks later Alberti and Mallo gave them as a wedding present a large-format painting that the couple carried across Madrid on foot.[298] Juan Guerrero Ruiz recounts a visit on 18 December made by Alberti and Mallo to his house, to retrieve some manuscripts of poems that Alberti had given to him.[299] Very, very shortly thereafter, their relationship would come to an end.

Alberti and María Teresa León

In 1928, María Teresa León (1903–1988) had published her first book of stories, *Cuentos para soñar* (Burgos: Hijos de Santiago Rodríguez), and undertaken a long tour of Argentina, accompanied by her husband; they separated on their return to Spain at the beginning of 1929.[300] It was in the middle of 1930, however, when she really came into the public eye, with a second book of stories, *La bella del mal amor* (Burgos: Hijos de Santiago Rodríguez), as well as several lectures given in different locales, including one entitled "Estética del amor." The collection was widely reviewed, on 4 July a celebratory "cocktail-concierto" was held at the Ritz Hotel, and she received an encomiastic write-up from Rafael Marquina in *La Gaceta Literaria*.[301]

As regards the timing of her first encounter with Alberti, the evidence is somewhat contradictory. Most testimonies point to a date very late in 1930, and also suggest that once this occurred, things progressed very quickly. Alberti asserts that "I was barely twenty-eight years old when I met her,"[302] and he was born on 16 December 1902. A *terminus ad quem* is their departure together for Mallorca at the beginning of January 1931.

We know that they met at a literary gathering at someone's house during which Alberti read his play *Santa Casilda* (the work that, with Mallo, Alberti had previously shared with the Morla Lynches):

> I met her in the year 1929 [in fact, 1930] ... at the home of a writer whose name was Alberto Valero Martín. I noticed her immediately because she was a very intelligent young woman, but also one of the most beautiful women in Spain ... She was lovely, wonderful, we quickly became close, and thereafter started a life together.[303]

Alberti's earlier account, in *La arboleda perdida*, is more lyrical:

> It was in somebody's home, which I had been taken to but I do not remember by whom. There she appeared before me, blond, beautiful ... That same night, through the streets ... I was already breathing filled up with her, swollen, rejoicing, exalting in her lingering murmur, impelled toward something that I felt was sure and true.[304]

For her part, León remembered that they met:

At the home of a female friend of mine … He was reading *Santa Casilda* and no one was saying anything. Because the people who were listening were fairly frivolous, and the only person who started to talk with him about old ballad cycles and about all those things was me. And he was thrilled, obviously, because I was talking about what he liked so much at that time. Besides, my family is from Burgos; everything coincided with Santa Casilda. And then, when he finished, I said to him: "I'm going home. The car is outside. Do you want me to take you somewhere?" He said: "Yes." And he came with me. We arrived at my house, at my mother's house, and then, at the door, he says: "It's a very fine night. Why don't we take a stroll?" And we started walking down Rosales, and it struck three when we were still walking down Rosales and talking about Spanish ballad cycles.[305]

Again, this matches the earlier, more evocative account provided in León's memoirs, *Memoria de la melancolía*:

That avenue was called Rosales. In that one stroll my life had been decided. Why did we walk together, just after being introduced, in that sweet night, so favourable to lovers? That girl who had gone back to her parents' home after a failed marriage does not know why. She was never able to explain to herself why her eyes fixed on those of the young man … She started out by listening. The young man was reading a theatrical work that recounted a miracle … Thinking it over, she walks in the night beside that unknown young man who wanted to accompany her … and they continue talking calmly, shaking the minutes off their shoulders so that they do not feel them passing … She does not remember clearly if the light of day began to break and then, before separating, they looked at each other, tired from staying up all night but radiant.[306]

León was the niece of Ramón Menéndez Pidal and María Goyri, and according to her cousin Gonzalo Menéndez-Pidal, "immediately following that first encounter, just after they had met, Rafael came to our home with María Teresa and they spent two or three days with us, in San Rafael."[307] León remembered things rather differently:

Shortly thereafter [the reading] I left for the home of Ramón
Menéndez Pidal, in San Rafael, that was the home of my aunt. My
aunt María Goiri. I had gone with my mother. And one morning ...
I went down to open the front door and I found Rafael, sitting there
on the doorstep.[308]

Memoria de la melancolía offers a more lyrical version:

She opened the door and there he was. That young man who had
read that play at the home of her female friends was sitting there on
the doorstep, yes, the young poet interested in Santa Casilda ... The
breeze from the Alto del León[309] was blowing. How can this be the
house of the president of the Academia Española? the young man
was shouting. I've been singing ballads since dawn, and nothing ...
Can I come in? Yes, he could come in ... The slight Andalusian
accent was a good match beside the spring, the pine trees, the mint
plants ... looking at oneself in the stream, seeing one's poor, battered
life pass by, seeing how, on kissing, it was disappearing.[310]

Although her cousin and León both mention San Rafael, they also
differ. Gonzalo offers no date, and specifies that they arrived together.[311]
From María Teresa's description, it seems to be summertime (given
the climate of the Guadarrama), she goes there alone, and the visit is
unexpected and unannounced. According to this alternative chronology,
the reading of *Santa Casilda* would have taken place in late spring or
early summer 1930, with the San Rafael visit shortly thereafter, and then
several months would have elapsed before the two of them decided to act
on their mutual attraction. It is noteworthy that from Cercedilla, where
he was spending time with Mallo, Alberti wrote to Cossío about seeing
Pidal frequently during the summer of 1930, but makes no mention of
María Teresa: "I make many visits to Ramón M. Pidal, who is summering
in San Rafael. For the children of the Instituto-Escuela – 1,200 – he is
going to arrange for me to give a reading of *La pájara pinta*. I will give it
in the main auditorium of the University."[312]

Alberti was with León on 15 December, awaiting the results of an up-
rising against the government launched from the Cuatro Vientos airport

on the heels of Fermín Galán's and Ángel García Hernández's efforts in Jaca, but it was soon thwarted.[313] However, Alberti and Mallo visited Guerrero on 18 December, and Alberti and León left for Mallorca around 4 January, so it seems that Alberti did not finally break with Mallo until the very last days of 1930. One source indicates that Alberti announced his decision to Mallo one afternoon while they were strolling together in Madrid's Jardín Botánico.[314]

However long or short the "overlap," Alberti experienced considerable inner turmoil over the two conflicting love interests:

> the cave-like state in which I was living and the strong light of day that her hair shone on my hands made me go up toward the sun and feel that spring had not died in the world ...
>
> I was extricating myself from another tormenting love, which still tugged at me and made me hesitate before I took refuge in that [other] port ... I struggled, shouted, wept, dragged myself along the ground.[315]

His tone was very different when, many years later, he evoked the same set of circumstances for his second wife: "We were very young and the truth is that we were very much in love. But then María Teresa appeared and she swept away everything that had come before."[316]

At the very beginning of January 1931, then, Alberti and León suddenly, almost clandestinely, left for Mallorca.[317] Juan Guerrero Ruiz was *au courant*. On 7 January, he told Jiménez the following:

> I recount to him briefly the story of Rafael Alberti running away to Mallorca with María Teresa León, which occurred two or three days ago, and he says that he does not understand the need to go off like that when already in Madrid they were "runaways," but at the end of the day "may they be happy and may God protect them." Imagining that this will have made Maruja Mallo deeply upset, he says that it makes him consider holding back the publication of his critical notes, since in the one about false Satanism he was alluding to the influence in the poetry of Alberti of the painting and the poetry of Dalí, and the painting and the costume design of Maruja

Mallo, and that under these circumstances he would not want this to upset her.[318]

And Salinas reported to Guillén on 11 January that

> Alberti was about to premiere his *Santa Casilda*. But the thing is, brace yourself!, that eight days ago he ran off in the company of a beautiful lady, a woman of letters, but a bad writer, María Teresa León, to Mallorca, as was to be expected, leaving me to deal with *Santa Casilda* and Maruja Mallo. It's the AAAAffair. An act of folly. What he's done is not yet known around here because Rafael disappeared without saying anything at his home. But I know everything, as always. I think that he'll return, in time to have the premiere. The kid is travelling, evidently, with all expenses paid, and with this act crowns his moral history. At all events the gesture has pleased me, because it shows me that there is something for Alberti even more important than vanity and the desire for success. The bad part of it is that *other thing*.[319]

The phrase "leaving me to deal with *Santa Casilda* and Maruja Mallo" is particularly important: evidently, up until the last moment Alberti was planning on premiering the work with the Santiago Artigas-Josefina Díaz company, which had undertaken a long Latin American tour before returning to Spain on 6 January.[320] Likewise, Mallo was very much involved in plans for the staging, and Salinas implies that for her, both professionally and personally, Alberti's *scappata* came as a complete surprise.[321]

In *La arboleda perdida*, Alberti portrays León as the one who takes him to Mallorca, as is confirmed, more prosaically, by Salinas ("he is going all expenses paid"): "to allow myself finally, after so much struggle, to be happily carried off and to wake up one morning on the beaches of Sóller, beside the blue, unique Mediterranean of the Balearic Islands."[322] Salinas calls it "the AAAAffair," and Alberti confirms that "malicious echoes of what many in Madrid believed to be just a fling started to reach us ... They were out looking for a scandal, as this George Sand – a writer, married, and as yet not divorced – was very well-known."[323] León offers a similar memory: "'Who is this George Sand who had abducted

Chopin-Alberti? Another idyll in Valldemosa?,' they wrote scandalously in one newspaper."[324] However, to date I have only found in the press one mildly ironic, indirect allusion, imagining a telegram that Alberti might send from the Balearic Islands.[325] They returned to Madrid a couple of weeks later, and on 26 January Alberti gave yet another reading of *Santa Casilda*, now at the Residencia de Señoritas.[326] Writing to Cossío, Diego reported on 25 January that "I have finished the selection for the *Antología* and I'm waiting for the last texts to be sent in. Alberti sent me things from Sóller (Mallorca). He must be back in Madrid by now."[327]

Juan Ramón Jiménez's essay in *La Gaceta Literaria* on 15 January was strikingly vituperative in tone, and evidently he – or Giménez Caballero – had had second thoughts about holding it back to spare Mallo's feelings.[328] In the second section, "Satanismo inverso," Jiménez makes a distinction between an "agile Satanism" and an "unhealthy, wretched ... Satanism of obscene aesthetics, of black mass, of Masonic mumbo-jumbo of the uncultured variety." He had hoped that with Remy de Gourmont this latter had ended, but unfortunately not:

This Satanism that is a vain farce, which I believed unable to return so soon, and [especially] in a period of nakedness, clarity, and intelligence like our own, nowadays unfortunately fills at least a half overall of the young people's art. (Among us: Salvador Dalí, on the other hand in control of his technique and his imagination; one or other friend of his, still very rough around the edges; María Mallo, highly skilled in coupling together picture-prints of garbage; Rafael Alberti, lamentably cut off from his own fine, natural being by the greenish-white transfer-prints[329] of Maria Mallo and the pen and the paintbrush of Salvador Dalí, who are swamping the new Spanish spring with their ingenuous, philistine mock-dreadfulness, which they have absorbed from the worst of German Expressionism and the most spectacular of French Surrealism.)[330]

As ever, Salinas had his finger on the pulse of events: "Alberti, who has already returned from his Chopin-esque escapade in Mallorca, in a lecture called J.R. a sylvan fairy and a confused busybody. Those articles of his really ticked off the youngsters.[331] And I understand it."[332] The letter is from 1 February, so the "lecture" would refer to Alberti's recent appearance at the Residencia de Señoritas on 26 January.

Still, for Alberti, Mallo, Dalí, and León, Jiménez's vitriolic attacks were largely irrelevant. Mallo left for Paris, alone, late in 1931, with a grant from the Junta para Ampliación de Estudios to study stage design, while Alberti finally abandoned *Santa Casilda* and quickly substituted *El hombre deshabitado* for a February premiere after León had introduced him to the Mexican actress María Teresa Montoya.[333] But all that is another story.

Conclusion

Romantic relationships and marriages between individuals working in the creative arts were not uncommon. Celso Lagar married the sculptor Hortense Bégué, Daniel Vázquez Díaz married the sculptor Eva Preetsman Aggerholm, the writer Rosa Chacel (who started out as a sculptor) married the painter Timoteo Pérez Rubio, and this was far from the only marriage to result from relationships between students enrolled at the Escuela Especial. These examples could be multiplied many times over. As remarked upon above, it is actually rather surprising that Mallo and Alberti did not meet sooner than the middle of 1925, but once they did the relationship became a major factor in their lives for the next five years, spanning a period – the second half of the 1920s – that saw the creation of two of Mallo's most important series of works, *Verbenas* (and *Estampas*) and *Cloacas y campanarios*, and also of what is arguably Alberti's most famous collection of poetry, *Sobre los ángeles*. It is surely true that none of those works would have been as they were, and conceivably might not even have existed at all, had the two not been in the intimate relationship documented here. Also of great interest are the various collaborative projects, all of which unfortunately remained at some inconclusive point in their evolution, that of *Yo era un tonto/Los cómicos del cine* probably offering us today the best, though still incomplete, idea of what it might have looked like had it been brought to fruition. Ultimately, Mallo and Alberti are examples of two hubs with their corresponding networks who for a substantial period of time came together to form what might be thought of as a joint hub. Members of Mallo's circle, whom Alberti did not already know, would have been introduced to him, and vice versa; additionally, operating jointly, they went on to form other bonds during the period 1925–30. Their silence, relative or absolute, about the relationship over the many subsequent decades only speaks more loudly of its importance to both of them.

EPILOGUE

The five case studies presented here, with their different principal figures and the wide range of other individuals clustered around them, offer many examples of the tightly knit community that is the focus of this book. Although the subjects of the case studies are diverse, there are a number of instances of direct acquaintance or friendship between them, and we can be sure that none of them was distanced by more than one degree of separation. Thus, even if Barradas did not meet them directly, he is connected with Manuel Ángeles Ortiz or Julio Moisés via a number of artist friends in common, Victorina Durán and Delhy Tejero both knew Mallo from the Escuela Especial, and only a scarcity of biographical information about Joaquina Zamora Sarrate prevents us from extending that datum to her as well, and so on and so forth. Indeed, the more knowledge that we have about an individual from this period, the more we are able to appreciate how deeply imbricated they were in the cultural circles of the day. This is particularly true of someone like García Lorca – the most highly researched person to be mentioned here, who was a personal friend of Barradas, Manuel Ángeles Ortiz, Mallo, García Maroto, and Alberti, and who was acquainted with a large percentage of the many other figures mentioned in this book, ranging from Juan Ramón Jiménez, to all the members of the Rinconcillo group who moved to Madrid, to Dalí and many other student artists at the Escuela Especial, and on and on. Thus, while in most standard descriptions of these years Lorca is represented as a hub – a veritable magnet – around which many others from the worlds of arts and letters circulated, it is salutary also to consider an alternative view, whereby he is seen not as the centre of multiple radiating spokes but rather as a sinuous thread weaving laterally through a large assortment of different milieus.

Likewise, there are many examples of the importance of certain locations and the functions that they perform. Sites of sociability are key in this story, both for initial encounters and developing friendships, and it is important to note that both chance and volition are involved here: Barradas and Alberto happened to frequent the same café and happened to meet, whereas others were attracted to a certain *tertulia* because of its reputation or were persuaded to go along because of a friend. Places of study, too, are crucial, as illustrated by the Academia Libre or the Escuela Especial, where many more or less like-minded people came together and where many friendships, and indeed a number of romances, developed. In these five chapters residential sites are, comparatively speaking, the least prominent of the three, but we should not underestimate their importance, as seen in the hub constituted by Ángeles Ortiz's studio in the Pasaje de la Alhambra or the first encounter between María Luisa González Rodríguez and Luis Buñuel at the summer student residence, nor should it be forgotten that detailed consideration of the role of the Residencia de Estudiantes has been deliberately sidelined here.

Evidently, these kinds of case studies could be multiplied many times over, extending to other writers, artists, and practitioners of all the other arts. The scope for exploration is virtually limitless. There are numerous figures who are self-recommending in that they are illustrative of many of the features associated with the closely linked circles that are my focus. Thus, for example, José María Hinojosa, a poet on the margins of the group of the so-called Generation of 1927, who moved between Málaga, Madrid, and Paris; Ernesto Giménez Caballero, a writer, critic, essayist, and editor of *La Gaceta Literaria*; Guillermo de Torre, whose trajectory took him from his early days at the centre of the Ultra movement, to his role as a critic, his marriage with Norah Borges, the time spent in Buenos Aires, and then his work at the Centro de Estudios Históricos in the 1930s; Rosa Chacel, who bridged the art and literary worlds and, after returning from the time spent in Rome (1922–27), moved through many spheres of Madrid's cultural scene; Daniel Vázquez Díaz, who after his move back to Madrid in 1918 was friendly with the *ultraístas*, Barradas, Maroto, Alberti, Giménez Caballero, and a great many others; or that small knot of progressive art critics made up most notably of Manuel Abril, José Francés, and Juan de la Encina.

Furthermore, beyond serving to enhance our knowledge and understanding of this particularly active and productive period in Spanish cultural history, it is my hope that the kinds of analysis applied here, involving human networks and sites of engagement, might have broader methodological implications and value, inasmuch that they should be applicable to many cultural scenes – any of those where direct interpersonal contact was a key feature of how they functioned. In theory, then, one might study the literary and artistic culture of Vienna, Berlin, Paris, London, or New York through this lens, but more specifically it should be particularly appropriate for those cities that in the nineteenth and twentieth centuries were somewhat smaller in population size. These would have tended to create the particular set of circumstances necessary to bring about that situation described in the book's introduction, where everybody who belonged to these circles would indeed have known just about everybody else. Besides Madrid, one thinks of places like Barcelona, Lisbon, Zurich, Amsterdam, Frankfurt, Munich, Dresden, Prague, Chicago, San Francisco, Quebec City, Montreal, Toronto, Vancouver, or Mexico City and Buenos Aires (before they underwent massive expansion). This kind of approach, therefore, should have the potential for wide cross-applicability as well as being instrumental in directing more attention to cultural scenes operating in the many lesser-studied urban spaces.

APPENDIX 1

Contributors to the Magazine *Alfar*[1]

Miscellaneous Contributors

Manuel Abril: 24, 25, 27, 32, 34, 36, 45, 47, 48, 49, 51, 60

Alberto: 28, 31, 33, 38

Carmen Barradas: 25, 31

Jorge Luis Borges: 36, 40, 41, 59

Luis Buñuel: 26, 29

Salvador Dalí: 32, 36, 40

José Francés: 25

Gabriel García Maroto: 33

Enrique Garrán: 34, 36

Ramón Gómez de la Serna: 27, 31, 32, 33, 34, 35, 40, 43, 58

Antonio de Ignacios: 23, 24, 28, 33

Benjamín Jarnés: 31, 32, 34, 35, 36, 38, 40, 41, 43, 44, 45, 47, 53, 54, 54, 59, 60

Huberto Pérez de la Ossa: 28, 31, 34, 38, 42, 44, 47

Ultraísta Poets

Rogelio Buendía: 41, 43, 46, 49

Rafael Cansinos Assens: 36

César A. Comet: 31, 53, 58, 60

Evaristo Correa Calderón: 23

Pedro Garfias: 24, 25, 26, 34, 37

Juan G. Olmedilla: 30

Jaime Ibarra: 54, 57, 58

Ernesto López-Parra: 32

Tomás Luque: 29

Eugenio Montes: 26, 28

Luis Mosquera: 50

1 Numerals refer to issue numbers. Those analyzed and listed here run from number 23 (November 1922) through number 60 (August–September 1926), the span of Casal's editorship.

Emilio Mosteiro: 58

Eduardo de Ontañón: 32, 33, 38, 46

Miguel Pérez Ferrero: 57, 59, 60

Eliodoro Puche: 31

José Rivas Panedas: 36

Guillermo de Torre: 26, 27, 28, 29, 30, 32, 34, 35, 37, 39, 42, 45, 50, 52, 60

Adriano del Valle: 39, 41, 42, 44, 46, 50, 53, 55, 58

Francisco Vighi: 42, 53

Poets Close to *Ultraísmo*

Mauricio Bacarisse: 47, 49, 60

Francisco Luis Bernárdez: 27, 28, 31, 45, 46

Juan Chabás: 29, 31, 36, 38, 43, 49, 52, 53, 54, 54, 56

Gerardo Diego: 40, 45, 47, 47, 50, 60

Antonio Espina: 37, 53, 57

Juan Gutiérrez Gili: 28, 54, 56, 57

Francisco Martínez Corbalán: 41, 46

Artists Affiliated with or Close to *Ultraísmo*

Francisco Bores: 29, 31, 32, 36, 38, 42, 44, 47, 50, 54

Norah Borges: 27, 27, 28, 32, 33, 36, 39, 44, 49

Sonia Delaunay: 35

Ángel Ferrant: 25, 32, 34, 35, 36, 37, 38, 39, 42, 46

Marjan Paszkiewicz: 37, 38, 41, 44, 60

Daniel Vázquez Díaz: 38, 39, 41, 42, 44

APPENDIX 2

Books and Periodical Publications by Gabriel García Maroto

Books by Gabriel García Maroto

Del jardín del arte. Joyas esmaltadas por el pintor Gabriel García Maroto en el año de MCMXI. Madrid: Imprenta Helénica, 1911.

La caravana pasa. Libro escrito para alivio de caminantes, solaz de mozas enamoradas y entretenimiento de pícaros y hampones. La Solana: Imprenta de Rogelio de la O, 1912.

El año artístico. Relación de sucesos acaecidos al arte español en el año mil novecientos doce. Madrid: Imprenta de José Fernández Arias, 1913.

Pro-arte. El prestigio de un cuadro. Madrid: Imprenta de José Fernández Arias, 1913. Pamphlet.

La canción interior. La Solana: Imprenta de Rogelio de la O, 1914.

El naturalismo, el regionalismo y la decadencia del arte. Salamanca: El Autor, 1914. Pamphlet.

Teoría de las artes nobles. Elementos de filosofía e historia del arte español. Vol. 1, *La pintura en España.* La Solana: Imprenta de Rogelio de la O, 1914.

Federico Beltrán y la Exposición Nacional de Bellas Artes de MCMXV. Madrid: Imprenta Española, 1915.

El libro de todos los días. Barcelona: Oliva de Vilanova Impresor, 1915.

Los senderos: Poemas. Barcelona: Biblioteca Dragonné/Imprenta de Pedro Ortega, 1916.

Catálogo de la exposición de pinturas y dibujos de Maroto. (Con un poema en verso del mismo autor). Palma de Mallorca: Salón de la Veda, 1923.

Madrid visto por un pintor. 37 escorzos, temas para cuadros futuros por Maroto con un retrato de este por Barradas. Madrid: Revista de Occidente/Imprenta Maroto, 1925. Series: La vida en torno, 1.

Toledo visto por un pintor: 40 escorzos, temas para cuadros futuros. Madrid: Revista de Occidente/Imprenta Maroto, 1925. Series: La vida en torno, 2.

El plástico. Madrid. Esbozos. Madrid: Revista de Occidente, 1926.

La revolución artística mexicana: Una lección. Madrid: El Autor/Imprenta E. Giménez, 1926.

*La nueva España 1930: Resumen de la vida artística española desde el año
    1927 hasta hoy.* Madrid: Ediciones Biblos, 1927. Facsimile reprint: *La nueva
    España, 1930.* Edited by José Luis Morales y Marín. Madrid: Tecnos, 1988.

Ed. *Almanaque de las artes y las letras para 1928.* Madrid: Biblioteca Acción,
    [1927].

Andalucía vista por el pintor Maroto: 105 dibujos y 25 glosas. Madrid: Biblos, 1927.

Castilla. Madrid: Biblioteca Acción, 1927.

La España mágica. Madrid: Biblioteca Acción, 1927. Series: La vida en torno.

Jesús entre nosotros. Con 33 dibujos en color de Maroto. *Textos del Evangelio
    según la versión del Padre Petit.* Madrid: Biblioteca Acción, 1927.

Manuel de Falla. 5 dibujos de Maroto. 5 autógrafos del maestro. Madrid:
    La Gaceta Literaria, 1927. Series: La vida en torno.

Un pueblo de Mallorca. Madrid: Biblioteca Acción, 1927.

La ría de Bilbao. Madrid: La Gaceta Literaria, 1927.

Verbena de Madrid: 15 dibujos de Maroto. Madrid: La Gaceta Literaria, 1927.

25 dibujos de temas andaluces. Málaga: Litoral, 1927.

*65 dibujos, grabados y pinturas, con una autocrítica y diferentes opiniones
    acerca de este autor.* Madrid: Biblos, 1927.

Ed. *Galería de poetas nuevos de México* [cover]/*Nueva antología de poetas
    mexicanos* [title page]. Selección y grabados de Maroto. Madrid: La Gaceta
    Literaria, 1928.

Veinte dibujos mexicanos. Comentario de Jaime Torres Bodet. Madrid:
    Biblioteca Acción, 1928.

Antonia Mercé, la Argentina. New York: Instituto de las Españas en los Estados
    Unidos, 1930. Co-authored with Ángel del Río, Federico García Lorca, and
    Federico de Onís.

20 grabados en madera: Cuba. Havana: [n.p.], October 1931.

Acción artística popular: 24 grabados en madera. Morelia: Edición del
    Gobierno del Estado de Michoacán, 1932.

Seis meses de acción artística popular, Michoacán, México. Morelia: Edición
    del Gobierno del Estado de Michoacán, 1932.

*Al servicio de los sordos mudos. Cómo se enseña. Nuevas maneras de enseñar.
    Una actitud social educativa.* Madrid: [n.p.], 1934.

Los caricaturistas y la guerra española. Madrid: Ediciones Españolas, 1937.

Un jefe del Ejército Popular: Teniente Coronel Joaquín Pérez Salas. Pozoblanco:
    Colectiva Linares, 1937.

Hombre y pueblo. Mexico City: Publicaciones "Hora de México," 1940.
  Series: Hora de México, 1.

El Valle de México. Gesto y resonancia. Mexico City: Industria Gráfica, 1941.

México en guerra. Esquema de una interpretación. Mexico City: Editorial
  Independencia, 1943. Published under the pseudonym Maclovio Flores.

Acción plástica popular. Educación y aprendizaje a escala nacional. Con
  ciento cinco reproducciones. Mexico City: Editorial Plástica Americana,
  1945. Series: Plástica Mexicana, 1.

Arquitectura popular de México. Mexico City: INBA, 1954. Co-authored with
  Enrique Yáñez.

Promoción de México. Caminos hacia su integración. Raíces. Esfuerzos.
  Testimonios. Mexico City: Guías Mexicanas-Enciclopedia Nacional, 1958.

Periodical Publications by Gabriel García Maroto

"Crónica. Noche en Toledo." *La Tarde* (Toledo) 1, no. 16 (12 March 1909): 1.

"Sobre la Exposición." *El País*, 12 September 1910, 1.

"Sobre la Exposición. El jurado de pintura." *El País*, 16 September 1910, 1.

"Sobre la Exposición. III." *El País*, 5 October 1910, 1.

"Sobre la Exposición. IV." *El País*, 20 October 1910, 2.

"Exposición de Arte Decorativo." *El País*, 17 October 1911, 2.

"De arte. El escultor Julio-Antonio." *Vida Manchega. Revista Semanal*
  Ilustrada (Ciudad Real) 1, no. 1 (7 March 1912): n.p.

"Exposición Villodas." *El País*, 20 March 1912, 2.

"De Bellas Artes. Chicharro renuncia a luchar con Pinazo. – Nobleza obliga."
  El País, 14 April 1912, 1.

"Para la Exposición. Federico Beltrán, pintor de retratos." *El País*, 22 April 1912, 1.

"Divagaciones sentimentales." *Vida Manchega. Revista Semanal Ilustrada*
  (Ciudad Real) 1, no. 12 (20 June 1912): n.p.

"Ángel Andrade. Pintor ilustre." *Vida Manchega. Revista Semanal Ilustrada*
  (Ciudad Real) 1, no. 20 (15 August 1912): n.p.

"El Museo del Prado. Los humos de la fábrica." *El País*, 24 January 1913, 2.

"La ronda." *Vida Manchega. Revista Semanal Ilustrada* (Ciudad Real) 2, no. 57
  (8 May 1913): n.p.

"Ignacio Zuloaga." *El Adelantado de Segovia*, 19 May 1913.

"Oraciones." *El Adelanto*, 30 September 1913, 2.

"La lluvia maligna." *El Adelanto*, 3 November 1913, 1.

"Letras salmantinas. Inquietudes." *El Adelanto*, 26 November 1913, 2.

"Letras salmantinas. Inquietudes." *El Adelanto*, 13 February 1914, 1.

"De colaboración. Arte y artistas." *El Adelanto*, 29 April 1914, 1.

"Gracias al Señor." *Vida Manchega. Revista Regional Ilustrada* (Ciudad Real) 3, no. 117 (10 July 1914): n.p.

"Páginas ingenuas. Mi hermano Cándido." *Vida Manchega. Revista Semanal Ilustrada* (Ciudad Real) 3, no. 122 (25 September 1914): n.p.

"Acordes." *El Adelanto*, 18 April 1918, 1.

"Campanas bautismales. Glosario de la vida humilde." *La Voz de Liébana. Decenario Regional de Intereses Generales* (Potes) 15, no. 608 (5 August 1918): 3–4 [Maroto's text paginated 1–4].

[Untitled.] *La Voz de Liébana. Decenario Regional de Intereses Generales* (Potes) 15, no. 624 (15 January 1919): 3–4 [Maroto's text paginated 53–6].

"Desde París. El Teatro de 'El Viejo Palomar.'" *La Esfera* 7, no. 339 (3 July 1920): n.p.

"Desde París. Bourdelle en el Salón Nacional." *La Esfera* 7, no. 342 (24 July 1920): n.p.

"Temas aldeanos. Viene el rey." *España* 6, no. 279 (4 September 1920): 11–12.

"Los bellos caminos españoles. Un viaje al valle de Liévana." *La Esfera* 7, no. 351 (25 September 1920): n.p.

"Temas aldeanos. El invierno en la villa." *La Esfera* 8, no. 365 (1 January 1921): n.p.

"Color y ritmo. I. Falta de atención. II. El franciscanismo y el valor estético de Darío de Regoyos." *Índice. (Revista Mensual)*, no. 1 (1921): 13–14.

"Temas sin importancia. Ecequiel, mi amigo." *La Esfera* 10, no. 471 (13 January 1923): n.p.

"El teatro español en París. *El señor de Pigmalión*, de Jacinto Grau." *La Esfera* 10, no. 487 (5 May 1923): n.p.

"Polémica artística. Esquema de una conferencia. El pintor Maroto replica a Baroja." *Heraldo de Madrid*, 7 April 1925, 4.

"Polémica artística. Esquema de una conferencia. El pintor Maroto replica a Baroja. Baroja le contesta a Vegue." *Heraldo de Madrid*, 8 April 1925, 4.

"El viaducto (Escorzos)." *Revista de Occidente* 9, no. 26 (August 1925): 191–7.

"En torno a la Exposición Alejandro Ferrant (Sociedad Amigos del Arte)." *Arte Español. Revista de la Sociedad Española de Amigos de Arte* 15, no. 3 (1926): 130–3.

"Nuevo descubrimiento de España. Tierras de Segovia." *Revista de las Españas*, segunda época, 1, no. 2 (August 1926): 101–6.

"Escorzos. Elegía de Sepúlveda." *La Esfera* 13, no. 663 (18 September 1926): 20.

"El concurso nacional de escultura. Ángel Ferrant." *Nuevo Mundo* 33, no. 1711 (5 November 1926): n.p.

"Al margen de una interesante exposición artística. Medalla de Ignacio Zuloaga." *Nuevo Mundo* 33, no. 1714 (26 November 1926): n.p.

"Arte y artistas. Prisma de Ignacio Zuloaga." *Nuevo Mundo* 33, no. 1715 (3 December 1926): n.p.

"Escorzos. Toledo visto por un pintor." *La Esfera* 14, no. 678 (1 January 1927): 81.

"Escorzos. Convento en Castilla." *La Esfera* 14, no. 680 (15 January 1927): 4.

"Arte. El arte de hoy. I. La dominante óptica." *La Gaceta Literaria* 1, no. 2 (15 January 1927): 5.

"La joven pintura mexicana." *Nuevo Mundo* 34, no. 1722 (21 January 1927): n.p.

"Nuevo descubrimiento de España. La ría de Bilbao." *Revista de las Españas* 2, nos 5–6 (January–February 1927): n.p.

"Carnaval en Castilla." *La Esfera* 14, no. 687 (5 March 1927): 34.

"Arte y artistas. Exposición de artistas andaluces. Diálogo entre él y yo." *Nuevo Mundo* 34, no. 1731 (25 March 1927): n.p.

"Arte y artistas. Maestros y críticos. La enseñanza del arte. Carta abierta a los críticos de arte españoles." *Nuevo Mundo* 34, no. 1733 (8 April 1927): n.p.

"Tierras de Segovia. Mercado en la ciudad." *Heraldo de Madrid*, 22 April 1927, 7.

"Tierras de Segovia. La posada. II." *Heraldo de Madrid*, 29 April 1927, 7.

"Tierras de Segovia. Pueblos del camino. III." *Heraldo de Madrid*, 6 May 1927, 7.

"Un debate apasionado. Campeonato para un meridiano intelectual." *La Gaceta Literaria* 1, no. 17 (1 September 1927): 3.

"Verbena madrileña." *Nuevo Mundo* 34, no. 1755 (9 September 1927): n.p.

"Iglesias de México: las cúpulas." *La Esfera* 14, no. 714 (10 September 1927): 10–11.

"Un pueblo de Castilla." *La Gaceta Literaria* 1, no. 19 (1 October 1927): 2.

"Castilla. La romería." *Nuevo Mundo* 34, no. 1763 (4 November 1927): n.p.

"Juan de la Encina. Crítico de arte, conservador y reconstructor o el alguacil alguacilado." *La Gaceta Literaria* 1, no. 22 (15 November 1927): 1–2.

"La revolución artística mexicana: una lección." *Forma* (Mexico) 1, no. 4 (1927): 8–16.

"*Goya en zig-zag.*" *Contemporáneos*, no. 4 (September 1928): 101–4.

NOTES

Introduction

1   For many evocative photographs of leading members of this older group, see Lasaga's *El Madrid de José Ortega y Gasset*.

2   On the city's "village feel," and the high likelihood of bumping into an acquaintance on the street, see Sinclair, *Trafficking Knowledge*, 182. For Madrid as urban space, see Ugarte, *Madrid 1900*; Parsons, *A Cultural History of Madrid*; Ramos, *Construyendo la modernidad*; and Larson, *Constructing and Resisting Modernity*. Other aspects are treated by Barrantes Martín, *Ciudad y modernidad*, and Diéguez Patao, *La generación del 25*.

3   Dozo and Fréché, "Réseaux et bases de données," 87, 90–1.

4   See Mitchell, "Network Procedures," 73–5, and Milroy and Milroy, "Social Network and Social Class," 3–6. The Milroys distinguish between structural and interactional ties within the network; I am interested in the formation of the former and in the nature of the latter.

5   The notion of "social space" can be traced back to Durkheim. Bachelard, Lefebvre, Tuan, De Certeau, and Thacker, among others, have made significant contributions to our understanding of the twin concepts of place and space. Broadly speaking, what emerges is an association of place with fixity and affective belonging and of space with movement and change (Palomares-Salas, *The Spatiality*, 2, 3, 9, 30). In terms borrowed from De Certeau, therefore, the sites of engagement to which I refer could be seen, *mutatis mutandis*, as well-defined places that are also activated as porous spaces, given their dimension of social interaction (*The Practice of Everyday Life*, 117).

6   Furthermore, as Sapiro and Nooy each point out, Bourdieu is fundamentally interested in objective relations based on the properties that characterize individuals or organizations, relations whose identification leads to the detection of underlying structures, whereas the analysis of networks focuses on the pattern of easily observable connections created by a multiplicitiy of subjective interactions: Sapiro, "Réseaux, institution(s) et champ," 45–7, 49; Nooy, "Fields and Networks," 305, 309, 312, 315–16.

7   As I documented in *El veintisiete en tela de juicio*, 22–65, the label *la joven literatura* (literally, the young literature) was that most often adopted in 1920s Spain for the emerging writers, and for a considerable time it became the most widely accepted term.

8   As Dozo and Fréché recognize, any web needs to be charted not just in space but also over time: "Réseaux et bases de données," 87.

9   Anderson, *La recepción de las vanguardias*, 7–12.

10 See Anderson, *El momento ultraísta* and *La recepción de las vanguardias*.

11 See Anderson, *Ernesto Giménez Caballero*.

12   This Spanish term has no direct translation; on its range of meanings, see the subsection entitled "The *Tertulia* and the Café" in chapter 1.

13   The title of the book jointly edited by Navarrete Navarrete and Lozano Marín, *Redes literarias en la poesía española del primer tercio del siglo XX*, appears very promising, but its contents do not push the field forward in any methodologically significant way.

14   See Anderson, *El veintisiete en tela de juicio.*

15   García-Posada, *Acelerado sueño*, 37–8.

16   Ascunce, *Barcelona and Madrid*, 17–56.

17   Ibid., 25.

18   Ibid., 11–12, and see 155.

19   Ibid., xxv, xxvii, 28.

20   Ibid., 25–6.

21   Ibid., 25, and see 81. The Revistas de la Edad de Plata website now offers an extensive network analysis of little magazines from this period. http://nrevistasedp.edaddeplata.org/#/.

22   Ascunce, *Barcelona and Madrid*, 124.

23   Alison Sinclair, *Trafficking Knowledge in Early Twentieth-Century Spain*, 182.

Chapter One

1   Following Sirinelli's observations in "Le hazard," 103–5, Trebitsch identifies three "degrees" of sociability: interactions that are just part of everyday life; interactions that result from some kind of group mentality; and strictly political forms of social organization ("Avant-propos," 13–14). I prefer to envisage this as operating on a continuous spectrum that would encompass those discrete categories.

2   There is an extensive bibliography on the salon, including Huddleston, *Bohemian, Literary and Social Life*; Mannheim, *Essays on the Sociology of Culture*; Elias, *The Civilizing Process*; Landes, *Women and the Public Sphere*; Habermas, *The Structural Transformation*; Harth, *Cartesian Women*; Goodman, *The Republic of Letters*; Pekacz, *Conservative Tradition*; Kale, *French Salons*; and Leroy, "La mondaine littéraire." For other French salons contemporary with Stein's, see Tedeschini Lalli, "A Knot of Salons."

3   For the earlier period, see the book by the foremost writer of *crónicas de salones*, Eugenio Rodríguez Ruiz de la Escalera (1856–1933), published under his pen name of Monte-Cristo, *Los salones de Madrid*, as well as Espina, *Las tertulias de Madrid*, 61–8, 96–102, 192.

4   Cansinos Assens, *La novela de un literato*, vol. 1, *1882–1914*, 194–8, 274–80, 333–6, 363–7, 369–74, 394–5, 432–6, 443–7, 448–51, 470–2.

5   The dictionary of the Real Academia Española (Spanish Royal Academy) makes little distinction between *tertulia* and one near synonym, *cenáculo*, though the latter term is definitely more archaic and can suggest a group with more closely aligned viewpoints; another term, *peña*, refers more to

the group of people involved (rather than the gathering), a group with some degree of internal cohesion and whose members meet with some regularity.

6   There is at least one documented case of a peripatetic *tertulia*, which circulated around six or seven different cafés over consecutive Saturdays. See González-Ruano, *Memorias*, 98, and Ayala, *Recuerdos y olvidos*, 90.

7   Rittner, Haine, and Jackson, eds, *The Thinking Space*.

8   Pinsker, *A Rich Brew*.

9   *Los cafés históricos*, 20–2, 199–202. See also Mannheim, *Essays on the Sociology of Culture*, 138–40.

10 The relevant sections are "El café," 9–157, "Algunos cafés vivos," 158–83, "Cafés extranjeros," 183–94, and "Más sobre los cafés y figones típicos de Madrid," 194–262.

11 *Heraldo de Madrid*, 20 August 1929, 7; 27 August 1929 [not seen; page number unavailable]; 3 September 1929, 12; 10 September 1929, 12; 17 September 1929, 12; 24 September 1929, 7; 1 October 1929, 7; 8 October 1929, 7; 22 October 1929, 10; 29 October 1929, 12; 5 November 1929, 10; 12 November 1929, 12; 19 November 1929, 7.

12 Forcada Cabanellas, *De la vida literaria*, 89–102.

13 *Panorama de Madrid. Florilegio de los cafés; Panorama de Madrid. Tertulias literarias*.

14 Save for the register of names of attendees kept by Gómez de la Serna (Reyes, *Tertulia de Madrid*, 100), and which must have served as the basis for the two books about his own *tertulia*, *Pombo* and *La sagrada cripta de Pombo*.

15 *Los cafés históricos*, 13.

16 *Las tertulias románticas en España*.

17 *Tertulias y grupos literarios*.

18 *Aquellas tertulias de Madrid*.

19 Díaz, *Madrid. Tabernas, botillerías y cafés*; Río López, *Los viejos cafés de Madrid*.

20 *Las tertulias de Madrid*.

21 "La tertulia de café," in *Arte y oficio de hablar*, 87–112.

22 *Tertulias, mentideros y programas de radio*. The next logical step would be an analysis of "talk shows" on television.

23 Gómez-Santos, *Crónica del Café Gijón*; Umbral, *La noche que llegué*; Tudela et al., *Café Gijón*.

24 Alaminos López, *Ramón y Pombo*.

25 Díaz Cañabate, *Historia de una tertulia*.

26 Bonet Correa, *Los cafés históricos*. For a briefer, academic approach, see Otero Carvajal, "Ciencia y cultura en Madrid."

27 *The Spatiality*, 75–105.

28 *Las tertulias de Madrid*, 32.

29 "Jardines de Recreo," Madripedia, accessed 24 May 2022, https://madripedia.wikis.cc/wiki/Jardines_de_Recreo; "Los Jardines de Recreo," El paisaje

de Madrid, 28 May 2014, http://elpaisajedemadrid.blogspot.com/2014/05/
los-jardines-de-recreo.html.

30   Not casinos in the English sense of the word; they were closer to the notion
     of a gentlemen's club, though not as exclusive.

31   *Las tertulias de Madrid*, 33–4, 45–7, 90–2.

32   *Sucedió*, 202–3.

33   See chapter 3.

34   Anderson, *El momento ultraísta*, 102–3, 524, 529.

35   Ibid., 143–4.

36   Cansinos Assens, *La novela de un literato*, vol. 1, *1882–1914*, 38–57.

37   Espina, *Las tertulias de Madrid*, 196–208.

38   See "El Parnasillo," Teatro Español y Naves del Español, accessed 24 May
     2022, https://www.teatroespanol.es/espacios/el-parnasillo.

39   Espina, *Las tertulias de Madrid*, 211–13. In this regard, Martínez Martín
     highlights the importance of the *tertulia* at the Librería de Fernando Fe:
     Vivir de la pluma, 175.

40   Cansinos Asséns, *La novela de un literato*, vol. 1, *1882–1914*, 376–8.

41   Huidobro, "Al fin se descubre mi maestro," 3; Torre, "Guillaume Apollinaire,"
     19–20; Torre, "La polémica del creacionismo," 115.

42   Torre, *Tan pronto ayer*, 67.

43   "Rafael Cansinos Assens," 218.

44   "Concha Espina."

45   F.A. [Francisco Ayala], "Las tertulias literarias. La Granja," 115. At first sight,
     it seems as if Luengo López's article, "Tazas calientes manchadas de car-
     mín," will address this issue, and indeed he does mention, briefly, Chacel and
     Mallo, as well as María Blanchard, and identifies La Granja El Henar (86) as
     one of the first cafés where it was more usual to see women participating in
     tertulias. However, much of the essay is concerned with conventional public
     opinion about unaccompanied women and the so-called *cafés de camareras*
     (cafés with waitresses).

46   My sense is that the notion of *artes industriales* here and elsewhere covers at
     least part of the areas of design, applied arts, and decorative arts.

47   Eiroa San Francisco, "El Lyceum Club," 206.

48   Durán, *Sucedió*, 217.

49   Ibid., 219.

50   Still, one can be sure that an interloper who sat at the café table of a *tertulia*
     in session would hardly have been welcome.

51   The Fígaro in question is the early nineteenth-century writer Mariano José
     de Larra. See Anderson, *El momento ultraísta*, 75, 129, 129n17, 143.

52   There is a splendid group photo of the event in Sánchez Ron et al., eds,
     El laboratorio de España, 136–7.

53   Feast in Honour of Figaro; Banquet for All the Members of the Pombo *Ter-
     tulia* in Alphabetical Order; Banquet in Honour of Mr Nobody; First Pombo

Lectisternium; Banquet of Period Physiognomies and Costume, or Dinner for Ancestors.

54 Anderson, *El momento ultraísta*, 86.

55 Laget, in "'La cuestión palpitante y manducante,'" provides a well-documented history.

56 The bibliography on the Ateneo is fairly extensive, and includes Forcada Cabanellas, "Del Ateneo de Madrid," in *De la vida literaria*, 113–27; García Martí, *El Ateneo de Madrid*; Araujo-Costa, *Biografía del Ateneo de Madrid*; Ruiz Salvador, *El Ateneo Científico, Literario y Artístico de Madrid*; Ruiz Salvador, *Ateneo, dictadura y república*; Villacorta Baños, *El Ateneo Científico, Literario y Artístico de Madrid*; Abellán, *El Ateneo de Madrid*; Olmos, *Ágora de la libertad*; and Ezama Gil, *Las musas suben a la tribuna*.

57 Espina rehearses some of its history and significance in *Las tertulias de Madrid*, 213–20. For other interesting comments, see Sinclair, *Trafficking Knowledge*, 182, 187.

58 González-Ruano reports being able to enter easily without being a member: *Memorias*, 103. He goes on to give a colourful account of several members of the institution.

59 As just one possible example of many, Guillermo de Torre situates his first meeting with Alfonso Reyes, Pedro Salinas, and Melchor Fernández Almagro there: *Tan pronto ayer*, 413, 446–7, 489.

60 Armiñán, *Biografía del Círculo de Bellas Artes*; Espina, *Las tertulias de Madrid*, 161–3; Salcedo, "Los orígenes del CBA"; Salcedo, "El edificio del CBA"; Temes, *El Círculo de Bellas Artes*; Rodríguez Ruíz and Blanca Sánchez, eds, *El Círculo de Bellas Artes de Madrid*.

61 Melchor de Almagro San Martín, "El P.E.N. Club español despierta de su letargo," *Ahora*, 15 November 1935, n.p.; Gómez de la Serna, *Automoribundia*, 478. According to Almagro San Martín, the organizing committee, desirous of recruiting Gómez de la Serna, created the unique position of *sumiller*.

62 *Lista provisional de socios del P.E.N.*; *Lista rectificada de socios del P.E.N.*

63 The opulence of the July 1922 banquet can be judged from an excellent photograph reproduced in the Almagro San Martín article. One can appreciate the predominant nature of the membership of the club from the composition of the original organizing committee and the lists of attendees at banquets given by Almagro San Martín.

64 Adriaensen and Ceballos Viro, "De kortstondige gevallen van de PEN-clubs"; Laget, "The Spanish Center of the International PEN."

65 *Automoribundia*, 477–8.

66 Gállego Rubio, "La Biblioteca de la Universidad Literaria de Madrid," 113.

67 Ibid., 115.

68 "La Universidad isabelina," Universidad Complutense de Madrid, accessed 24 May 2022, https://www.ucm.es/resena-historica-la-universidad-isabelina; "La Universidad del Sexenio Democrático y la Restauración," Universidad Complutense de Madrid, accessed 24 May 2022, https://www.ucm.es/la-

universidad-del-sexenio-democratico-y-la-restauracion; "Del Desastre del 98 a la Guerra civil," Universidad Complutense de Madrid, accessed 24 May 2022, https://www.ucm.es/del-desastre-del-98-a-la-guerra-civil; Sanz Esteban, "Historia del caserón de San Bernardo"; Palomera Parra, "La organización académica y administrativa."

69 Gállego Rubio, "La Biblioteca de la Universidad Literaria," 118.

70 Hernández Sandoica, "La Universidad de Madrid," paints an insightful and overall depressing picture of the Universidad Central from its establishment in Madrid through to the turn of the century, followed by slow and patchy modernization in the first decades of the twentieth century.

71 Instituto Nacional de Estadística, *Anuarios Estadísticos*, 1920–21, 1930–31.

72 *Tan pronto ayer*, 400–1.

73 Ortiz Ballesteros, *Paseando por Madrid con el Real Conservatorio*; Sarget Ros, "Rol modélico del Conservatorio de Madrid I"; Sarget Ros, "Rol modélico del Conservatorio de Madrid II"; "Historia de las enseñanzas artísticas de música en España"; Granda, "RESAD. Historia de una escuela centenaria."

74 Anderson and Dougherty, "Continuity and Innovation in Spanish Theatre."

75 As of the reform of 1917, the established subjects for study were practical declamation/recitation, costume, history of dramatic literature, and ancient and modern history of fencing and its practice.

76 A full listing is given in "Centros de la JAE," JAE/CSIC 2010, accessed 24 May 2022, http://www.jae2010.csic.es/centros.php.

77 Abad, "La obra filológica."

78 See the documentary film *¿Qué es España?*, made in 1926 by Luis Araquistáin for a Latin American lecture tour undertaken by him and Cayetano Coll y Cuchí. There were alterations and additions made in 1929, in preparation for a second tour of the same area undertaken by Rodolfo Llopis in 1930. There has been doubt surrounding the original date of filming, but this is attested to by an announcement in *Los Quijotes* (San Juan, Puerto Rico) 1, no. 31 (14 August 1926): 3, where Araquistáin and his documentary are mentioned. See Fuentes, "La arboleda encontrada," and Menéndez-Onrubia, "Galdós y el 'prodigioso invento' del cinematógrafo." In the incomplete reconstruction (available online at http://www.restauracionesfilmoteca.com/cine-espanol/no-ficcion/que-es-espana/), there is a section dedicated to the Centro: we see Menéndez Pidal, Ricardo Orueta, Américo Castro, and Dámaso Alonso, among others, sitting in an office, and group shots in the garden of the building.

79 López-Ocón Cabrera, "La dinámica investigadora del Centro de Estudios Históricos"; López Sánchez, *Heterodoxos españoles*; Limón, "El Palacio de Hielo." The administrative offices of the JAE also moved to the Palacio de Hielo.

80 Torre, *Tan pronto ayer*, 21, 111. Torre studied for his law degree mainly at the Universidad Central, though he took his last exams through the Universidad de Granada. His professional interest in diplomacy oriented toward Spanish

America may have been boosted by his enduring romance with Norah Borges.

81 Rodríguez Rubio, "Historia de las Escuelas Oficiales de Idiomas"; Nistal Ramón and Yuste López, "Fondos de la Escuela Central de Idiomas."

82 Escolano Benito, "Las escuelas normales."

83 Colmenar Orzaes, "Espacio y tiempo escolar."

84 Ferrer, "La Escuela de Estudios Superiores"; Flecha García, "Las aspirantes al magisterio secundario."

85 Sánchez Blanco and Hernández Huerta, "La Asociación para la Enseñanza de la Mujer"; Capel Martínez and Magallón Portolés, "Un sueño posible," 228–30.

86 Mestre et al., "Los estudios superiores de diseño"; Sabio, "Las escuelas de arte"; Rico, "La mujer y las Escuelas de Artes y Oficios."

87 Romano, "Las Escuelas de Artes y Oficios."

88 Grammar and handwriting, elements of mathematics, geography, history, physics, elements of chemistry, natural sciences, standard law, notions of civic education, and music.

89 Artistic drawing, geometric drawing and elements of decorative composition (painting), modelling and elements of decorative composition (sculpture), introductory history of the decorative and industrial arts, dressmaking (dresses and linens), practical instruction in lace with artificial flowers, pyrography, embossing work, and embroidery; mechanical industries, industrial analyses; stenography, typing, notions of telegraphy and telephony, postal geography, scientific biographies, English, German, French, commercial accounting and its practices, commercial legislation, and elements of agriculture and flower cultivation.

90 Hygiene, child care, home remedies, caring for the ill; then economics, household accounting, making linens and upkeep of linens in daily use, hat making, and culinary art.

91 Pérez-Villanueva Tovar, "La Escuela del Hogar y Profesional de la Mujer"; González Sanz, "Los métodos de dibujo."

92 Navascués Palacio, "La creación de la Escuela de Arquitectura."

93 Almarza Burbano, "Francisco de Paula Aldana Monte."

94 "Escuela de Cerámica de La Moncloa y Escuela de Arte Francisco Alcántara," Arte en Madrid, accessed 24 May 2022, https://artedemadrid.wordpress.com/2013/11/19/escuela-de-ceramica-de-la-moncloa-y-escuela-de-arte-francisco-alcantara/.

95 "Anuarios Estadísticos, De 1921 a 1930/Anuario 1921–1922," Instituto Nacional de Estadística, accessed 24 May 2022, https://www.ine.es/inebaseweb/treeNavigation.do?tn=148740&tns=149200#149200.

96 "Anuarios Estadísticos, De 1921 a 1930/Anuario 1930," Instituto Nacional de Estadística, accessed 24 May 2022, https://www.ine.es/inebaseweb/treeNavigation.do?tn=43032&tns=43394#43394.

97   The documentary film *¿Qué es España?*, previously cited, contains a sequence on the ILE; it shows a group of pupils in the garden, several of the teachers, and the then director, Manuel B. Cossío.

98   Zulueta and Alicia Moreno, *Ni convento ni college*, 60. When he was unable to get a room in the Residencia de Estudiantes, Lorca lodged at the Pensión Pi y Margall in the fall of 1928 and the first months of 1929: García Lorca, *Epistolario completo*, 604.

99   Carande, "Fortuny, 14," 75–6.

100 Méndez, *Caminos inversos*, 20.

101 Díez de Revenga, "José de Ciria," 70.

102 García Lorca, *Epistolario completo*, 340.

103 Méndez and Ulacia, *Memorias habladas, memorias armadas*, 85–6. She mis-identifies the street as calle Constantino Fernández, whereas it was actually on calle Constantino Rodríguez, 7 (nowadays calle de los Libreros). Other notables who stayed there include José María Souviron, Ramón Acín, and Ramón Gaya.

104 Peña Hinojosa, "Nota previa," 14; Sánchez Rodríguez, "José María Hinojosa."

105 Hinojosa, *Epistolario*, 45, 141; M. Moreno, ed., *José María Hinojosa*, 13–14.

106 M. Moreno, ed., *José María Hinojosa*, 170 (6 May 1927); Hinojosa, *Epistolario*, 72, 141 (22 September 1927).

107 Sánchez Rodríguez, *Este film inacabado*, 25; Sánchez Rodríguez, "José María Hinojosa."

108 It began in 1910 with one large detached house located at calle Fortuny, 14. Subsequently, it added the houses at Fortuny 10, 8, and 12, and in 1915 was able to move to what became its permanent home on calle Pinar. Further construction continued there for many years and included buildings for both the Residencia and for other JAE initiatives.

109 The bibliography on the Residencia de Estudiantes is extensive; see Pérez de Ayala, ed., "La Residencia de Estudiantes"; Sáenz de la Calzada, *La Residencia de Estudiantes 1910–1936*, revised as *La Residencia de Estudiantes. Los residentes*; Pérez-Villanueva Tovar, *La Residencia de Estudiantes. Grupos universitario y de señoritas*, revised as *La Residencia de Estudiantes 1910–1936*; Pérez-Villanueva Tovar, "La Residencia de Estudiantes"; Sinclair, "'Telling It Like It Was'?"; Ribagorda, *El coro de Babel*; Jiménez Fraud, *Epistolario*. See also the documentary *¿Qué es España?* cited above, which contains a very evocative section on the Residencia. There is extensive footage of sports events on the playing fields then alongside the Residencia, shots of José Moreno Villa and his room in one of the pavilions, a scene in the dining room during lunch, the library (the building that housed it was subsequently remodelled, so these are particularly valuable), the laboratories, and finally some of its publications.

110 Flecha García, "Alumnas y equipos directivos de la Residencia Teresiana"; Peralta Ortiz, "Orígenes y características de una residencia."

111 Glick, "Fundaciones americanas y ciencia española"; Rueda, "Gregorio del Amo"; Ribagorda, "La Fundación Del Amo."

Chapter Two

1 Lorenzo Arribas, "Atocha."
2 A number of useful plans and photographs are available here: "La olvidada fuente de la Glorieta de Atocha (Plaza del Emperador Carlos V)," Historia Urbana de Madrid, 2 September 2016, https://historia-urbana-madrid.blogspot.com/2016/09/la-olvidada-fuente-de-la-glorieta-de.html.
3 The first plot and then, later, the second can be seen clearly on historical city plans from different time periods, such as those of Teixeira (1656), available at https://commons.wikimedia.org/wiki/File:Pedro_Teixeira_Albernaz_(1656)_plano_de_Madrid.png; Tomás López (1762), at https://www.museodelprado.es/en/the-collection/art-work/madrid-map/c264da66-05ad-49cb-a796-caf78101a679; Tomás López (1785), at https://es.m.wikipedia.org/wiki/Archivo:Plano_de_Madrid_1785_de_Tomas-Lopez.jpg; and Carlos Ibáñez e Ibáñez de Ibero (1879), at https://www.ign.es/web/catalogo-cartoteca/resources/html/001629.html (notice here the garden layout inside the patio of the second rectangle, preserved today in the Reina Sofía museum).
4 Muñoz Alonso, "De hospital a museo."
5 Sáiz Carrero, "Historia del Hospital General," 668.
6 There are references in the Madrid press from 1843 onward to a Café de Oriente situated in the Plaza de Isabel II, but this is unrelated and had closed down by the 1880s. Nor should the café that interests us be confused with the modern-day establishment on the west side of town with the same name, derived from the close-by Plaza de Oriente.
7 Archivo General de la Villa de Madrid, refs 7-285-1, 7-286-1, and 7-423-98; there "Solar A" is identified as "plot coming from the Hospital." The city plan of 1879, referenced above, shows a blank space in the first rectangle, which supports this conjecture.
8 "Café de Oriente," *El Liberal*, 23 June 1887, 3.
9 Ibid.
10 "Círculos políticos. Asuntos del día," *El Día*, 26 February 1888, 3; "Banquete federal," *La República*, 28 February 1888, 1; "De ayer a hoy," *El Día*, 4 November 1888, 1; "Ecos del día," *La Época*, 3 December 1888, 1.
11 *Anuario del comercio*, 346.
12 "El señor Don José Rodríguez y Fernández," *Heraldo de Madrid*, 22 February 1906, 6; Archivo General de la Villa de Madrid, refs 16-309-121, 17-469-47; "Madrid en verano. Café Restaurant de Oriente," *El Liberal*, 23 August 1911, 2.
13 "[Advert]," *ABC*, 11 November 1915, 2.
14 N. Hernández Luquero, "El amable libro viejo," *Heraldo de Madrid*, 12 October 1919, 2.

15 "Una pregunta, lector ... ¿Qué vio usted ayer? Un solar convertido en ester-
    colero," *La Libertad*, 14 August 1928, 2.

16 "Una estrella en el camino," 20n1, with several good photos of the Dorna at
    20, 25.

17 There are many modern-day photos available, both of the exterior and inte-
    rior, on websites such as Tripadvisor, Foursquare City Guide, as well as the
    images attached to reviews on Google Maps.

18 Archivo General de la Villa de Madrid, miscellaneous correspondence to the
    Ayuntamiento de Madrid relating to Atocha 118, letter from María Maciá,
    24 February 1910: "it continues to have ten openings." As Bonet Correa
    writes, "All the cafés from the Restoration and the period of the regency of
    María Cristina have slender and slim cast iron columns and high coffered
    ceilings with plasterwork," *Los cafés históricos*, 49.

19 The closest that we come to a "period" reference is found in González-Ruano,
    Memorias. There he refers with his usual irony to "that strange and rundown
    café that ... was called at that time nothing less than the 'Great Social Café
    of the East'" (97).

20 See F.A. [Francisco Ayala], "Atocha (Hotel Nacional)," 136. However, the
    chronology that he proposes is problematic, and he seems to conflate the
    Café de Oriente with the Nacional.

21 See, for example, see "Calle Atocha y Hotel Nacional, entre 1920 y 1925. Hauser
    y Menet. Tarjeta postal," Imagenes del viejo Madrid, accessed 22 May 2022,
    http://www.viejo-madrid.es/paginas/20/1920-121.html, and "La Glorieta de
    Atocha desde la calle de Claudio Moyano," Memoria de Madrid, accessed
    22 May 2022, http://www.memoriademadrid.es/buscador.php?accion=
    VerFicha&id=10111.

22 Aguerre, ed., *Barradas. Colección MNAV*, 285.

23 The principal church in Zaragoza is the Basílica de Nuestra Señora del Pilar.
    See the first-hand account that Barradas gives to Casal in a letter of 4 April
    1919: García and García-Sedas, "Rafael Barradas y Julio J. Casal," n.p.

24 This account is synthesized from a number of sources: Brihuega, "Saturno en
    el sifón"; Faxedas Brujats, "Barradas' Vibrationism and Its Catalan Context";
    Grau, "Barradas en el MNAV"; García Guatas, "Barradas"; Lomba Serrano,
    "Barradas en Aragón"; Rodrigo, "*El pescador de maravillas submarinas*";
    Pereda, *Barradas*.

25 Antonio stayed on in Barcelona until February 1919, as witnessed by Torres-
    García's letters to Barradas: García-Sedas, ed. *Joaquín Torres-García y Rafael
    Barradas*, 133–51.

26 "Aniversario de la independencia del Uruguay. Composición alusiva a la in-
    dependencia del Uruguay. Dibujo," *El Fígaro*, 25 August 1918, 8; "Las fiestas
    de Madrid. – La de la 'Melonera,'" *El Fígaro*, 11 September 1918, 15; "[Dibujo],"
    in Fernando Mota, "Para los niños. En busca de la ciudad luminosa en la que
    impera la verdad," *El Fígaro*, 15 October 1918, 3; "Reconstrucciones infantiles.
    Dibujos y texto," *El Fígaro*, 15 October 1918, 3.

27 Brihuega, "Saturno en el sifón," 23; Antonio de Ignacios, *Historial Rafael Barradas*, 70. For instance: *Travesuras de Tilón y sus amigos* (Madrid: Editorial Pagés y Compañía, 1918).

28 Anderson, *El momento ultraísta*, 239–40, 346n16, 751.

29 García, ed., *Correspondencia Rafael Cansinos Assens/Guillermo de Torre 1916–1955*, 57.

30 Torres-García acknowledges receipt of a letter from Barradas, almost certainly the first one written after his move to Madrid: García-Sedas, ed., *Joaquín Torres-García y Rafael Barradas*, 133.

31 Ibid.

32 Faxedas Brujats, "Barradas' Vibrationism and Its Catalan Context," n.p.

33 Lagar had first defined this style in a text in the catalogue of his exhibition at Dalmau (January–February 1915). A derivation of Cubism, as the name suggests it employed flat planes and a considerable use of colour: see Faxedas Brujats, "Barradas' Vibrationism and Its Catalan Context."

34 Many of the works had been exhibited in Barcelona at the Laietanes Gallery, 1–15 April 1918; immediately beforehand, at the same gallery, Barradas had celebrated his first solo show, which opened on 20 March.

35 These "calligrammes" function as a kind of schematic art criticism: *Salón del Ateneo. Exposición planista. Celso Lagar. Esculturas animalistas de Hortensia Bégué ... Invitación* (Madrid, 1918).

36 García-Sedas, ed., *Joaquín Torres García y Rafael Barradas*, 142.

37 Anderson, *El momento ultraísta*, 192–202, 361–71.

38 Fernando López Martín, "La exposición de Celso Lagar. Comentarios vibracionistas por F. [*sic*] Barradas," *El Fígaro*, 5 December 1918, 4.

39 See *Casa de apartamentos* [oil on canvas; dated 1919 and exhibited at Mateu in April of that year], Museo Nacional de Artes Visuales, accessed 22 May 2022, http://acervo.mnav.gub.uy/obras.php?q=ni:3128. This drawing was later turned into a full-scale painting: Pereda, *Barradas*, 95; Aguerre, ed., *Barradas. Colección MNAV*, 195.

40 "Comentarios de actualidad. La pintura moderna y sus propulsores. Celso Lagar," *El Parlamentario*, 13 December 1918, 3; Anderson, *El momento ultraísta*, 354.

41 "¿Qué opina usted acerca del porvenir político e intelectual de España? Los intelectuales dicen ... Rafael Cansinos Assens," *El Parlamentario*, 27 November 1918, 1; Anderson, *El momento ultraísta*, 336–43, 372–6.

42 See the brief sections on Barradas (111, 232) and that on "Celso Lagar y sus planismos" (352–5) in Francés, *El año artístico*. For general information on his biography and career, see Villalba Salvador, "El crítico de arte José Francés."

43 García-Sedas, ed., *Joaquín Torres-García y Rafael Barradas*, 137.

44 Ibid., 146.

45 Ibid., 148.

46 Ignacios, *Historial Rafael Barradas*, 70.

47 Fuster del Alcázar, "Barradas y la escena," 23; Fuster del Alcázar, "Rafael Barradas y Catalina Bárcena," 6.

48 Brihuega, "Saturno en el sifón," 23; Fuster del Alcázar, "Barradas y la escena," 23; Peláez Martín, "Barradas en el teatro de arte," 92–3.

49 Ignacios, *Historial Rafael Barradas*, 75–6. There is a contract between Martínez Sierra and Barradas dated 3 June 1919, stipulating an advance payment of two hundred pesetas monthly for drawings for the Biblioteca Estrella, though this may just formalize a pre-existing arrangement: Fuster del Alcázar, "Barradas y la escena," 26; Alba Nieva, "Cuerpo y figurín," 373.

50 The first was Bernardin de Saint-Pierre, *Pablo y Virginia*, translated by Manuel Abril, illustrated by Barradas, ornamentation by Manuel Fontanals (Madrid: Estrella, 1919).

51 García-Sedas, ed., *Joaquín Torres-García y Rafael Barradas*, 136–7.

52 "Friend" in the sense of someone well-disposed toward them or, in this case, their artistic production.

53 García-Sedas, ed., *Joaquín Torres-García y Rafael Barradas*, 139–40.

54 Ibid., 146.

55 Barradas letter to Torres-García, 25 February 1919, in García-Sedas, ed., *Joaquín Torres-García y Rafael Barradas*, 155–6.

56 Ignacios, *Historial Rafael Barradas*, 70, 75.

57 Catalogue, reproduced in Bonet and Pérez, eds, *El ultraísmo y las artes plásticas*, 195; Jardi, *Rafael Barradas a Catalunya*, 36.

58 Silvio Lago, "La vida artística. Exposiciones en Madrid," *La Esfera* 6, no. 279 (3 May 1919): n.p.

59 Torre, "Frisos críticos. Directrices novísimas pictóricas. El *vibracionismo* de Barradas," *Perseo*, no. 1 (May 1919).

60 García-Sedas, ed., *Joaquín Torres-García y Rafael Barradas*, 180.

61 Alberto Lasplaces, "Rafael Barradas en Madrid," *El Día*, Suplemento (Montevideo), año VIII, no. 320, 26 February 1939.

62 García-Sedas, ed., *Joaquín Torres-García y Rafael Barradas*, 182; the visit occurred on 16 October 1919.

63 Ignacios, *Historial Rafael Barradas*, 87.

64 Ibid., 81.

65 Ibid., 83.

66 Alfredo Médici, the Uruguayan tenor with whom Barradas had travelled to Europe.

67 García-Sedas, ed., *Joaquín Torres-García y Rafael Barradas*, 191.

68 Ibid., 196–7.

69 "Reconstrucciones infantiles. Dibujos y texto," cited above. The best-known example of this kind of two-dimensional theatre (*teatro planista*) is that constructed by Hermegildo Lanz for the theatrical entertainment held in the Lorca family home in Granada on Epiphany, 1923. The term also recalls Lagar's avant-garde artistic style of *planismo*.

70   In the letter he outlines four proposals: a piece for Christmas programming, a "finale number," a "very amusing little comedy" done in a "clownish" style, and the puppet show for a matinée program: Alba Nieva, "Cuerpo y figurín," 379.

71   Caricatures in *ABC*, 20 January 1920, 6, and 27 February 1920, 6; photograph in *Nuevo Mundo* 27, no. 1363 (27 February 1920): n.p.; reproduction of original drawing, "Teatro de los niños," in Martínez Sierra, *Un teatro de arte en España*, 161.

72   "Eslava," *El Imparcial*, 18 February 1920, 5.

73   García-Sedas, ed., *Joaquín Torres-García y Rafael Barradas*, 202–3.

74   Fuster del Alcázar, "Barradas y la escena," 27; García-Sedas, ed., *Joaquín Torres-García y Rafael Barradas*, 198n14.

75   "Noticias e informaciones teatrales," *La Correspondencia de España*, 11 March 1920, 7; J.A., "Los teatros. Eslava. *El maleficio de la mariposa*", *El Sol*, 23 March 1920, 11.

76   Peláez Martín, "Barradas en el teatro de arte," 94, 97n37.

77   Anderson, "¿Entre prodigio y protegido?" His tardiness in returning from Granada after the New Year was a source of considerable frustration for Martínez Sierra.

78   García-Sedas, ed., *Joaquín Torres-García y Rafael Barradas*, 198n4; Alarcó, ed., *Rafael Barradas y Juan Gutiérrez Gili (1916–1929)*, 77; Bonet and Pérez, eds, *El ultraísmo y las artes plásticas*, 195.

79   Carmona, "Rafael Barradas y el 'arte nuevo' en España, 1917–1925," 122–4.

80   C.-C., "Exégesis del momento. Exposición Barradas en el Ateneo," *La Ilustración Española y Americana* 64, no. 10 (15 March 1920): 157; Manuel Abril, "Barradas," *Vell i Nou. Revista Mensual d'Art* época II, 1, no. 8 (November 1920): 279–85.

81   "Funciones para hoy," *El Imparcial*, 30 April 1920, 5; "Cartel para el día 3," *La Correspondencia de España*, 1 May 1920, 5; "Gacetillas," *La Correspondencia de España*, 1 May 1920, 6; "Veladas teatrales," *La Época*, 1 May 1920, 1; "Los teatros. Gacetillas," *El Sol*, 1 May 1920, 9; "Cartelera," *El Correo Español*, 16 May 1920, 4.

82   Fuster del Alcázar, "Barradas y la escena," 29.

83   Alba Nieva, "Cuerpo y figurín," 374.

84   A likely departure date of 10 or 12 May was mentioned: García-Sedas, ed., *Joaquín Torres-García y Rafael Barradas*, 209.

85   García-Sedas, ed., *Joaquín Torres-García y Rafael Barradas*, 207–8, 209. Torres-García announced his departure date as 15 May.

86   J.Ll.A., "Comiat a En J. Torres-Garcia," *La Veu de Catalunya*, 14 May 1920, 8.

87   "Notas breves. Catalina," *La Publicidad*, 21 May 1920, 1.; "L'eminent actriu Caterina Bárcena," *L'Esquella de la Torratxa* 42, no. 2151 (28 May 1920): 301; "Crònica. Exposició de retrats de la Bárcena," *La Veu de Catalunya*, 25 June 1920, 9.

88   García-Sedas, ed., *Joaquín Torres-García y Rafael Barradas*, 210n5; Bonet and Pérez, eds, *El ultraísmo y las artes plásticas*, 195.

89   J. Sacs, "Nuestras crónicas de arte. Cubismos, tómbolas y caligrafías. Barradas," *La Publicidad*, 30 May 1920, 6; "Notas breves. Puertaferrisa, 18," *La Publicidad*, 3 June 1920, 1; "Exposició Barradas a Casa en Dalmau," *La Veu de Catalunya*, 5 June 1920, 5; R.B., "Exposició Barradas," *La Revista* 6, no. 115 (1 July 1920): 182.

90   Pereda, *Barradas*, 120.

91   García-Sedas, ed., *Joaquín Torres-García y Rafael Barradas*, 213, 214.

92   Anderson, *El momento ultraísta*, 148, 239, 346, 354, 563, 653–4, 684, 687–9, 691, 693. For a tentative listing of *ultraístas* and others close to the group, see 112–20.

93   Brihuega, "Saturno en el sifón," 25.

94   "Desde Buenos Aires. Adiós a Barradas."

95   Barrera López, "Pedro Garfias," 14.

96   Herrera Navarro, "Documentos inéditos sobre la vanguardia artística española," 485.

97   García Lorca, *Epistolario completo*, 109; his mother's saint's day was 5 April. Among the *ultraístas* Guillermo de Torre and José de Ciria y Escalante would be possibilities, and among Residencia friends, Luis Buñuel.

98   "Banquete a Paszkiewicz," *Vltra*, no. 10 (10 May 1921): n.p.

99   "Velada ultraísta," *La Tribuna*, 30 April 1921, 9.

100 "Kaleidoscopio. Nuestra segunda Velada," *Vltra*, no. 10 (10 May 1921): n.p.

101 "Noticias. Homenaje a Eva de Aggerholm y a Vázquez Díaz," *La Libertad*, 7 May 1921, 7.

102 "Arte y artistas. Banquete en honor de Vázquez Díaz y Eva Aggerholm," *ABC*, 18 May 1921, 21.

103 Rodrigo, *"El pescador de maravillas submarinas,"* 14.

104 The correspondence between Barradas in Madrid and Gili in Barcelona ends in September: Rodrigo, *"El pescador de maravillas submarinas,"* 18–19.

105 He also began publishing in *Vltra*, from no. 20 (15 December 1921) onward.

106 Anderson, "La revista *Tableros* dentro de la trayectoria ultraísta."

107 "Un banquete en el Hotel Palace. En honor de Luis Araquistáin," *El Sol*, 29 January 1922, 3; "Contra la inmoralidad y el matonismo. Homenaje a Luis Araquistáin," *La Voz*, 30 January 1922, 3; Padró Nieto, "El banquete a Luis Araquistáin."

108 "En favor de los hambrientos rusos. El festival en el teatro del Centro," *La Época*, 21 February 1922, 2; "Espectáculos. Centro," *El Liberal*, 24 February 1922, 2; "El festival a beneficio de los niños rusos," *El Sol*, 25 February 1922, 1.

109 "En favor de la Rusia hambrienta. La exposición de Bellas Artes," *La Voz*, 13 February 1922, 1.

110 García and García-Sedas, *Julio J. Casal (1889–1954)*; García and García-Sedas, "Rafael Barradas y Julio J. Casal": see, for instance, the letter of 4 April 1919.

111   A facsimile is available at https://2012.academia.gal/hemeroteca-virtual#pax-inas_numero.do?id=2752&d-447263-p=13&current_page=2. Dated 1920, the drawing depicts a crowded scene with the reversed letters of "E F A C" on a window.

112   Different incarnations of this magazine, under different names, were published from the end of 1920 onward. In the first years it was largely a commercial publication; its name was changed to *Revista de la Casa América-Galicia* in September 1922, and from the November number onward (unnumbered, but corresponding to number 23) there was a notable shift in the contents toward very modern literary and artistic matters, a clear sign of Casal's influence.

113   Bonet, "Barradas y el Ultraísmo," 12.

114   Herrera Navarro, "Documentos inéditos sobre la vanguardia artística española," 485; Bonet and Pérez, eds, *El ultraísmo y las artes plásticas*, 195.

115   "Gacetillas. Eslava," *La Acción*, 15 December 1921, 5; J.L. de M., "Los Teatros. Eslava. *Linterna mágica*," *El Liberal*, 17 December 1921, 3. At some point Burmann's name disappeared from the list.

116   H.R., "Vigía," *Vltra*, no. 21 (1 January 1922): n.p. Humberto Rivas was the de facto director of *Vltra*.

117   "Gacetillas teatrales. Eslava. Funciones especiales para niños," *La Correspondencia de España*, 26 December 1921, 7; A., "Veladas teatrales. Eslava: Inauguración del Teatro de los Niños," *La Época*, 30 December 1921, 1.

118   "Informaciones teatrales. Gacetillas. Nuevas aventuras de Pinocho," *La Correspondencia de España*, 30 January 1922, 6; J.A., "Información teatral. Eslava. Nuevo programa del Teatro de los Niños," *El Sol*, 5 February 1922, 2. A photo of one of the scenes clearly showing Barradas's set and costumes can be found in "De la vida madrileña," *La Semana Gráfica* 2, no. 45 (11 February 1922): n.p.

119   Pedro, *España renaciente*, 97–100; González-Ruano, *Memorias*, 105; Buñuel, *Mi último suspiro*, 62.

120   González-Ruano, *Memorias*, 105. According to Ruano, they congregated around an extremely rich Extremaduran pig farmer, Antonio Daza, who bought them rounds of drinks.

121   Buñuel, *Mi último suspiro*, 62. Confirmed by Torre, who remembers Buñuel as one of the group: *Tan pronto ayer*, 498, 552.

122   Pérez Bazo, *Juan Chabás y su tiempo*, 32–3; Casal, "Nota biográfica," 22.

123   Bonet and Pérez, eds, *El ultraísmo y las artes plásticas*, 199.

124   According to Torre, the *tertulia* was indeed "presided over by the painter Barradas": *Tan pronto ayer*, 497.

125   Casal, "Nota biográfica," 22.

126   [Evaristo] Correa Calderón, "Retrato de José Francés," *Revista de Casa América-Galicia* [no. 23] (November 1922): 3.

127   Forcada Cabanellas, *De la vida literaria*, 144.

128   Ignacios, *Historial Rafael Barradas*, 62.

129 Torre, "Desde Buenos Aires. Adiós a Barradas"; cf. Torre, *Tan pronto ayer*, 497.

130 Torre, *Tan pronto ayer*, 497–8.

131 Ibid., 542, and see 541.

132 *Bores nuevo. Los años veinte y treinta*, 43.

133 Aub, *Luis Buñuel, novela*, 88.

134 García Monge, "Garfias y Borges," 10; Gibson, *Luis Buñuel*, 119.

135 For a detailed study of the Platerías *tertulia*, see Anderson, "Estudio preliminar," 22–4.

136 Anderson, *El momento ultraísta*, 142–54.

137 Ibid., 202.

138 Gómez de la Serna, *Pombo*, 145–6. Lagar reappears briefly in *La sagrada cripta de Pombo*, with a reproduction of a sketch "Una fantasía de Celso Lagar sobre Pombo" (435) and a small photograph of the painter (471).

139 Gómez de la Serna, *La sagrada cripta de Pombo*, 272. A copy of the magazine *Horizonte* is also on the table, dating the drawing to late 1922 or 1923.

140 Ibid., 283, 285, 288, 679 ("Apuntes que hace Barradas mientras se conversa," "Más improvisaciones de Barradas sobre los papeles que se tiran," "Más apuntes de Barradas," "Otro apunte de mí, por Barradas"). In the third of this sequence, lower left, Dalí's face is clearly discernible.

141 Ibid., 347.

142 José de Ciria y Escalante, "La tertulia de Pombo," *La Atalaya*, 6 March 1921.

143 There are two versions of this, a draft and a clean fair copy. The former is available at https://www.museoreinasofia.es/en/collection/artwork/pombo, and the latter at http://acervo.mnav.gub.uy/obras.php?q=ni:3191.

144 "Los banquetes. Una innovación curiosa," *El Sol*, 11 March 1923, 1. The rest of the committee was made up of Rafael Urbano, Comet, Montes, Buñuel, Rafael Sánchez Ventura, Chabás, Alfonso García Valdecasas, and Augusto Fernández.

145 It is reproduced in Gómez de la Serna, *La sagrada cripta de Pombo*, 739.

146 García and García-Sedas, "Rafael Barradas y Julio J. Casal," n.p.

147 Alberto Lasplaces, "Rafael Barradas en Madrid," *El Día*, Suplemento (Montevideo), año VIII, no. 320, 26 February 1939. Lasplaces had first tried to find him in May 1920 (Pereda, *Barradas*, 123), but Barradas was then in Barcelona, so the visit must have occurred in the fall, after Lasplaces's return to Madrid from Paris.

148 He appears with a hat in the better-known image: Pereda, *Barradas*, 229; *Rafael Barradas* (Galería Jorge Mara), 18; Brihuega and Lomba, eds, *Barradas. Exposición antológica, 1890–1929*, 55; and hatless in the other: Pereda, *Barradas*, 58, though the water carafe, pipe, and glass are identical in both.

149 *Tan pronto ayer*, 498.

150 García-Sedas, ed., *Joaquín Torres-García y Rafael Barradas*, 159.

151 Ibid., 190.

152 Alarcó, ed., *Rafael Barradas y Juan Gutiérrez Gili (1916–1929)*, 38.

153   "Ante la muerte del pintor Rafael Barradas," *Heraldo de Madrid*, 16 February
      1929, 16.

154   *Tan pronto ayer*, 498. The "already named" refers to a list of *ultraístas*.

155   Rogers, "García Lorca and His Friends," 19, 20, 22–5; García Buñuel, *Recor-
      dando a Luis Buñuel*, between 70–1.

156   Alarcó, ed., *Rafael Barradas y Juan Gutiérrez Gili*, 81.

157   Aguerre, ed., *Barradas. Colección* MNAV, 100; *García Lorca*, Museo Nacional
      de Artes Visuales, accessed 25 May 2022, http://acervo.mnav.gub.uy/obras.
      php?q=ni:3216. Lorca's use of the "G" initial instead of the full name García
      marks this as a relatively early signature, around 1921–22. See also Ortiz
      Saralegui, "Federico García Lorca y Rafael Barradas."

158   Aguerre, ed., *Barradas. Colección* MNAV, 206–7; *García Maroto y García Lorca*,
      Museo Nacional de Artes Visuales, accessed 25 May 2022, http://acervo.
      mnav.gub.uy/obras.php?q=ni:3116.

159   F.B., "Los poetas nuevos. Juan Gutiérrez-Gili en el Ateneo," *La Corresponden-
      cia de España*, 2 April 1923, 5; Alarcó, ed., *Rafael Barradas y Juan Gutiérrez
      Gili*, 90; Bonet and Pérez, eds, *El ultraísmo y las artes plásticas*, 284.

160   For a wealth of biographical information on Alberto, see Brihuega, ed.,
      Alberto Sánchez 1895–1962. Dibujos, and Brihuega and Lomba, eds, *Alberto
      1895–1962*.

161   Valentín de Pedro, "El escultor Alberto. Un hijo del pueblo, panadero y artista,
      como Gorki," *Informaciones*, 12 June 1925, 1. See also Francisco Mateos, "El
      escultor Alberto," *El Socialista*, 25 February 1926, 4, and Sánchez, *Palabras
      de un escultor*, "Notas biográficas," 72.

162   Sánchez, *Palabras de un escultor*, "Carta a Luis Lacasa, September 1958," 19, 26.

163   Sánchez, *Palabras de un escultor*, "Notas biográficas," 73.

164   For instance: Brihuega, ed., *Alberto Sánchez 1895–1962. Dibujos*, 13; García
      Guatas, "Barradas," 58.

165   García Guatas, "Barradas," 61; Jardi, *Rafael Barradas a Catalunya i altres
      artistes que passaren la mar*, 39. See also Gil Bel, "Barradas," *Noreste* 4, no. 12
      (Fall 1935): 3.

166   Jarnés, *Epistolario 1919–1939*, 11.

167   Sánchez, *Palabras de un escultor*, "Recuerdos de Rafael Barradas," 40.

168   A decade later, Alberto would be commissioned by Lorca to design some of
      the sets for La Barraca.

169   García-Lorca, ed., *Signos de amistad*, 76. See also chapter 6 of this volume.

170   "El sillero" and "Estudio para bajorrelieve" in the *Revista*, no. 28 (March 1923)
      and no. 31bis (August 1923), and "Panadero en descanso" and "Estudio" in
      Alfar, no. 33 (October 1923) and no. 38 (March 1924).

171   "Dibujo," *Alfar*, no. 31bis (August 1923); Brihuega and Lomba, eds, *Alberto
      1895–1962*, 30.

172   "Café de Atocha," *Ronsel*, no. 3 (July 1924): 7; Brihuega and Lomba, eds, *Alberto
      1895–1962*, 30, 191.

173   Ródenas de Moya, "Benjamín Jarnés," xvi–xvii.

174 Domínguez Lasierra, *Benjamín Jarnés*, 77.

175 Pérez Marqués, "Cartas a J. López Prudencio"; Jarnés, *Epistolario, 1919–1939*.

176 Cansinos Assens, *La novela de un literato*, vol. 3, *1923–1936*, 170–1.

177 He made his debut in the *Revista de Occidente* with "El río fiel," no. 23 (May 1925): 145–69.

178 Jarnés, "Luco de Jiloca," *Alfar*, no. 34 (November 1923): 7–8; in the same number Barradas published a portrait of Jarnés's brother: "Mosen Pedro Jarnés," 9.

179 Gómez de la Serna, *La sagrada cripta de Pombo*, 671.

180 Two other photos are reproduced in Pereda, *Barradas*, 147, and *Rafael Barradas* (Galería Jorge Mara), 20; and in Pereda, *Barradas*, 182, and *Rafael Barradas* (Galería Jorge Mara), 20. It is worth noting that in his pen portrait of Jarnés, Cansinos Assens has him sitting in a wicker armchair on the terrace of the Café de Oriente: *La novela de un literato*, vol. 3, *1923–1936*, 165.

181 There are also photos of Barradas alone, hatless, and sitting on the curb of the sidewalk, with the same background, as well as of him posing with his mother: Pereda, *Barradas*, 38, 133. Likewise, the same close friends also figure in other group photographs, like one of Barradas, Jarnés, Garrán (back row), unidentified, and Alberto (front row), once more with the same background: Pereda, *Barradas*, 132; Brihuega and Lomba, eds, *Alberto 1895–1962*, 28. Notice that here, three are wearing overcoats.

182 Manegat, "Tres artistas amigos"; Pereda, *Barradas*, 78.

183 "La Redacción de *El Correo Español*," *El Correo Español*, 31 March 1920, 1.

184 Juan Gutiérrez-Gili offered an impressionistic survey of his biography and novelistic output in "Perfiles jóvenes. Huberto Pérez de la Ossa."

185 "Desde Buenos Aires. Adiós a Barradas."

186 Pereda, *Barradas*, 139; notice the lamppost, more prominent here, but which also appears in some of the other shots.

187 The best reproduction to date is to be found in *Rafael Barradas* (Galería Jorge Mara), 24, where the image is even less cropped than in the version that I was able to obtain.

188 Pereda, *Barradas*, 150.

189 There is a fine photograph of the artist standing in front of his works on display in *La Acción*, 6 December 1921, 3. The most detailed review is provided by Ángel Vegue y Goldoni, "Crónica de arte. Exposiciones," *El Imparcial*, 9 December 1921, 3, who also notes that Sánchez Felipe started off as a mason and then turned to art.

190 "Rincones del Madrid viejo," 19 March 1922, 1; "Plaza de los carros (Madrid)," 18 February 1923, 1.

191 Jarnés, *Epistolario 1919–1939*, 11.

192 "Un artista notable. Sánchez Felipe, a Cuba," *La Acción*, 10 September 1923, 4.

193 Cansinos Assens, *La novela de un literato*, vol. 3, *1923–1936*, 169.

194 García Maroto, *Promoción de México*, 33; García Lorca, *Epistolario completo*, 101. See also chapter 5 of this volume.

195 García Lorca, *Epistolario completo*, 109.

196   Where Maroto earned criticism and Ruiz praise from Evaristo Correa Calderón: "Comentario a la Exposición Nacional de Bellas Artes," *La Ilustración Española y Americana* 64, no. 20 (30 May 1920): 308–19. Two years later, Maroto organized an event to express admiration for the works that Ruiz showed at the 1922 Exposición Nacional: "Noticias," *El Imparcial*, 2 June 1922, 5.

197   "Banquete en Pombo. En honor de Solana," *La Voz*, 6 January 1921, 6.

198   Later, for a show of twenty-five drawings of Madrid and Toledo by Maroto, at the Salón Nancy (26 October 26–? November 1925), Barradas contributed a portrait of the artist.

199   There are several interesting articles: Ángel Samblancat, "Barradas, el proteico," *El Diluvio*, 22 November 1922, 17; F.P., "Actualidad artística en España," *Revista de Bellas Artes* 11, no. 14 (December 1922): 20; Francisco Alcántara, "La vida artística. En el Ateneo. Los cuadros de García Maroto, Cristóbal Ruiz, Barradas y Winthuysen," *El Sol*, 9 December 1922, 2; Juan de la Encina, "Crítica de arte. Cuatro artistas modernos," *La Voz*, 12 December 1922, 1; Blanquerna, "La Exposicion de Pintura del Ateneo," *La Correspondencia de Espana*, 15 December 1922, 1; Juan de la Encina, "De arte. Cuatro artistas modernos," *La Voz*, 16 December 1922, 1; Antonio Espina, "La exposición del Ateneo," *España* 8, no. 349 (23 December 1922): 12–13; Adolfo Salazar, "De soslayo. Un pintor químicamente puro," *El Sol*, 5 January 1923, 2; Silvio Lago [José Francés], "Vida artística. Cuatro pintores modernos," *La Esfera* 10, no. 473 (27 January 1923): n.p. Blanquerna singled out Maroto and Barradas for praise; Encina found Maroto and Barradas "los más afines"; while Salazar mused on Barradas's connections with Cubism.

200   The program can be found in "Gacetilla musical. Recital de composiciones de Carmen Barradas," *El Sol*, 22 December 1922, 7. Inspired by the event, Adolfo Salazar wrote a long article about her and her music: "La vida musical. Una compositora: Carmen Barradas," *El Sol*, 28 December 1922, 2.

201   Gibson, *The Shameful Life of Salvador Dalí*, 129–31.

202   See chapter 6.

203   There were, naturally, a number of other women in other years still studying there: official government figures for 1922–23 list 13 among a total of 100 enrolled pupils: Instituto Nacional de Estadística-Instituciones Especiales de Enseñanaza. See also chapter 4 of this volume.

204   Escribano, "Maruja Mallo, una bruja moderna," 46.

205   Ferris, *Maruja Mallo*, 62.

206   Gibson, *The Shameful Life*, 131–4.

207   García Lorca, *Epistolario completo*, 171–3.

208   Dalí was likely aware of Barradas while still living in Figueres; his household subscribed to *La Publicidad*, and Joan Sacs published a substantial review of the 1920 Dalmau exhibition there: "Nuestras crónicas de arte. Cubismos, tómbolas y caligrafías. Barradas," *La Publicidad*, 30 May 1920.

209   This style started appearing in Barradas's work around 1920. See Santos Torroella, "Barradas–Lorca–Dalí"; Santos Torroella, "Barradas y el clownismo con Dalí y García Lorca al fondo," *Guadalimar*; Santos Torroella, "Barradas y el *clownismo* con Dalí y García Lorca al fondo," in *Rafael Barradas*.

210   Dalí, *The Secret Life of Salvador Dalí*, 175.

211   Ferris, *Maruja Mallo*, 63, 67; Vicent, "Maruja Mallo, la diosa de los cuatro brazos."

212   For a facsimile, see *Sueños noctámbulos*, Salvador-dali.org, accessed 25 May 2022, https://www.salvador-dali.org/es/obra/adquisiciones/289/suenos-noctambulos.

213   The work connects stylistically with several others from 1922; also, Lorca is noticeably absent from the group.

214   Bonet, "Maruja Mallo 'La forma expresa el contenido de una época.'"

215   *Salvador Dalí y Maruja Mallo en el Café de Oriente*, Salvador-dali.org, accessed 25 May 2022, https://www.salvador-dali.org/es/museos/teatro-museo-dali-de-figueres/exposiciones/61/de-suenos-paseos-nocturnos-y-vivencias; Brihuega and Lomba, eds, *Alberto 1895–1962*, 28.

216   Mangini, *Maruja Mallo*, 147; Costa, *De sueños, paseos nocturnos y vivencias*.

217   After Pilar's mother's death, her youngest sister came to stay with them in Madrid.

218   Brihuega and Lomba, eds, *Alberto 1895–1962*, 28.

219   Mallo, "Dalí"; Ferris, *Maruja Mallo*, 67.

220   The literal meaning of the magazine's name, *Alfar*, is "potter's workshop," and hence "the potters."

221   Pereda Valdés, ed., *Antología de la moderna poesía uruguaya*, 121.

222   "Desde Buenos Aires. Adiós a Barradas."

223   For full details, see appendix 1: "Contributors to the magazine *Alfar*."

224   "Agasajo al poeta uruguayo Julio J. Casal," *El Sol*, 11 December 1923, 4.

225   A copy of Casal's earlier collection, *Cincuenta y seis poemas*, bears a signed dedication from the author to Lorca. On the front cover there is a doodle of a face done by Dalí, and inside there is a three-quarter-length drawing of Dalí by Lorca: Vehi, ed., *Del primer Dalí al Manifest Groc*, 152–3.

226   "Agasajo al poeta uruguayo Julio J. Casal," *La Libertad*, 13 December 1923, 5.

227   "Desde La Coruña. La revista *Alfar*," *La Libertad*, 28 December 1924, 4.

228   *Tan pronto ayer*, 498. See Anderson, "*Libro de poemas versus* Ultra."

229   Castillo Marc Sardá, *Conversaciones con José "Pepín" Bello*, 68.

230   Santos Torroella, "Barradas y el *clownismo* con Dalí y García Lorca al fondo," in *Rafael Barradas*, 26.

231   Tomás Borrás, "En la ciudad. Los diez 'Parnasillos,'" *La Voz*, 21 July 1921, 1.

232   Another transitory "ism" into which Barradas situated a brief phase of his artistic output.

233   Benjamín Jarnés, "El antipapa de Oriente. Barradas," *Revista de Casa América-Galicia*, no. 31bis (August 1923): n.p. See also Jarnés's later remembrance: "Rafael Barradas," *Revista de Occidente* 23, no. 69 (March 1929): 389–91.

234 Cansinos Assens, *La novela de un literato*, vol. 3, *1923–1936*, 162–75.

235 Widely reported in the press on 21 May 1924, Alfonso Vidal y Planas was sent to prison for twelve years for the murder the previous year of Luis Antón del Olmet in a room of the Teatro Eslava.

236 Cansinos Assens, *La novela de un literato*, vol. 3, *1923–1936*, 162.

237 Ibid., 163.

238 Ibid., 164–5.

239 Ibid., 165. The month after his article about Barradas, Jarnés dedicated one to Cansinos: "El poeta de la ternura indeterminada," *Revista de Casa América-Galicia*, no. 32 (September 1923): 18.

240 An artist-illustrator of the period famous for his somewhat risqué drawings of women.

241 Cansinos Assens, *La novela de un literato*, vol. 3, *1923–1936*, 165.

242 Ibid., 166.

243 "Rincones de Madrid. Cuchilleros," 3.

244 Cansinos Assens, *La novela de un literato*, vol. 3, *1923–1936*, 166.

245 Ibid., 166–7.

246 Ibid., 168–9.

247 He had a poem printed in *Revista de Casa América-Galicia*, no. 32 (September 1923).

248 Pérez Ferrero, *Unos y otros*, 39–43. See also Méndez Bejarano, *Diccionario de escritores, maestros y oradores naturales de Sevilla y su actual provincia*, vol. 2, primera parte, 251–2, who provides the following information: born in 1899 in Sevilla, Raedo published one slim volume of poetry, *Flores de luna* (Bilbao, 1921), and announced another, *Selene*, as well as three novels and a compilation volume. Méndez Bejarano describes the poetry as possessing *modernista*, Futurist, *ultraísta*, and analogous veins of inspiration.

249 Cansinos indicates that Pizarro had published a book of *Cuentos extremeños*; there is a rare reference to *Óleos, prosas de la raza y novelas cortas* (Badajoz, 1921), which may possibly be the same volume.

250 Cansinos Assens, *La novela de un literato*, vol. 3, *1923–1936*, 171.

251 Ibid.

252 Ibid., 172.

253 Ibid., 170–1.

254 Ibid., 173.

255 Ibid., 172.

256 Ibid., 174.

257 Jarnés, *Epistolario 1919–1939*, 12.

258 Brihuega and Lomba, eds, *Barradas. Exposición antológica*, n.p.

259 *Atocha*, Museo Nacional Centro de Arte Reina Sofía, accessed 25 May 2022, https://www.museoreinasofia.es/en/collection/artwork/atocha; González Madrid, ed., *Rafael Barradas, 1914–1929*, 58.

260 Brihuega and Lomba, eds, *Barradas. Exposición antológica*, n.p.

261 Ibid., n.p.

262   Aguerre, ed., *Barradas. Colección* MNAV, 133; *Estación del mediodía*, Museo Nacional de Artes Visuales, accessed 25 May 2022, http://acervo.mnav.gub.uy/obras.php?q=ni:3130.

263   García Puig, "Barradas," 19–22.

264   *Rafael Barradas* (Galería Jorge Mara), 71; Brihuega and Lomba, eds, *Barradas. Exposición antológica*, n.p.

265   *Hombre en la taberna*, Museo Nacional de Artes Visuales, accessed 25 May 2022, http://acervo.mnav.gub.uy/obras.php?q=ni:3145; Pereda, *Barradas*, 72.

266   *Rafael Barradas* (Galería Jorge Mara), 73; Brihuega and Lomba, eds, *Barradas. Exposición antológica*, n.p.

267   González Madrid, ed., *Rafael Barradas, 1914–1929*, 59.

268   *Rafael Barradas* (Galería Palatina), 11.

269   *Composición vibracionista*, Museo Nacional Centro de Arte Reina Sofía, accessed 25 May 2022, https://www.museoreinasofia.es/coleccion/obra/composicion-vibracionista; *Rafael Barradas* (Galería Jorge Mara), 47; Brihuega and Lomba, eds, *Barradas. Exposición antológica*, n.p.

270   Bonet Correa, *Los cafés históricos*, front cover and 263; Aguerre, ed., *Rafael Barradas. Hombre flecha.*

271   Pereda, *Barradas*, 73; Brihuega and Lomba, eds, *Barradas. Exposición antológica*, n.p.

272   Gómez de la Serna, *La sagrada cripta de Pombo*, 290. The text mainly incorporates advertising copy and reads "CAFÉ | Y CERVECERÍA | SOCIAL | DE ORIENTE | KOLA CORTALS | LICOR HIGIÉNICO | PAPEL | DE | FUMAR | NIKOLA." A schematic self-portrait appears bottom right.

273   Brihuega and Lomba, eds, *Barradas. Exposición antológica*, n.p.

274   *Hombre en la taberna*, Museo Nacional de Artes Visuales, accessed 25 May 2022, http://acervo.mnav.gub.uy/obras.php?q=ni:1611; Aguerre, ed., *Barradas. Colección* MNAV, 74.

275   *Home al café (Atocha)*, Museo Nacional Centro de Arte Reina Sofía, accessed 25 May 2022, https://www.museoreinasofia.es/coleccion/obra/hombre-cafe-atocha; González Madrid, ed. *Rafael Barradas, 1914–1929*, 63.

276   Enrique Vaquer, "Crónicas de arte. El VIII Salón de Humoristas," *La Época*, 10 June 1922, 5.

277   Lists of names are given in "Anoche en Pombo. Homenaje a Díez-Canedo," *La Voz*, 21 November 1922, 4; "Ágape a Díez-Canedo," *España* 8, no. 345 (25 November 1922): 6.

278   "Banquete a Jacinto Grau," *La Voz*, 17 March 1923, 8.

279   Letters to Casal place Barradas in Madrid on 15 June and back in the capital by 15 October: García and García-Sedas, "Rafael Barradas y Julio J. Casal." Barradas writes to Jarnés on 11 September that he is feeling better and is looking forward to returning to Madrid: Jarnés, *Epistolario 1919–1939*, 11.

280   Ignacios, *Historial Rafael Barradas*, 92.

281   García and García-Sedas, "Rafael Barradas y Julio J. Casal."

282   "Guía de espectáculos. Teatros," *El Imparcial*, 15 October 1924, 8.

283   García and García-Sedas, "Rafael Barradas y Julio J. Casal."

284   See chapters 5 and 6 for more details on this exhibition.

285   Fuster del Alcázar, "Rafael Barradas y Catalina Bárcena," 4–6. Later, in Oc-
       tober, Barradas wrote to Martínez Sierra offering his services, and while in
       his response the latter softened the tone adopted in his July letters, it is clear
       that he had moved on: Pereda, *Barradas*, 180.

286   Luis Capdevila, "Exequias líricas a Rafael Barradas," *El Diluvio*, 23 February
       1929, 15.

287   Bárcena had a son, Fernando Vargas (b. 1910), almost certainly fathered by
       the veteran actor Fernando Díaz de Mendoza. Barradas praised Fernando's
       youthful artistic works to Torres-García in 1919: García-Sedas, ed., *Joaquín
       Torres-García y Rafael Barradas*, 191. In the 1920s he gave him lessons and
       even arranged for him to exhibit, at age fifteen, in the Sociedad de Artistas
       Ibéricos: Fuster del Alcázar, "Barradas y la escena," 29.

288   A good photograph of the Eslava exhibit can be found in Pereda, *Barradas*,
       172.

289   *Exposition Internationale des Arts Décoratifs et Industriels Modernes. Cata-
       logue Général Officiel*, 366.

290   "La Exposición Internacional de Artes Decorativas de París. Los artistas es-
       pañoles premiados," *La Época*, 18 November 1925, 3. Burmann also won a
       "grand prix."

291   Reyero Hermosilla, *Gregorio Martínez Sierra y su teatro de arte*, 26.

292   Fuster del Alcázar, "Rafael Barradas y Catalina Bárcena," 6 and 6n7; a letter
       from Martínez Sierra to Barradas places the former back in Madrid as of 24
       October: Pereda, *Barradas*, 180.

293   García-Sedas, ed., *Joaquín Torres-García y Rafael Barradas*, 109. A letter
       from Martínez Sierra to Barradas puts the latter in Barcelona in late October
       and refers to a likely upcoming trip to Paris that he will be making (Pereda,
       Barradas, 180). In an undated letter García Maroto wrote to Barradas ask-
       ing, "Are you off to Paris? Off to popular triumph, to active intervention in
       milieux with strong resonances?" (Aguerre, ed., *Rafael Barradas. Hombre
       flecha*, 213).

294   Pereda, *Barradas*, 174.

295   See his letter to Torres-García of 3 March 1926, written from Hospitalet,
       in García-Sedas, ed., *Joaquín Torres-García y Rafael Barradas*, 224–5. On
       13 March Barradas opened an exhibition of his work at the Dalmau gallery,
       composed mainly of drawings done in the South of France. Earlier Dalí had
       placed Barradas in Barcelona in late November and mid-December 1925, in
       a letter sent to Lorca and a postcard sent to José Bello: Santos Torroella, ed.,
       "Salvador Dalí escribe a Federico García Lorca," 24; Santos Torroella, ed.,
       "Las cartas de Salvador Dalí a José Bello Lasierra," x.

296   Brihuega, "Una estrella en el camino del arte español," 39–40; Lasso, "Escritos
       III," 236–7.

297 Santiago de la Cruz, "Aspectos de Madrid. Las 'peñas' literarias," *Heraldo de Madrid*, 3 September 1929, 12.

Chapter Three

1 Document 7-378-4, Archivo de la Villa, Madrid.

2 On the topic of pleasure gardens, or recreational gardens, in fashion in the nineteenth century, see "Los Jardines de Recreo," El paisaje de Madrid, 28 May 2014, http://elpaisajedemadrid.blogspot.com/2014/05/los-jardines-de-recreo.html, where the Alhambra theatre gardens are mentioned.

3 In the last decade of the nineteenth century, the Teatro Alhambra underwent a name change to Teatro Moderno, although many continued to refer to it by its original name. In 1905, it was demolished in order to construct two apartment houses.

4 For more details on its architectural configuration, see M.R. Jiménez, "El Pasaje de la Alhambra y sus pintores," Antiguos cafés de Madrid, 27 April 2018, http://antiguoscafesdemadrid.blogspot.com/2018/04/el-pasaje-de-la-alhambra-y-sus-pintores.html.

5 See ibid. a good photo of the building they occupied.

6 Anon., "El deshojar de la margarita y la política municipal"; Carandell, "El caso del Pasaje de la Alhambra"; Carandell, "Epílogo para el Pasaje de la Alhambra"; Sampelayo, "El Pasaje de la Alhambra se va"; Ramírez de Lucas, "Arquitectura y urbanismo."

7 José Fernández Bremón, "Crónica general," *La Ilustración Española y Americana* 32, no. 16 (30 April 1888): 2.

8 P. Millán, "Nuestros pintores. Casto Plasencia," *El País*, 3 May 1888, 1–2. See also J. Ortega Munilla, "Madrid. (Noticias de pintura)," *Los Lunes de El Imparcial*, 21 May 1888, 5.

9 "En el estudio de Plasencia," *La Iberia*, 28 October 1888, 2. See also A. Sánchez Pérez, "Madrid contemporáneo. I. El estudio de Plasencia," *La Ilustración Ibérica. Semanario Científico, Literario y Artístico* (Barcelona) 7, no. 344 (3 August 1889): 486–7.

10 "En el estudio de Plasencia," *La Época*, 19 June 1889, 3. See also "Nuestros grabados. Bellas Artes," *La Ilustración Española y Americana* 33, no. 25 (8 July 1889): 7.

11 A. Sánchez Pérez, "Madrid contemporáneo. I. El estudio de Plasencia," *La Ilustración Ibérica. Semanario Científico, Literario y Artístico* (Barcelona) 7, no. 344 (3 August 1889): 486. Another similar description is to be found in R. Blanco Asenjo, "Dos talleres y un cuadro. (A la memoria del ilustre y malogrado Plasencia)," *La Ilustración Ibérica. Semanario Científico, Literario y Artístico* (Barcelona) 8, no. 405 (4 October 1890): 634. An excellent photo of the interior of the studio and its diverse accoutrements, as of 1888, is available at http://ceres.mcu.es/pages/Viewer?accion=4&AMuseo=MSM&Ninv=83952.

12   R. Blanco Asenjo, "Dos talleres y un cuadro. (A la memoria del ilustre y malogrado Plasencia)," *La Ilustración Ibérica. Semanario Científico, Literario y Artístico* (Barcelona) 8, no. 405 (4 October 1890): 634.

13   "Jiménez Aranda, José," Museo del Prado, accessed 26 May 2022, https://www.museodelprado.es/aprende/enciclopedia/voz/jimenez-aranda-jose/95205715-1109-4642-adbd-969d2ae6198a. For more details, see Pérez Calero, *José Jiménez Aranda.*

14   "Noticias varias," *El Correo Militar,* 7 January 1892, 2.

15   Pavlova Todorova, "Consola, 1905, de Joaquín Sorolla," 5.

16   "Ecos madrileños," *La Época*, 2 May 1897, 1.

17   See Museo Sorolla, accessed 26 May 2022, http://ceres.mcu.es/, inventory numbers 80011, 80012, 80016, 80236, 80672, 80676, 80677, 81189, 81190, 81191, 81196, 81197, 81198, 81199, 81200, 81668, 81670, 82865, 83952, 85995, 85996, 86523, 86524.

18   "Estudio de Sorolla en el Pasaje de La Alhambra, Madrid," Museo Sorolla, accessed 26 May 2022, http://ceres.mcu.es/pages/Viewer?accion=4&AMuseo=MSM&Ninv=81189.

19   "Estudio de Sorolla en el Pasaje de La Alhambra, Madrid," Museo Sorolla, accessed 26 May 2022, http://ceres.mcu.es/pages/Viewer?accion=4&AMuseo=MSM&Ninv=80672. Based on a passing reference, I suspect that for part of the decade (1893–1903) Sorolla let his friend Cecilio Plá y Gallardo use some of the space or that Plá occupied a contiguous studio: see "Asaltos de armas. En honor de Merignac," *La Época*, 27 January 1901, 2.

20   "Pasaje de La Alhambra," Museo Sorolla, accessed 26 May 2022, http://ceres.mcu.es/pages/Viewer?accion=4&AMuseo=MSM&Ninv=00584.

21   Pavlova Todorova, "Consola, 1905, de Joaquín Sorolla," 11–12. In 1911 Sorolla had the house built on Paseo General Martínez Campos that we know today as the Museo Sorolla.

22   Francisco Alcántara, "Notas de arte," *El Imparcial*, 6 January 1909, 1.

23   Ibid. Alcántara notes that while the building in the Pasaje is not old, it can already be considered as historic.

24   Note the reference to the Duque de Tovar, already mentioned here: "Asaltos de armas. En honor de Merignac," *La Época*, 27 January 1901, 2. Sorolla was a personal friend of the duke and painted a famous portrait of his daughter María Figueroa.

25   On the previous history of such institutions, see Pérez Calero, "La Academia Libre."

26   His actual name was Manuel Ortiz Gallardo; he added Ángeles following the pattern of using two first names established by Julio Antonio and Juan Cristóbal: Moya Morales, "Los nombres de Manuel Ángeles Ortiz".

27   Rodrigo, *Memoria de Granada*, 200–2. From Granada, José Mora Guarnido announces the wedding and the new Madrid address to Fernández Almagro: Escoriza Escoriza, "La generación de plata," 102.

28 García Lorca, *Epistolario completo*, 62–5. Lorca and Ángeles Ortiz were childhood friends: Rodrigo, *Memoria de Granada*, 31–2.

29 Letters from Gregorio Martínez Sierra in Madrid to Lorca in Granada, 1920: Archivo Federico García Lorca, Centro Federico García Lorca, Granada, inventory numbers COA-645, COA-646, and COA-647; García Lorca, *Epistolario completo*, 66; Mora Guarnido, *Federico García Lorca y su mundo*, 125.

30 See the article by Lorca, "Notas de arte. Sainz de la Maza," *Gaceta del Sur* (Granada), 27 May 1920, 1. There are several letters written by Lorca to his parents through April, but these dry up completely from May onward: *Epistolario completo*, 69–77. In a slightly earlier letter Lorca had announced that "until the month of May I won't be able to leave here" (68). After the premiere of *El maleficio* his parents wanted him to return to Granada, but Federico defended his decision to stay longer (72–5).

31 Rodrigo, *Memoria de Granada*, 203. Carmona points out that through Lorca, Ortiz would have met Martínez Sierra and Catalina Bárcena and then also Barradas: "Manuel Ángeles Ortiz en los años del 'Arte Nuevo.' 1918–1939," 21–2.

32 Rodrigo, *Memoria de Granada*, 106–47. This was the name given to the *tertulia* whose "home base" was the Café Alameda in Granada; see Escoriza Escoriza, ed., *La generación de plata*, 17–35, 61–121.

33 For an evocation of the friends' time in Madrid, see Mora Guarnido, *Federico García Lorca y su mundo*, 116–22.

34 Rodrigo, *Memoria de Granada*, 202, 204.

35 García Lorca, *Epistolario completo*, 66.

36 Ibid., 67.

37 Ibid., 69. 2 April is Saint Francis of Paola's day.

38 Lozano Miralles, ed., *Crónica de una amistad*, 36.

39 García Lorca, *Epistolario completo*, 80n180, 83n190.

40 Ibid., 85; Antonio Rodríguez Espinosa, Lorca's old primary school teacher and family friend lived in Madrid.

41 Ibid., 87.

42 Ibid., 89.

43 Rodrigo, *Memoria de Granada*, 204–6.

44 Carmona comments, "it is hard to know what Ángeles Ortiz undertook in the French capital during this first trip and it is also difficult to establish with precision the chronology of his work between 1920 and 1922": "Manuel Ángeles Ortiz en los años del 'Arte Nuevo,'" 23.

45 García Lorca, *Epistolario completo*, 115.

46 Rodrigo, *Memoria de Granada*, 209, 215; Anon., "Biografía," in *Manuel Ángeles Ortiz*, 191.

47 Lozano Miralles, ed., *Crónica de una amistad*, 46.

48 Escoriza Escoriza, "La generación de plata," 78. Cristóbal is referenced in more detail below.

49 García Lorca, *Epistolario completo*, 143. At his father's insistence, Lorca would not return at all to Madrid during 1922, in order to concentrate on finishing his undergraduate degree in law at the Universidad de Granada.

50 Carmona, "Manuel Ángeles Ortiz en los años del 'Arte Nuevo,'" 24n29.

51 Rodrigo, *Memoria de Granada*, 210–1.

52 Ibid., 215; Anon., "Biografía," in *Manuel Ángeles Ortiz*, 191.

53 Rodrigo, *Memoria de Granada*, 211.

54 Prados and Lorca had met when they were teenagers, when Lorca's family was vacationing on the south coast; they had met again at the Residencia de Estudiantes at the beginning of 1920.

55 Caffarena, *Manuel Ángeles Ortiz*, 25–6.

56. Rodrigo, *Memoria de Granada*, 212.

57 Ibid., 29, 215; Anon., "Biografía," in *Manuel Ángeles Ortiz*, 191.

58 Rodrigo, *Memoria de Granada*, 215.

59 Ibid., 218.

60 Ibid., 222–3. The same design was also reproduced on the cover of the pamphlet that printed, anonymously, Falla's musicological notes on *El "cante jondo" (canto primitivo andaluz)*: see Escoriza Escoriza, "La generación de plata," plates between 96 and 97.

61 In the sense of a manuscript's illuminations.

62 Rodrigo, *Memoria de Granada*, 120–1. In this, Lorca may have been influenced by Barradas's quite similar ideas.

63 García Lorca, *Epistolario completo*, 153–4.

64 José Francés, "Los bellos ejemplos. En Granada resucita el guignol," *La Esfera*, 10, no. 475 (10 February 1923): n.p.

65 Rodrigo, *Memoria de Granada*, 235. Rodrigo ascribes the letter to 24 October, but the collective postcard to Lorca described immediately below appears to be from the eighteenth and already places Ángeles Ortiz in Paris. This postcard cannot be from the twenty-eighth (rather than the eighteenth), given that Prados wrote to Lorca on that date from Ulm: Tinnell, "Epistolario," 43.

66 Rodrigo, *Memoria de Granada*, 234–6.

67 Archivo de la Fundación García Lorca, document COA-804. García Chacón, "'Unidos por una goma elástica,'" offers a transcription and a small reproduction of the postcard, 121–2.

68 Hernández, *Emilio Prados*, 1:31. On arriving in Freiberg, Emilio found there another friend of his and Lorca's from the Residencia de Estudiantes, José Antonio Rubio Sacristán.

69 Anon., "Biografía," in *Manuel Ángeles Ortiz*, 191; Rodrigo, *Memoria de Granada*, 236, 241.

70 Hernández, *Emilio Prados*, 1:31. On their travels around Germany they sent several postcards to Federico and his brother Francisco: Tinnell, "Epistolario," 43–5.

71 See the biography at Soriaaedo.com, accessed 26 May 2022, http://www.soriaaedo.com/biografia.html.

72 One of the very few monographs about this painter, simply entitled *Julio Moisés*, lists no author.

73 "Julio Moisés Fernández de Villasante," Real Academia de la Historia, accessed 27 May 2022, http://dbe.rah.es/biografias/11417/julio-moises-fernandez-de-villasante; Recio Aguado, "Arte en la academia," 299.

74 To the point that some critics even construe the name incorrectly, believing that it refers to a landscape school – an *escuela de paisaje* (confused with *pasaje*).

75 "Noticias," *La Voz*, 7 March 1924, 6.

76 "Arte y artistas. El IV Salón Internacional de fotografía," *Gran Vida. Revista Ilustrada* 22, no. 248 (February 1924): 49.

77 "De arte. Manifestaciones de vida," *La Correspondencia de España*, 5 May 1924, 1.

78 "De arte. Homenaje a Julio Moisés," *La Libertad*, 21 January 1925, 4.

79 Pérez Segura, "Tejada y la pintura moderna en España," 40.

80 Ibid., 57–8; Sáenz de Tejada Benvenuti, "Cronología," 277.

81 On the top floor the dividing wall between numbers 7 and 9 had been removed, creating one very large space: Sáenz de Tejada Benvenuti, "Cronología," 272.

82 Pérez Segura, "Tejada y la pintura moderna en España," 22.

83 Ibid., 23; Sáenz de Tejada Benvenuti, "Cronología," 272.

84 An ornate, full-colour *Boceto para el estudio del Horno de la Mata*, painted by Sáenz de Tejada, is reproduced in Escribano, ed., *Carlos Sáenz de Tejada*, 35.

85 Pérez Segura, "Tejada y la pintura moderna en España," 22–3; here the text is attributed to a newspaper article by Manaut Viglietti, "Carlos Sáenz de Tejada. Evocación," but it does not actually appear there. Curiously, the same passage, with a number of minor textual variants, is reproduced in J.L.M.M., "Biografía. Ismael Cuesta (1899–1982)," with no attribution of source.

86 J. Blanco Coris, "Arte y artistas. En el estudio de Ismael Cuesta," *Heraldo de Madrid*, 23 April 1921, 1.

87 Pérez Segura, "Tejada y la pintura moderna en España"; J.L.M.M., "Biografía. Ismael Cuesta (1899–1982)."

88 J.L.M.M., "Biografía. Ismael Cuesta (1899–1982)."

89 Pérez Segura, "Tejada y la pintura moderna en España," 23; Manaut Viglietti, "Carlos Sáenz de Tejada. Evocación." A good photograph of Sáenz de Tejada, Bores, and Cuesta together inside the studio can be seen at http://ismaelcuesta.blogspot.com/.

90 Pérez Segura, "Joaquín Peinado en los escenarios," 32, and "Cronología," 89.

91 Pérez Segura, "Joaquín Peinado en los escenarios," 34, 36, and "Tejada y la pintura moderna en España," 39. Pérez Segura records Tejada receiving a scholarship to El Paular for 1921 ("Joaquín Peinado en los escenarios," 34; "Tejada y la pintura moderna en España," 38), and Esteban Drake lists him as a recipient also for 1922 and 1923 (*De El Paular a Segovia 1919–1991*, 100,

104). Likewise, Esteban Drake lists Peinado as going to El Paular in those same three years: 1921, 1922, and 1923 (*De El Paular a Segovia 1919–1991*, 99, 100, 104).

92 Pérez Segura, "Tejada y la pintura moderna en España," 58; Carmona, "Bores ultraísta," 15.

93 "El incendio de anoche," *El Liberal*, 21 January 1925, 3; "Sucesos de Madrid. Un voraz incendio ha destruido el estudio de un pintor," *Heraldo de Madrid*, 21 January 1925, 2. According to the newspaper reports, the space was in the name of Tejada's uncle, Antonio Mora. The cause was the sawdust-fuelled heating stove, which had caused two previous, though less serious, fires: Sáenz de Tejada Benvenuti, "Cronología," 272.

94 Pérez Ferrero, *Unos y otros*, 172.

95 Ibid., 171–2. The Saboya, or Savoya, was squeezed in between the theatre and another well-known café, La Elipa: González-Ruano, *Memorias*, 157.

96 Bonet and Pérez, *El ultraísmo y las artes plásticas*, 227. The book's cover was designed by Salvador Bartolozzi.

97 Located on calle Carranza, 13. See "Con Cecilio Pla," Jesualdo Gallego Navajas (blog), accessed 27 May 2022, http://jesualdogallegonavajas.blogspot.com/p/con-cecilio-pla.html.

98 Marchand, ed., "Propos de l'artiste," 15–16; Bores, "Notas autobiográficas," 13; Dechanet, "Biografía" (1999), 167; Dechanet, "Biografía" (2003), 21; Carmona, "Bores ultraísta," 15; Tusell, "Francisco Bores," 100.

99 Marchand, ed., "Propos de l'artiste," 17; Osma, "Bores," 5–6; Carmona, "Bores ultraísta," 15; Dechanet, "Biografía" (1999), 168.

100 A. de L., "La Exposición Nacional de Bellas Artes," *La Libertad*, 28 June 1922, 4–5.

101 Pérez Bazo, *Juan Chabás*, 14.

102 Mangini, *Maruja Mallo y la vanguardia española*, 147 (no source is identified).

103 Carmona, "Bores ultraísta," 47. Dechanet expands the list to include the Gijón, Pombo, Lhardy, La Granja de El Henar, and Lyon d'Or ("Biografía" [1999], 168), which seems more like a list of notable *tertulias* rather than ones that we know for certain Bores frequented.

104 Carmona, "Naturaleza y cultura," 48.

105 Ibid.

106 Pérez Ferrero, "Sáenz de Tejada, recuerdos de otros días."

107 Faraldo, *Benjamín Palencia*, quoted by Corredor-Matheos, *Vida y obra de Benjamín Palencia*, 40.

108 García Lorca, *Epistolario completo*, 273.

109 *Bores nuevo. Los años veinte y treinta*, 39–40. The effort came to naught, perhaps because of their reluctance to join in, perhaps because of the onset of the summer months.

110 It was 1924, according to *Eduardo Vicente: El pintor de Madrid*, 3–4; 1925, according to Anon., "A modo de currículum vitae de Eduardo Vicente," 217–18.

111 *Eduardo Vicente: El pintor de Madrid*, 3–4; Dechanet, "Biografía" (1999), 168.

112 Most of this information comes from Quesada Dorador, "Juan Cristóbal (1896–1961)," 15–23.

113 See "Biografía (1896–1920)," Juancristobalescultor.es, accessed 27 May 2022, https://juancristobalescultor.es/biografia-1896-1920/. In 1919 he transferred it to the calle Don Ramón de la Cruz, 56.

114 Antonio de Hoyos y Vinent, "Exposiciones," *El Día*, 24 February 1917, 3; José Francés, "De Bellas Artes. La exposición del Ateneo," *Mundo Gráfico* 7, no. 279 (28 February 1917): n.p.

115 Other works of note are busts of Falla and Miguel Pizarro.

116 Recio Aguado, "Arte en la academia," 299.

117 "En honor del Sr. Edwards Bello," *El Fígaro*, 26 March 1920, 6.

118 "Homenaje a Eva de Aggerholm y a Vázquez Díaz," *La Libertad*, 7 May 1921, 7; "Banquete a dos artistas," *La Acción*, 16 May 1921, 3; "Banquete en honor de Vázquez Díaz y Eva Aggerholm," *La Libertad*, 17 May 1921, 3; "Biografía (1921–1930)," Juancristobalescultor.es, accessed 27 May 2022, https://juancristobalescultor.es/biografia-1921-1930/

119 Dalí was suspended on 18 October 1923 but was allowed to return to do his second-year coursework during the 1924–25 academic year.

120 Moreno Villa, *Vida en claro*, 161.

121 Santos Torroella, *Dalí residente*, 39.

122 "Comarcal. Figueras, 22," *Diario de Gerona*, 24 May 1924, 5. He was freed twenty days later.

123 Andrés Segovia, Emilio Carrere, Rafael Lasso de la Vega, and Pedro Luis de Gálvez, according to "Enrique Estévez Ochoa," Real Academia de la Historia, accessed 27 May 2022, http://dbe.rah.es/biografias/85346/enrique-estevez-ochoa; Ramón Gómez de la Serna, Mauricio Bacarisse, and José Bergamín according to "Enrique Estévez Ochoa," Wikipedia, last edited 19 November 2021, https://es.wikipedia.org/wiki/Enrique_Est%C3%A9vez_Ochoa. See also "Enrique Ochoa: Pintor de El Puerto," 31 October 2010, Gente del puerto, https://www.gentedelpuerto.com/2010/10/31/819-enrique-ochoa-pintor-de-el-puerto/.

124 Falcón, *Asalto a los cielos*, 34–5. See also chapter 6 of this volume.

125 Fouchet, *Wifredo Lam*, 54; "Biography," Wildredo Lam (blog), accessed 27 May 2022, https://www.wifredolam.net/en/biography.html.

126 Sánchez, "El artista adolescente," 6.

127 Borràs, "Lam in Spain," 18–19.

128 Fouchet, *Wifredo Lam*, 76–8; Núñez Jiménez, *Wifredo Lam*, 87–9; "Cronología 1923–1938," Wilfredolam.net, accessed 27 May 2022, https://www.wifredolam.net/es/cronologia/1923-1938.html.

129 Nuevo Cal and Álvarez González, *Maruja Mallo*, 3–4; Nuevo Cal and Ínsua López, *Maruja Mallo*, 48. See also chapter 6 of this volume.

130 Escribano, "Maruja Mallo, una bruja moderna," 46. According to Meléndez Táboas, two other women entered at that time, Milagros Tercero and

Encarnación Rubio y Gómez, though they might have taken the entrance exam at a different moment: "Maruja Mallo entre sus condiscípulas," 117–18.

131 Mangini, *Maruja Mallo y la vanguardia española*, 50, 147; it is difficult to know exactly what year this datum corresponds to (before or after 1924). See also Rivas, "Maruja Mallo, pintora del más allá," 16, and chapter 2 of this volume.

132 Conversation with Maruja Mallo, quoted in Borràs, "Palencia, introductor del surrealismo," 8.

133 See chapter 6.

134 Cabañas Bravo, "La Historia del Arte en el Centro de Estudios Históricos de la JAE," 146.

135 Moreno Villa, *Vida en claro*, 101.

136 Moreno Villa, *Memoria*, 340–1.

137 Moreno Villa, *Vida en claro*, 114–17. He sent six drawings to the collective exhibition collecting money for the Russian people threatened by hunger, which was held in the Ateneo Obrero of Gijón in March 1922: Pérez de Ayala, ed., *José Moreno Villa (1887–1955)*, 208; see also the number of the magazine *Prisma* (Paris) corresponding to April 1922.

138 Pérez de Ayala, "Miscelánea biográfica," 107.

139 Carmona, "José Moreno Villa," 38.

140 Moreno Villa, *Vida en claro*, 161–2. The date is confirmed by what he had written years previously, in a manuscript of 1939: "My dedication to painting was formalized in the year 1924 as a result of the problems that cubism posed to my mind" (Moreno Villa, *Memoria*, 280).

141 Moreno Villa, "La exposición desde lejos," *Hermes*, nos 46–7 (1919): 308–10, in Moreno Villa, *Temas de arte*, 178.

142 Moreno Villa, "Hombres, hechos, intereses, ideas. Exposición Barradas en el Ateneo de Madrid," *Hermes*, no. 57 (March 1920): 161, in Moreno Villa, *Temas de arte*, 181.

143 Moreno Villa, "Hombres, hechos, intereses, ideas. Exposición Vázquez Díaz en Madrid," *Hermes*, no. 69 (March 1921): 235–6, in Moreno Villa, *Temas de arte*, 199–200.

144 Moreno Villa, "Puntos de arte. La rosa, la columna y la nube," *El Sol*, 24 October 1924, 2, in Moreno Villa, *Temas de arte*, 226.

145 Moreno Villa, "Orientaciones artísticas. El arte de mi tiempo," *El Norte de Castilla*, 14 May 1925, 1, in Moreno Villa, *Temas de arte*, 242.

146 Corredor-Matheos, *Vida y obra de Benjamín Palencia*, 14–19.

147 Benjamín Palencia in "Juan Ramón Jiménez, juzgado por sus contemporáneos y discípulos," 38; Soler Serrano, "[Entrevista con Benjamín Palencia]"; Corredor-Matheos, "Benjamín Palencia," 194.

148 Hoz and Madariaga, *Pancho Cossío*, 127, 202.

149 Florisel, "Una lamentable exposición," *Renovación Española* 1, no. 36 (3 October 1918): n.p.

150 *España* 9, no. 397 (24 November 1923): 10; *Revista de Occidente* 1, no. 5 (November 1923): 163–70; *España* 10, no. 410 (16 February 1924): 8.

151 Pérez Segura, "Tejada y la pintura moderna en España," 58; Sáenz de Tejada Benvenuti also reproduces a photograph, dated to 1923, of the two together at a fair: "Cronología," 277.

152 Campoy, "Crítica de exposiciones," 21.

153 Recio Aguado, "Arte en la academia," 299.

154 Esteban Drake, *De El Paular a Segovia 1919–1991*, 99.

155 Some of his designs are reproduced in Martínez Sierra, *Un teatro de arte en España, 1917–1925*.

156 Anon., "Cronología," in *Penagos (1889–1954)*, 67.

157 The most detailed biographical account is provided by Arcediano and García Díez, *Carlos Sáenz de Tejada*, 22–52; see also Sáenz de Tejada Benvenuti, "Cronología," 269. His father was in the diplomatic service.

158 Pérez Segura, "Tejada y la pintura moderna en España," 17–20; Sáenz de Tejada Benvenuti, "Cronología," 269–70; Arcediano and García Díez, *Carlos Sáenz de Tejada*, 30–3. Sáenz de Tejada Benvenuti mentions Álvarez de Sotomayor as another mentor: "Cronología," 274, 275.

159 Arcediano and García Díez, *Carlos Sáenz de Tejada*, 34.

160 Other sources give 1916 as the date, but 1915 appears to be the most solidly documented.

161 Sáenz de Tejada Benvenuti, "Cronología," 275.

162 See Escribano, ed., *Carlos Sáenz de Tejada*, for a full treatment. His uncle on his mother's side, Antonio de Lezama, helped him join *La Libertad*: Arcediano and García Díez, *Carlos Sáenz de Tejada*, 30.

163 As it turns out, by his own uncle(!): Antonio de Lezama, "De arte. Salón de Otoño de la Asociación de Pintores y Escultores", *La Libertad*, 5 December 1920, 5.

164 Pérez Segura, "Tejada y la pintura moderna en España," 58.

165 Arcediano and García Díez, *Carlos Sáenz de Tejada*, 49; Vázquez Astorga, "El diario madrileño," 427 and 427n18.

166 He sent four paintings that were hung in the room, Sala X, shared with Salvador Dalí: Arcediano and García Díez, *Carlos Sáenz de Tejada*, 50.

167 He received a fellowship from the Junta para Ampliación de Estudios to extend his studies, and also got married immediately before leaving: Sáenz de Tejada Benvenuti, "Cronología," 278–9.

168 Pérez Ferrero, "Sáenz de Tejada, recuerdos de otros días."

169 Bonet, "Santa Cruz. El cuarto mosquetero," 11–22; Grandes, "De Paco Santa Cruz a Francisco López," 145–51.

170 Anon., "A modo de currículum vitae de Eduardo Vicente," 217.

171 Doldán, "Esteban Vicente y Eduardo Vicente Madrid." There is some confusion as to whether Eduardo and Bonafé shared both studios, or if they only came on to the scene with the second one, on the Paseo del Prado: see Anon.,

"A modo de currículum vitae de Eduardo Vicente," 217, and *Eduardo Vicente: El pintor de Madrid*, 3.

172   Doldán, "Esteban Vicente y Eduardo Vicente Madrid"; Vicente, "Credo pictórico de Eduardo Vicente," 235; "Cabezas," "Mentidero de la Villa," *ABC*, 20 July 1975, 30.

173   Pérez Ferrero, *Unos y otros*, 223; Anon., "A modo de currículum vitae de Eduardo Vicente," 217–18; *Eduardo Vicente: El pintor de Madrid*, 3–4; Doldán, "Esteban Vicente y Eduardo Vicente Madrid."

174   Vicente, "Credo pictórico de Eduardo Vicente," 235.

175   *La pintura de Eduardo Vicente*, 10.

176   Vicente, "Credo pictórico de Eduardo Vicente," 235.

177   "Notas de arte. Exposición del Liceo de la Juventud," *La Época*, 17 April 1925, 3; Rafael Marquina, "Bellas Artes. Las exposiciones. Liceo de la Juventud," *Heraldo de Madrid*, 17 April 1925, 5; "De arte. Exposición del Liceo de la Juventud," *La Voz*, 17 April 1925, 2.

Chapter Four

1   For a panoramic summary of the history of the JAE, see Sánchez Ron, "La Junta para Ampliación de Estudios e Investigaciones Científicas ochenta años después." On its intellectual origins in the ILE, see Cacho Viu, "La Junta para Ampliación de Estudios"; Sánchez de Andrés, "La Junta para Ampliación de Estudios dentro del proyecto institucionista"; and García-Velasco, "Un proyecto para la modernización de España." Cacho Viu's comments on the educational philosophy and liberal political agenda of the JAE were later nuanced by García-Velasco in an identically titled article, "La Junta para Ampliación de Estudios."

2   A brief sequence featuring Castillejo appears in the documentary film *¿Qué es España?*. On Castillejo's intellectual formation, see Abellán Velasco, "José Castillejo, profesor de derecho romano."

3   Sánchez Ron, "Encuentros y desencuentros," 100.

4   Romero de Pablos and Sánchez Ron, "Cronología," 32; Carande, "Fortuny, 14," 75; García Camarero, "La Junta para Ampliación de Estudios." Later it moved to calle Almagro, 26.

5   The CEH additionally organized summer courses from 1912 onward, and in 1920 set up the Instituto de las Españas in New York under the directorship of Federico de Onís: García-Velasco, "El reencuentro con la modernidad," 65–6; Vázquez Ramil, *Mujeres y educación*, 89. Other diverse aspects of the CEH are treated in the nine articles in volume 2 of Sánchez Ron and José García-Velasco, eds, *100 años de la JAE*.

6   The broad history of these general developments has been covered well in a number of recent studies: Cacho Viu, "La Junta para Ampliación de Estudios," 16–23; Alarcó, ed., *Laboratorios de la nueva educación*; Basabe and

López Cobo, "La Residencia de Señoritas"; Codina-Canet and San Segundo, "Fuentes documentales y archivo"; García-Velasco, ed., *Redes internacionales*; Romero de Pablos and Sánchez Ron, "Cronología"; Sánchez Ron, ed., *La Junta para la Ampliación de Estudios*; Sánchez Ron, "La Junta para Ampliación de Estudios"; Vázquez Ramil, *Mujeres y educación.*

7   Fortuny was only three to four blocks away from the JAE's central offices at calle Almagro, 26.

8   Ramil Vázquez, "La Residencia de Señoritas," 508, 512. The street numbering had changed from 12 and 14; the Residencia de Estudiantes had started in Fortuny, 14, then over successive years had added 10, 8, and 12. Carande offers an evocative description of the tiny bedrooms and other sparse living conditions in "Fortuny, 14," 75, when it housed the original Residencia de Estudiantes in 1910.

9   Cueva, "Los Grupos de Niños y Niñas de la Residencia de Estudiantes," 41.

10 Vázquez Ramil, "La Residencia de Señoritas," 508; Vázquez Ramil, *Mujeres y educación*, 159–60; Cueva, "Los grupos de niños y niñas de la Residencia de Estudiantes," 41.

11 Zulueta and Moreno, *Ni convento ni college*, 33–4.

12 When Delhy Tejero first came to study in Madrid, her father arranged for her to live at a girls' boarding school run by nuns. Another alternative was the Academia Teresiana, established in 1914: see Cuesta, Turrión, and Merino, "Dos residencias universitarias femeninas"; Flecha García, "Alumnas y equipos directivos"; and Peralta Ortiz, "Orígenes y características."

13 For other factors entering into the initiative, see Cueva, "La Residencia de Señoritas," and Cueva, "Traspasando fronteras, nuevos horizontes," 286–8. The overall issue of limited access to (higher) education for women is treated by Vázquez Ramil, *Mujeres y educación*, 107–27.

14 Carmen de Munárriz, "La Residencia de Señoritas en la intimidad," *Estampa* 3, no. 118 (15 April 1930): n.p.

15 Cueva, "Traspasando fronteras, nuevos horizontes"; Vázquez Ramil, *Mujeres y educación*, 129–55; Pérez-Villanueva Tovar, "María de Maeztu en la Residencia de Señoritas."

16 Cueva, "Los Grupos de Niños y Niñas de la Residencia de Estudiantes," 42; Cueva, "Los Grupos de Niños y Niñas de la Residencia de Estudiantes en el origen del Instituto-Escuela," 416–29; Pérez-Villanueva Tovar, *La Residencia de Estudiantes*, 283–5.

17 Zulueta and Moreno, *Ni convento ni college*, 67, 90, 132–3; Vázquez Ramil, "La Residencia de Señoritas," 512; Vázquez Ramil, *Mujeres y educación*, 162, 275; Guerrero, "Un lugar de memoria," 301; Pérez-Villanueva Tovar, *La Residencia de Estudiantes*, 283–7. The Instituto de Segunda Enseñanza Fortuny is located on these calle Fortuny lots today.

18 On Alice Gordon see the extensive coverage provided by Zulueta, *Misioneras, feministas, educadoras*, 39–41, 66, 75–95, 97–116, 117–37.

19 The private ILE school offered a program of progressive, sometimes experimental, coeducation classes at the primary and secondary levels. See Zulueta, *Misioneras, feministas, educadoras*, 172–3.

20 Zulueta, *Misioneras, feministas, educadoras*, 139–40.

21 The ILE survives in its contemporary form as the Fundación Francisco Giner de los Ríos.

22 Zulueta and Moreno, *Ni convento ni college*, 79–86; Huguet, "Modernidad y género."

23 Technically, these were two abutting lots, one on each of the mentioned streets: Guerrero, "Un lugar de memoria," 306; Zulueta, *Misioneras, feministas, educadoras*, 145. With their purchase the Instituto Internacional owned three-quarters of the city block.

24 Zulueta, *Misioneras, feministas, educadoras*, 148–51.

25 Ibid., 155–7.

26 Ibid., 157–60. With time, this address has become synonymous with the building.

27 Ibid., 165–8.

28 Ibid., 172, 241. Huntington served until 1916, but after relinquishing the directorship remained on the Instituto Internacional's board. The religious mission/school part of the enterprise became entirely separate and transferred to Barcelona in 1910.

29 Piñón, "El Instituto Internacional en España," 258. Zulueta, *Misioneras, feministas, educadoras*, reproduces a pamphlet from the period summarizing the educational opportunities: Magisterio, Bachillerato, Conservatorio, "a completely English education" (i.e., primary), kindergarten, and English classes, as well as accommodation for participants in the JAE's summer courses for foreigners (169–72, 176). On the growth of the institution, see 174–9.

30 Zulueta, *Misioneras, feministas, educadoras*, 181–2, 216, 219–20.

31 García-Velasco, "El reencuentro con la modernidad," 58–9; Zulueta, *Misioneras, feministas, educadoras*, 217. Rental agreements were renewed through the 1920s, and the JAE eventually concluded the purchase of Fortuny, 53, in 1927: Zulueta and Moreno, *Ni convento ni college*, 110, 113. Memorial Hall remained in the possession of the Boston-based International Institute for Girls in Spain; in the post-Franco era, Fortuny, 53 became the headquarters of the Fundación Ortega y Gasset.

32 Cueva, "Los Grupos de Niños y Niñas de la Residencia de Estudiantes," 42.

33 Zulueta and Moreno, *Ni convento ni college*, 89–96; Vázquez Ramil, *Mujeres y educación*, 166, 191; Guerrero, "Un lugar de memoria," 306.

34 Cueva, "Los Grupos de Niños y Niñas de la Residencia de Estudiantes," 42–4.

35 Zulueta, *Misioneras, feministas, educadoras*, 221–2, 229–37.

36 Vázquez Ramil, "La Residencia de Señoritas," 512; Vázquez Ramil, *Mujeres y educación*, 203.

37 Pérez-Villanueva Tovar, "La Residencia de Señoritas," 149–53; Vázquez Ramil, *Mujeres y educación*. The tables provided by Vázquez Ramil show university

enrollment increasing from 1 in 1915 to 39 in 1921 and to 102 by 1927 (*Mujeres y educación*, 200, 209).

38 Pérez-Villanueva Tovar, "La Residencia de Señoritas," 149.

39 Ontañón, "El Instituto-Escuela, experiencia educativa." It was set up to provide primary education in three grades, ages 8 through 10, and secondary in six grades, ages 11 through 17; kindergarten was added later. In 1918, only the first four grades were offered, with the intention that existing pupils would go on to populate the higher grades in subsequent years (214).

40 Vázquez Ramil, *Mujeres y educación*, 95; Ontañón, "El Instituto-Escuela, experiencia educativa," 217.

41 An article from 1926 contains evocative photographs of the Residencia de Estudiantes site and buildings, Jiménez de la Espada, his wife Isabel Suárez, and a group of boys, the vestibule and a bedroom, boys around a piano, and the dining room at lunchtime: R., "En la Residencia de Niños."

42 García-Velasco, "El reencuentro con la modernidad," 57–9; Zulueta and Moreno, *Ni convento ni college*, 114; Vázquez Ramil, *Mujeres y educación*, 96.

43 Cueva, "Los Grupos de Niños y Niñas de la Residencia de Estudiantesr," 42, 44.

44 Essentially, José Castillejo, seconded by the pedagogue Luis Álvarez Santullano, then director of the Grupo de Niños.

45 Zulueta and Moreno, *Ni convento ni college*, 102n89, 114, 133–5; Vázquez Ramil, *Mujeres y educación*, 166, 169, 193–5, 208, 277; Pérez-Villanueva Tovar, *La Residencia de Estudiantes*, 284. Rooms for the girls were provided at Fortuny, 53, from 1917; they were moved to Rafael Calvo, 1, in 1922 (to make way for more residents of the Residencia de Señoritas), in 1923 to the top floor of Miguel Ángel, 8, and finally, in 1928, to calle Ríos Rosas, 7.

46 Zulueta and Moreno, *Ni convento ni college*, 10, 135; *Vázquez Ramil, Mujeres y educación*, 194. Centres for the Instituto-Escuela were established at the Olivar de Atocha (Cerrillo de San Blas), just south of the Buen Retiro park, and on the calle Pinar campus. New buildings were opened just north of the Residencia de Estudiantes complex in the 1930s, which in the Franco era were transformed into the Instituto Ramiro de Maeztu.

47 Zulueta and Moreno, *Ni convento ni college*, 132, 139; Vázquez Ramil, *Mujeres y educación*, 188, 193, 195.

48 Zulueta and Moreno, *Ni convento ni college*, 139–40; Vázquez Ramil, *Mujeres y educación*, 93, 195, 278.

49 "Los hogares del resurgimiento español. La Residencia de las Señoritas Estudiantes," *Nuevo Mundo* 30, no. 1512 (12 January 1923): n.p.

50 César G. Iniesta, "La mujer en la edad moderna. Nuestra Residencia de Señoritas," *Heraldo de Madrid*, 20 March 1928, 8–9.

51 Rafael Villaseca, "Las que estudian. En la Residencia de Señoritas, hablando con María de Maeztu," *ABC*, 7 April 1929, 15–7.

52 Juan del Sarto, "Grandes obras españolas. La Biblioteca de la Residencia de Señoritas," *Crónica* 1, no. 6 (22 December 1929): n.p.

53   J.S., "La Residencia de Señoritas, hogar madrileño de la intelectualidad femenina española y extranjera … ," *Crónica* 2, no. 17 (2 March 1930): n.p.

54   Carmen de Munárriz, "La Residencia de Señoritas en la intimidad," *Estampa* 3, no. 118 (15 April 1930): n.p.

55   These "period" pieces can usefully be supplemented by the online exhibition *En vanguardia: La Residencia de Señoritas en su centenario (1913–1936)*, and in particular the multimedia experience "La Residencia de Señoritas en primer persona," available at http://www.residencia.csic.es/expomujeres/webdoc/index.html.

56   Iniesta, "La mujer en la edad moderna"; J.S., "La Residencia de Señoritas." Vázquez Ramil identifies the source in *Mujeres y educación*, 152 and 152n65.

57   Vázquez Ramil consulted the copy preserved in the archive of the Residencia de Señoritas.

58   Villaseca, "Las que estudian," 16, 17.

59   The most detailed study of this aspect is by López Cobo, "El 'espíritu de la casa,'" where she examines the various factors that Maeztu had to contend with, the evolution of the internal functioning in response to – eventually – a tenfold increase in residents, as well as the (in)famous "blue book," which laid out information on all the norms of the establishment.

60   Cacho Viu comments on what he calls the "explicit behaviourism," and notes that a further benefit of such a policy was to shield, pre-emptively, the Residencia from right-wing, moralistic attacks: "La Junta para Ampliación de Estudios," 19–21.

61   López Cobo, "El 'espíritu de la casa,'" 543.

62   Cueva, "La Residencia de Señoritas," 218, 220. The core subjects were English, French, German, library science, pedagogy, psychology, practical chemistry, supplemented by Latin, mathematics, philosophy, and dressmaking: López Cobo, "El 'espíritu de la casa,'" 541.

63   Ribagorda, "La vida cultural," 190–6; Zulueta and Moreno, *Ni convento ni college*, 175–8; Vázquez Ramil, *Mujeres y educación*, 233, 243–69. Several distinguished visitors – such as Gabriela Mistral, Victoria Ocampo, and Marie Curie – lodged at the Residencia, during which time the residents were able to meet and interact with them: Ribagorda, "Una historia en la penumbra."

64   Zulueta and Moreno, *Ni convento ni college*, 62, 179–83.

65   Ibid., 115; Pérez-Villanueva Tovar, "La Residencia de Señoritas," 158; Vázquez Ramil, *Mujeres y educación*, 202.

66   Pérez-Villanueva Tovar, *La Residencia de Estudiantes*, 649.

67   Zulueta and Moreno, *Ni convento ni college*, 183–4; Pérez-Villanueva Tovar, "La Residencia de Señoritas," 158; Pérez-Villanueva Tovar, *La Residencia de Estudiantes*, 650.

68   "Historia de la academia," Real Academia de Bellas Artes de San Fernando, accessed 30 May 2022, https://realacademiabellasartessanfernando.com/es/academia/historia.

69   Ibid.

70 "Historia de la UCM – Facultad de Bellas Artes," Universidad Complutense de Madrid, accessed 30 May 2022, https://www.ucm.es/historia_ucm_facultad_bellas_artes; Vian Herrero, "La biblioteca de la Facultad de Bellas Artes," 255–6. The program of study was divided into pictorial anatomy, perspective, studies of ancient art, drawing from life and drapery, colouring, landscape, composition applied to painting and sculpture, figure modelling, and theory and history of fine arts.

71 Cabanillas Casafranca and Serrano de Haro, "La mujer en la Escuela de Bellas Artes," 116, correct the later date given by Diego, *La mujer y la pintura del XIX español*, 190, 192. See also Lomba Serrano, *Bajo el eclipse*, 60–1.

72 Diego, *La mujer y la pintura del XIX español*, 192–4.

73 Ibid., 194; Ramos Altamira, *Ricardo Vilar i Negre*, 55.

74 Cabanillas Casafranca and Serrano de Haro, "La mujer en la Escuela de Bellas Artes," 118; Lomba Serrano, *Bajo el eclipse*, 61. Depending on the then current nomenclature, these would include life drawing, figure modelling, pictorial anatomy, and colouring and composition.

75 Diego, *La mujer y la pintura del XIX español*, 191.

76 Cabanillas Casafranca and Serrano de Haro, "La mujer en la Escuela de Bellas Artes," 119; Diego, *La mujer y la pintura del XIX español*, 69, 190, 191. One of the six in the cohort of 1884–85, Regina Pérez Alemán, had applied to be admitted to these classes in 1884, but the request was denied: Ramos Altamira, *Ricardo Vilar i Negre*, 55.

77 Cabanillas Casafranca and Serrano de Haro, "La mujer en la Escuela de Bellas Artes," 119.

78 Figures in column 1 are from the *Anuarios Estadísticos* of the Instituto Nacional de Estadística. Figures in column 2 are from Villarejo Hervás, "'Adorno' y profesionalización artística femenina," 80, whose numbers are based on the enrollment records of the Escuela Especial de Pintura, Escultura y Grabado de Madrid, Archivo Histórico de la Biblioteca de la Facultad de Bellas Artes, Universidad Complutense de Madrid, signaturas 199–1 and 199–2. Figures in column 3 are from Lomba Serrano, *Bajo el eclipse*, "Anexo 1," 260–2, who provides listings of names for each year based on the *libros de matrícula*. The numbers, generally a little lower, likely bear witness to slight inconsistences in record keeping or different ways of counting certain categories of students.

79 Estradé Gutiérrez, "La enseñanza de la pintura"; García-Luengo Manchado, "La promoción de 1915."

80 Estradé Gutiérrez, "La enseñanza de la pintura," 334–5; Real Decreto, "Reglamento de la Escuela Especial de Pintura, Escultura y Grabado de Madrid," *Gaceta de Madrid*, no. 113 (23 April 1922): 299–303.

81 Estradé Gutiérrez, "La enseñanza de la pintura," 217–9, 332, 336.

82 *López-Obrero*, cited in Inglada, *Alfonso Ponce de León*, 38. See also López-Obrero, "Los alumnos de la Escuela de Pintura," 8.

83 On this resistance to reform, see Arañó Gisbert, "La enseñanza de las Bellas Artes."

84 Chacel, *Acrópolis*.

85 Dalí, *The Secret Life*, 163–4.

86 López-Obrero, "Los alumnos de la Escuela de Pintura," 8.

87 Sarto, "Visitas de CRÓNICA." There are three excellent photographs: of two life-drawing classes, one with a female model and one with a male model, and of a sculpting class copying a classical statue.

88 López-Obrero specifies that you had to go up more than ninety steps.

89 López-Obrero, "Los alumnos de la Escuela de Pintura," 8.

90 Inglada, *Alfonso Ponce de León*, "Apéndice 4," 176.

91 Archivo General, Universidad Complutense de Madrid; Archivo Histórico de la Biblioteca de la Facultad de Bellas Artes, Universidad Complutense de Madrid; Archivo de Secretaría de Alumnos de la Facultad de Bellas Artes, Universidad Complutense de Madrid; Soto Cano, ed., *Homenaje a Paulino Vicente*. He was away from Madrid for almost the whole period 1920–23.

92 Only the website dedicated to the sculptor Juan Cristóbal mentions him as a friend at the EEPEG: See "Biografía (1896–1920)," Juancristobalescultor.es, accessed 30 May 2022, https://juancristobalescultor.es/biografia-1896-1920/.

93 Villarejo Hervás, "'Adorno' y profesionalización artística femenina," 38. Flecha García gives the names of two students, Asunción Gallego Durán and María Cruz Herreros Cervera, who around 1927 were living at the Residencia Teresiana: "Alumnas y equipos directivos," 301. Herreros Cervera would go on to become an art teacher at an Escuela del Magisterio.

94 Pérez-Villanueva Tovar, "La Residencia de Señoritas," 152.

95 Vázquez Ramil, *Mujeres y educación*, 373–451.

96 Vázquez Ramil, *Mujeres y educación*, 406. I can find no record of her being enrolled at the Escuela Especial.

97 Pérez-Villanueva Tovar, *La Residencia de Estudiantes*, 604. No names are provided.

98 Murga Castro, "Muros para pintar."

99 These other names include Carmen Graells Corriols, Paula Serrano Pastor, and Estrella Agraz Gutiérrez.

100 I am grateful to Almudena de la Cueva for this information.

101 See Alix and González Orbegozo, eds, *Dibujantas*, 222–6.

102 What little biographical information is available suggests that she may have studied at the Escuela Especial at a much earlier moment in her life, during the 1910s: see Afonso Fernández, *Mis investigaciones*, 314, 357.

103 Murga Castro and Gaitán Salinas, "Introducción," 18.

104 Durán, *Mi vida*, vol. 1, *Sucedió*, 181–3.

105 Ibid., 183–6; she had been taking classes in drawing since age twelve (156).

106 Ibid., 176.

107 Archivo General, Universidad Complutense de Madrid; Archivo Histórico de la Biblioteca de la Facultad de Bellas Artes, Universidad Complutense de Madrid.

108 Letters from Durán to María de Maeztu, of July 1916 and January 1917, cited by Murga Castro, "Muros para pintar," 91n8, and Murga Castro and Gaitán Salinas, "Introducción," 24n27.

109 Murga Castro and Gaitán Salinas, "Introducción," 24.

110 Of these last years, Durán explains that "When I finished all the classes, a decree added more in order to qualify for a university degree as art teacher. That year only the elegant painter [Francisco] Pompey, Matilde Calvo and I enrolled in those [extra] courses," and she comments that she welcomed the extension as it allowed her more time at the conservatory: Durán, *Mi vida*, vol. 1, *Sucedió*, 197. In Spanish the term is *profesor[a] de dibujo*, literally professor of drawing.

111 Durán, *Mi vida*, vol. 1, *Sucedió*, 185–7.

112 Ibid., 203–5.

113 Ibid., 197–201, 201–3.

114 Ibid., 199, 202.

115 Ibid., 187–91, quote at 190.

116 Durán describes the position as *auxiliar meritoria*: ibid., 209.

117 Ibid., 209–10; Murga Castro, "Muros para pintar," 91.

118 Durán, *Mi vida*, vol. 1, *Sucedió*, 215.

119 Some of the information in this paragraph is derived from the online archive of the Junta para Ampliación de Estudios, available at http://archivojae.edad-deplata.org/jae_app/. Unfortunately, this website is somewhat outdated and still relies on a program (Adobe Flash Player) no longer supported by many browsers. Readers wishing to consult the archive may benefit from the brief video introduction available at http://www.residencia.csic.es/100digital/jae/index.htm.

120 Durán, *Mi vida*, vol. 1, *Sucedió*, 250–1. As secretary, she figures significantly in the article by Javier Sánchez-Ocaña, "Una institución curiosa: La Escuela del Hogar y Profesional de la Mujer," *Heraldo de Madrid*, 26 January 1928, 8–9.

121 Murga Castro, "Muros para pintar," 91. See also the multiple references in Murga Castro and Gaitán Salinas, "Introducción," 21, 24–5, 31, 31–2, 32–3, 33, 33–4.

122 "Banquete a la señorita Victorina Durán," *La Época*, 3 January 1929, 1; "Banquete a Victorina Durán," *La Época*, 5 February 1929, 1; Durán, *Mi vida*, vol. 1, *Sucedió*, 225. Several professors from the Escuela Especial had been involved in her being appointed to the position: see Meléndez Táboas, "Maruja Mallo entre sus condiscípulas," 125.

123 Durán, *Mi vida*, vol. 1, *Sucedió*, 191.

124 Chacel, *Obra completa*, vol. 8, *Autobiografías*, 271; Balló, *Las sinsombrero*, 212; Kirkpatrick, *Mujer, modernismo y vanguardia*, 262. Previously, Chacel had studied art first at the Escuela de Artes y Oficios and then at the Escuela del Hogar y Profesional de la Mujer.

125 Archivo General, Universidad Complutense de Madrid; Archivo Histórico de la Biblioteca de la Facultad de Bellas Artes, Universidad Complutense de Madrid.

126 Durán, *Mi vida*, vol. 1, *Sucedió*, 164, 191–2.

127 Villarejo Hervás, "'Adorno' y profesionalización artística femenina," 41–6; Archivo, Junta para Ampliación de Estudios.

128 Durán, *Mi vida*, vol. 1, *Sucedió*, 192. Muñoz Degrain was professor of land-scape painting at the EEPEG from 1895 to 1919; he also gave private lessons: Lomba Serrano, *Bajo el eclipse*, 50.

129 Archivo, Junta para Ampliación de Estudios.

130 Bautista Cordero, "Márgara Villegas, traductora de John Dos Passos."

131 Durán, *Mi vida*, vol. 1, *Sucedió*, 192.

132 Ibid.

133 Gaitán Salinas and Murga Castro, "Victorina Durán y Maruja Mallo," 402.

134 Durán, *Mi vida*, vol. 1, *Sucedió*, 192.

135 Ibid., 203.

136 Ibid., 192.

137 Ibid., 203–5.

138 Ibid., 197.

139 Ibid., 232–4.

140 Ibid., 215–16.

141 Ibid., 214.

142 I have not been able to identify this individual; Durán says only that "she was an amateur painter": *Mi vida*, vol. 2, *El Rastro*, 149.

143 These biographical sketches of Durán's friends have been compiled and syn-thetized from various complementary sources, including the JAE archives (http://www.residencia.csic.es/100digital/en/jae/index.htm), the Madrid press of the period, (http://hemerotecadigital.bne.es/index.vm), as well as the other books cited elsewhere in this chapter.

144 Chacel, *Obra completa*, vol. 8, *Autobiografías*, 271. González was dating and would go on to marry the linguist Salvador Fernández Ramírez (296).

145 Carretón Cano, "Victorina Durán y el círculo sáfico de Madrid," 9.

146 In the registry of the Residencia de Señoritas, a María Paz González is listed as resident in the fall of 1921 and studying not art but general culture. I am grateful to Almudena de la Cueva for this information. It is impossible to confirm if this is the Paz González mentioned by Chacel.

147 Durán, *Mi vida*, vol. 1, *Sucedió*, 192; Chacel, *Obra completa*, vol. 8, *Autobiografías*, 271, 279–80.

148 Durán, *Mi vida*, vol. 1, *Sucedió*, 195–7; Chacel, *Obra completa*, vol. 8, *Autobiografías*, 281, 285.

149 Durán, *Mi vida*, vol. 1, *Sucedió*, 193.

150 Ibid.

151 Ibid., 194–5.

152   Dalí, *The Secret Life*, 162.

153   Carretón Cano, "Victorina Durán y el círculo sáfico," 9.

154   Fuentes González, *Delhy Tejero*, 17; Gutiérrez-Carbajal, "Trayectoria artística de Delhy Tejero," 414.

155   Vila Tejero, "Delhy Tejero. Biografía," 281.

156   Fuentes González, *Delhy Tejero*, 19, 43.

157   Villalba Salvador, "Arte entre líneas," 99.

158   Ibid., 99n231.

159   This is the same establishment where Pérez Herrero received her secondary education. For Tejero, see Villalba Salvador, "Arte entre líneas," 99; M.G.O., "Delhy Tejero – Adela Tejero Bedate," 328.

160   Fuentes González, *Delhy Tejero*, 22.

161   Alcaide and Pérez, "Delhy Tejero," 17.

162   Antoniorrobles, "Las artistas en la conquista de Madrid. Delhy Tejero, profesora de la Escuela de Artes y Oficios," *Crónica* 4, no. 125 (3 April 1932): n.p.

163   Villalba Salvador, "Arte entre líneas," 99.

164   Cabañas Bravo, "Delhy Tejero," 34; M.G.O., "Delhy Tejero – Adela Tejero Bedate," 328; Fuentes González, *Delhy Tejero*, 26.

165   Secretaría de Alumnos de la Facultad de Bellas Artes, Universidad Complutense de Madrid.

166   Ibid. See also Gutiérrez-Carbajal, "Trayectoria artística de Delhy Tejero," 414.

167   *Heraldo de Madrid*, 18 March 1926; see Villalba Salvador, "Arte entre líneas," 99n233.

168   Fuentes González, *Delhy Tejero*, 26.

169   Archivo de Secretaría de Alumnos de la Facultad de Bellas Artes, Universidad Complutense de Madrid; Cabanillas Casafranca and Amparo Serrano de Haro, "La mujer en la Escuela de Bellas Artes," 122. She also repeated one more (colouring and composition) in which in 1927–28 she had received an annotation of "D. de M." (*debe de mejorar* [needs to improve]).

170   *El Liberal*, 5 December 1926, 1.

171   Vila Tejero, "Adela Tejero Bedate," 165.

172   López-Obrero, "Los alumnos de la Escuela de Pintura," 9.

173   I am grateful to Almudena de la Cueva for this information. Gutiérrez-Carbajal suggests that she also had a room for 1930–31 but took no meals there: "Trayectoria artística de Delhy Tejero," 415. However, numerous other sources indicate that Tejero was abroad, studying at the École Supérieure Logelain in Brussels, from January–June 1931: see, for instance, Fuentes González, *Delhy Tejero*, 39, and Cabañas Bravo, "Delhy Tejero," 36–7. She took up her post as interim special professor of mural painting at the central Escuela de Artes y Oficios in August 1931: Fuentes González, *Delhy Tejero*, 27.

174   Alcaide and Pérez, "Delhy Tejero," 16.

175   *Suplemento a La Escuela moderna*, no. 3166 (11 May 1927): 2; *Suplemento a La Escuela moderna*, no. 3351 (16 February 1929): 6. See also Gutiérrez-Carbajal, "Trayectoria artística de Delhy Tejero," 415.

176   L.R., "Los primeros pasos de una artista que llegará lejos." See the applications for *pensiones* in the online archive of the Junta para Ampliación de Estudios (submitted in October 1929 and again in 1930) avaiable at http://www.residencia.csic.es/100digital/en/jae/index.htm.

177   Tejero, *Los Cuadernines*, 37.

178   Ibid., 36 and 36n1. The beginning of the entry reads as follows: "The sixth of October, 1929 I arrived in Madrid with 225 pesetas that I was given at home. Up to the fifteenth I was at the Castro's house." It can be no coincidence that precisely on October 6 she submitted to the Escuela Especial documents requesting her official ratification as an art teacher: Fuentes González, *Delhy Tejero*, 26 and 26n15.

179   Pseudonym of Ricardo García López (1890–1984).

180   A fine colour illustration of a fairy princess can be seen in Enrique González Fiol, "La estrella y los caracoles," *La Esfera* 17, no. 863 (19 July 1930): 11.

181   L.R., "Los primeros pasos de una artista que llegará lejos"; Fuentes González, *Delhy Tejero*, 46, 73–5; Alario Trigueros, "Delhy Tejero," 307. Francis Bartolozzi followed a very similar trajectory: before finishing at the EEPEG, she started doing illustrations for children's stories published by Editorial Calleja, branched out into magazines, such as *Estampa* and *Crónica*, and then started creating her own characters for children's stories that she wrote and illustrated: see Lozano Úriz, "Una vida," 8.

182   L.R., "Los primeros pasos de una artista que llegará lejos." Three months later Tejero would note that "between 15 November 1929 and 30 June 1930 I have earned 1.385 pts.," *Los Cuadernines*, 36.

183   Archivo, Residencia de Señoritas, Fundación Ortega y Gasset, Madrid.

184   Cueva and Márquez Padorno, eds, *Mujeres en vanguardia*, 356, 364.

185   The exhibition first opened in January 1930, and every couple of months the artists and works shown were changed; Tejero was there in the third installment that started in May: "Notas de arte. La Unión de Dibujantes," *El Siglo Futuro*, 2 May 1930, 3, and E. Estévez-Ortega, "La actualidad artística. Una visión de España de Walt Louderback. Una Exposición de Dibujantes," *La Esfera* 17, no. 854 (17 May 1930): 10.

186   "Exposición Nacional de Bellas Artes," *La Libertad*, 11 June 1930, 7, noted her skill as a watercolourist.

187   "Los premios de la Exposición," *La Libertad*, 12 July 1930, 2.

188   Zulueta and Moreno, *Ni convento ni college*, 229–30.

189   Ibid., 35; Vázquez Ramil, *Mujeres y educación*, 93, 278.

190   Cueva and Márquez Padorno, eds, *Mujeres en vanguardia*, 367.

191   *Vázquez Ramil, Mujeres y educación*, 386; Rico Carabias, "Josefina Carabias y la Residencia de Señoritas Estudiantes," *Boletín*.

192   Rico, "Josefina Carabias y la Residencia de Señoritas Estudiantes," in *Ni tontas ni locas*, 243–4.

193   See Durán, *Mi vida*, vol. 1, *Sucedió*, 199.

194   Alario Trigueros, "Delhy Tejero," 314 and 314n48.

195 Others also mentioned in passing include Pilar Gamonal, Amparo Vallina, and Pura Verdú Tormo: Lozano Bartolozzi, "Artistas plásticas españolas," 295, and López-Obrero, "Los alumnos de la Escuela de Pintura," 9.

196 Mallo would have contact with the Residencia de Señoritas years later, when she gave drawing classes there during the 1935–36 academic year: Gaitán Salinas and Murga Castro, "Victorina Durán y Maruja Mallo," 406.

197 Varo, *Remedios Varo*, 38.

198 Tejero, *Una muchacha y una maleta*, 79–80.

199 Ibid., 81.

200 Escribano, "Maruja Mallo, una bruja moderna," 46.

201 Sarto, "Visitas de CRÓNICA."

202 See Balló, *Las sinsombrero*, 39–57. Some rare examples of her work can be seen in Inglada, *Alfonso Ponce de León*, 44–5.

203 Moreiro, "Arte. Maruja Mallo"; Bonet, "Maruja Mallo"; Escribano, "Maruja Mallo, una bruja moderna," 45–55; Mallo, "Dalí (1979)," 223.

204 Varo, *Remedios Varo*, 37.

205 Varo, *Remedios Varo*, 38–9. Like Victorina Durán and Mallo (see chapter 6), Varo also frequented some of the literary and artistic *tertulias*, as well as the Círculo de Bellas Artes: *Remedios Varo*, 40.

206 Lozano Úriz, "Una vida," 7; Lozano Úriz, *Un matrimonio de artistas*, 26–7.

207 Varo, *Remedios Varo*, 38.

208 Chacel, *Obra completa*, vol. 8, *Autobiografías*, 285.

209 Varo, *Remedios Varo*, 38–9: interview with Bartolozzi. Lizárraga and Lozano were friends and lodged in the same *pensión* together: Lozano Bartolozzi, "Artistas plásticas españolas," 293.

210 Lozano Bartolozzi, "Artistas plásticas españolas," 296.

211 López-Obrero, "Los alumnos de la Escuela de Pintura," 9.

212 Cueva and Márquez Padorno, eds, *Mujeres en vanguardia*, 356: the location is misidentified as the Residencia de Señoritas.

213 Lomba Serrano, "Joaquina Zamora," 34.

214 Ibid., 35–6.

215 Ibid., 34.

216 Ibid. Lomba Serrano reproduces a fine class photo from the 1925–26 year of a group of students gathered around one of the professors; Zamora is one of eight women students.

217 Ibid. Lomba Serrano further notes that Zamora received private classes from Benedito as well as from Cecilio Plá: *Bajo el eclipse*, 52.

218 I am grateful to Almudena de la Cueva for this information. Zamora is only listed as resident for 1927–28 by Vázquez Ramil, *Mujeres y educación*, 451, whereas Murga Castro implies that she was there for the whole time, 1924–28: "Muros para pintar," 96. Cabanillas Casafranca and Serrano de Haro also place her there between 1924 and 1928, probably because that span corresponds to her years of study at the EEPEG: "La mujer en la Escuela de Bellas Artes," 132.

219 See above: this is the exhibition in which Tejero also participated.

220 Lomba Serrano, "Joaquina Zamora," 36–8.

221 Ibid., 38–42.

222 Salaberria Lizarazu, "La larga marcha de Juan Vicens," 7. She lived in his house for a period of her time there.

223 Prado Herrera, "Universitarias en Salamanca."

224 Vázquez Ramil, *Mujeres y educación*, 406. María Luisa finished her undergraduate coursework in classical languages, Greek and Latin, in 1921, and at that point transferred to Madrid: Montes López and Gallego Morón, "María Luisa González," 223; "Personajes en el Archivo de RTVE: La Residencia de Estudiantes," RTVE Play, 3 September 2010, https://www.rtve.es/play/audios/personajes-en-el-archivo-de-rtve/residencia-estudiantes-generacion-del-27-retrato-epoca-parte-1/866906/.

225 Gállego Rubio, "Dos bibliotecarias complutenses"; Salaberria Lizarazu, "La larga marcha de Juan Vicens," 7.

226 "María Luisa González," 224; "Personajes en el Archivo de RTVE: La Residencia de Estudiantes," RTVE Play, 3 September 2010, https://www.rtve.es/play/audios/personajes-en-el-archivo-de-rtve/residencia-estudiantes-generacion-del-27-retrato-epoca-parte-2/866919/.

227 My thanks to Almudena de la Cueva for help in untangling the details in the interview given by María Luisa González.

228 Archive, Junta para Ampliación de Estudios.

229 Gállego Rubio, "Dos bibliotecarias complutenses"; Salaberria Lizarazu, "La larga marcha de Juan Vicens"; Pérez de Ayala, "Joaquín Peinado escribe," 8.

230 Salaberria Lizarazu, "La larga marcha de Juan Vicens," 10.

231 Martínez Rus, "La Librairie Espagnole de León Sánchez Cuesta," 109–13.

232 Montes López and Gallego Morón, "María Luisa González," 224.

233 Salaberria Lizarazu, "La larga marcha de Juan Vicens," 9; Calvo Alonso-Cortés, "Homenaje a María Luis González," 21.

234 Buñuel, *Mi último suspiro*, 72.

235 Ibid.; see also Alberti, *La arboleda perdida. Libros III y IV de memorias*, 308, and Aub, *Conversaciones con Buñuel*, 309.

236 Gállego Rubio, "Dos bibliotecarias complutenses."

237 Gibson, *Federico García Lorca*, vol. 1, *De Fuente Vaqueros a Nueva York (1898–1929)*, 367–8; Moreno Villa, *Memoria*, 488.

238 See Fernández Utrera, *Buñuel en Toledo*.

Chapter Five

1 Serrano de la Cruz Peinado, "Por tercera vez," 11.

2 Juan de la Encina, "De arte. Estampas de España," *La Voz*, 5 June 1926, 1. I presume the reference is to Nietzsche.

3 García Maroto, *La nueva España. 1930*, 2. Henceforth, in all bibliographical references Maroto's name will be abbreviated as "GGM." Details of his many

books and articles cited here can be found in appendix 2: "Books and Periodical Publications by Gabriel García Maroto."

4   Alejo Carpentier, "Maroto. Viajero de 3ª," *Diario de la Marina*, 15 January 1928, 33.

5   GGM, *Promoción de México*, 17–20. This book is as close as Maroto ever came to writing an autobiography; it contains a wealth of useful information, though it was written at several decades' remove from the events described and in a literary style that is consistently florid, often convoluted, and occasionally tortured. See also Serrano de la Cruz Peinado, "Hacia el reconocimiento debido," 140–1; GGM, *La nueva España. 1930*, 2.

6   GGM, *Promoción de México*, 20.

7   Serrano de la Cruz Peinado, "Hacia el reconocimiento debido," 142; see GGM, "Ángel Andrade."

8   GGM, *Promoción de México*, 23.

9   Gabriel G.C. Maroto, "Crónica. Noche en Toledo"; cf. GGM, *Promoción de México*, 22–3; Alejo Carpentier, "Maroto. Viajero de 3ª," *Diario de la Marina*, 15 January 1928, 33.

10 Serrano de la Cruz Peinado, "Hacia el reconocimiento debido," 143–4.

11 GGM, *Promoción de México*, 25.

12 *El País*, 12 September 1910 through 20 October 1910.

13 GGM, *Promoción de México*, 25.

14 "Exposición de Bellas Artes. Conferencia interesante," *El Liberal*, 4 November 1910, 2; "Exposición de Bellas Artes. Conferencia de G. García Maroto," *Heraldo de Madrid*, 6 November 1910, 1; "En el Palacio de Cristal. Conferencia de Gabriel García Maroto," *El País*, 6 November 1910, 1. It is unlikely but possible that he knew Marinetti's Futurist manifesto from 1909.

15 GGM, *Promoción de México*, 23–4.

16 GGM, "De Bellas Artes. Chicharro renuncia a luchar con Pinazo."

17 GGM, *Promoción de México*, 25, 26.

18 "Los Independientes. Convocatoria," *El Liberal*, 7 February 1913, 3.

19 Several would go on to become recognized writers and journalists, and Segovia a celebrated guitarist.

20 M. Santos Cantero, "Bagatelas," *Vida Manchega* 2, no. 49 (13 March 1913): n.p.

21 A., "La pintura española," *Heraldo de Madrid*, 19 April 1913, 1.

22 GGM, *Promoción de México*, 26.

23 Serrano de la Cruz Peinado, "Hacia el reconocimiento debido," 147; GGM, *Promoción de México*, 26.

24 GGM, *Promoción de México*, 27, 28.

25 Alberto Valero Martín, "Gabriel García Maroto," *Vida Manchega* 2, no. 79 (9 October 1913): n.p.; "[García Maroto, pintando el hermoso cuadro *El coplero* ...]," *Vida Manchega* 2, no. 84 (13 November 1913): n.p.

26 Caj., "En la Universidad. La velada de ayer del Ateneo de Salamanca. El romance popular y los cantos charros," *El Adelanto*, 14 November 1913, 1–2; "En el Ateneo. La velada de anoche," *El Adelanto*, 18 November 1913, 1.

27 "Algo sobre estética. Al margen de un folleto," *El Adelanto*, 7 April 1914, 1–2.

28 Serrano de la Cruz Peinado, "Hacia el reconocimiento debido," 149; GGM, *Promoción de México*, 28 and 28n23.

29 GGM, "Páginas ingenuas. Mi hermano Cándido."

30 Serrano de la Cruz Peinado, "Hacia el reconocimiento debido," 150.

31 GGM, *Promoción de México*, 28–9.

32 One of her paintings is reproduced in Serrano de la Cruz Peinado, ed., *Gabriel García Maroto y la renovación*, 96.

33 GGM, *Promoción de México*, 29 and 29n27.

34 Serrano de la Cruz Peinado, "Hacia el reconocimiento debido," 150–1.

35 Antonio Robles, "Lo que se recuerda con más admiración," *Heraldo de Madrid*, 17 June 1927, 9; Serrano de la Cruz Peinado, "Hacia el reconocimiento debido," 151.

36 GGM, *Promoción de México*, 30.

37 Serrano de la Cruz Peinado, "Hacia el reconocimiento debido," 152.

38 GGM, *Promoción de México*, 30; Serrano de la Cruz Peinado, "Hacia el reconocimiento debido," 152.

39 Essentially a fictive entity, it did not publish any other books, and his wife's second surname was Dragonné or Dragoné.

40 GGM, *Promoción de México*, 31.

41 Ibid.

42 "Libros y revistas," *España* 4, no. 153 (14 March 1918): 14.

43 GGM, "Acordes." The poems are dedicated to Enrique Nogueras, a friend of Unamuno.

44 "La familia Narezo (I)"; GGM, *Promoción de México*, 30.

45 GGM, *Promoción de México*, 32.

46 This indecision dates back to his adolescence: "my specific aspiration [was] made up of two factors that I perceived as complementary: art and literature, visual and written expression. All confused and muddled up, on occasions juxtaposed and claiming, depending on how things went, absolute priority or my relative attention": ibid., 21–2.

47 Maroto does mention "a group of poems that clearly responded to the captivating experience of living in conjunction with the so-called Isle of Gold," composed around 1923 in Mallorca: ibid., 36. One of these poems, "Amanecer," was printed in his *Almanaque de las artes y las letras*, 169.

48 No. 608 (5 August 1918) through no. 624 (15 January 1919), a total of twelve installments.

49 The two "chapters" of the novel are titled "Viaje en un coche de línea" and "El poema de la casa amada."

50 Francisco Alcántara, "La vida artística. En el Ateneo. Pinturas y dibujos de García Maroto," *El Sol*, 15 April 1919, 2, provides the longest excerpt.

51 J. Blanco Coris, "Arte y artistas. Exposición García Maroto," *Heraldo de Madrid*, 14 April 1919, 1.

52   Rafael Urbina, "El teatro, los libros y el arte en España," *Cosmópolis*, no. 8 (August 1919): 669–89.

53   José Francés commented positively on Maroto's pieces at both: "La Exposición de Bellas Artes. Notas en el catálogo," *La Atalaya*, 24 August 1919, 1, and "La Exposición de Bilbao. La pintura española," *La Esfera* 6, no. 302 (11 October 1919): n.p.

54   "Un concurso. Los carteles del Círculo de Bellas Artes," *Nuevo Mundo* 27, no. 1360 (6 February 1920): n.p., with a reproduction of his poster.

55   *Nuevo Mundo* 27, no. 1370 (16 April 1920) features a cover designed by Maroto, but he did not win a prize: José Francés, "El arte editorial. Nuestra portada," *Nuevo Mundo* 27, no. 1371 (23 April 1920): n.p. Another of his designs was used for the front cover of *Nuevo Mundo* 27, no. 1382 (9 July 1920).

56   Correa Calderón, "Comentario a la Exposición Nacional de Bellas Artes," *La Ilustración Española y Americana* 64, no. 20 (30 May 1920): 308–19.

57   Maroto also featured in the decorative arts section and received a modest prize.

58   GGM, "Desde París. El Teatro de 'El Viejo Palomar'"; GGM, "Desde París. Bourdelle en el Salón Nacional." The first article is dated to May, and the second to June. Juan Ramón Jiménez thanked him for the dedication of the first one and congratulated him on his designs in the Exposición Nacional: Jiménez, *Epistolario*, vol. 2, *1916–1936*, 148–9.

59   On Maroto's efforts to find help for his daughter, see GGM, *Promoción de México*, 32.

60   "Al vuelo," *La Voz de Liébana. Revista Regional*, segunda época, 16, no. 668 (31 August 1920): 8. The couple's third surviving child, José, was not born until 1922.

61   "Al vuelo," *La Voz de Liébana*, segunda época, 16, no. 670 (30 September 1920): 7; "Al vuelo," *La Voz de Liébana. Revista Regional*, segunda época, 16, no. 672 (31 October 1920): 7.

62   The first mention in the press of the "Colección Aventuras" occurred on 29 December: "[advert: "Para Año Nuevo y para Reyes"], *La Voz*, 29 December 1920, 7.

63   GGM, "Los bellos caminos españoles"; GGM, "Temas aldeanos. El invierno en la villa"; drawings by Maroto included in Fernando Mota, "Cómo miran los niños la vida …," *La Esfera* 8, no. 367 (15 January 1921): n.p.; GGM, "Temas sin importancia."

64   The earliest surviving one from Jiménez is from 8 July 1920. In late September and October, they exchanged several communications: Jiménez, *Epistolario*, vol. 2, *1916–1936*, 148–9, 162–3, 165, 173.

65   *Epistolario*, vol. 2, *1916–1936*, 165. Curiously, Teresa Gómez Trueba does not mention Maroto in "¿Qué fue antes, el título o el libro? Análisis genético del proyecto inédito de Juan Ramón Jiménez *En la rama del verde limón*," *Creneida*, no. 2 (2014): 218–45.

66   *Epistolario*, vol. 2, *1916–1936*, 173–4.

67 Serrano de la Cruz Peinado, "Hacia el reconocimiento debido," 155.

68 GGM, *Promoción de México*, 32–3.

69 Alfonso Reyes, "La imprenta medieval," *Monterrey. Correo Literario de Alfonso Reyes* (Rio de Janeiro), no. 2 (1930): 1.

70 Francisco Alcántara, "La vida artística. La aventura artístico-industrial de Gabriel García Maroto," *El Sol*, 17 January 1922, 7. Maroto mentions an article by Enrique Díez-Canedo published in *La Nación* (Buenos Aires), which I have not located: GGM, *Promoción de México*, 33.

71 "Sección especial por palabras," *El Imparcial*, 3 March 1921, 5.

72 Jiménez, *Epistolario*, vol. 2, *1916–1936*, 205. In 1915, Jiménez and Zenobia had embarked on a major publishing project of Tagore translations; they worked with several printers, including Encuadernación Calleja and Fortanet: Young, "The Invention of an Andalusian Tagore," 42n1; Sánchez García, "Juan Ramón Jiménez y el mercado editorial."

73 Jiménez, *Epistolario*, vol. 2, *1916–1936*, 219.

74 Ibid., 220.

75 Ibid., 234.

76 *Índice. (Revista Mensual)*, nos 1 and 2 (1921): unpaginated pink advertising pages inside back cover.

77 Reproduction in Trapiello, *Imprenta moderna*, 123. Trapiello dedicates a few pages to Maroto's press, 108–12, 137–40.

78 GGM, "Color y ritmo."

79 Jiménez, *Epistolario*, vol. 2, *1916–1936*, 223, 229, 230.

80 Ibid., 233, 237, 235n552.

81 Ibid., 229–31, 237–8, 241–2, 247–8, 250.

82 Ibid., 242.

83 Ibid., 248.

84 GGM, *Promoción de México*, 33.

85 Guerrero Ruiz, *Juan Ramón de viva voz*, vol. 1, *1913–1931*, 51. The large number on the front cover of number 3 was clearly hand drawn, a practice abandoned for number 4, where the format changes.

86 "*Índice*," *El Sol*, 22 December 1921, 4; "Publicaciones recibidas," *Vltra* 2, no. 21 (1 January 1922): n.p. In the next diary entry, from 7 March 1922, Guerrero wrote, "There remain for 1921 the three numbers already published, with yellow covers": *Juan Ramón de viva voz*, vol. 1, *1913–1931*, 51–2.

87 GGM, *Promoción de México*, 33.

88 Valender, "García Maroto y el *Libro de poemas*," 158; GGM, *Promoción de México*, 35.

89 García Lorca, *Epistolario completo*, 109.

90 Ibid., 96–7.

91 Ibid., 101.

92 García Lorca, *Epistolario completo*, 116; the letter to his family is written on Imprenta Maroto letterhead.

93 Valender, "García Maroto y el *Libro de poemas*."

94   GGM, *Promoción de México*, 34.

95   Ibid.

96   Ibid.

97   Ibid., 34–5.

98   Canito, "Entrevistas. Juan Guerrero, cónsul de la poesía."

99   Valender, "García Maroto y el *Libro de poemas*," 162; García Lorca, *Epistolario completo*, 115.

100 García Lorca, *Epistolario completo*, 117.

101 Young, "The Invention of an Andalusian Tagore," 44n3; García Lorca, *Epistolario completo*, 105–6.

102 See the entries for 1921 in the chronological representation of Rabindranath Tagore's biography available at http://www.rabindratirtha-wbhidcoltd.co.in/Rabisarani/event/VZlSXRlVONlUsRmeT1WNXJ1aKVVVB1TP.

103 Maroto remembers serving as the art director for a production of Tagore's *El cartero del rey* at the Residencia, but his identification of Buñuel in the role of Ragupati, a major character in *Sacrificio*, demonstrates that his memory was faulty: GGM, *Promoción de México*, 35. Lorca was cast as Jaising; there is no record of who was going to play King Govinda.

104 Dinverno, *"Suites,"* 12.

105 García Lorca, *Epistolario completo*, 119; the colophon is dated 15 June.

106 Maurer, "¡Ay, Maroto!: Noticias de una amistad," 33.

107 García Lorca, *Epistolario completo*, 125–6n348.

108 Ibid., 125.

109 Lozano Miralles, ed., *Crónica de una amistad*, 44. The emphasis on *"our"* clearly distinguishes this scheme from Jiménez's *Índice*; Maroto's state of mind likely relates to his severe money problems.

110 Letter of 13 October: Lozano Miralles, ed., *Crónica de una amistad*, 46.

111 García Lorca, *Epistolario completo*, 130–1.

112 See Almagro's letter of 17 February 1922 in Lozano Miralles, ed., *Crónica de una amistad*, 53: "Are you keen to create the magazine?"

113 Francisco Alcántara, "La vida artística. La aventura artístico-industrial de Gabriel García Maroto," *El Sol*, 17 January 1922, 7.

114 Maroto reproduced Unamuno's self-portrait (done ca 1894) in *Almanaque de las artes*, 9; he refers to these drawings in *Promoción de México*, 27, and reproduced there the same self-portrait. Apparently, Maroto included them in the exhibition unbeknownst to Unamuno. Having missed the show, in January 1922 Alfonso Reyes wrote to Unamuno about them, who understandably was mystified: García Blanco, "El escritor mejicano," 167.

115 Maurer, "De la correspondencia de García Lorca," 62: "a session[?] of my paintings and by *other people*, and you are among these latter."

116 Serrano de la Cruz Peinado, "Hacia el reconocimiento debido," 155.

117 "El hambre en Rusia. Por tres duros se puede salvar una vida. Llamamiento a las mujeres españolas," *El Sol*, 11 February 1922, 4; "'Quince pesetas pueden

salvar una vida.' En favor de la Rusia hambrienta. España debe acudir a esta obra de humanidad," *El Sol*, 18 February 1922, 1.

118   "Nuestro homenaje," *La Canción Popular. Revista Musical* 1, no. 9 (September 1922): n.p.

119   See chapter 2, note 199, for a full listing of articles. *Día perlado* is reproduced in Serrano de la Cruz Peinado, ed., *Gabriel García Maroto y la renovación*, 63.

120   GGM, *Promoción de México*, 35.

121   Peláez, "Epistolario selectivo."

122   Preserved in the Archivo de la Fundación Federico García Lorca.

123   Serrano de la Cruz Peinado, "Hacia el reconocimiento debido," 157–8.

124   Silvio Lago, "Vida artística. Cuatro pintores modernos," *La Esfera* 10, no. 473 (27 January 1923): n.p.

125   Juan de la Encina, "La nueva generación artística," *La Voz*, 26 January 1923, 1.

126   Juan de la Encina, "De arte. Un mecenas catalán," *La Voz*, 1 February 1923, 1.

127   "Homenaje a un pintor. Banquete a Juan de Echevarría," *El Sol*, 23 February 1923, 2.

128   Juan de la Encina, "Crítica de arte. Una carta y una idea," *La Voz*, 24 February 1923, 1.

129   Juan de la Encina, "De arte. Una carta a un pintor," *La Voz*, 28 February 1923, 1.

130   France had had a Salon des Indépendants since 1884, founded with the slogan *sans jury ni recompense.*

131   Juan de la Encina, "De arte. Una carta a un pintor," *La Voz*, 28 February 1923, 1; Juan de la Encina, "De arte. Hay que crear el Salón de Independientes," *La Voz*, 7 March 1923, 1. For more on Encina, the 1925 exhibition, and what led up to it, see Alzuri Milanés, "Juan de la Encina crítico de arte," 37–9; for his criticism of the Exposiciones Nacionales, see Jiménez-Blanco Carrillo de Albornoz, "Juan de la Encina, director del Museo de Arte Moderno," 46–7.

132   D'Ors, *Mi Salón de Otoño*, 6. D'Ors goes on to describe his own personal, purely hypothetical, exhibition.

133   D'Ors, *Mi Salón de Otoño*, 9–10.

134   "Banquete a Jacinto Grau," *El Sol*, 11 March 1923, 4; "Banquete a Jacinto Grau," *La Correspondencia de España*, 15 March 1923, 8; "Banquete a Jacinto Grau," *La Voz*, 17 March 1923, 8.

135   Francisco Alcántara, "La vida artística. Los paisajes mallorquines de Manuel Fernández Peña en el Salón Arte Moderno," *El Sol*, 23 March 1923, 6.

136   GGM, "El teatro español en París. *El señor de Pigmalión.*" This was doubtless written in March.

137   Serrano de la Cruz Peinado, "Hacia el reconocimiento debido," 158.

138   A.V. y G. [Ángel Vegue y Goldoni], "Bellas Artes. Exposición Maroto," *El Imparcial*, 3 February 1925, 5; Juan de la Encina, "De arte. La exposición Maroto," *La Voz*, 7 February 1925, 1.

139 "Virgilio Garcia Peñaranda (Molina de Segura, Múrcia 1898–Palma 1971)," Miquelcinema, 12 February 2011, http://miquelcinema.blogspot. com/2011/02/virgilio-garcia-penaranda-molina-de.html.

140 Deià is nearly equidistant from Sóller (where Alberti and León would travel a few years later – see chapter 6) and Valldemossa (where Chopin and Sand had famously spent time).

141 GGM, *Promoción de México*, 35; Serrano de la Cruz Peinado, "Hacia el reconocimiento debido," 158.

142 Several canvases are reproduced in Serrano de la Cruz Peinado, ed., *Gabriel García Maroto y la renovación*, 70–6.

143 An extract from the text appears in ibid., 49–50.

144 According to Brihuega, over 1925–27 Maroto had a studio in the La Guindalera neighbourhood of Madrid: "Gabriel García Maroto y *La Nueva España 1930*," 268–9. As of fall 1925, Maroto gave his home address as Paseo (nowadays calle) de Francisco Silvela, 20: Aguerre, ed., *Rafael Barradas. Hombre flecha*, 213. The calle de Francisco Silvela borders the La Guindalera neighbourhood on its west side.

145 A.V. y G. [Ángel Vegue y Goldoni], "Bellas Artes. Exposición Maroto," *El Imparcial*, 3 February 1925, 5.

146 "Noticias," *El Imparcial*, 7 February 1925, 7; "Vida cultural. Las conferencias de ayer. El arte contemporáneo," *El Imparcial*, 8 February 1925, 3; "Bellas artes. Conferencia del pintor Maroto," *Heraldo de Madrid*, 9 February 1925, 4.

147 Juan de la Encina, "De arte. La exposición Maroto," *La Voz*, 7 February 1925, 1; Francisco Alcántara, "La vida artística. Los cuadros de Maroto," *El Sol*, 11 February 1925, 4; Ángel Vegue y Goldoni, "Bellas artes. Exposición Maroto. Orientaciones modernas," *El Imparcial*, 14 February 1925, 3.

148 "Notícies i exposicions d'art," *La Veu de Catalunya*, 4 April 1925, 11; C.C., "Carnet de les arts. Les ultimes exposicions," *La Publicitat*, 18 April 1925, 1.

149 See, for example, Rafel Benet, "Croniques d'art. Altres exposicions," *La Veu de Catalunya*, 16 April 1925, 3.

150 On 31 March 1923, Guillermo de Torre wrote to Barradas asking for an update on the new endeavour: "What's happening with the Society of Independents? Shortly after the initiative emerged, I wrote to Maroto, reminding him of our analogous initiative from two years ago, with [Adolfo] Salazar, the Delaunays, etc., and expressing my unwavering and fervent support for all efforts in this direction": Aguerre, ed., *Rafael Barradas. Hombre flecha*, 212.

151 Brihuega, "La ESAI y el arte español," 20. Both exhibition spaces – Arte Moderno and Amigos del Arte – were housed in the Palacio de Bibliotecas y Museos.

152 "Homenaje a un artista. Banquete a Sunyer," *El Imparcial*, 7 February 1925, 6; "Ecos de todas partes. El comensal desconocido," *Heraldo de Madrid*, 12 February 1925, 1. The identical report appears in multiple newspapers, so it is possible Maroto was omitted by mistake.

153 Manuel Abril, "Cómo fue," *Alfar* 5, no. 51 (July 1925): 27–30; Manuel Abril, "Rumbos, exposiciones y artistas. Exposición, en San Sebastián, de arte moderno," *Blanco y Negro* 41, no. 2104 (20 September 1931): 19–23. Discounting Maroto, all of them are known to have attended the Sunyer banquet.

154 "De arte. Un manifiesto interesante," *La Libertad*, 1 April 1925, 4; "Sociedad de Artistas Españoles," *El Sol*, 2 April 1925, 6.

155 José Bergamín, Emiliano Barral, Ricardo Canals, Francisco Durrio, Joaquín Enríquez, Óscar Esplá, Manuel de Falla, Federico García Lorca, Adolfo Salazar, Ángel Sánchez Rivero, and Joaquín Sunyer.

156 One assumes that organizing duties were shared between some or all of the six, and perhaps others. A letter from March, sent by Maroto to Manuel Ángeles Ortiz, attests to his participation and the desire to include in the exhibition painters then resident in Paris (Pérez Segura, "Joaquín Peinado en los escenarios," 39). Pancho Cossío and Joaquín Peinado heeded his invitation. A drawing by Maroto adorned the front cover of the official program of the event: Brihuega and Lomba, eds, *Alberto 1895–1962*, 31.

157 Last-minute disagreements led to two signatories who were also major artists, Sunyer and Vázquez Díaz, not sending works.

158 Juan de la Encina, "Crítica de arte. Ricardo Baroja," *La Voz*, 27 March 1925, 1.

159 "Polémica artística. Ricardo Baroja hace frente a todos los críticos y arremete contra ellos. De Ricardo Baroja a 'Juan de la Encina,'" *Heraldo de Madrid*, 31 March 1925, 1.

160 "Polémicas artísticas. Contestando a Ricardo Baroja," *Heraldo de Madrid*, 1 April 1925, 1.

161 GGM, "Polémica artística. Esquema de una conferencia. El pintor Maroto replica a Baroja"; GGM, "Polémica artística. Esquema de una conferencia. El pintor Maroto replica a Baroja. Baroja le contesta a Vegue."

162 Luis Araquistáin, "Comentarios. La crítica y el genio", *La Voz*, 21 April 1925, 1; A.V. y G. [Ángel Vegue y Goldoni], "Vida cultural. Las conferencias de ayer. En la Casa del Libro," *El Imparcial*, 26 April 1925, 3; "Conferencias. En la Casa del Libro," *El Sol*, 27 April 1925, 2.

163 It lasted from 27 March through 28 April, with dozens of pieces appearing in various Madrid newspapers. In its wake, the *Heraldo de Madrid* started to plan several independent exhibitions: "Las huellas de una polémica. Propósitos del *Heraldo*. Las Exposiciones de Arte," *Heraldo de Madrid*, 23 May 1925, 1.

164 Ybarra, ed., *La Sociedad de Artistas Ibéricos*.

165 The longest article dedicated to him was Juan de la Encina, "Crítica de arte. Los Artistas Ibéricos. Gabriel G. Maroto," *La Voz*, 2 July 1925, 1.

166 Brihuega, "La ESAI y el arte español," 23.

167 "Bellas artes. Conferencia del pintor Sr. García Maroto," *Heraldo de Madrid*, 26 June 1925, 6; "Conferencias. D. Gabriel García Maroto," *El Sol*, 26 June 1925, 4.

168 García Lorca, *Epistolario completo*, 281–2n834. Palencia echoes the summary of the talk given in the *El Sol* report.

169   *Nuevo Mundo*'s coverage appeared on 26 June; together with a relatively brief
       text, it reproduced works by Barradas, Sáenz de Tejada, Peinado, Guezala,
       Moreno Villa, Zelaya, Fernando, Bores, Palencia, García Ascot, and Dalí:
       "En el Retiro se celebra la Exposición de Artistas Ibéricos," *Nuevo Mundo* 32,
       no. 1640 (26 June 1925): n.p.
170   *Bores nuevo. Los años veinte y treinta*, 39.
171   Ibid., 40.
172   Serrano de la Cruz Peinado, "Hacia el reconocimiento debido," 161.
173   GGM, "El viaducto (Escorzos)."
174   Maroto also spun individual images off into postcards: see the reproductions
       in Serrano de la Cruz Peinado, ed., *Gabriel García Maroto y la renovación*,
       134–6.
175   Madrid, Toledo, and then "Bilbao, Ávila and Segovia, Granada, Sevilla, Sal-
       amanca; temples of Spain, Córdoba, Mallorca, Galicia, Asturias, Cataluña,
       Aragón; people of Spain, children, female nudes, humble things, the ports of
       Spain and trades": Ángel Vegue y Goldoni, "Temas artísticos. Los dibujos de
       García Maroto. Un libro y una Exposición," *El Imparcial*, 4 November 1925,
       2. See also Juan de la Encina, "De arte. Estampas de España," *La Voz*, 5 June
       1926, 1, on Maroto's plans to travel the highways and byways of Spain.
176   Ángel Vegue y Goldoni, "Temas artísticos. Los dibujos de García Maroto. Un
       libro y una Exposición," *El Imparcial*, 4 November 1925, 2.
177   GGM, "Notas de ayer," in *La España mágica*, 245–7.
178   Juan de la Encina, "De arte. Viendo y leyendo," *La Voz*, 16 November 1925, 1.
179   Luis de Zulueta, "Arte nuevo. La fuente y el vaso," *La Libertad*, 5 November
       1925, 1.
180   "En Artistas Vascos. Exposición Maroto," *El Liberal* (Bilbao), 7 October 1925,
       3; Visitante, "Exposición Maroto," *El Nervión*, 20 October 1925, 3. Two sculp-
       tures by Ángel Ferrant were also displayed.
181   GGM, *Promoción de México*, 38; Juan de la Encina, "De arte. Coloquios a la
       deriva. (Andalucía vista por un pintor)," *La Voz*, 5 September 1927, 1.
182   GGM, *Andalucía vista por el pintor Maroto*, 8.
183   José Francés, "El perfil de los días. Maroto o la disconformidad," *Nuevo
       Mundo* 32, no. 1658 (30 October 1925): n.p.
184   Juan de la Encina, "De arte. Por las exposiciones," *La Voz*, 4 May 1926, 1.
185   Serrano de la Cruz Peinado, "Hacia el reconocimiento debido," 161.
186   Rafael Marquina, "La Exposición Nacional (Notas estrictas y desinteresa-
       das)," *Heraldo de Madrid*, 8 June 1926, 4.
187   "La Exposición de Bellas Artes. El Jurado concedió ya los premios a los ar-
       tistas. Y dicen que ni son todos los que están, ni están todos los que son," *La
       Voz*, 8 June 1926, 8.
188   Maroto could be referring to the article of 8 June; Marquina also published
       on the ninth, decrying the results of the jury: R.M., "Exposición Nacional de
       Bellas Artes. Relación oficial de recompensas," *Heraldo de Madrid*, 9 June
       1926, 2.

189   "Cosas de la Exposición. Otra carta," *La Voz*, 11 June 1926, 2.

190   For a recap, see Silvio Lago, "La Exposición Nacional. Epílogo lamentable," *La Esfera* 13, no. 650 (19 June 1926): n.p.

191   I can find no trace of the promised publication of the expanded letter.

192   Juan de la Encina, "De arte. Estampas de España," *La Voz*, 5 June 1926, 1.

193   In his review Encina refers to Antonio Ponz's *Viaje de España*, eighteen volumes, 1772–1794, which Maroto had used as a point of comparison in his text for the Salón Nancy exhibition of October 1925: see GGM, "Notas de ayer," in *La España mágica*, 246.

194   Ángel Vegue y Goldoni, "Temas artísticos. Los dibujos de García Maroto. Un libro y una Exposición," *El Imparcial*, 4 November 1925, 2.

195   GGM, "En torno a la Exposición Alejandro Ferrant."

196   GGM, *Promoción de México*, 36, 37.

197   Ibid., 37.

198   Ibid., 38.

199   E. Giménez Caballero, "Madrid: Sílex y caireles," *El Sol*, 17 July 1926, 1.

200   GGM, "Nuevo descubrimiento de España. Tierras de Segovia"; GGM, "Escorzos. Elegía de Sepúlveda."

201   "Exposiciones. La joven pintura mejicana," *La Voz*, 20 December 1926, 3.

202   "Vida cultural. Conferencias de arte. En la Exposición de niños mejicanos," *El Imparcial*, 23 December 1926, 6; "Conferencias. El arte mejicano," *La Libertad*, 23 December 1926, 5. Substantial excerpts were later reproduced by Maroto in GGM, *Acción plástica popular*, 17–21, where he gives the title as "La joven pintura mexicana: Una lección." The passages allow us to appreciate his rapturous tone, and the emphasis (at least here) on the Mexican Revolution and the recent flowering of art with its roots in the culture of the Indigenous population. Cf. GGM, *Promoción de México*, 44–5.

203   GGM, *Acción plástica popular*, 17.

204   Juan de la Encina, "Crónicas de arte. Las pinturas infantiles. Una carta abierta," *La Voz*, 16 December 1926, 1; Juan de la Encina, "De Arte. Los niños mejicanos," *La Voz*, 23 December 1926, 1; Juan de la Encina, "De arte. Coloquios a la deriva," *La Voz*, 29 December 1926, 1; Juan de la Encina, "De arte. Coloquios a la deriva," *La Voz*, 3 January 1927, 1; Juan de la Encina, "Crítica de arte. Coloquios a la deriva," *La Voz*, 5 January 1927, 1.

205   Juan de la Encina, "Crítica de arte. Coloquios a la deriva," *La Voz*, 5 January 1927, 1.

206   Antonio Ballesteros de Martos, "Revista de libros. Arte. *La revolución artística mejicana. Una lección*, por Gabriel García Maroto. Edición del autor. Madrid," *El Sol*, 28 January 1927, 2.

207   GGM, "La joven pintura mexicana."

208   "Comité redactor de *La Gaceta Literaria*," *La Gaceta Literaria* 1, no. 1 (1 January 1927): 1; GGM, *Promoción de México*, 50.

209   Benjamín Jarnés, "Escaparate de libros. Carteles y pasquines," *La Gaceta Literaria* 1, no. 15 (1 August 1927): 4.

210   Antonio Espina, "Arte. Exposición Maroto," *La Gaceta Literaria* 1, no. 15 (1 August 1927): 5.

211   "Primer cumpleaños de LA GACETA LITERARIA," *La Gaceta Literaria* 2, no. 25 (1 January 1928): 1–2.

212   Enrique González Rojo, "Los alumnos-pintores de Ramos Martínez," *La Gaceta Literaria* 1, no. 1 (1 January 1927): 1.

213   "Conferencias. La de GGM en el Palacio de Biblioteca," *La Gaceta Literaria* 1, no. 1 (1 January 1927): 5.

214   GGM, "Arte. El arte de hoy. I. La dominante óptica." The "I" suggested that there would be more installments, which were not forthcoming.

215   There is a considerable secondary bibliography: see, for instance, Londero, "Vanguardia y nacionalismo"; Alemany Bay, *La polémica del meridiano*; and De Castro, "The Intellectual Meridian Debate."

216   GGM, "Un debate apasionado." Maroto illustrated it with an "Alegoría de Juan de la Encina."

217   GGM, "Juan de la Encina." For a biographical sketch and an appraisal of Encina's stature as an art critic, see Alzuri Milanés, "Juan de la Encina crítico de arte" and the section "Biografía" in the same catalogue. Francisco Alcántara provides a contemporary evocation of Encina in "La vida artística. Crítica al margen de 'Juan de la Encina,'" *El Sol*, 9 July 1924, 4.

218   Maroto would later review his book on Goya: GGM, "*Goya en zig-zag.*"

219   Although Maroto's taste in art had changed, and although now he held up different artists as paragons of their craft, the basic flaws in the system remained the same. It is illuminating to read those articles from 1910 alongside the book of 1927.

220   GGM, *Promoción de México*, 46.

221   Juan de la Encina, "Crítica de arte. Coloquios a la deriva," *La Voz*, 5 January 1927, 1.

222   E. Giménez Caballero, "Visitas literarias. Cuatro pintores al kaleidoskopio," *El Sol*, 17 March 1927, 1.

223   There is a modern facsimile edition from 1988. Reproductions of the cover, the title page, and the start of one chapter can be seen in Trapiello, *Imprenta moderna*, 166–7.

224   GGM, *La nueva España. 1930*, 5.

225   GGM, *Promoción de México*, 46.

226   GGM, *La nueva España. 1930*, 5, 7.

227   GGM, *Acción plástica popular*, 22. Here Maroto refers to himself in the third person via this pseudonym.

228   Juan de la Encina, "Crítica de arte. Coloquios a la deriva. (¿La vuelta de Murillo?)," *La Voz*, 28 March 1927, 1.

229   Ernesto Giménez Caballero, "Revista literaria ibérica," *Revista de las Españas* 2, nos 7–8 (March–April 1927): 212–15.

230   Rafael Marquina, "La feria de los libros. *La nueva España-1930*, GGM," *Heraldo de Madrid*, 26 April 1927, 7; Juan Chabás, "Resumen literario. Noticias

literarias. Libros nuevos. Revistas," *La Libertad*, 29 April 1927, 6; G. de Torre, "Escaparate de libros. Libros españoles. GGM: *1930. La nueva España* (con 92 grabados). – Ediciones Biblos. Madrid," *La Gaceta Literaria* 1, no. 9 (1 May 1927): 4; J. Díaz Fernández, "Revista de libros. Arte. Maroto: *La nueva España: 1930*. Dibujos, grabados y pinturas. Editorial Biblos. Madrid," *El Sol*, 11 May 1927, 2.

231 J. Díaz Fernández, "Revista de libros. Arte. Maroto: *La nueva España: 1930*. Dibujos, grabados y pinturas. Editorial Biblos. Madrid," *El Sol*, 11 May 1927, 2.

232 Juan Antonio Gaya Nuño, "A los veinticinco años de un libro sobre política de las artes," *Ínsula* 7, no. 77 (May 1952): 9.

233 GGM, *La nueva España. 1930*, 60–71.

234 GGM, *Acción plástica popular*, 34.

235 GGM, "El concurso nacional de escultura. Ángel Ferrant"; GGM, "Al margen de una interesante exposición artística"; GGM, "Arte y artistas. Prisma de Ignacio Zuloaga"; GGM, "Arte y artistas. Exposición de artistas andaluces"; GGM, "Arte y artistas. Maestros y críticos." The exhibition of Andalusian artists was the first fruit of the *Heraldo de Madrid* initiative.

236 "Exposición de Litografías Artísticas," *La Época*, 7 March 1927, 4.

237 Ángel Vegue y Goldoni, "Bellas artes. Las cerámicas de Fernando Arranz," *El Imparcial*, 23 April 1927, 8.

238 A.V. y G., "Bellas Artes. Exposición Maroto," *El Imparcial*, 30 June 1927, 5.

239 Francisco Alcántara, "La vida artística. Los dibujos de Maroto," *El Sol*, 13 July 1927, 2.

240 Ibid.

241 Antonio Espina, "Arte. Exposición Maroto," *La Gaceta Literaria* 1, no. 15 (1 August 1927): 5.

242 GGM, "Escorzos. Toledo visto por un pintor"; GGM, "Escorzos. Convento en Castilla"; GGM, "Nuevo descubrimiento de España. La ría de Bilbao"; GGM, "Carnaval en Castilla"; GGM, "Tierras de Segovia. Mercado en la ciudad"; GGM, "Tierras de Segovia. La posada. II"; GGM, "Tierras de Segovia. Pueblos del camino. III"; GGM, "Verbena madrileña"; GGM, "Castilla. La romería."

243 GGM, "Un pueblo de Castilla," with two small sketches.

244 Enrique Díez-Canedo made this point in E.D.-C., "Revista de libros. *Litoral. Cuadernos mensuales*, publicados bajo la dirección de Emilio Prados y Manuel Altolaguirre. – Málaga. (2.25 el número)," *El Sol*, 11 March 1927, 2.

245 The cover and four of the five images are reproduced in Serrano de la Cruz Peinado, ed., *Gabriel García Maroto y la renovación*, 132–3.

246 Perhaps a distant antecedent of Giménez Caballero's film *Esencia de verbena* (1929). The entire contents of the portfolio – the fifteen photoengravings – are reproduced in Serrano de la Cruz Peinado, ed., *Gabriel García Maroto y la renovación*, 124–31.

247 Regarding his itinerary, see GGM, *Promoción de México*, 36, 37. The full title on the slip cover of the volume was given as *Andalucía vista por el pintor Maroto. Córdoba. Granada. Málaga. Sevilla. Jaén. Paisajes. Gentes.*

105 dibujos, dessins, drawings. 25 glosas, gloses, glosses. Among others, it contained the five drawings from *Manuel de Falla.*

248   GGM, *Promoción de México*, 38. Maroto goes on to include here excerpts from two of the prose glosses, "Castillos" and "Mujeres" (38–9, 39–40).

249   As did Andrenio, "Aspectos. Una visión de Andalucía. Literaria y pictórica," *La Voz*, 3 October 1927, 1.

250   Juan de la Encina, "De arte. Coloquios a la deriva. (Andalucía vista por un pintor)," *La Voz*, 5 September 1927, 1.

251   E. Giménez Caballero, "Revista literaria ibérica," *Revista de las Españas* 2, no. 12 (August 1927): 541–2.

252   Rafael Marquina, "La feria de los libros. *Andalucía.* – Maroto," *Heraldo de Madrid*, 13 September 1927, 7.

253   Antonio Espina, "Del repertorio andaluz. Glosas y dibujos," *La Gaceta Literaria* 1, no. 18 (15 September 1927): 5.

254   Melchor Fernández Almagro, "Andalucía vista por el pintor Maroto," *Revista de Occidente* 5, no. 54 (December 1927): 422–3.

255   Evidently, these two collections, again with "text and drawings" by Maroto, focused on areas that he had treated earlier in his own painting and in drawings published in periodicals.

256   GGM, "Notas de ayer," in *La España mágica*, 247.

257   GGM, "Para Ángel Ferrant, en Viena," in *La España mágica*, 9–10.

258   E. Giménez Caballero, "Revista literaria ibérica," *Revista de las Españas* 2, nos 15–16 (November–December 1927): 695.

259   GECÉ, "Revista de libros. *La España mágica,*" *El Sol*, 7 March 1928, 2.

260   GGM, *Promoción de México*, 42.

261   Gustavo Bueno Sánchez, "Ediciones Biblos 1927–1928," Filosofía en español, accessed 13 May 2022, http://www.filosofia.org/ave/003/c117.htm.

262   Maroto's very early enthusiasm for the reformist writer and politician Joaquín Costa, who had links with La Solana, is documented by Serrano de la Cruz Peinado, "Hacia el reconocimiento debido," 141.

263   GGM, *Promoción de México*, 42.

264   A reproduction of the cover of Fedin's *Las ciudades y los años*, designed and executed by Maroto, can be seen in Trapiello, *Imprenta moderna*, 162.

265   Bueno Sánchez, "Ediciones Biblos 1927–1928," provides a comprehensive listing.

266   GGM, *Acción plástica popular*, 21. He refers, of course, to Primo de Rivera.

267   G.C. "Escaparate de libros. Libros rusos," *La Gaceta Literaria* 1, no. 8 (15 April 1927): 4.

268   See the advertisement in *La Gaceta Literaria* 1, no. 14 (15 July 1927): 5.

269   E.G.C., "La América nueva. Un gran romance mejicano," *La Gaceta Literaria*, 1, no. 17 (1 September 1927): 3.

270   "La cruzada contra el bolchevismo. Cuantos tengan algo que defender y conservar han de solidarizarse frente a las maniobras soviéticas," *La Nación*, 22 April 1927, 1–2.

271 "Una carta y unas observaciones. El ejercicio de la crítica y los intereses industriales," *La Nación*, 26 April 1927, 4.

272 All numbers can be consulted on the Hemeroteca Digital site (http://hemerotecadigital.bne.es/index.vm) of the Biblioteca Nacional in Madrid.

273 See Santonja, *Del lápiz rojo al lápiz libre*, 99–149.

274 P.F.M., "*Andalucía* vista por el pintor Maroto: Ediciones Biblos," *Post-Guerra* 1, no. 4 (25 September 1927): 15.

275 Santonja, *Del lápiz rojo al lápiz libre*, 124–5.

276 GGM, *Promoción de México*, 63.

277 The first advert appeared in *La Gaceta Literaria* 1, no. 22 (15 November 1927): 4, and announced publication for the end of the month. The advert featured (in black and white) a large reproduction of the book's front cover.

278 GGM, *Promoción de México*, 51.

279 GGM, ed., *Almanaque*, 2.

280 Ibid., 8.

281 *Nunisme* is often associated with Pierre-Albert Birot; from the Greek *nun*, meaning the present.

282 GGM, ed., *Almanaque*, 8.

283 Ibid., 11.

284 Ibid., 5, 61, 135, 171.

285 Ibid., 17, 23, 41, 83, 113, 119, 145, 151, 161, 195, 207, 215.

286 Ibid., 34–9.

287 In the logo/flyer for *La Gaceta Literaria* made by Maroto, the shaded outline of South America, labelled "América," sits atop the solid shape of Spain, with a steamship beside the two of them. This design is reproduced in GGM, ed., *Almanaque*, 112, as an advert for the magazine.

288 Beyond the influence of Giménez Caballero, Sáez Delgado also posits that the inclusive spirit of the Sociedad de Artistas Ibéricos exhibition was carried on by Maroto: "*El almanaque de las artes*," 319–22.

289 Sáez Delgado points out that Almada Negreiros exhibited at the Salón de la Unión Iberoamericana immediately before Maroto, in the summer of 1927, and both shows were reviewed by Espina in *La Gaceta Literaria*: "*El almanaque de las artes*," 323–4.

290 Benjamín Jarnés, "El almanaque de Maroto," *La Gaceta Literaria* 2, no. 25 (1 January 1928): 5.

291 GECÉ, "Revista de libros. Calendarios de literatura," *El Sol*, 22 January 1928, 2.

292 Guillermo de Torre, "Almanaques literarios," *Caras y Caretas*, no. 1534 (25 February 1928): n.p.

293 GGM, *Promoción de México*, 59, 60.

294 Ibid., 29–30.

295 GGM, "Iglesias de México: Las cúpulas."

296 GGM, *Promoción de México*, 59.

297 GGM, "Un debate apasionado."

298 GGM, *Promoción de México*, 59.

299   GGM, *Acción plástica popular*, 34.

300   Ibid. That he was in political and hence potentially legal trouble with the Primo de Rivera authorities may connect with other motives at which Serrano de la Cruz Peinado hints rather darkly: "His virtues (or defects, depending on how you looked at it) were the cause of no little resentment and no few confrontations and fears, which led Maroto to find himself obliged to leave for Mexico at the end of 1927": "Por tercera vez, y … ¿definitiva?," 16.

301   "Comida íntima. En honor del pintor Maroto," *El Liberal*, 15 December 1927, 3.

302   "Maroto, a Méjico," *La Gaceta Literaria* 1, no. 24 (15 December 1927): 7; GGM, *Promoción de México*, 60.

303   Rafael Suárez Solís, "Gabriel García Maroto va a México. Estará dos días en La Habana," *Diario de la Marina*, 29 December 1927, 30.

304   Manuel Aznar, "La España de hoy. Notas de actualidad," *Diario de la Marina*, 1 January 1928, 32; GGM, *Promoción de México*, 60.

305   Cf. GGM, *Acción plástica popular*, 34.

306   "El pintor español Maroto en México," *Diario de la Marina*, 9 January 1928, 30; GGM, *Promoción de México*, 60.

307   Serrano de la Cruz Peinado, "Hacia el reconocimiento debido," 170–1.

308   Alejo Carpentier, "Maroto. Viajero de 3ª," *Diario de la Marina*, 15 January 1928, 33.

309   See Valender, "García Maroto y los Contemporáneos," and GGM, *Promoción de México*, 61–4. Alongside the *Veinte dibujos mexicanos*, the other early fruit of this period was a poetic anthology, GGM, ed., *Galería de los poetas nuevos de México* [cover]/*Nueva antología de poetas mexicanos* [title page].

310   See GGM, *Acción plástica popular*, 34–9.

311   GGM, *Promoción de México*, 26.

312   Ibid., 40–1.

313   Ibid., 46.

314   GGM, *Acción plástica popular*, "Semblanza de un desconocido," 11.

315   GGM, *Acción plástica popular*, "La huella de un educador. I. Autocrítica," 15–16.

316   Ibid.

Chapter Six

1   Laurenson-Shakibi, "*Amor imposible, cosas en común*," 41.

2   These private art lessons were probably from Andrés Sandoval: Meléndez Táboas, "Formación y primeros trabajos de Maruja Mallo," 1619. For Mallo's time at the Escuela de Artes y Oficios, see Ferris, *Maruja Mallo*, 44; Nuevo Cal and Ínsua López, *Maruja Mallo: De prometedora pioneira*, 29.

3   Nuevo Cal and Álvarez González, *Maruja Mallo. Vida e exilio*, 3–4; Nuevo Cal and Ínsua López, *Maruja Mallo: De prometedora pioneira*, 48.

4   Archive, Real Academia de San Fernando, Universidad Complutense de Madrid.

5   Meléndez Táboas, "Formación y primeros trabajos de Maruja Mallo," lists all the titles. Some contemporary reviews are: R.O. [Ramón Ovies], "Exposición

de Arte Avilesino. Figuras de la Exposición. Maruja Gómez," *La Voz de Avilés*, 22 August 1922; Silvio Itálico [Benito Álvarez-Buylla Lozana], "Exposición de Arte Avilesino," *La Voz de Avilés*, 5 September 1922, 1; Francés, "Notas de un catálogo"; José María Malgor, "La Sociedad 'Amigos del Arte' y la IV Exposición de Artistas Avilesinos," *La Voz de Asturias*, 29 August 1926, 5. See also Nuevo Cal and Ínsua López, *Maruja Mallo: De prometedora pioneira*, 30–5.

6   "Notas de un catálogo."

7   Nuevo Cal and Ínsua López, *Maruja Mallo: De prometedora pioneira*, 39. The addresses given in her records place her there between 1922 and 1926: archive, Real Academia de San Fernando, Universidad Complutense de Madrid.

8   Meléndez Táboas, "Formación y primeros trabajos de Maruja Mallo," 1620.

9   Archive, Real Academia de San Fernando, Universidad Complutense de Madrid. Because of Dalí's suspension in October of his second year, from that point forward their classes were out of sync. Meléndez Táboas offers many details regarding those five classes in "Maruja Mallo entre sus condiscípulas," 118–21.

10   See *Sueños noctámbulos*, Salvador-dali.org, accessed 25 May 2022, https://www.salvador-dali.org/es/obra/adquisiciones/289/suenos-noctambulos.

11   See chapter 2.

12   García Lorca, *Epistolario completo*, 171–2. Nuevo Cal and Ínsua López state that her elder brother José (b. 1900) was a *residente* and coincided with Lorca and Pepín Bello (*Maruja Mallo: De prometedora pioneira*, 48), but I cannot find any record of him there.

13   *Salvador Dalí y Maruja Mallo en el Café de Oriente*, Salvador-dali.org, accessed 25 May 2022, https://www.salvador-dali.org/es/museos/teatro-museo-dali-de-figueres/exposiciones/61/de-suenos-paseos-nocturnos-y-vivencias.

14   1907–1999, librarian, journalist, and later Communist activist.

15   See chapter 3. Certain illustrations done by Ochoa for magazines, which Mallo had seen when younger, had served as inspiration for her: Meléndez Táboas, "Formación y primeros trabajos de Maruja Mallo," 1619.

16   Falcón, *Asalto a los cielos*, 34–5. The date is uncertain – at some point between September 1922 and 1924 (when Falcón moved to London).

17   "Maruja Mallo entre sus condiscípulas," 124. Apparently, José Moreno Carbonero, the professor in charge of the subject (since 1892), had problems with women students drawing male nudes (see chapter 4), causing Mallo to seek outside assistance.

18   Falcón, *Asalto a los cielos*, 35.

19   Nuevo Cal and Ínsua López, *Maruja Mallo: De prometedora pioneira*, 45. The three works were entitled *Montserrat*, *Retrato*, and *Cabeza*: Meléndez Táboas, "Formación y primeros trabajos de Maruja Mallo," 1620–1.

20   Gibson, *Federico García Lorca*, vol. 1, *De Fuente Vaqueros a Nueva York (1898–1929)*, 544, 668n47. Mallo gave Gibson to understand that she and

Aladrén dated for a while. On Aladrén more generally, see Gibson, *Federico García Lorca*, vol. 1, *De Fuente Vaqueros a Nueva York (1898–1929)*, 544–9.

21 Archive, Real Academia de San Fernando, Universidad Complutense de Madrid; Mallo, "Dalí," 223; Balló, *Las sinsombrero*, 39–57.

22 Rivas, "Maruja Mallo, pintora del más allá," 16; Nuevo Cal and Ínsua López, *Maruja Mallo: De prometedora pioneira*, 48.

23 Moreno Villa, *Vida en claro*, 161; see also chapter 3 of this volume.

24 Méndez, *Memorias habladas*, 43, 48, 51–3. Méndez's poem "Tenerife," dedicated to Mallo, from *Inquietudes* (Madrid: Juan Pueyo, 1926), appears to describe Mallo's painting *La isleña* or another (unknown) canvas very close to it.

25 Nuevo Cal and Ínsua López, *Maruja Mallo: De prometedora pioneira*, 61–2. A photo of Maruja, her sister Emilia, and a number of female friends picnicking in the Canaries can be seen at https://nl.pinterest.com/pin/632826185120999831/.

26 Mangini, *Maruja Mallo*, 73, 311–2n123; Nuevo Cal and Ínsua López, *Maruja Mallo: De prometedora pioneira*, 60, 65–6. Her brother Cristino registered her for classes on 25 September, but then she added more in person on the thirtieth: archive, Real Academia de San Fernando, Universidad Complutense de Madrid.

27 Meléndez Táboas, "Formación y primeros trabajos de Maruja Mallo," 1620; Nuevo Cal and Ínsua López indicate that she was there in August with her mother, who was briefly back on the mainland: *Maruja Mallo: De prometedora pioneira*, 70.

28 "Obituario," *El Progreso*, 28 December 1926, 1; "De sociedad. Viajeros," *La Prensa*, 9 January 1927, 3; "De sociedad. Viajeros," *La Prensa*, 3 March 1927, 3; "Ecos de sociedad. Viajes," *La Gaceta de Tenerife*, 13 November 1928, 2. Subsequently, he was posted to Almería, Villacañas, and, in mid-1930, to Motril: "La Gaceta. Disposiciones oficiales," *El Orzán*, 22 June 1930, 3.

29 Mangini, *Maruja Mallo*, 53, 305n60; Nuevo Cal and Ínsua López, *Maruja Mallo: De prometedora pioneira*, 70.

30 Details of which classes she took in which years, and of the professors teaching those classes, are given in Meléndez Táboas, "Maruja Mallo entre sus condiscípulas," 121–4, 126–7.

31 Nuevo Cal and Ínsua López, *Maruja Mallo: De prometedora pioneira*, 68.

32 Mallo was born in Viveiro, which is located in the province of Lugo; "Crónicas de la vida gallega," *Diario de la Marina*, 5 July 1926, 4; Libro de Actas, no. 148, Diputación Provincial de Lugo, 15 June 1926; Bal, "Conocimiento de Maruja Mallo"; Pérez de Ayala, "Álbum biográfico. Maruja Mallo," 77; Nuevo Cal and Ínsua López, *Maruja Mallo: De prometedora pioneira*, 68.

33 Nuevo Cal and Ínsua López, *Maruja Mallo: De prometedora pioneira*, 79, 120–1.

34 Meléndez Táboas, "Formación y primeros trabajos de Maruja Mallo," 1621, gives the nine titles. Some contemporary reviews: X. del S., "La Exposición

de Arte Gallego. Vestíbulo," *El Eco de Santiago*, 13 August 1926, 1: "Ana María Gómez, varios retratos fuertemente dibujados"; X. del S., "La Exposición de Arte Gallego. Sala IX," *El Eco de Santiago*, 30 August 1926, 1: "Figura de niña, pintada por Ana María Gómez, está plena de felices intentos." See also Nuevo Cal and Ínsua López, *Maruja Mallo: De prometedora pioneira*, 69–70.

35 The four major works from the *Verbenas* series can be located in the following: *La verbena* (1927), Museo Nacional Centro de Arte Reina Sofía, accessed 2 June 2022, https://www.museoreinasofia.es/en/collection/artwork/verbena-fair, and *La Verbena de Pascua* (1927), *Verbena* (1928), and *Kermesse* (1928), in Corredoira López, ed., *Maruja Mallo*, at (respectively) 62, 63, and 65. Three of the *Estampas* are also reproduced in Corredoira López, ed., *Maruja Mallo*, 68–73, and others can be viewed online.

36 Mercedes Valero de Cabal, "Pintora cubista?," *Región*, 13 August 1927, 16, and two works reproduced at 2–3; "La Feria de Muestras. Las exposiciones artísticas," *El Noroste*, 13 August 1927, 3; José María Malgor, "Ante la exposición de Maruja Gómez Mallo," *La Voz de Avilés*, 25 August 1927, 2. Mallo was in attendance for the exhibition, and shortly after it closed she and her brother Cristino left to visit family in Galicia: "De sociedad," *El Noroeste*, 30 August 1927, 1.

37 J. Díaz Fernández, "Acerca de Maruja Mallo, pintora de vanguardia," *El Noroeste*, 21 August 1927, 3.

38 García de Valdeavellano, "Maruja Mallo en su carrousel." During the visit Mallo herself drew attention to the change in her style from a year ago.

39 Luis García de Valdeavellano, "Crónicas de arte. La joven pintura española," *La Época del Domingo*, 1 October 1927, 1.

40 "Artes. Maruja Mallo por el camino de Spies," *La Prensa* (Santa Cruz de Tenerife), 6 January 1928, 3; Pestana Nóbrega, "Maruja Mallo." Mallo likely met another Canary Islands native, Agustín Espinosa, when they both coincided in Madrid in 1922–24; Espinosa was mainly in the Canaries from 1924 onward. She may have reconnected with him in the summer of 1925, when she likely also met Pestana Nóbrega; both men were part of the group behind the magazine *La Rosa de los Vientos*. In 1929, on the cover flap of Espinosa's book *Lancelot, 28°–7°* (Madrid: Ediciones A.L.F.A.), the same publishing house announced as forthcoming *El arte de Maruja Mallo* (40 dibujos con un prólogo de Agustín Espinosa), which unfortunately never appeared.

41 That is, redolent of Ramón Gómez de la Serna.

42 *Cartas a Germaine*, 661. Days earlier, on 2 December, Mallo, alongside all four of her visitors and many others, had attended the opening of Moreno Villa's art show in a Chrysler car dealership: Francisco Alcántara, "La vida artística. Exposición Moreno Villa. II," *El Sol*, 15 December 1927, 2.

43 Fernández Almagro and Gallego Burín, *Literatura y política*, 116. Escoriza Escoriza traces connections between Gregorio Martínez Sierra's wife, María de la O Lejárraga, and Falla, Granada, and members of the Rinconcillo group, and between María de la O and Mallo, leading to Mallo connecting with

Fernández Almagro and Gallego Burín: "La generación de plata," 95–6 and plate between 96 and 97. There are two photographs of the three of them in 1928 strolling in a Madrid street and in the Retiro park.

44 Gómez de la Serna, "Maruja Mallo," 9. All these visits were to the relatively new apartment on Ventura Rodríguez, where Maruja had a room to herself, unlike a number of her siblings: Mangini, *Maruja Mallo*, 53, 305n60.

45 Pérez Ferrero, "Baraja de estampas."

46 "Notre Dame de la aleluya." Giménez Caballero also commissioned her to design the cover for his 1928 book *Hércules jugando a los dados* (Madrid: La Nave), which features an illustration very much in the style of the *Estampas*.

47 José María Quiroga Pla, "Avisos al lector. Más en torno a un pintor nuevo," *El Norte de Castilla*, 20 April 1928; reprinted in *Mediodía*, no. 13 (October 1928): 3–6. Photos of Mallo from the period are reproduced in Corredoira López, ed., *Maruja Mallo*, 310, 315.

48 Mallo, in Escribano, "Maruja Mallo, una bruja moderna," 49.

49 Mallo, "Ortega y Gasset," 221.

50 No invitation seems to have survived, and there does not appear to have been a catalogue. The date can be calculated from Valdeavellano's review: L.G. de V., "Notas de arte. Exposición Maruja Mallo," *La Época*, 30 May 1928, 1. According to Nuevo Cal and Ínsua López (*Maruja Mallo: De prometedora pioneira*, 101), it was open each day from 11:00 to 1:00 and 4:00 to 8:00. A letter from Ernestina de Champourcin to Carmen Conde places its *inauguración* – perhaps a *vernissage* of sorts – at 11:00 a.m. on the twenty-fifth: *Epistolario (1927–1995)*, 94.

51 Mallo, *Lo popular en la plástica española*, 7.

52 Including *Alfar, L'Amic de les Arts, Blanco y Negro, La Época, Gaceta de Bellas Artes, La Gaceta Literaria, Ilustração. Publicação quinzenal, El Liberal, La Libertad, Mediodía, Región, Revista de Avance, Revista de la Raza, Revista de las Españas, Revista de Occidente, El Sol, Verso y Prosa*, and *La Voz*.

53 The sixteen canvases were not shown as a group until May 1932, at an exhibition held at the Galerie Pierre (Pierre Loeb's gallery) in Paris. They were subsequently dispersed, and as far as I can ascertain, no modern exhibition has reunited all of them. The current whereabouts of several are unknown. Although there is some variation in the titles given: *Antro de fósiles, Basuras, Campanario, Cardos y esqueleto, Cloaca, Espantapájaros, Espantapeces, Estornino muerto, Fósiles, Grajo y excrementos, Huella, Huella y esqueleto/ Esqueleto y huella, Huellas/Huellas abominables, Lagarto y cenizas, Rana/ Sapo y excrementos, Tierra y excrementos*, Aranda Barca's undergraduate thesis ("Maruja Mallo [1902–1995] y su etapa surrealista en Madrid") manages to bring together in an appendix small reproductions of all sixteen.

54 Mallo, "La Escuela de Vallecas"; Alberti, "Tribuna: *La arboleda perdida*"; Alberti, *La arboleda perdida III y IV*, 92. Alberto [Sánchez] situates these walks as starting "from 1927, more or less": "Sobre la Escuela de Vallecas," 49, and see 53. From October 1925 through the end of 1929, Palencia intermittently

spent several periods in Paris, at one point sharing a studio with Pancho Cossío; little is documented regarding the precise dates, but Carmona provides the best coverage ("Naturaleza y cultura," 48–54) and Luis Buñuel's letters provide several precise indications (*Correspondencia escogida*, 44, 56). Palencia has a notable drawing entitled *Paisaje de Vallecas* that is dated to 1928: Esteban Leal, ed., *Benjamín Palencia*, 67. For more on the Escuela de Vallecas, and for members of the group beyond Alberto and Palencia, see the exhibition catalogue prepared by Alaminos López, *La Escuela de Vallecas*; important among them would be Pancho Lasso, Juan Manuel Díaz-Caneja, Antonio Rodríguez Luna, and Eduardo Díaz Yepes.

55   Mallo, *Lo popular en la plástica española*, 23, 27; she continues on in a similar vein for several more paragraphs. Manuel Abril comments extensively on the change and reproduces some samples of the new work in "Rumbos, exposiciones y artistas."

56   Guillén, *Cartas a Germaine*, 733.

57   L.G. de V., "Notas de arte. Exposición José de Togores," *La Época*, 27 November 1928, 4.

58   E. de M., "En el Lyceum Club. Una vespertina teatral," *El Imparcial*, 8 January 1929, 3. See Ernestina de Champourcin's comments on the design and its realization: *Epistolario (1927–1995)*, 263; her own play *Fábrica de estrellas* was also performed.

59   Anon., "Maruja Mallo, la pintora revolucionaria"; Mallo, *Lo popular en la plástica española*, 12. This work is also known by a slightly different alternative title, *El colorín colorado*.

60   Mallo, *Lo popular en la plástica española*, 12; Gómez Mesa, "Cinema y arte nuevo." Several of them appeared in *La Gaceta Literaria*, *Nueva Revista*, and *Popular Film* over 1929–30. An album of fifteen lithographs entitled *Le cinéma comique* was to be published by the Jeanne Bucher Gallery in Paris in 1931 or 1932, but never appeared (a subscription form survives: Corredoira López, ed., *Maruja Mallo*, 319).

61   Cao Moure, ed., *1929. Lugo*, 57–8; Corredoira López, ed., *Maruja Mallo*, 67.

62   "La Casa de los Tiros y la Exposición Regional de Arte Moderno," *La Época*, 2 November 1929, 3; Orion, "Notas de arte. Visitas a la Exposición Regional," *El Defensor de Granada*, 30 November 1929, 1; Juan Torrez Díaz, "La Casa de los Tiros residencia oficial del Patronato Nacional del Turismo y la Exposición Regional de Arte Moderno," *Granada Gráfica. Revista Ilustrada*, no. 14 (December 1929): n.p.; Escoriza Escoriza, "La generación de plata," 87–8, 95–6, plates between 96 and 97, 118–21.

63   Nuevo Cal and Ínsua López, *Maruja Mallo: De prometedora pioneira*, 121.

64   Juan de la Encina, "De arte. Vanguardia de verano. II," *La Voz*, 13 September 1930, 1.

65   The part of the show featuring contemporary Spanish artists continued on to the San Diego Museum of Art in early 1931.

66   Alberti, *La arboleda perdida. Libros I y II*, 129–30, 162.

67   Archive, Fundación Gregorio Prieto, Madrid. In the summer of 1919, Alberti and his father spent time in the sierra of San Rafael: Alberti, *La arboleda perdida. Libros I y II*, 118. Alberti comments briefly on his close friendship with Prieto in Mateo, *Rafael Alberti. De lo vivo y lejano*, 67.

68   Alberti, *Un amigo de la juventud*, 35–6. Alberti dates the visit "to the beginning of winter [of 1919]" (*La arboleda perdida. Libros I y II*, 119), but the letter demonstrates it was a little later.

69   Alberti, *La arboleda perdida. Libros I y II*, 136.

70   Ibid., 108–9, 122–3. Amado Nervo was one of several favoured poets: ibid., 109, 126–7; Alberti, *Un amigo de la juventud*, 35. For more information on the two friends, see Alberti, *Un amigo de la juventud*, 9–27.

71   "El *Cuaderno de Mari Celina* y otros poemas." Alberti writes, "poems kept on coming out of me as if they had flowed from a mysterious spring that I carried within me and could not contain": *La arboleda perdida. Libros I y II*, 137. It is not clear whether in July Alberti was in Madrid or San Rafael: in *La arboleda perdida. Libros I y II* he says that he spent the summer preparing to retake exams for the *bachillerato* (122), but there is a letter written by him in San Rafael dated to 11 September 1920: Alberti, *Un amigo de la juventud*, 37–8.

72   Alberti, *La arboleda perdida. Libros I y II*, 146.

73   Alberti, *Un amigo de la juventud*, 127–8; Alberti, *La arboleda perdida. Libros I y II*, 147–8.

74   Anon., "El Salón de Otoño"; Aguirre, "Segundo Salón de Otoño"; Aguirre, "Nota humorística del Segundo Salón de Otoño" (1 October 1921); Aguirre, "Nota humorística del Segundo Salón de Otoño" (15 October 1921).

75   Alberti, *La arboleda perdida. Libros I y II*, 149–50.

76   Alonso, "Rafael entre su arboleda," 1.

77   Alberti, *La arboleda perdida. Libros I y II*, 149–52; Aub, *Conversaciones con Buñuel*, 284; "En el Ateneo. Exposición Rafael Alberti," *El Sol*, 20 March 1923, 4. Alberti states that he was followed at the Ateneo by Francisco Cossío, but Cossío's show actually opened there in January of that year.

78   Alberti, *La arboleda perdida. Libros I y II*, 152–3; Aub, *Conversaciones con Buñuel*, 284. The compositions are dated to San Rafael, August 1922, while *Horizonte*, no. 3, is dated 15 December 1922, so Alberti's reminiscence that "the spring breezes were circling the windows" (*La arboleda perdida. Libros I y II*, 152) is hard to explain.

79   Alberti dates it to "January or February of 1922" (*La arboleda perdida. Libros I y II*, 151) and Aleixandre to the spring of that same year (Aleixandre, "Rafael Alberti, pintor," 683), rather than the correct March 1923.

80   Alberti, *La arboleda perdida. Libros I y II*, 162.

81   Buñuel, *Mi último suspiro*, 63; Aub, *Conversaciones con Buñuel*, 284–5; at some point, Alberti also joined the famous Orden de Toledo: *Mi último suspiro*, 72; Alberti, *La arboleda perdida. Libros I y II*, 215.

82 Jiménez Gómez, *Lorca y Alberti*, 44; Alberti, *Un amigo de la juventud*, 58–9, 94, 129; letters to Prieto, 1 July, 2 August, 2 September, and 5 September 1923; late July/2 August, 22 August, 6–7 September, and 24 September 1924 (archive, Fundación Gregorio Prieto, Madrid). Among the *Poemas anteriores a "Marinero en tierra"* there are poetic texts included in letters to Espinosa dated in San Rafael to 14 August 1922 and 17 August 1923 (Alberti, *Obras completas. Poesía I*, 662–3; Alberti, *Un amigo de la juventud*, 58–9, 75–6).

83 Letters to Prieto, 27 April and 10 May 1923 (archive, Fundación Gregorio Prieto, Madrid); Alberti, *Un amigo de la juventud*, 63–76, 91, 132; Alberti, *La arboleda perdida. Libros I y II*, 142.

84 Prieto repeatedly asserted that he had met Lorca at his exhibition at the Museo de Arte Moderno, at that time housed in the Biblioteca Nacional, which opened on 12 April 1924 ("Arte y artistas. Exposición Prieto," *La Acción*, 11 April 1924, 3); see, for instance, Prieto, *Lorca y la generación del 27*, 34.

85 Aub, *Conversaciones con Buñuel*, 284; Alberti, *La arboleda perdida I y II*, 168–9.

86 Archive, Fundación Gregorio Prieto, Madrid. Here Alberti also mentions a "print of the Virgin and the Wise King," which is a painting that he gifted Lorca, inscribed, "To Federico G. Lorca | this print of the south | at the inauguration of our | friendship – Rafael Alberti 1924" (Jiménez Gómez, *Lorca y Alberti*, 46; painting reproduced on 51; currently it is hung in the Huerta de San Vicente, Granada). In the same letter Alberti records a request from Lorca to produce a second painting, of "the apparition of the Virgin of Beautiful Love to the poet Federico García Lorca"; this commission *is* later remembered by Alberti (Alberti, *La arboleda perdida. Libros I y II*, 168). During the summer of 1924 Lorca wrote to Prieto asking if Alberti was in San Rafael (García Lorca, *Epistolario completo*, 232).

87 Alberti, "Balcones. 1. 2. 3."

88 Alberti, *La arboleda perdida. Libros I y II*, 169.

89 Ibid., 174.

90 Ibid., 170–2; Aub, *Conversaciones con Buñuel*, 287.

91 Although that would have been his first choice, Hinojosa did not live at the Residencia de Estudiantes (see chapter 1). According to Hernández ("Presentación del epistolario," 18), Prados, who knew Hinojosa from Málaga and from the magazine *Ambos*, introduced him into the Residencia circle over the fall and winter of that year. There are photographs of Hinojosa in Toledo with Buñuel, Dalí, Moreno Villa, etc., from 1924. See also the group-signed postcard to Juan Guerrero Ruiz from 4 December 1924, which puts Lorca, Alberti, Hinojosa, Bello, Dalí, and Chacón together in Juan Vicéns's room at the Residencia (García Lorca, *Epistolario completo*, 255–6). From 1925 on, Bergamín would become a firm friend of Alberti, through the Civil War and beyond (Alberti, *La arboleda perdida. Libros I y II*, 202).

92 Letter to Prieto, July 1924 (archive, Fundación Gregorio Prieto, Madrid).

93   "Exposición Gregorio Prieto," *El Sol*, 5 January 1925, 4. For the portrait that Prieto did of Alberti, see *Retrato de Rafael Alberti*, Museo Gregorio Prieto, accessed 2 June 2022, https://gregorioprieto.org/obras/retrato-de-rafael-alberti-3/.

94   Gutiérrez-Vega, *Corresponsales españoles*, 16; Alberti, *La arboleda perdida. Libros I y II*, 176. Alberti had previously intended to spend October 1922 to June 1923 in Rute with his sister, but this plan never came to fruition (Alberti, *Un amigo de la juventud*, 58, 129).

95   Alberti, *La arboleda perdida. Libros I y II*, 183–4; Gutiérrez-Vega, *Corresponsales españoles*, 23, 25, 28, 29, 31. César González-Ruano makes some very curious remarks and rather pejorative insinuations about Alberti's early friendship with Chacón, and Chacón's support for Alberti in competing for the prize: *Memorias*, 129.

96   Gutiérrez-Vega, *Corresponsales españoles*, 31–3.

97   Archive, Fundación Gregorio Prieto, Madrid. If the time indication given is accurate, Alberti would have returned from Rute right around Easter, which fell in 1925 on 12 April. Alberti's numerous letters to Chacón from Rute abruptly stop after 30 March, and then restart with a letter from Madrid on 8 May (to Chacón in Burgos): Gutiérrez-Vega, *Corresponsales espanoles*, 35–7. In a letter from Chacón y Calvo to Juan Guerrero Ruiz, of 29 April, he says that Alberti has been visiting him daily during his recent illness: García Lorca, *Epistolario completo*, 270n794.

98   Alberti, *La arboleda perdida. Libros III y IV*, 33.

99   García Lorca, *Epistolario completo*, 289.

100   Alberti, *Marinero en tierra*, 123. According to Alberti, he and Jiménez had first met around spring 1923, in a meeting mediated by Chabás: Alberti, *La arboleda perdida. Libros I y II*, 204.

101   The closeness of Hinojosa to the whole group is demonstrated by the dedications in the collection, to Alberti, Dalí, Juan Vicéns, Buñuel, José María Chacón, José Bello, Altolaguirre, Lorca, Moreno Villa, Prados, Bergamín, and García Maroto.

102   Anon., "[untitled]," *Gaceta de Madrid*; "Premios nacionales de Literatura," *La Época*, 8 June 1925, 1.

103   Altolaguirre, *Epistolario 1925–1959*, 30.

104   It is unclear when or how Altolaguirre and Alberti met in person as adults. Altolaguirre remembers him playing as a child with his elder brother (*Obras completas*, vol. 1, *El caballo griego*, 46), while Alberti recounts having met Luis over the winter of 1919–20 (Alberti, *La arboleda perdida. Libros I y II*, 119); elsewhere Altolaguirre states, "I knew Rafael from when I was a child" (*Obras completas*, vol. 1, *El caballo griego*, 66). A letter from Alberti to Chacón y Calvo and Altolaguirre, dated 8 May 1925, is addressed to "Dearest José María and Manolito" (Altolaguirre, *Epistolario 1925–1959*, 28). At this time Alberti had met Prados only once (Alberti, *Cuaderno de Rute [1925]*, 116).

105   Alberti, *La arboleda perdida. Libros I y II*, 221, 227.

106   Ibid., 227; advertisements in the press, *La Libertad*, 11 November 1925, 7,
       El Sol, 20 November 1925, 2. The first review that I have found came out in
       December: S. de R., "Autores y libros. Revista bibliográfica. Alberti (Rafael).
       – *Marinero en tierra* (poesías)," *La Nación*, 12 December 1925, 2. Most others
       did not appear until 1926.
107   Alberti, *La arboleda perdida. Libros I y II*, 228–9; Jiménez Gómez, *Lorca y
       Alberti*, 73; Alberti, *Cuaderno de Rute (1925)*, 109, 115; Alberti, *Un amigo de
       la juventud*, 110.
108   Alberti, *La arboleda perdida. Libros I y II*, 231; Jiménez Gómez, *Lorca y Al-
       berti*, 96–7.
109   Alberti, *La arboleda perdida. Libros I y II*, 233. A letter from Alberti to Ce-
       lestino Espinosa from December 1925 already mentions his desire to go to
       Almería and laments his lack of funds; a thank-you letter, from Almería,
       March 1926, acknowledges belatedly the 300 pesetas sent by Espinosa: Al-
       berti, *Un amigo de la juventud*, 110–11.
110   Alberti, *La arboleda perdida. Libros I y II*, 233–4. According to his letter to
       Espinosa from Almería, "I dedicate my time to 'amore.' The women from Al-
       mería are wonderful. I go to the Park every morning. There I act like a posh
       dandy": *Un amigo de la juventud*, 112.
111   Alberti, *La arboleda perdida. Libros I y II*, 234–5, 237–8; Morelli, ed., *Gerardo
       Diego y el III Centenario de Góngora*, 43.
112   Postcard from Gerardo Diego to Juan Guerrero Ruiz, 18 April 1926: "yesterday
       I had the pleasure of meeting Alberti" (García Lorca, *Epistolario completo*,
       346n1012); Alberti's version of their first encounter in 1925 must therefore be
       incorrect (Alberti, *La arboleda perdida. Libros I y II*, 201). They must have
       been in epistolary contact since summer 1925, as on 13 July, Altolaguirre
       wrote to Diego telling him that he had informed Alberti of his "desire for
       friendship": Altolaguirre, *Epistolario 1925–1959*, 32.
113   Gómez de Tudanca, "Prólogo," 13; Alberti, *La arboleda perdida. Libros I y II*,
       239; Alberti, *Correspondencia a José María de Cossío*, 23–5.
114   Alberti, *Correspondencia a José María de Cossío*, 23, 25; Sánchez Cuesta, Sa-
       linas, and Guillén, *Correspondencia*, 224, 230. Alberti described the dramatic
       work as a *guirigay lírico-bufo-bailable*, literally a "lyrical-buffo-danceable
       rumpus."
115   Altolaguirre, *Epistolario 1925–1959*, 42. Hernández ("Presentación del episto-
       lario de Emilio Prados," 20–1) hypothesizes a possible brief trip to Málaga in
       November, for which at the moment there is no documentary evidence.
116   Morelli, ed., *Gerardo Diego y el III Centenario de Góngora*, 51, 67–76, 84,
       91; García Lorca, *Epistolario completo*, 352–3n1029, 370n1080; Alberti, *Cor-
       respondencia a José María de Cossío*, 25, 28; Guillén, *Cartas a Germaine*,
       634–6, 638.
117   Alberti, *La arboleda perdida. Libros I y II*, 241–4; Felipe Sassone, "Literatos y
       toreros," *ABC*, 24 May 1927, 6.

118   Alberti, *La arboleda perdida. Libros I y II*, 253; Alberti took part in the bull-
      fight at the end of which Ignacio Sánchez Mejías announced his retirement.
119   García Lorca, *Epistolario completo*, 533n353; Guillén, *Cartas a Germaine*,
      667–71.
120   Alberti, *La arboleda perdida. Libros I y II*, 261; Guillén, *Cartas a Germaine*,
      673.
121   Alberti, *Correspondencia a José María de Cossío*, 31–3; Salinas and Guillén,
      Correspondencia (1923–1951), 83–4.
122   Alberti, *La arboleda perdida. Libros I y II*, 251.
123   Ibid., 261.
124   Ibid., 263–5. See Gagen, "Rafael Alberti's 'Muerte y juicio,'" 944–5, for a
      slightly different take on the chronology.
125   Alberti, *La arboleda perdida. Libros I y II*, 274–5.
126   "Notas de arte. Exposición de Mariano de Cossío," *La Nación*, 3 April 1928, 4.
127   Diego and Cossío, *Epistolario*, 171.
128   Ibid., 176.
129   Alberti, *La arboleda perdida. Libros I y II*, 266.
130   Cossío exaggerates a little when he writes, "Rafael Alberti was my guest here
      and it was here that he wrote almost all of *Sobre los ángeles*": *Estudios sobre
      escritores montañeses*, 62. On other poems that he worked on while staying
      there, see Fernández, "Los poemas de Rafael Alberti," 88–95.
131   On 5 May Alberti wrote to Pedro Lorenzo, the mayor of the town, "We have
      fond memories of the days that we spent in Torrelavega": *Correspondencia a
      José María de Cossío*, 85.
132   Diego and Cossío, *Epistolario*, 248.
133   Piñer, *Memoria de Gerardo Diego*, 88n66.
134   Alberti, *La arboleda perdida. Libros I y II*, 268; Fernández, "Introducción,"
      26. In Alberti's postscript to Cossío's letter of the end of May 1928, he refers
      to this visit; "your Altolaguirres" are Luis Piñer and Basilio Fernández: Diego
      and Cossío, *Epistolario*, 173.
135   Diego and Cossío, *Epistolario*, 248; Alberti, *La arboleda perdida. Libros I y
      II*, 266–7.
136   Alberti, *La arboleda perdida. Libros I y II*, 267–8.
137   Ibid., 268. At Altamira a new cave had just been discovered: "Importante
      descubrimiento. Cerca de la cueva de Altamira es hallada otra, en la que se
      advierten vestigios de la vida del hombre primitivo," *Heraldo de Madrid*, 25
      May 1928, 4.
138   Altolaguirre, *Epistolario 1925–1959*, 128. This was the moment when the fi-
      nances of *Litoral*/Imprenta Sur reached a critical state; Altolaguirre passed
      the manuscript on to Prados, who for a time was singly in charge and who
      hoped to launch with it "a new poetic collection" (129).
139   Diego and Cossío, *Epistolario*, 174–6, 248–9.

140 This situation is similar to the contrast, often remarked upon, of the tone found in Lorca's letters home from New York and the moods reflected in the poems of *Poeta en Nueva York*.

141 *La arboleda perdida I y II*, 269.

142 Alberti, *Correspondencia a José María de Cossío*, 33, 35.

143 Guillén and Cossío, *Correspondencia*, 134–6 and 135–6n11; Guillén, *Cartas a Germaine*, 729–31, 737, 760; Alberti, *Correspondencia a José María de Cossío*, 36; Altolaguirre, *Epistolario 1925–1959*, 129. A few days before 18 September 1928, Alberti wrote to Prados offering him *Sobre los ángeles* in lieu of *Cal y canto*, and by 25 October Prados knew that Alberti was opting for *Revista de Occidente* for *Cal y canto* (Neira, "Epistolario de la Casona de Tudanca," 16). Likewise, with Imprenta Sur's continuing economic precariousness, Alberti finally accepted a more alluring offer from C.I.A.P. for *Sobre los ángeles*.

144 "Conferencias y reuniones. Exposición de Benjamín Palencia," *El Sol*, 24 October 1928, 2; Anon., "Palencia, Alberti, Bergamín"; Guillén, *Cartas a Germaine*, 740–1. On 29 October, Alberti wrote to Cossío as follows: "The other morning I had, in the Benjamín Palencia exhibition, a riotous success with my book, our book, *Sobre los ángeles*. There were some 150 people": Alberti, *Correspondencia a José María de Cossío*, 36.

145 The exhibition ran from the eighteenth to the thirtieth: "Noticias," *La Libertad*, 18 October 1928, 6.

146 Jiménez Gómez, *Lorca y Alberti*, 156. Alberti, Salinas, and Guillén had been able to spend a few hours with Diego on 19 November, during a stopover that he made in Madrid: Diego and Cossío, *Epistolario*, 177–8.

147 Alberti, *Correspondencia a José María de Cossío*, 37; Bergamín, "El canto y la cal en la poesía de Rafael Alberti"; Quiroga Pla, "Ulises adolescente."

148 Anon., "[advertisement]," *La Gaceta Literaria*; Azorín, "Los ángeles. Poesía," *ABC*, 6 June 1929, 3.

149 "[advertisement]," *El Sol*, 30 July 1929, 2.

150 Anon., "6.ª sesión del Cineclub."

151 Morla Lynch, *En España*, 70, 79.

152 Alberti, *La arboleda perdida. Libros I y II*, 274, 281; Alberti, *La arboleda perdida. Quinto libro AP V*, 25. Three poems were published in *Litoral* in June 1929, one in *Atlántico* also in June, four in *Revista de Occidente* in October, and another in *Nueva Revista* in December.

153 Alberti, *La arboleda perdida. Libros I y II*, 280. A. Hernández-Catá tells us that "this summer I saw him walking from Guadarrama to Cercedilla decked out in a pearl grey pullover and a beret adorned with a star" ("Horizontes. El suicidio de un poeta"), the implication being that the star was red. A "notebook" with poetic manuscripts, including poems from *Sermones y moradas*, is dated to Cercedilla, 15 June 1929: Alberti, *Obras completas. Poesía I*, 790, 795.

154 "Los estudiantes. Poesías de Alberti," *El Liberal*, 29 October 1929, 3; "Noticias," *El Liberal*, 29 October 1929, 4.

155 Anon., "La batalla del Lyceum." This had been arranged by Champourcin, who gave her own account to Conde in a letter of the thirteenth (*Epistolario [1927–1995]*, 329–30), and later defended him in *La Gaceta Literaria* ("Un 'suceso' literario").

156 "Cómicos y autores. Una lectura," *La Libertad*, 22 November 1929, 5.

157 Alberti, *La arboleda perdida. Libros I y II*, 277–8.

158 Ibid., 290–1. Still, V.X. was already familiar with the poem in an article published on 24 December 1929: "La más joven poesía."

159 "Bazar", *Heraldo de Madrid*, 7 January 1930, 10. Only one would be published: *Tres cómicos de cine. Charlot, Clara Bow y Harold Lloyd* (Madrid: Zeus, 1931), by César Muñoz Arconada.

160 Mateos Miera, "Introducción," 111–41; Salinas and Guillén, *Correspondencia (1923–1951)*, 106; Guerrero Ruiz, *Juan Ramón de viva voz*, vol. 1, *1913–1931*, 121.

161 "Radiodifusión. Emisiones de Madrid. Para mañana," *La Nación*, 8 January 1930, 2.

162 Alberti, *La arboleda perdida. Libros I y II*, 291–2.

163 J.G.O., "Aunque firma una traducción literaria de *Maya*, Azorín prefiere las adaptaciones libres," *Heraldo de Madrid*, 25 January 1930, 7; José Luis Salado, "Literatura. Los nuevos. Rafael Alberti, de niño, quería ser pintor," *Heraldo de Madrid*, 30 January 1930, 8.

164 J.G., "De música. Orquesta sinfónica," *El Liberal*, 21 March 1930, 2; Ad. S., "La edición musical," *El Sol*, 21 December 1930, 2.

165 "La compañía Díaz-Artigas marcha a América," *ABC*, 3 April 1930, 10.

166 "Noticias," *El Liberal*, 1 April 1930, 4; "Una función benéfica," *La Voz*, 1 April 1930, 2.

167 "Poesías y comentarios," *ABC*, 4 May 1930, 33.

168 "Las conferencias de Keyserling," *El Sol*, 8 May 1930, 8.

169 Alberti, *Correspondencia a José María de Cossío*, 38–9; Morla Lynch, *En España*, 80–1.

170 Diego and Cossío, *Epistolario*, 186.

171 Alberti, *Correspondencia a José María de Cossío*, 40.

172 More poems were published in March 1930 and January and February 1931; the play was premiered by the María Teresa Montoya company in February 1931: Alberti, *La arboleda perdida. Libros I y II*, 281.

173 Jiménez, "Acento. Poetas de antro y dianche." See Guerrero Ruiz, *Juan Ramón de viva voz*, vol. 1, *1913–1931*, 74.

174 Guerrero Ruiz, *Juan Ramón de viva voz*, vol. 1, *1913–1931*, 78. Boldly, Alberti offered it to Guerrero for a new magazine that he and Jiménez were planning.

175 See Guerrero Ruiz, *Juan Ramón de viva voz*, vol. 1, *1913–1931*, 90.

176 For period photographs of the Palacio de Velázquez, see Memoria de Madrid, accessed 3 June 2022, http://www.memoriademadrid.es/buscador.php?accion=VerFicha&id=10541&num_id=3&num_total=5, and http://www.memoriademadrid.es/buscador.php?accion=VerFicha&id=10543&num_id=17&num_total=331#.

177 Ybarra, ed., *La Sociedad de Artistas Ibéricos*; Pérez Segura, "La sociedad de artistas ibéricos (1920–1936)."

178 This section is a re-elaboration of my article "Maruja Mallo and Rafael Alberti, 1925–1928."

179 Méndez, *Memorias habladas*, 41–6.

180 Ibid., 46–8.

181 Lorca appears in a formal group photograph in *El Imparcial*, 29 May 1925, 3, and Dalí in another, *El Liberal*, 29 May 1925, 1.

182 Letter from Chacón to Juan Guerrero, cited in García Lorca, *Epistolario completo*, 279n820.

183 Pérez Ferrero, "Sáenz de Tejada, recuerdos de otros días."

184 Pérez Ferrero, "El largo exilio del pintor Bores."

185 Vicent, "Maruja Mallo."

186 Hinojosa left Madrid for Málaga and Campillos later in June: Neira, *Viajero de soledades*, 109.

187 "Ecos de sociedad. Viajes," *Gaceta de Tenerife*, 19 June 1925, 2.

188 Mallo writes that after the third day or date, people already "nos pusieron el panfleto encima." The idiom is uncommon but seems to mean that from then on, they were identified by others as a couple.

189 Alberti, *La arboledad I y II*, 193–4.

190 "They have been saying for a long time now that the prize for poetry will go to me. I don't know": letter to Prieto, 12/26 May 1925, archive, Fundación Gregorio Prieto, Madrid.

191 Alberti, "Tribuna: *La arboleda perdida*." She would study one more year at the EEPEG.

192 Méndez, *Memorias habladas*, 47.

193 Aub, *Conversaciones con Buñuel*, 243.

194 Lorca left for Granada on 16 June, the day following his reading: García Lorca, *Epistolario completo*, 279n820.

195 Valender, "Concha Méndez escribe," 133.

196 Ibid.

197 Ibid., 135, 136, and see also 137–9.

198 Gutiérrez-Vega, *Corresponsales españoles*, 38.

199 Ulacia finds in Méndez's oblique references "probably an allusion to Rafael Alberti": "Concha Méndez y Luis Buñuel," 14.

200 Valender, "Concha Méndez escribe," 143.

201 Champourcin and Conde, *Epistolario (1927–1995)*, 182.

202 Méndez, *Memorias habladas*, 51, 61.

203 Ibid., 56.

204 Archive, Fundación Gregorio Prieto, Madrid.

205 Méndez, *Memorias habladas*, 52. The scene was of an organ grinder's assistant dancing with an aristocratic lady.

206 Vicent, "Maruja Mallo"; Alberti, "Tribuna: *La arboleda perdida*"; Mallo, "La escuela de Vallecas."

207   Bayo, "Alberti por Alberti," 10; Alberti, *Correspondencia a José María de Cossío*, 23, 25; García Montero, "Biografía," 126; Guillén, *Cartas a Germaine*, 634; Ruiz Silva, "Música y literatura en la Generación del 27," 38–9; Mateos Miera, "Alberti en el teatro de las vanguardias," 66.

208   Alberti, "Tribuna: *La arboleda perdida*"; Mallo, *Lo popular en la plástica española*, 12. At other moments, Palencia was also identified as involved as a designer: Sánchez Cuesta, Salinas, and Guillén, *Correspondencia*, 224, 230; Jiménez Gómez, *Lorca y Alberti*, 107. Alberti wrote two letters to Óscar Esplá about *La pájara pinta* in early August and then 1 September 1926, and both were amply illustrated by Palencia: Ruiz Silva, "Música y literatura en la Generación del 27," plates between 38 and 39.

209   Alberti, *La arboleda perdida. Libros I y II*, 281. As with *La pájara pinta*, Palencia was also involved in this project: the manuscript of *El colorín colorado* states "Sets, costumes, and masks by Benjamín Palencia" (Mateos Miera, "Poesía y ballet," 573). It is another unclassifiable work, with many elements of avant-garde musical theatre.

210   Alberti, "Tribuna: *La arboleda perdida*." In *La arboleda perdida. Quinto libro*, he refers to "the time when I was crazy about ... making love on the freezing park benches" (26); cf. Alberti, "Su recuerdo está en mi corazón."

211   *Maruja Mallo*, 121.

212   *Maruja Mallo: De prometedora pioneira*, 97–8.

213   [Francisco Ayala], "Las tertulias literarias. La Granja."

214   "La generación de plata," 95–6.

215   For Alberti's visit to Arniches to thank him, facilitated by Bergamín, see Alberti, *La arboleda perdida. Libros I y II*, 202–4. For the Huerta de Mena, see Concha Diez-Pastor Iribas, "¿Por qué hay que proteger Huerta de Mena?," *Hortaleza Periódico Vecinal*, 3 April 2022, https://www.periodicohortaleza.org/por-que-hay-que-proteger-la-finca-de-los-almendros-huerta-de-mena/.

216   Santos Torroella, *Dalí residente*, 188.

217   Amado, "Carta abierta a Rafael Alberti," 14.

218   Amado, "Introducción a una correspondencia," 10.

219   "Biografía," 133.

220   *Litoral Alberti*.

221   Interestingly, Alberti includes a "Madrigal al billete de tranvía" in *Cal y canto*.

222   *Litoral Alberti*; Amado, "Carta abierta a Rafael Alberti," 12. Given the cryptic nature of the poem, Laurenson-Shakibi's reading of it, "*Amor imposible, cosas en común*," 45, is plausible but far from conclusive. See also her earlier study, "Angels, Art and Analysis."

223   Amado, "Carta abierta a Rafael Alberti," 11.

224   Soria Olmedo, ed., *Alberti. "Sobre los ángeles*," 76.

225   Connell, "*Sobre los ángeles*: Form and Theme," 10.

226   In Diego's *Carmen*, numbers 3–4.

227 Further, Alberti stated to Bayo that "I started to write *Sobre los ángeles* when I was just finishing *Cal y canto*. Before finishing it I already had a lot of poems written, like 'El paraíso perdido' or 'El cuerpo deshabitado'": *Sobre Alberti*, 36.

228 "Tribuna: *La arboleda perdida*."

229 In her study, Mateo omits all mention of Mallo and concentrates exclusively on Amado; she also attributes to the failed relationship "almost all of the anguish and desperation in the book," which seems unwarranted and excessive: Mateo, "Introducción," 89–90.

230 Bayo, "Alberti por Alberti," 13.

231 Corredor-Matheos, "Prólogo," 20.

232 "Tribuna: *La arboleda perdida*."

233 Connell, "*Sobre los ángeles*: Form and Theme," 10.

234 Tejada, "Una entrevista con Rafael Alberti," 8. Still, in 1996 Alberti reported that Victoria "not long ago wrote me a beatific postcard" (*La arboleda perdida. Quinto libro*, 27). It is unclear where the surname Bárcena comes from; at the end of 1929, Victoria married a lawyer, Moisés Garrido Martínez: "Bodas recientes", *ABC*, 29 December 1929, 89.

235 "Tribuna: *La arboleda perdida*."

236 Alberti, *La arboledad perdida I y II*, 263–6.

237 Ibid., 263–4.

238 Months later, in February 1929, Alberti wrote to Cossío, "Tell Escolástico that *my beloved* has got another boyfriend and that she is the stupidest girl in Spain" (*Correspondencia a José María de Cossío*, 37–8), which seems to be a reference to Victoria and her fiancé. Gagen argues that it was the breakdown of these relationships that truly sparked the crisis; likewise, in *Sobre los ángeles* he finds a number of oblique references to Victoria and some to Maruja ("The Consequences of Concupiscence," 13–14), but it remains problematic to identify a *tú* addressed in a poem with a specific person in real life.

239 *Correspondencia a José María de Cossío*, 85, 86.

240 Ibid., 86.

241 Alberti, *La arboleda perdida I y II*, 264.

242 "Tribuna: *La arboleda perdida*."

243 Soria Olmedo, ed., *Alberti. "Sobre los ángeles*," 29.

244 Marisa had studied with Daniel Vázquez Díaz in 1925, and Mauricio often served as her model.

245 In the many newspaper reports, Carmen Manso is sometimes identified as a cousin of Mauricio, but I have been unable to verify any family connection.

246 "Un joven saca un automóvil de su propiedad, sin permiso de sus padres; el coche vuelca en la carretera y resultan tres personas heridas," *Heraldo de Madrid*, 12 June 1928, 1; "Un vuelco en Alcobendas. Varias personas lesionadas," *El Imparcial*, 13 June 1928, 12.

247 Connell, "*Sobre los ángeles*: Form and Theme," 10.

248 Ibid.

249   The family's concern was probably heightened because Mauricio's father, driven by his chauffeur, had been involved in a fatal car accident with a teenager in January: "Sobre un atropello. Se nos ruega unas aclaraciones," *El Imparcial*, 25 January 1928, 6.

250   "Vuelca un automóvil y trata de matarse el conductor," ABC, 13 June 1928, 21; "Atropellos y choques. Se suicida después de volcar," *El Sol*, 13 June 1928, 3.

251   "Tribuna: *La arboleda perdida.*"

252   Alberti, *La arboleda perdida. Libros I y II*, 264.

253   *Correspondencia a José María de Cossío*, 33.

254   Connell, "*Sobre los ángeles*: Form and Theme," 10. Connell goes on to detect more oblique references in other poems, 11.

255   "Biografía," 136.

256   *Maruja Mallo*, 142.

257   Ibid., 332n80.

258   "*Amor imposible, cosas en común*," 45.

259   The author is punning on the verb *acuchillar*, literally to stab, but which also refers to the style of Renaissance clothing decoration known as slashing.

260   "Maruja Mallo," 10–11.

261   *Maruja Mallo*, 142. The reference is to the Mallo family residence at Ventura Rodríguez, 3; members of the family of the Marqués de Salamanca were associated with that apartment building, but the Palacio, nowadays turned into a bank building, was actually on Recoletos. Nuevo Cal and Ínsua López, in *Maruja Mallo: De prometedora pioneira*, 70, make the same error.

262   *Correspondencia a José María de Cossío*, 34.

263   Ibid., 35.

264   Ibid., 34.

265   *Cartas a Germaine*, 733.

266   *Epistolario (1927–1995)*, 257.

267   Ibid., 262. Champourcin uses the word *tonto*, alluding to the collection *Yo era un tonto ...* that Alberti was working on.

268   This character only appears very briefly in the surviving scenes of the play (Alberti, *La pájara pinta*, 60), but is mentioned frequently in statements made by Alberti (Bayo, "Alberti por Alberti," 8; Alberti, "Tribuna: *La arboleda perdida*"; Torres, "Rafael Alberti, en el 'lecho del torero herido'"). The illustration is reproduced in Corredoira López, ed., *Maruja Mallo*, 101, and is also available in "Maruja Mallo y Rafael Alberti, un amor creativo y un olvido premeditado," Arrinconarte – El rincón del arte (blog), 12 May 2011, http://arrinconarte-elrincondelarte.blogspot.com/2011/05/maruja-mallo-y-rafael-alberti-un-amor.html

269   Mateos Miera, "Alberti en el teatro de las vanguardias," 69; in his interview with Bayo, Alberti refers to "a painted curtain where they appeared, like in a popular strip cartoon": "Alberti por Alberti," 8. See also Santeiro, "Nueva humanización del arte," who notes that in the period of Mallo's almost monochromatic *Cloacas y campanarios*, "for her drawings she still retains

all the colours: the drawings that illustrate *La pájara pinta* by R. Alberti, for example."

270 Good reproductions can be viewed in "Maruja Mallo y Rafael Alberti, un amor creativo y un olvido premeditado," Arrinconarte – El rincón del arte (blog), 12 May 2011, at http://arrinconarte-elrincondelarte.blogspot. com/2011/05/maruja-mallo-y-rafael-alberti-un-amor.html.

271 Torre, Pérez Ferrero, and Salazar y Chapela, eds, *Almanaque literario 1935*, 37, 46, 49, 253.

272 For a close reading of this poem, see Anderson, "Rafael Alberti and Maruja Mallo in 1929."

273 Jiménez Gómez, *Lorca y Alberti*, 163.

274 Alberti, *La arboleda perdida. Quinto libro*, 25.

275 Hernández-Catá, "Horizontes. El suicidio de un poeta."

276 Letter of 25 July 1929, *Epistolario (1927–1995)*, 310.

277 Martín Gijón, *Una poesía de la presencia*, 24–5; Alberti, "Tribuna: *La arboleda perdida*."

278 Vivanco, "Rafael Alberti en su palabra acelerada," 16. Vivanco is vague about dates: Soria Olmedo, ed., *Alberti. "Sobre los ángeles,"* 29, situates this in 1928, but 1929 seems more plausible. According to another source, Alberti spent part of one summer sleeping rough and then shaving and eating at Vivanco's family house and spending the days with him: Valverde, "Rafael Alberti and Luis Felipe Vivanco."

279 Anon., "La batalla del Lyceum."

280 "Cómicos y autores. Una lectura," *La Libertad*, 22 November 1929, 5.

281 José Gimeno, "'Cine' especializado. La sexta sesión del Cineclub," *El Imparcial*, 18 May 1929, 8.

282 "Horizontes. El suicidio de un poeta."

283 Ibid.

284 Anon., "La batalla del Lyceum." Cf. Mateo, *Rafael Alberti. De lo vivo y lejano*, 117.

285 Alberti, "Un 'suceso' literario." In later editions, the poem's title was shortened to "En el día de su muerte a mano armada."

286 Salinas and Guillén, *Correspondencia (1923–1951)*, 105.

287 "Una conversación con Bragaglia," *ABC*, 16 January 1930, 11.

288 *En España con Federico García Lorca*, 80. Unfortunately, these do not appear to have survived.

289 *En España con Federico García Lorca*, 81.

290 *Correspondencia a José María de Cossío*, 38. The banquet had been held on 26 June at the Hotel Nacional, Madrid.

291 *Correspondencia a José María de Cossío*, 39.

292 Diego and Cossío, *Epistolario*, 186.

293 Mangini, *Maruja Mallo*, 150–1.

294 Nuevo Cal and Ínsua López, *Maruja Mallo: De prometedora pioneira*, 150. Although there is no evidence, the news could have caused her concern about her immediate future and career.

295 Anon., "Noticias de última hora," 2.

296 "Conferencias," *El Sol*, 10 September 1930, 8; R.G., "En San Sebastián."

297 Alberti, "'Chuflillas de "El niño de la palma."' 'Joselito en su gloria.' 'Seguidillas a una extranjera.'"

298 Mateos Miera, "Rafael Alberti y la música," 91.

299 Guerrero Ruiz, *Juan Ramón de viva voz*, vol. 1, *1913–1931*, 84.

300 Ferris, *Palabras contra el olvido*, 75.

301 R.M., "María Teresa León."

302 Alberti, "Cuando tú apareciste … ," ii–iii.

303 Bustos, "Alberti: 'Con María Teresa termina una vida ejemplar,'" 56. Bayo identifies the host as Sofía Valero de Mazas, who appears to be Alberto's sister: *Sobre Alberti*, 43.

304 *La arboleda I y II*, 300.

305 Aub, *Conversaciones con Buñuel*, 313.

306 *Memoria de la melancolía*, 31–2.

307 Prado, *Los nombres de Antígona*, 222. Ironically, the full name of the town is Los Ángeles de San Rafael; it is situated further out in the Guadarrama. This might have been the occasion on which Alberti read *Santa Casilda* to the Menéndez Pidal family: Marrast, *Aspects du théâtre*, 21.

308 Aub, *Conversaciones con Buñuel*, 313.

309 A mountain pass in the Guadarrama range.

310 *Memoria de la melancolía*, 33–4.

311 Furthermore, Prado goes on to add, "the new couple, in search of more privacy than they could have at the Menéndez Pidal home, decided to go off to spend some days in Mallorca": *Los nombres de Antígona*, 223.

312 *Correspondencia a José María de Cossío*, 39. A performance of *La pájara pinta* in the Campo del Moro by "pupils of the Instituto Escuela" was finally held on 24 April 1933: "En el Campo del Moro. La fiesta escolar de esta tarde," *Luz*, 24 April 1933, 16.

313 Alberti, *La arboleda perdida. Libros I y II*, 302–3. Alberti's play, *Fermín Galán*, is from 1931.

314 Pablo Jiménez, "La magia exacta."

315 Alberti, *La arboleda perdida. Libros I y II*, 300. Similar sentiments and a similar vocabulary are to be found in Alberti, "Cuando tú apareciste … ," ii.

316 Mateo, *Rafael Alberti*, 121–2.

317 As León writes, "We fled to an island, toward the isle of good fortune"; she goes on to describe the stay in some detail: *Memoria de la melancolía*, 90.

318 Guerrero Ruiz, *Juan Ramón de viva voz*, vol. 1, *1913–1931*, 112.

319 Salinas and Guillén, *Correspondencia (1923–1951)*, 124. A few months later, after seeing a performance of *Fermín Galán*, Salinas would again have less than kind words for "the lady who's in love" (138).

320 "La compañía Díaz-Artigas regresa de América," *Heraldo de Madrid*, 6 January 1931, 6; see also Alberti, *Correspondencia a José María de Cossío*, 40–1. Marrast reports an undated private reading of the play at Salinas's home

at which several others were present, including Adriano del Valle and Juan Guerrero Ruiz: *Aspects du théâtre*, 20–1.

321　In 1931, both Mallo and Alberti applied to the Junta para Ampliación de Estudios for funds to travel to France to study modern staging practices. Although both applications postdate the breakup (Mallo's is from 3 February 1931, Alberti's 12 August: archive, Junta para Ampliación de Estudios), given their similarity, it seems likely that an original or preliminary plan had been for them to go together.

322　*La arboleda perdida I y II*, 300.

323　Ibid.

324　*Memoria de la melancolía*, 91.

325　Samuel Ros, "Humorismo. El género epistolar y su sustituto," *Heraldo de Madrid*, 15 January 1931, 9.

326　"La 'Santa Casilda,' de Rafael Alberti," ABC, 27 January 1931, 36.

327　Diego and Cossío, *Epistolario*, 187.

328　"Acento. Historias de España. Evolución superinocente. Satanismo inverso. Nueva academia española." This essay was being planned as of 19 December: Guerrero Ruiz, *Juan Ramón de viva voz*, vol. 1, *1913–1931*, 83, and see also 112.

329　Jiménez appears to be punning here: *calcomanía* is a decal or transfer; *calcar* means to make an exact copy, so etymologically the word could be taken to imply a mania for making precise copies.

330　Jiménez, "Acento. Historias de España … " 3.

331　The *Gaceta Literaria* pieces of 15 November 1930 and 15 January 1931, plus "Poesía escrita. Juan José Domenchina (1930)," *Heraldo de Madrid*, 22 January 1931, 8.

332　Salinas and Guillén, *Correspondencia (1923–1951)*, 127.

333　Alberti, *La arboleda perdida. Libros I y II*, 303.

BIBLIOGRAPHY

Abad, Francisco. "La obra filológica del Centro de Estudios Históricos." In *1907–1987. La Junta para Ampliación de Estudios e Investigaciones Científicas 80 años después*, vol. 2, edited by José Manuel Sánchez Ron, 503–17. Madrid: CSIC, 1988.

Abellán, José Luis. *El Ateneo de Madrid: historia, política, cultura, teosofía.* Madrid: La Librería, 2006.

Abellán Velasco, Manuel. "José Castillejo, profesor de derecho romano." In *100 años de la JAE. La Junta para Ampliación de Estudios e Investigaciones Científicas en su centenario*, vol. 1, edited by José Manuel Sánchez Ron and José García-Velasco, 257–91. Madrid: Fundación Francisco Giner de los Ríos/Residencia de Estudiantes, 2010.

Abril, Manuel. "Rumbos, exposiciones y artistas. Maruja Mallo." *Blanco y Negro* 40, no. 2067 (28 December 1930): 16–20.

Adriaensen, Brigitte, and Álvaro Ceballos Viro. "De kortstondige gevallen van de PEN-clubs tijdens het interbellum in Spanje. Een geschiedenis van politieke en regionale polarisatie." *Nederlandse Letterkunde* 16, no. 3 (December 2011): 258–75.

Afonso Fernández, Adalberto. *Mis investigaciones ... y algo más.* Vol. 3. Bloomington, IN: Palibrio, 2012.

Aguerre, Enrique, ed. *Barradas. Colección MNAV.* Montevideo: Museo Nacional de Artes Visuales, 2013.

– ed. *Rafael Barradas. Hombre flecha.* Buenos Aires: Museo de Arte Latinoamericano de Buenos Aires, 2021.

Aguirre. "Nota humorística del Segundo Salón de Otoño." *Gaceta de Bellas Artes* 12, no. 177 (1 October 1921): 8–9.

– "Nota humorística del Segundo Salón de Otoño." *Gaceta de Bellas Artes* 12, no. 178 (15 October 1921): 8–9.

Aguirre, Lorenzo. "Segundo Salón de Otoño. Artistas que han remitido obras. Pintura." *Gaceta de Bellas Artes* 12, no. 177 (14) (1 October 1921): 2–7.

Alaminos López, Eduardo, ed. *La Escuela de Vallecas: Mito y realidad. Una poética de la emoción y lo telúrico.* Madrid: Ayuntamiento de Madrid, 2013.

– *Ramón y Pombo. Libros y tertulia (1915–1957).* Madrid: Ulises, 2020.

Alarcó, Belén, ed. *Rafael Barradas y Juan Gutiérrez Gili (1916–1929).* Madrid: Residencia de Estudiantes, 1996.

–, ed. *Laboratorios de la nueva educación en el centenario del Instituto-Escuela.* Madrid: Fundación Francisco Giner de los Ríos/Institución Libre de Enseñanza, 2019.

Alario Trigueros, María Teresa. "Delhy Tejero y la figura de 'la mujer moderna.'" In *Delhy Tejero. Representación. Exposición antológica*, edited by José Marín-Medina, 305–17. Valladolid: Junta de Castilla y León/Caja España, 2009.

Alba Nieva, Isabel María. "Cuerpo y figurín. Poéticas de la modernidad en la escena española (1866–1926)." PhD diss., Universidad de Málaga, 2015.

Alberti, Rafael. "Balcones. 1. 2. 3." *Alfar* 4, no. 40 (May 1924): 12.

– *Marinero en tierra.* Madrid: Biblioteca Nueva, 1925.

– "Marinero en tierra." *Sí (Boletín bello español)*, no. 1 (1925): 1–8.

– "Soledad tercera (Fragmento)." *La Gaceta Literaria* 1, no. 11 (1 June 1927): 2.

– "Los dos ángeles." *Carmen*, nos 3–4 (March 1928): n.p.

– "Oda a Platko." *La Voz de Cantabria*, 27 May 1928, 1.

– "'Auto de fe.' 'Hallazgos en la nieve.' 'Mensaje.'" *Litoral*, no. 9 (June 1929): 5–9.

– "La primera ascensión de Maruja Mallo al subsuelo." *La Gaceta Literaria* 3, no. 61 (1 July 1929): 1.

– "'Carta de Maruja Mallo a Ben Turpin.' 'Telegrama de Luisa Fazenda a Bebe Daniels y Harold Lloyd.' 'Charles Bower, inventor.'" *La Gaceta Literaria* 3, no. 65 (1 September 1929): 3.

– "'Telegrama de Raimond Haptton a Wallace Beery.' 'Falso homenaje a Adolphe Menjou.' 'Five O'clock Tea.'" *La Gaceta Literaria* 3, no. 66 (15 September 1929): 5.

– "'Un tragaluz sin vidrio.' 'Dos niños.' 'Fragmento de un deseo.' 'Elegías.' 'Adiós a las luces perdidas.'" *Revista de Occidente* 7, no. 76 (October 1929): 33–7.

– "Un 'suceso' literario. La conferencia de Rafael Alberti." *La Gaceta Literaria* 3, no. 71 (1 December 1929): 5.

– "Elegía a Garcilaso (Luna 1503–1536)." *Nueva Revista. Notación Literaria*, no. 2 (24 December 1929): 3.

– *Cal y canto.* Madrid: Revista de Occidente, 1929.

– *Sobre los ángeles.* Madrid: Compañía Ibero-Americana de Publicaciones, 1929.

– "'Chuflillas de "El niño de la palma."' 'Joselito en su gloria.' 'Seguidillas a una extranjera.'" *ABC*, 9 November 1930, 13.

– "Navidad. 'I. Las tres negaciones.' 'II. El buen ventero.' 'III. Nana.' 'IV. Al y del.'" *Blanco y Negro* 40, no. 2066 (21 December 1930): 16–17.

– "'I. El ángel confitero.' 'II. La hortelana del mar.' 'III. El platero.' 'IV. El pescador.' 'V. El zapatero.' 'VI. El sombrerero.'" *ABC*, 26 December 1930, 7.

– *Lope de Vega y la poesía contemporánea, seguido de La pájara pinta.* Edited by Robert Marrast. Paris: Centre de Recherches de l'Institut d'Études Hispaniques, 1964.

– *La arboleda perdida. Libros I y II de memorias.* Barcelona: Seix Barral, 1975.

– *Cuaderno de Rute (1925)*, *Litoral* (Málaga) 6, nos 70–2 (1977).

– *La pájara pinta.* Edited by Carlos Ruiz Silva. *La Pluma* 2ª época, no. 8 (1982): 45–103.

– "Tribuna: *La arboleda perdida.* De las hojas que faltan." *El País*, 29 September 1985, 13.

– *La arboleda perdida. Libros III y IV de memorias.* Barcelona: Seix Barral, 1987.

– "Cuando tú apareciste … " In María Teresa León, *Memoria de la melancolía*, i–v. Barcelona: Círculo de Lectores, 1987.

– *Litoral Alberti.* Monographic special issue, *Litoral* (Málaga) (April 1993).

– "Su recuerdo está en mi corazón." *ABC*, 7 February 1995, 81.

– *La arboleda perdida. Quinto libro (1988–1996)*. Madrid: Anaya & Mario Muchnik, 1996.

– *El colorín colorado (Nocturno español en un solo cuadro)*. Edited by Eladio Mateos Miera. *La Razón*, Suplemento "El Cultural" 1, no. 6 (13 December 1998): 14–17.

– *Correspondencia a José María de Cossío, seguido de "Auto de fe" y otros hallazgos inéditos*. Edited by Rafael Gómez de Tudanca and Eladio Mateos Miera. Valencia: Pre-Textos, 1998.

– *Un amigo de la juventud: Cartas de Rafael Alberti a Celestino Espinosa*. Edited by María Paz Sanz Álvarez. Madrid: Sociedad Estatal de Conmemoraciones Culturales, 2002.

– *Obras completas. Poesía I*. Edited by Jaime Siles. Barcelona: Seix Barral/Sociedad Estatal de Conmemoraciones Culturales, 2003.

Alcaide, J.L., and F.J. Pérez Rojas. "Delhy Tejero, una artista de los años treinta." In *Delhy Tejero 1904–1968. Ciento once dibujos*, edited by Eduardo Alaminos López, 11–26. Madrid: Museo Municipal de Arte Contemporáneo de Madrid, 2005.

Aleixandre, Vicente. "Rafael Alberti, pintor." In Rafael Alberti, *Poesía (1924–1967)*, edited by Aitana Alberti, 683–6. Madrid: Aguilar, 1977.

Alemany Bay, Carmen. *La polémica del meridiano intelectual de Hispanoamérica: 1927. Estudio y textos*. Alicante: Universidad de Alicante, 1998.

Alix, Josefina, and Marta González Orbegozo, eds. *Dibujantas*. Madrid: Museo ABC, 2019.

Almarza Burbano, María Elisa. "Francisco de Paula Aldana Montes (1870–1938) pintor e ilustrador malagueño. (Segunda parte)." *Isla de Arriarán*, no. 34 (December 2009): 243–82.

Alonso, Dámaso. "Rafael entre su arboleda." *Ínsula* 18, no. 198 (May 1963): 1, 16.

Altolaguirre, Manuel. *Obras completas*. Vol. 1, *El caballo griego. Crónicas y artículos. Estudios literarios*. Edited by James Valender. Madrid: Istmo, 1986.

– *Epistolario 1925–1959*. Edited by James Valender. Madrid: Residencia de Estudiantes, 2005.

Alzuri Milanés, Miriam. "Juan de la Encina crítico de arte." In *Juan de la Encina y el arte de su tiempo. 1883–1963*, edited by Miriam Alzuri Milanés and María Dolores Jiménez-Blanco Carrillo de Albornoz, 21–41. Madrid: Museo Nacional Centro de Arte Reina Sofía/Museo de Bellas Artes de Bilbao, 1998.

Amado, José María. "Introducción a una correspondencia." *Litoral*, nos 109–11 (1982): 9–15.

– "Carta abierta a Rafael Alberti." In *Litoral Alberti*. Monographic special issue, *Litoral* (Málaga) (April 1993): 11–15.

Anderson, Andrew A. "¿Entre prodigio y protegido?: El joven Lorca en Madrid (1919–1920)." *Boletín de la Fundación Federico García Lorca* 9, no. 17 (1995): 91–101.

– *El veintisiete en tela de juicio. Examen de la historiografía generacional y replanteamiento de la vanguardia histórica española*. Madrid: Gredos, 2005.

– *Ernesto Giménez Caballero: The Vanguard Years (1921–1931)*. Newark, DE: Juan de la Cuesta, 2011.

– *El momento ultraísta. Orígenes, fundación y lanzamiento de un movimiento de vanguardia.* Madrid: Iberoamericana; Frankfurt: Vervuert, 2017.

– *La recepción de las vanguardias extranjeras en España: cubismo, futurismo, dadá. Estudio y ensayo de bibliografía.* Sevilla: Renacimiento, 2018.

– "Estudio preliminar." In *El ultraísmo en España. Ensayos críticos*, by Manuel de la Peña, 9–35. Sevilla: Renacimiento, 2019.

– "La revista *Tableros* dentro de la trayectoria ultraísta." *Mediodía. Revista Hispánica de Rescate*, no. 2 (2019): 118–33.

– "Maruja Mallo and Rafael Alberti, 1925–1928: New Evidence and Observations." *Bulletin of Hispanic Studies* 97, no. 8 (2020): 843–58.

– "*Libro de poemas versus* Ultra: Direcciones de la poesía española, 1918–1921." In *Umbrales de vanguardia*, edited by Carlos García, 61–89. Madrid: Albert editor, 2021.

– "Rafael Alberti and Maruja Mallo in 1929 and 'La primera ascensión de Maruja Mallo al subsuelo.'" *Cincinnati Romance Review*, no. 51 (2021): 1–19.

Anderson, Andrew A., and Dru Dougherty. "Continuity and Innovation in Spanish Theatre, 1900–1936." In *The Cambridge History of the Theatre in Spain*, edited by David T. Gies and María Delgado, 282–309. Cambridge: Cambridge University Press, 2012.

Anon. "El Salón de Otoño." *Gaceta de la Asociación de Pintores y Escultores* 11, nos 154–5 (15 October 1920): 2–3.

– "[untitled]." *Gaceta de Madrid*, no. 163 (12 June 1925): 1719.

– "Palencia, Alberti, Bergamín." *La Gaceta Literaria* 2, no. 45 (1 November 1928): 8.

– "6.ª sesión del Cineclub." *La Gaceta Literaria* 3, no. 57 (1 May 1929): 1.

– "[advertisement]." *La Gaceta Literaria* 3, no. 59 (1 June 1929): 6.

– "La batalla del Lyceum. Las musas de vanguardia se rebelan contra su poeta." *Heraldo de Madrid*, 11 November 1929, 1.

– "Noticias de última hora sobre el veraneo de escritores españoles. En Madrid y otras playas." *La Gaceta Literaria* 4, no. 89 (1 September 1930): 1–2.

– "Maruja Mallo, la pintora revolucionaria, sostiene que las Escuelas, en general, son estafas al candor público." *Cosmópolis* 6, no. 38 (April 1931): 40–1.

– "El deshojar de la margarita y la política municipal." *ABC*, 13 October 1968, 7–8.

– "Cronología." In *Penagos (1889–1954)*, edited by Rafael de Penagos and Alicia Navarro, 65–69. Madrid: Fundación Cultural Mapfre Vida/Centro Cultural del Conde Duque, 1989.

– "Biografía." In *Manuel Ángeles Ortiz*, edited by Lina Davidov and Eugenio Carmona, 189–207. Madrid: Museo Nacional Centro de Arte Reina Sofía, 1996.

– "A modo de currículum vitae de Eduardo Vicente." In *Eduardo Vicente*, edited by Natacha Seseña, 217–25. Madrid: Museo Municipal, 1999.

Anuario del comercio, de la industria, de la magistratura y de la administración de España. Madrid: Bailly-Baillière e hijos, 1902.

Aranda Barca, Marta. "Maruja Mallo (1902–1995) y su etapa surrealista en Madrid." Unpublished honour's thesis, Universidad de Zaragoza, 2016.

Arañó Gisbert, Juan Carlos. "La enseñanza de las Bellas Artes como forma de ideología cultural." *Arte, Individuo y Sociedad*, no. 2 (1989): 9–30.

Araujo-Costa, Luis. *Biografía del Ateneo de Madrid.* Madrid: Imprenta Samarán, 1949.

Arcediano, Santiago, and José Antonio García Díez. *Carlos Sáenz de Tejada.* Vitoria: Fundación Caja de Ahorros de Vitoria y Alava, 1993.

Armiñán, Luis de. *Biografía del Círculo de Bellas Artes, 1880–1973.* Madrid: Imprenta Foresa, 1973.

Ascunce Arenas, Aránzazu. *Barcelona and Madrid: Social Networks of the Avant-Garde.* Lewisburg, PA: Bucknell University Press, 2012.

Aub, Max. *Conversaciones con Buñuel. Seguidas de 45 entrevistas con familiares, amigos y colaboradores del cineasta aragonés.* Madrid: Aguilar, 1985.

– *Luis Buñuel, novela.* Edited by Carmen Peire. Granada: Cuadernos del Vigía, 2013.

F.A. [Francisco Ayala]. "Atocha (Hotel Nacional)." In *Almanaque de las artes y las letras para 1928,* edited by Gabriel García Maroto, 136. Madrid: Biblioteca Acción, 1928.

– "Las tertulias literarias. La Granja." In *Almanaque de las artes y las letras para 1928,* edited by Gabriel García Maroto, 114–15. Madrid: Biblioteca Acción, 1928.

Ayala, Francisco. *Recuerdos y olvidos.* Vol. 1, *Del paraíso al destierro.* Madrid: Alianza, 1982.

Bachelard, Gaston. *La Poétique de l'espace.* Paris: Presses Universitaires de France, 1958.

Bal, Jesús. "Conocimiento de Maruja Mallo." *El Pueblo Gallego,* 5 October 1928, 13; reprinted in "Conocimiento de Maruja Mallo." *Revista del Centro Gallego* (Montevideo) 8, no. 143 (December 1928): 21.

Balló, Tània. *Las sinsombrero. Sin ellas, la historia no está completa.* Barcelona: Espasa, 2016.

Barrantes Martín, Beatriz. *Ciudad y modernidad en la prosa hispánica de vanguardia.* Valladolid: Universidad de Valladolid, 2007.

Barrera López, José María. "Pedro Garfias. Cartas a Rafael Cansinos Assens (1918–1920)." *Ínsula,* no. 653 (May 2001): 13–16.

Basabe, Nere, and Azucena López Cobo. "La Residencia de Señoritas. La contribución de la JAE a la educación de la mujer. 'Despejo y disposición.' La educación de la mujer española entre dos siglos." *Circunstancia. Revista de Ciencias Sociales del Instituto Universitario de Investigación Ortega y Gasset* 5, no. 14 (September 2007): n.p.

Bayo, Manuel. "Alberti por Alberti." *Primer Acto,* no. 150 (November 1972): 6–19.

– *Sobre Alberti.* Madrid: CVS Ediciones, 1974.

Benjamín Palencia y el surrealismo. 1926–1936. Madrid: Guillermo de Osma, 1994.

Bergamín, José. "El canto, y la cal en la poesía de Rafael Alberti." *La Gaceta Literaria* 3, no. 54 (15 March 1929): 2.

"Biografía." In *Juan de la Encina y el arte de su tiempo. 1883–1963,* edited by Miriam Alzuri Milanés and María Dolores Jiménez-Blanco Carrillo de Albornoz, 97–109.

Madrid: Museo Nacional Centro de Arte Reina Sofía/Museo de Bellas Artes de Bilbao, 1998.

Bonet, Juan Manuel. "Maruja Mallo 'La forma expresa el contenido de una época.'" *El País*, 30 January 1977.

– "Barradas y el ultraísmo." In *Barradas – Torres-García*, 11–18. Madrid: Guillermo de Osma, 1991.

–, ed. *Francisco Santa Cruz (1899–1957). La vanguardia oculta*. Madrid: Museo de Arte Contemporáneo, 2009.

– "Santa Cruz. El cuarto mosquetero (Un retrato en fichas)." In *Francisco Santa Cruz (1899–1957). La vanguardia oculta*, edited by Juan Manuel Bonet, 11–34. Madrid: Museo de Arte Contemporáneo, 2009.

Bonet, Juan Manuel, and Carlos Pérez, eds. *El ultraísmo y las artes plásticas*. Valencia: IVAM Centre Julio González, 1996.

Bonet Correa, Antonio. *Los cafés históricos*. Madrid: Cátedra, 2012.

Bores, Francisco. "Notas autobiográficas." In *Francisco Bores, 1898–1972. Exposición antológica*, 13–14. Madrid: Ministerio de Educación y Ciencia–Dirección General del Patrimonio Artístico Cultural, 1976.

Bores nuevo. Los años veinte y treinta. Madrid: Guillermo de Osma; Barcelona: Oriol Galeria d'Art, 1996.

Borràs, Maria Lluïsa. "Palencia, introductor del surrealismo." In *Benjamín Palencia y el surrealismo. 1926–1936*, 5–15. Madrid: Guillermo de Osma, 1994.

– "Lam in Spain." In *Wifredo Lam: Catalogue Raisonné of the Painted Work*. Vol. 1, *1923–1960*, edited by Lou Laurin-Lam, 18–53. Lausanne: Acatos, 1996.

Bourdieu, Pierre. *The Field of Cultural Production. Essays on Art and Literature*. Edited by Randal Johnson. New York: Columbia University Press, 1993.

– *The Rules of Art. Genesis and Structure of the Literary Field*. Translated by Susan Emanuel. Stanford, CA: Stanford University Press, 1996.

Brihuega, Jaime. "Gabriel García Maroto y *La Nueva España 1930* que los españoles leyeron en 1927." *Cuadernos de Estudios Manchegos*, no. 19 (1989): 263–76.

– "Saturno en el sifón. Barradas y la vanguardia española." In *Barradas. Exposición antológica, 1890–1929*, edited by Jaime Brihuega and Concha Lomba, 13–45. Zaragoza: Gobierno de Aragón; Barcelona: Generalitat de Catalunya; Madrid: Comunidad de Madrid, 1992.

– "La ESAI y el arte español en la bisagra de 1925." In *La Sociedad de Artistas Ibéricos y el arte español de 1925*, edited by Lucía Ybarra, 15–31. Madrid: Museo Nacional Centro de Arte Reina Sofía; Barcelona: Àmbit Servicios Editoriales, 1995.

–, ed. *Alberto Sánchez 1895–1962. Dibujos*. Bilbao: Museo de Bellas Artes de Bilbao, 1997.

– "Una estrella en el camino del arte español. Trayectoria de Alberto hasta la Guerra Civil." In *Alberto 1895–1962*, edited by Jaime Brihuega and Concepción Lomba, 19–72. Madrid: Aldeasa/Museo Nacional Centro de Arte Reina Sofía, 2001.

Brihuega, Jaime, and Concha Lomba, eds. *Barradas. Exposición antológica, 1890–1929*. Zaragoza: Gobierno de Aragón; Barcelona: Generalitat de Catalunya; Madrid: Comunidad de Madrid, 1992.

Brihuega, Jaime, and Concepción Lomba, eds. *Alberto 1895–1962*. Madrid: Aldeasa/ Museo Nacional Centro de Arte Reina Sofía, 2001.

Bueno Sánchez, Gustavo. "Ediciones Biblos 1927–1928." Filosofía en español, accessed 13 May 2022. http://www.filosofia.org/ave/003/c117.htm.

Buñuel, Luis. *Mi último suspiro. (Memorias)*. Esplugues de Llobregat: Plaza & Janés, 1982.

– *Correspondencia escogida*. Edited by Jo Evans and Breixo Viejo. Madrid: Cátedra, 2018.

Cabañas Bravo, Miguel. "Delhy Tejero: Una imaginación ensimismada en las décadas centrales del siglo XX." In *Delhy Tejero 1904–1968. Ciento once dibujos*, edited by Eduardo Alaminos López, 27–54. Madrid: Museo Municipal de Arte Contemporáneo de Madrid, 2005.

– "La Historia del Arte en el Centro de Estudios Históricos de la JAE." In *Tiempos de investigación. JAE-CSIC, cien años de ciencia en España*, edited by Miguel Ángel Puig-Samper Mulero, 143–53. Madrid: CSIC, 2007.

Cabanillas Casafranca, África, and Amparo Serrano de Haro. "La mujer en la Escuela de Bellas Artes de San Fernando (1873–1967)." *Academia. Boletín de la Real Academia de Bellas Artes de San Fernando*, no. 121 (2019): 111–36.

"Cabezas." "Mentidero de la Villa." *ABC*, 20 July 1975, 30.

Cacho Viu, Vicente. "La Junta para Ampliación de Estudios, entre la Institución Libre de Enseñanza y la generación de 1914." In *1907–1987. La Junta para Ampliación de Estudios e Investigaciones Científicas 80 años después*, vol. 2, edited by José Manuel Sánchez Ron, 3–26. Madrid: CSIC, 1988.

Caffarena, Ángel. *Manuel Ángeles Ortiz. Pintor-poeta*. Málaga: Librería Anticuaria El Guadalhorce, 1970.

Calvo Alonso-Cortés, Blanca. "Homenaje a María Luis González y Juan Vicens de la Llave." *Educación y Biblioteca* 12, no. 108 (2000): 17–22.

Campoy, A.M. "Crítica de exposiciones. Benjamín Palencia, íntimo." *ABC de las Artes*, 18 January 1981, 19, 21.

Canito, Enrique. "Entrevistas. Juan Guerrero, cónsul de la poesía." *Ínsula* 10, no. 112 (April 1955): 9.

Cansinos-Assens, Rafael. *La novela de un literato (Hombres-Ideas-Efemérides-Anécdotas …)*. Vol. 1, *1882–1914*. Edited by Rafael M. Cansinos. Madrid: Alianza, 1982.

– *La novela de un literato. (Hombres-Ideas-Efemérides-Anécdotas…)*. Vol. 3, *1923–1936*, edited by Rafael M. Cansinos. Madrid: Alianza, 1995.

Cao Moure, José, ed. *1929. Lugo y su provincia (Libro de oro)*. Vigo: PPKO, 1929.

Capel Martínez, Rosa María, and Carmen Magallón Portolés, "Un sueño posible: La JAE y la incorporación de las españolas al mundo educativo y científico." In *El laboratorio de España. La Junta para Ampliación de Estudios e Investigaciones Científicas, 1907–1939*, edited by José Manuel Sánchez Ron, Antonio Lafuente García, Ana Romero, and Leticia Sánchez de Andrés, 223–49. Madrid: Sociedad Estatal de Conmemoraciones Culturales/Residencia de Estudiantes, 2007.

Carande, Ramón. "Fortuny, 14." *Residencia. Revista de la Residencia de Estudiantes* (Mexico City), número conmemorativo (December 1963): 75–6.

Carandell, Luis. "El caso del Pasaje de la Alhambra." *Triunfo* 25, no. 437 (17 October 1970): 21–3.

– "Epílogo para el Pasaje de la Alhambra." *Triunfo* 27, no. 507 (17 June 1972): 12.

Carmona Mato, Eugenio. "José Moreno Villa y la renovación plástica española (1924–1936)." In *José Moreno Villa (1887–1955)*, edited by Juan Pérez de Ayala, 35–48. Madrid: Ministerio de Cultura, 1987.

– "Rafael Barradas y el 'arte nuevo' en España, 1917–1925." In *Barradas. Exposición antológica, 1890–1929*, edited by Jaime Brihuega and Concha Lomba, 107–39. Zaragoza: Gobierno de Aragón; Barcelona: Generalitat de Catalunya; Madrid: Comunidad de Madrid, 1992.

– "Naturaleza y cultura. Benjamín Palencia y el 'Arte Nuevo' (1919–1936)." In *Benjamín Palencia y el arte nuevo. Obras 1919–1936*, edited by Paloma Esteban Leal, 41–82. Madrid: Bancaja, 1994.

– "Manuel Ángeles Ortiz en los años del 'Arte Nuevo.' 1918–1939." In *Manuel Ángeles Ortiz*, edited by Lina Davidov and Eugenio Carmona, 17–38. Madrid: Museo Nacional Centro de Arte Reina Sofía, 1996.

– "Bores ultraísta, clásico, nuevo. 1921–1925." In *Francisco Bores. El ultraísmo y el ambiente literario madrileño 1921–1925*, 11–51. Madrid: Residencia de Estudiantes, 1999.

Carretón Cano, Vicente. "Victorina Durán y el círculo sáfico de Madrid. Semblanza de una escenógrafa del 27." *El Maquinista de la Generación* 2ª época, no. 9 (February 2005): 4–21.

Casal, Julio J. *Cincuenta y seis poemas*. Madrid: Tip. Artística, 1921.

– *Rafael Barradas*. Buenos Aires: Losada, 1949.

Castillo, David, and Marc Sardá. *Conversaciones con José "Pepín" Bello*. Barcelona: Anagrama, 2007.

Catálogo oficial de la Exposición Nacional de Pintura, Escultura y Arquitectura de 1910. Madrid: Artes Gráficas "Mateu," 1910.

Chacel, Rosa. *Acrópolis*. Barcelona: Seix Barral, 1984.

– *Obra completa*. Vol. 8, *Autobiografías*. Edited by Carlos Pérez Chacel and Antonio Piedra. Valladolid: Fundación Jorge Guillén, 2004.

Champourcin, Ernestina de. "Un 'suceso' literario. La conferencia de Rafael Alberti." *La Gaceta Literaria* 3, no. 71 (1 December 1929): 5.

Champourcin, Ernestina de, and Carmen Conde. *Epistolario (1927–1995)*. Edited by Rosa Fernández Urtasun. Madrid: Castalia, 2007.

Codina-Canet, María Adelina, and Rosa San Segundo. "Fuentes documentales y archivo de la Residencia de Señoritas de Madrid (1915–1936)." *Revista General de Información y Documentación* 25, no. 2 (2015): 493–515.

Colmenar Orzaes, María del Carmen. "Espacio y tiempo escolar en la Escuela Normal Central de Maestras de Madrid durante la etapa de la Restauración." *Revista Complutense de Educación* 5, no. 2 (1994): 47–58.

Connell, Geoffrey. "The Autobiographical Element in *Sobre los ángeles*." *Bulletin of Hispanic Studies* 60, no. 3 (1963): 160–73.

– "*Sobre los ángeles*: Form and Theme." *Spanish Studies*, no. 4 (1982): 1–14.

Corredoira López, Pilar, ed. *Maruja Mallo*, Buenos Aires: Museo Nacional de Bellas Artes/Santiago de Compostela: Xunta de Galicia, 1994.

Corredor-Matheos, José. *Vida y obra de Benjamín Palencia*. Madrid: Espasa-Calpe, 1979.

– "Prólogo." In *Canto de siempre (antología)*, by Rafael Alberti, 7–36. Madrid: Espasa-Calpe, 1980.

– "Benjamín Palencia: Esbozo biográfico." In *Benjamín Palencia y el arte nuevo. Obras 1919–1936*, edited by Paloma Esteban Leal, 193–206. Madrid: Bancaja, 1994.

Cossío, José María. *Estudios sobre escritores montañeses*. Santander: Instituto de Literatura José María de Pereda/Institución Cultural de Cantabria/Diputación Provincial de Santander, 1973.

Costa, Cuca R. *De sueños, paseos nocturnos y vivencias*. Figueres: Fundació Gala-Salvador Dalí, 2016.

Cuesta, Josefina, María José Turrión, and Rosa María Merino. "Dos residencias universitarias femeninas en España, 1914–1915." In *La Residencia de Señoritas y otras redes culturales femeninas*, edited by Josefina Cuesta, María José Turrión, and Rosa María Merino, 11–30. Salamanca: Universidad de Salamanca/Fundación José Ortega y Gasset–Gregorio Marañón, 2015.

Cueva, Almudena de la. "La Residencia de Señoritas y la educación superior de la mujer." *Boletín de la Institución Libre de Enseñanza* 2ª época, nos 78–80 (December 2010): 217–30.

– "Los Grupos de Niños y Niñas de la Residencia de Estudiantes. Una aproximación preliminar." *Boletín de la Institución Libre de Enseñanza* 2ª época, nos 85–6 (July 2012): 37–50.

– "Traspasando fronteras, nuevos horizontes. María de Maeztu y la Residencia de Señoritas." In *Redes internacionales de la cultura española, 1914–1939*, edited by José García-Velasco, 284–92. Madrid: Residencia de Estudiantes, 2014.

Cueva, Almudena de la, and Margarita Márquez Padorno, eds. *Mujeres en vanguardia. La Residencia de Señoritas en su centenario (1915–1935)*. Madrid: Residencia de Estudiantes, 2015.

– "Los Grupos de Niños y Niñas de la Residencia de Estudiantes en el origen del Instituto-Escuela." In *Los laboratorios de la nueva educación en el centenario del Instituto-Escuela*, edited by Belén Alarcó, 416–29. Madrid: Fundación Francisco Giner de los Ríos/Institución Libre de Enseñanza, 2019.

Dalí, Salvador. *The Secret Life of Salvador Dalí*. Translated by Haakon M. Chevalier. New York: Dial Press, 1942.

Davidov, Lina, and Eugenio Carmona, eds. *Manuel Ángeles Ortiz*. Madrid: Museo Nacional Centro de Arte Reina Sofía, 1996.

De Castro, Juan E. "The Intellectual Meridian Debate and Colonialist Nostalgia." In *The Spaces of Latin American Literature. Tradition, Globalization, and Cultural Production*, 33–47. London: Palgrave Macmillan, 2008.

De Certeau, Michel. *L'Invention du quotidian*. Vol. 1, *Arts de faire*. Paris: Union Générale d'Éditions, 1980; *The Practice of Everyday Life*. Translated by Steven Rendall. Berkeley: University of California Press, 1984.

Dechanet, Hélène. "Biografía." In *Bores esencial. 1926–1971*, edited by Eugenio Carmona and Hélène Dechanet, 167–89. Madrid: Museo Nacional Centro de Arte Reina Sofía, 1999.

— "Biografía." In *Francisco Bores. Catálogo razonado. Pintura 1917–1944*, 21–41. Madrid: MNCARS/Telefónica, 2003.

Díaz, Lorenzo. *Madrid. Tabernas, botillerías y cafés. 1476–1991*. Madrid: Espasa-Calpe, 1992.

Díaz Cañabate, Antonio. *Historia de una tertulia*. Valencia: Castalia, 1952.

Díaz-Plaja, Fernando. *Arte y oficio de hablar. (Una pasión española)*. Oviedo: Nobel, 1996.

Diego, Estrella de. *La mujer y la pintura del XIX español. (Cuatrocientas olvidadas y algunas más)*. Madrid: Cátedra, 1987.

Diego, Gerardo, and José María de Cossío. *Epistolario. Nuevas claves de la generación del 27*. Edited by Rafael Gómez de Tudanca. Alcalá de Henares: Universidad de Alcalá de Henares, 1996.

Diéguez Patao, Sofía. *La generación del 25. Primera arquitectura moderna en Madrid*. Madrid: Cátedra, 1997.

Díez de Revenga, Francisco Javier. "José de Ciria y Escalante y la revista *Reflector* en la primera vanguardia." *Monteagudo* 3ª época, no. 7 (2002): 69–79.

Dinverno, Melissa, ed. *"Suites." El viaje de la percepción*. Granada: Consorcio Centro Federico García Lorca, 2020.

Doldán, Ana. "Esteban Vicente y Eduardo Vicente Madrid: 1900–1936." *Informes USA* (Alcalá de Henares: Instituto Franklin-UAH), no. 19 (January 2014): n.p.

Domínguez Lasierra, Juan. *Benjamín Jarnés (1888–1949). Bibliografía*. Zaragoza: Institución "Fernando el Católico" (CSIC), 2013.

d'Ors, Eugenio. *Mi Salón de Otoño. Primera serie*. Madrid: Revista de Occidente, 1924.

Dozo, Björn-Olva, and Bibiane Fréché. "Réseaux et bases de données." In *Les Réseaux littéraires*, edited by Daphné de Marneffe and Benoît Denis, 86–108. Brussels: Le Cri/CIEL, 2006.

Durán, Victorina. *Mi vida*. Vol. 1, *Sucedió*. Edited by Idoia Murga Castro and Carmen Gaitán Salinas. Madrid: Residencia de Estudiantes, 2018.

— *Mi vida*. Vol. 2, *El Rastro. Vida de lo inanimado*. Edited by Idoia Murga Castro and Carmen Gaitán Salinas. Madrid: Residencia de Estudiantes, 2018.

Eduardo Vicente: El pintor de Madrid. Madrid: Quixote–Servicio del Arte Español, 1963.

Eiroa San Francisco, Matilde. "El Lyceum Club: Cultura, feminismo y política fuera de las aulas." In *La Residencia de Señoritas y otras redes culturales femeninas*, edited by Josefina Cuesta, María José Turrión, and Rosa María Merino, 197–225. Salamanca: Universidad de Salamanca/Fundación José Ortega y Gasset–Gregorio Marañón, 2015.

Elias, Norbert. *The Civilizing Process*. Vol. 1, *The History of Manners*. Translated by Edmund Jephcott. Oxford: Basil Blackwell, 1978.

Escolano Benito, Agustín. "Las escuelas normales, siglo y medio de perspectiva histórica." *Revista de Educación*, no. 269 (1982): 55–76.

Escoriza Escoriza, Emilio J. "La generación de plata. Primeros pasos de la vanguardia en Granada." In *La generación de plata. Primeros pasos de la vanguardia en Granada*, edited by Emilio J. Escoriza Escoriza, 61–121. Granada: Junta de Andalucía/Caja Granada, 2007.

Escribano, María. "Maruja Mallo, una bruja moderna." In *Maruja Mallo*, edited by Pilar Corredoira López, 45–55. Buenos Aires: Museo Nacional de Bellas Artes; Santiago de Compostela: Xunta de Galicia, 1994.

–, ed. *Carlos Sáenz de Tejada. Los años de "La Libertad."* Madrid: Fundación Cultural MAPFRE VIDA, 1998.

Espina, Antonio. *Las tertulias de Madrid*. Edited by Óscar Ayala. Madrid: Alianza, 1995.

Esteban Drake, Mesa. *De El Paular a Segovia 1919–1991*. Segovia: Diputación Provincial de Segovia / Ayuntamiento de Segovia, 1991.

Esteban Leal, Paloma, ed. *Benjamín Palencia y el arte nuevo. Obras 1919–1936*. Madrid: Bancaja, 1994.

–, ed. *Benjamín Palencia y el origen de la poética de Vallecas*. Toledo: Caja Castilla La Mancha, 2007.

Estradé Gutiérrez, Enrique. "La enseñanza de la pintura en la Escuela de Bellas Artes de San Fernando de Madrid, 1857–1936." PhD diss., Universidad Complutense de Madrid, 1997.

Exposition Internationale des Arts Décoratifs et Industriels Modernes. Catalogue Général Officiel. Paris: Ministère du Commerce et de l'Industrie, des Postes et des Télégraphes, 1925.

Ezama Gil, Ángeles. *Las musas suben a la tribuna. Visibilidad y autoridad de las mujeres en el Ateneo de Madrid (1882–1939)*. Logroño: Genueve Ediciones, 2018.

Falcón, Irene, in collaboration with Manuel Jiménez and Jesús Montero. *Asalto a los cielos. Mi vida junto a Pasionaria*. Madrid: Temas de Hoy, 1996.

Faraldo, Ramón D. *Benjamín Palencia*. Barcelona: Galerías Layetanas/Sociedad Alianza de Artes Gráficas, 1949.

Faxedas Brujats, M. Lluïsa. "Barradas' Vibrationism and Its Catalan Context." In "Southern Modernisms," edited by Joana Cunha Leal and Begoña Farré Torras. Special issue, *Journal of the International Association of Research Institutes in the History of Art*, no. 0135 (15 July 2016). https://journals.ub.uni-heidelberg.de/index.php/rihajournal/article/view/70202/63550.

Fernández, Emiliano. "Introducción." In *Poemas. 1927–1987*, by Basilio Fernández, 9–31. Gijón: Llibros del Pexe, 1991.

Fernández, Lidio Jesús. "Los poemas de Rafael Alberti en la Casona de Tudanca en 1928." In *Rafaël Alberti et les avant-gardes*, edited by Serge Salaün and Zoraida Carandell, 83–97. Paris: Presses Sorbonne Nouvelle, 2004.

Fernández Almagro, Melchor, and Antonio Gallego y Burín. *Literatura y política. Epistolario 1918–1940*. Edited by Antonio Gallego Morell and Cristina Viñes. Granada: Diputación Provincial de Granada, 1986.

Fernández Gallo, Cristina. "Concha Espina." *La Pajarera Magazine*, 21 February 2018. https://www.lapajareramagazine.com/concha-espina.

Fernández Utrera, María Soledad. *Buñuel en Toledo. Arte público, acción cultural y vanguardia*. Woodbridge, UK: Tamesis, 2016.

Ferrer, Salvador. "La Escuela de Estudios Superiores del Magisterio (1909–1932)." *Revista de Educación*, no. 240 (1975): 41–50.

Ferris, José Luis. *Maruja Mallo. La gran transgresora del 27*. Madrid: Temas de Hoy, 2004.

– *Palabras contra el olvido. Vida y obra de María Teresa León (1903–1988)*. Sevilla: Fundación José Manuel Lara, 2017.

Flecha García, Consuelo. "Las aspirantes al magisterio secundario en el proyecto de renovación pedagógica de la JAE." In *100 años de la JAE. La Junta para Ampliación de Estudios e Investigaciones Científicas en su centenario*, vol. 2, edited by José Manuel Sánchez Ron and José García-Velasco, 649–81. Madrid: Fundación Francisco Giner de los Ríos/Residencia de Estudiantes, 2010.

– "Alumnas y equipos directivos de la Residencia Teresiana de Madrid (1914–1936)." In *La Residencia de Señoritas y otras redes culturales femeninas*, edited by Josefina Cuesta, María José Turrión, and Rosa María Merino, 287–311. Salamanca: Universidad de Salamanca/Fundación José Ortega y Gasset–Gregorio Marañón, 2015.

Forcada Cabanellas, Manuel. *De la vida literaria. Testimonios de una época*. Prologue by Fausto Hernández. Rosario: Ciencia, 1941. Reprinted with prologue by Juan Bonilla and appendix by Pablo Rojas. Sevilla: Renacimiento, 2020. Page references are to the 2020 edition.

Fouchet, Max-Pol. *Wifredo Lam*. Barcelona: Polígrafa, 1989.

Francés, José. *El año artístico. 1918*. Madrid: Mundo Latino, 1919.

– "Notas de un catálogo. La Exposición de Artistas Avilesinos." *La Esfera* 9, no. 460 (28 October 1922): n.p.

Francisco Bores. El ultraísmo y el ambiente literario madrileño 1921–1925. Madrid: Residencia de Estudiantes, 1999.

Francisco Bores. Catálogo razonado. Pintura 1917–1944. Madrid: MNCARS/Telefónica, 2003.

Fuentes, Juan Francisco. "La arboleda encontrada. ¿Qué es España? Un documental atribuido a Luis Araquistáin." In *El laboratorio de España. La Junta para Ampliación de Estudios e Investigaciones Científicas, 1907–1939*, edited by José Manuel Sánchez Ron, Antonio Lafuente García, Ana Romero, and Leticia Sánchez de Andrés, 251–61. Madrid: Sociedad Estatal de Conmemoraciones Culturales/Residencia de Estudiantes, 2007.

Fuentes González, Isabel. *Delhy Tejero entre la tradición y la modernidad. 1904–1936*. Zamora: Diputación Provincial de Zamora/Ayuntamiento de Zamora/Instituto de Estudios Zamoranos "Florián de Ocampo," 1998.

Fuster del Alcázar, Enrique. "Barradas y la escena: La sugestión vibrante." In *Rafael Barradas, 1914–1929*, edited by María José González Madrid, 23–31. L'Hospitalet de Llobregat: Centre Cultural Metropolità Tecla Sala, 2004.

– "Rafael Barradas y Catalina Bárcena." In *Rafael Barradas (1890–1929)*, 3–6. Madrid: Guillermo de Osma, 2013.

Gagen, Derek. "The Consequences of Concupiscence. Love Poetry in *Sobre los ángeles*." *Romance Studies* 16, no. 2 (1998): 5–19.

– "Rafael Alberti's 'Muerte y juicio': Death, Judgement, and the Poetry of (Dis)belief." *Modern Language Review* 99, no. 4 (October 2004): 938–53.

Gaitán Salinas, Carmen. "Arte, educación y mujer. Embarque hacia el exilio de 1939." *Archivo Español de Arte* no. 353 (January-March 2016): 61–76.

Gaitán Salinas, Carmen, and Idoia Murga Castro. "Victorina Durán y Maruja Mallo: Encuentros y desencuentros de dos artistas exiliadas." *Arenal* 26, no. 2 (July–December 2019): 399–425.

Gallego Morell, Antonio. *Las tertulias románticas en España*. Madrid: Revista de Occidente, 1973.

Gállego Rubio, María Cristina. "La Biblioteca de la Universidad Literaria de Madrid y la Biblioteca de la Universidad Central: 1836–1897." In *Historia de la Biblioteca de la Universidad Complutense de Madrid*, edited by Juan Antonio Méndez Aparicio and María Cristina Gállego Rubio, 113–32. Madrid: Editorial Complutense, 2007.

– "Dos bibliotecarias complutenses en la Orden de Toledo de Luis Buñuel (Día de la mujer trabajadora, 8 de marzo de 2014)." Biblioteca y sociedad, Universidad Complutense de Madrid, 7 March 2014. http://webs.ucm.es/BUCM/blogs/bibliotecaysociedad/8657.php#.XvIWF7lYaAg.

García, Carlos, ed. *Correspondencia Rafael Cansinos Assens/Guillermo de Torre 1916–1955*. Madrid: Iberoamericana; Frankfurt am Main: Vervuert, 2004.

García, Carlos, and Pilar García-Sedas. *Julio J. Casal (1889–1954. Correspondencia con Ramón Gómez de la Serna y Guillermo de Torre (1921–1954)*. Madrid: Del Centro Editores, 2015.

– "Rafael Barradas y Julio J. Casal: Una amistad más allá de la vida." academia.edu, 2016.

García Blanco, Manuel. "El escritor mejicano Alfonso Reyes y Unamuno." *Cuadernos Hispanoamericanos*, no. 71 (November 1955): 155–79.

García Buñuel, Pedro Christian. *Recordando a Luis Buñuel*. Zaragoza: Diputación Provincial de Zaragoza/Ayuntamiento de Zaragoza, 1985.

García Camarero, Ernesto. "La Junta para Ampliación de Estudios e Investigaciones Científicas (1996)." Lecture given at the Revista Oral Calle Libre forum, 1996. http://www.jae2010.csic.es/documentos/articulos/articulo03.pdf.

García Chacón, Irene. "'Unidos por una goma elástica': Aspectos textuales y paratextuales de la correspondencia entre Manuel Ángeles Ortiz y Federico García Lorca." *Piedras Lunares. Revista Giennense de Literatura*, no. 2 (2018): 109–26.

García de Valdeavellano, Luis. "Maruja Mallo en su carrousel." *La Gaceta Literaria* 1, no. 17 (1 September 1927): 5.

García Guatas, Manuel. "Barradas: Ars longa vita brevis." *Artigrama*, no. 17 (2002): 49–69.

García Lorca, Federico. *Epistolario completo*. Edited by Andrew A. Anderson and Christopher Maurer. Madrid: Cátedra, 1997.

García-Lorca, Laura, ed. *Signos de amistad. La colección de Federico García Lorca.* Granada: Huerta de San Vicente; Madrid: Residencia de Estudiantes, 1998.

García-Luengo Manchado, Javier. "La promoción de 1915 de la Escuela Especial de Pintura, Escultura y Grabado de Madrid: Una visión global." *Boletín del Seminario de Estudios de Arte y Arqueología: Arte*, no. 79 (2013): 227–46.

García Maroto, Gabriel. *Promoción de México. Caminos hacia su integración. Raíces. Esfuerzos. Testimonios.* Mexico City: Guías Mexicanas, 1958.

García Martí, Victoriano. *El Ateneo de Madrid (1835–1935).* Madrid: Dossat, 1948.

García Monge, Carlos. "Garfias y Borges: Amigos ultraístas." *Huarte de San Juan. Filología y Didáctica de la Lengua*, no. 8 (2006): 9–15.

García Montero, Luis. "Biografía." In *Rafael Alberti: El poema compartido*, edited by Luis García Montero, 99–326. Granada: Junta de Andalucía–Consejería de Cultura, 2003.

García-Posada, Miguel. *Acelerado sueño. Memoria de los poetas del 27.* Madrid: Espasa, 1999.

García Puig, María Jesús. "Barradas: 'Café' con poesía pictórica." In *Rafael Barradas*, 19–22. Madrid: Galería Jorge Mara, 1992.

García-Sedas, Pilar, ed. *Joaquín Torres-García y Rafael Barradas. Un diálogo escrito: 1918–1928.* Prologue by Joaquim Molas. Barcelona: Parsifal, 2001.

García-Velasco, José. "La Junta para Ampliación de Estudios, la Institución Libre de Enseñanza y la modernización de la cultura española." *Boletín de la Institución Libre de Enseñanza* 2ª época, nos 63–4 (December 2006): 13–33.

– "Un proyecto para la modernización de España." In *El laboratorio de España. La Junta para Ampliación de Estudios e Investigaciones Científicas, 1907–1939*, edited by José Manuel Sánchez Ron, Antonio Lafuente García, Ana Romero, and Leticia Sánchez de Andrés, 157–99. Madrid: Sociedad Estatal de Conmemoraciones Culturales/Residencia de Estudiantes, 2007.

–. "El reencuentro con la modernidad. Estrategias y redes internacionales de la cultura española (1914–1939)." In *Redes internacionales de la cultura española, 1914–1939*, edited by José García-Velasco, 28–75. Madrid: Residencia de Estudiantes, 2014.

–, ed. *Redes internacionales de la cultura española, 1914–1939.* Madrid: Residencia de Estudiantes, 2014.

Gaya Nuño, Juan Antonio. "A los veinticinco años de un libro sobre política de las artes." *Ínsula* 7, no. 77 (May 1952): 9.

Gibson, Ian. *Federico García Lorca.* Vol. 1, *De Fuente Vaqueros a Nueva York (1898–1929).* Barcelona: Grijalbo, 1985.

– *The Shameful Life of Salvador Dalí.* New York: W.W. Norton, 1997.

– *Luis Buñuel. La forja de un cineasta universal, 1900–1938.* Madrid: Aguilar, 2013.

Giménez Caballero, Ernesto. "Notre Dame de la aleluya." *Papel de Aleluyas* 2, no. 5 (March 1928): n.p.

Glick, Thomas F. "Fundaciones americanas y ciencia española: La Fundación Del Amo, 1928–1940." In *Estudios sobre Julio Rey Pastor (1888–1962)*, edited by Luis Español González, 313–26. Logroño: Instituto de Estudios Riojanos, 1990.

Gómez de la Serna, Ramón. *Pombo*. Madrid: Imprenta de Mesón de Paños, 8, 1918. Reprint, Madrid: Comunidad de Madrid–Consejería de Educación/Visor Libros, 1999. Page references are to the 1999 edition.

– *La sagrada cripta de Pombo*. Madrid: Imprenta G. Hernández y Galo Sáez, 1924. Reprint, Madrid: Comunidad de Madrid–Consejería de Educación/Visor Libros, 1999. Page references are to the 1999 edition.

– "Maruja Mallo." In *59 grabados en negro y 9 láminas en color. 1928–1942*, by Maruja Mallo, 7–15. Buenos Aires: Losada, 1942.

– *Automoribundia (1888–1948)*. Edited by Celia Fernández Prieto. Madrid: Mare Nostrum, 2008.

Gómez de Tudanca, Rafael. "Prólogo." In Rafael Alberti, *Correspondencia a José María de Cossío, seguido de "Auto de fe" y otros hallazgos inéditos*, edited by Rafael Gómez de Tudanca and Eladio Mateos Miera, 13–19. Valencia: Pre-Textos, 1998.

Gómez Mesa, L. "Cinema y arte nuevo. Originalidad de Maruja Mallo." *Popular Film* (Barcelona) 5, no. 198 (15 May 1930): 3.

Gómez-Santos, Marino. *Crónica del Café Gijón*. Madrid: Biblioteca Nueva, 1955.

Gómez Trueba, Teresa. "¿Qué fue antes, el título o el libro? Análisis genético del proyecto inédito de Juan Ramón Jiménez *En la rama del verde limón*." *Creneida*, no. 2 (2014): 218–45.

González Madrid, María José, ed. *Rafael Barradas, 1914–1929*. L'Hospitalet de Llobregat: Centre Cultural Metropolità Tecla Sala, 2004.

González Ruano, César. *Memorias. Mi medio siglo se confiesa a medias*. Sevilla: Renacimiento, 2004.

González Sanz, Alejandro. "Los métodos de dibujo en las enseñanzas de artes aplicadas: Madrid 1900–1963." PhD diss., Universidad Complutense de Madrid, 2005.

Goodman, Dena. *The Republic of Letters: A Cultural History of the French Enlightenment*. Ithaca, NY: Cornell University Press, 1994.

Granda, Juanjo. RESAD. *Historia de una escuela centenaria*. Madrid: Real Escuela Superior de Arte Dramático, 2000. http://www.resad.es/images/historia-de-una-escuela-centenaria.pdf.

Grandes, Lorenzo de. "De Paco Santa Cruz a Francisco López. Cronología interrumpida." In *Francisco Santa Cruz (1899–1957. La vanguardia oculta*, edited by Juan Manuel Bonet, 143–57. Madrid: Museo de Arte Contemporáneo, 2009.

Grau, María Eugenia. "Barradas en el MNAV. Sobre cronologías ampliadas." In *Barradas. Colección MNAV*, edited by Enrique Aguerre, 282–97. Montevideo: Museo Nacional de Artes Visuales, 2013.

Guerrero, Salvador. "Un lugar de memoria de la geografía española de la Institución Libre de Enseñanza: los edificios de la Residencia de Señoritas." In *Mujeres en vanguardia. La Residencia de Señoritas en su centenario (1915–1935)*, edited by Almudena de la Cueva and Margarita Márquez Padorno, 296–315. Madrid: Residencia de Estudiantes, 2015.

Guerrero Ruiz, Juan. *Juan Ramón de viva voz*. Vol. 1, *1913–1931*. Edited by Manuel Ruiz-Funes Fernández. Valencia: Pre-Textos/Museo Ramón Gaya, 1998.

Guillén, Jorge, and José María de Cossío. *Correspondencia*. Edited by Julio Neira and Rafael Gómez de Tudanca. Valencia: Pre-Textos, 2002.

– *Cartas a Germaine (1919–1935)*. Edited by Margarita Ramírez. Barcelona: Galaxia Gutenberg/Círculo de Lectores, 2010.

Gutiérrez-Carbajal, Inés. "Trayectoria artística de Delhy Tejero." *Anuario del Instituto de Estudios Zamoranos "Florián de Ocampo,"* no. 21 (2004): 413–34.

Gutiérrez-Gili, Juan. "Perfiles jóvenes. Huberto Pérez de la Ossa." *La Gaceta Literaria* 2, no. 25 (1 January 1928): 4.

Gutiérrez-Vega, Zenaida. *Corresponsales españoles de José Mª Chacón*. Madrid: Fundación Universitaria Española, 1986.

Habermas, Jürgen. *The Structural Transformation of the Public Sphere. An Inquiry into a Category of Bourgeois Society*. Translated by Thomas Burger. Cambridge, MA: MIT Press, 1989.

Hansen, Hans Lauge. "La superposición metafórica entre ensalzamiento eufórico y degradación crítica en Rafael Alberti y Maruja Mallo." In *La metáfora en la poesía hispánica (1885–1936)*, edited by Hans Lauge Hansen and Julio Jensen, 175–93. Sevilla: Alfar, 1997.

Harth, Erica. *Cartesian Women: Versions and Subversions of Rational Discourse in the Old Regime*. Ithaca, NY: Cornell University Press, 1992.

Havard, Robert. "Rafael Alberti, Maruja Mallo, and Giménez Caballero: Materialist Imagery in *Sermones y moradas* and the Issue of Surrealism." *Modern Language Review* 93, no. 4 (1998): 1007–20.

– *The Crucified Mind. Rafael Alberti and the Surrealist Ethos in Spain*. London: Tamesis, 2001.

Hernández, Patricio. *Emilio Prados: La memoria del olvido*. 2 vols. Zaragoza: Universidad de Zaragoza, 1988.

– "Presentación del epistolario de Emilio Prados a Federico García Lorca." *Boletín de la Fundación Federico García Lorca* 11, nos 21–2 (December 1997): 9–24.

Hernández-Catá, A. "Horizontes. El suicidio de un poeta." *La Voz* (Madrid), 1 November 1929, 1.

Hernández Sandoica, Elena. "La Universidad de Madrid en el primer tercio del siglo XX." In *La Facultad de Filosofía y Letras de Madrid en la Segunda República. Arquitectura y Universidad durante los años 30*, edited by Santiago López-Ríos Moreno and Juan Antonio González Cárceles, 42–57. Madrid: Sociedad Estatal de Conmemoraciones Culturales/Ayuntamiento de Madrid/Ediciones de Arquitectura–Fundación Arquitectura COAM, 2008.

Hernanz Angulo, Beatriz. "El *Cuaderno de Mari Celina* y otros poemas: Prehistoria poética albertiana. Rafael Alberti en sus primerísimos orígenes." In *Literatura española, siglos XIX, XX y XXI. Literatura del exilio. Teoría literaria. Cine y literatura*, edited by Beatriz Mariscal and Blanca López de Mariscal, 213–24. Vol. 3 of *Actas del XV Congreso de la Asociación Internacional de Hispanistas. "Las dos orillas."* Mexico City: Fondo de Cultura Económica/Asociación Internacional de Hispanistas/Tecnológico de Monterrey, 2007.

Herrera Navarro, Javier. "Documentos inéditos sobre la vanguardia artística española (I. Tres cartas madrileñas de Barradas)." *Boletín de Arte*, no. 18 (1997): 483–93.

Hinojosa, José María. *Epistolario (1922–1936)*. Edited by Julio Neira and Alfonso Sánchez Rodríguez. Sevilla: Fundación Genesian, 1997.

"Historia de las enseñanzas artísticas de música en España." Conservatorio de Música "Cristóbal Halffter," Junta de Castilla y León: Conservatorio Profesional de Música Cristóbal Halffter (Ponferrada, León), accessed 18 May 2022. http://cpmhalffter.centros.educa.jcyl.es/sitio/index.cgi?wid_seccion=7&wid_item=169.

Hoz, Ángel de la, and Benito Madariaga. *Pancho Cossío. El artista y su obra*. Santander: Ayuntamiento de Santander/Caja Cantabria/Fundación Marcelino Botín/Intra/Universidad de Cantabria, 1990.

Huddleston, Sisley. *Bohemian, Literary and Social Life in Paris: Salons, Cafes, Studios*. London: George G. Harrap, 1928.

Huguet, Montserrat. "Modernidad y género en los inicios del siglo XX. Tradición misional y legado de las educadoras estadounidenses en España." In *La Residencia de Señoritas y otras redes culturales femeninas*, edited by Josefina Cuesta, María José Turrión, and Rosa María Merino, 71–115. Salamanca: Universidad de Salamanca/Fundación José Ortega y Gasset–Gregorio Marañón, 2015.

Huidobro, Vicente. "Al fin se descubre mi maestro." *Création*, no. 3 (February 1924), suplemento castellano a la revista *Création*. Pamphlet of 16 pp.

Ignacios, Antonio de. *Historial Rafael Barradas*. Montevideo: El Autor, 1953.

Inglada, Rafael. *Alfonso Ponce de León (1906–1936)*. Presented by Juan Manuel Bonet. Epilogue by Eugenio Carmona. Madrid: Aldeasa/Museo Nacional Centro de Arte Reina Sofía, 2001.

Instituto Nacional de Estadística. *Anuarios Estadísticos* [various years]. https://www.ine.es/inebaseweb/25687.do.

Isabel de Bustos, Clara. "Alberti: 'Con María Teresa termina una vida ejemplar.'" *ABC*, 16 December 1988, 56–7.

Jardi, Enric. *Rafael Barradas a Catalunya i altres artistes que passaren la mar*. Barcelona: Generalitat de Catalunya, Comissió Amèrica i Catalunya, 1992.

Jarnés, Benjamín. *Epistolario 1919–1939, y Cuadernos íntimos*. Edited by Jordi Gracia and Domingo Ródenas de Moya. Madrid: Residencia de Estudiantes, 2003.

Jiménez, Juan Ramón. "Acento. Poetas de antro y dianche. Federico García Lorca (1928). Dámaso Alonso (1928). Rafael Alberti (1929)." *La Gaceta Literaria* 4, no. 94 (15 November 1930): 7.

– "Acento. Historias de España. Evolución superinocente. Satanismo inverso. Nueva academia española." *La Gaceta Literaria* 5, no. 98 (15 January 1931): 3.

– *Epistolario*. Vol. 2, *1916–1936*. Edited by Alfonso Alegre Heitzmann. Madrid: Residencia de Estudiantes, 2012.

Jiménez, Pablo. "La magia exacta." *ABC*, 7 February 1995, 81.

Jiménez-Blanco Carrillo de Albornoz, María Dolores. "Juan de la Encina, director del Museo de Arte Moderno." In *Juan de la Encina y el arte de su tiempo. 1883–1963*, edited by Miriam Alzuri Milanés and María Dolores Jiménez-Blanco Carrillo de

Albornoz, 43–72. Madrid: Museo Nacional Centro de Arte Reina Sofía/Museo de Bellas Artes de Bilbao, 1998.

Jiménez Fraud, Alberto. *Epistolario*. Vol. 1, *1905–1936*. Edited by James Valender, José García-Velasco, Tatiana Aguilar-Álvarez Bay, and .Trilce Arroyo. Madrid: Unicaja/Residencia de Estudiantes, 2017.

Jiménez Gómez, Hilario. *Lorca y Alberti, dos poetas en un espejo (1924–1936)*. Madrid: Biblioteca Nueva; Cáceres: Diputación Provincial de Cáceres, 2003.

J.L.M.M. "Biografía. Ismael Cuesta (1899–1982)." Ismael Cuesta (blog), accessed 22 May 2022. http://ismaelcuesta.blogspot.com/p/biografia.html.

Julio Moisés. Barcelona: Joaquín Gil Guiñón, 1932.

Kale, Steven. *French Salons: High Society and Political Sociability from the Old Regime to the Revolution of 1848*. Baltimore, MD: Johns Hopkins University Press, 2004.

Kirkpatrick, Susan. *Mujer, modernismo y vanguardia en España (1898–1931)*. Madrid: Cátedra, 2003.

"La familia Narezo (I)." *Valle del Liébana: Revista digital del Valle de Liébana en Cantabria*, accessed 22 may 2022. http://www.valledeliebana.info/reportajes/personajes/losnarezo1.html.

La pintura de Eduardo Vicente. Torrelavega: Biblioteca José María de Pereda, 1949.

Laget, Laurie-Anne. "'La cuestión palpitante y manducante': Los ecos de la vida literaria en la prensa a través de la polémica sobre los banquetes (1923)." In *Literatura hispánica y prensa periódica (1875–1931)*, edited by Javier Serrano Alonso and Amparo de Juan Bolufer, 827–38. Santiago de Compostela: Universidade de Santiago de Compostela, 2009.

– "The Spanish Center of the International PEN through Its First *Sumiller*: From a Project of International Solidarity to an Expression of the Tensions of the Literary Society of Madrid (1922–1924)." In *Cultural Organizations, Networks and Mediators in Contemporary Ibero-America*, edited by Diana Roig-Sanz and Jaume Subirana, 200–12. New York: Routledge, 2020.

Landes, Joan B. *Women and the Public Sphere in the Age of the French Revolution*. Ithaca, NY: Cornell University Press, 1988.

Larson, Susan. *Constructing and Resisting Modernity: Madrid 1900–1936*. Madrid: Iberoamericana; Frankfurt am Main: Vervuert, 2011.

Lasaga, José, ed. *El Madrid de José Ortega y Gasset*. Madrid: Sociedad Estatal de Conmemoraciones Culturales/Residencia de Estudiantes, 2006.

Lassaigne, Jacques, ed. *Borès*. Paris: Louis Carré Éditeur, 1957.

Lasso, Francisco. "Escritos III. Autobiografía." In *Pancho Lasso. Retrospectiva*, edited by Josefina Alix, 236–7. Teguise, Lanzarote: Fundación César Manrique, 1997.

Laurenson-Shakibi, Helen. "Angels, Art and Analysis: Rafael Alberti's *Sobre los ángeles*." In *Crossing Fields in Spanish Culture*, edited by Federico Bonaddio and Xon de Ros, 103–17. Oxford: Legenda, 2003.

– "*Amor imposible, cosas en común*. Rafael Alberti and Maruja Mallo 1925–1929." *Bulletin of Spanish Studies* 84, no. 1 (2007): 37–55.

Lefebvre, Henri. *La Production de l'espace*. Paris: Anthropos, 1974.

León, María Teresa. *Memoria de la melancolía*. Prologue by Rafael Alberti. Barcelona: Círculo de Lectores, 1987.

Leroy, Géraldi. "La mondaine littéraire à la Belle Époque." *Les Cahiers de LIHTP. Sociabilités intellectuelles. Lieux, milieux, réseaux*, no. 20, edited by Nicole Racine and Michel Trebitsch (March 1992): 85–100.

Limón, Esteban. "El Palacio de Hielo: sede del Centro de Estudios Históricos." In *1907–1987. La Junta para Ampliación de Estudios e Investigaciones Científicas 80 años después*, vol. 2, edited by José Manuel Sánchez Ron, 605–22. Madrid: CSIC, 1988.

Lista provisional de socios del P.E.N. (Poetas, Ensayistas, Novelistas. Club internacional de escritores). Madrid: Tipografía de Nieto y Compañía, 1922.

Lista rectificada de socios del P.E.N. (Poetas, Ensayistas, Novelistas. Club internacional de escritores). Madrid: Tipografía de Nieto y Compañía, 1923.

Litoral Alberti. Monographic special issue, *Litoral* (Málaga) (April 1993).

Lomba Serrano, Concha. "Barradas en Aragón." In *Barradas. Exposición antológica, 1890–1929*, edited by Jaime Brihuega and Concha Lomba, 65–82. Zaragoza: Gobierno de Aragón; Barcelona: Generalitat de Catalunya; Madrid: Comunidad de Madrid, 1992.

– "Joaquina Zamora entre el regionalismo y los otros realismos 1916–1936." In *Joaquina Zamora. Exposición antológica*, edited by María de la Presentación Sanz del Amo in conjunction with Concepción Lomba Serrano and Alfredo Romero Santamaría, 33–51. Zaragoza: Diputación Provincial de Zaragoza, 1996.

– "Marisa Roësset, en la frontera (1924–1939)." *Archivo Español de Arte* 91, no. 362 (April–June 2018): 143–58.

– *Bajo el eclipse. Pintoras en España, 1880–1939*. Madrid: Consejo Superior de Investigaciones Científicas, 2019.

Londero, Eleanor. "Vanguardia y nacionalismo: La polémica del meridiano (Madrid–Buenos Aires, 1927)." *Iberoamericana* 13, no. 1 (1989): 3–19.

López Cobo, Azucena. "El 'espíritu de la casa' en la Residencia de Estudiantes. Características específicas del Grupo de Señoritas." In *100 años de la JAE. La Junta para Ampliación de Estudios e Investigaciones Científicas en su centenario*, vol. 2, edited by José Manuel Sánchez Ron and José García-Velasco, 531–49. Madrid: Fundación Francisco Giner de los Ríos/Residencia de Estudiantes, 2010.

López-Obrero, Ángel. "Los alumnos de la Escuela de Pintura." *Heraldo de Madrid*, 19 November 1928, 8–9.

López-Obrero. Córdoba: Galería de Arte, 5/Caja Provincial de Ahorros de Córdoba, 1994.

López-Ocón Cabrera, Leoncio. "La dinámica investigadora del Centro de Estudios Históricos de la JAE." In *La ciencia de la palabra: Cien años de la "Revista de Filología Española,"* edited by Pilar García Mouton and Mario Pedrazuela Fuentes, 19–53. Madrid: Consejo Superior de Investigaciones Científicas, 2015.

López Sánchez, José María. *Heterodoxos españoles. El Centro de Estudios Históricos, 1910–1936*. Madrid: Marcial Pons/Consejo Superior de Investigaciones Científicas, 2006.

Lorenzo Arribas, José Miguel. "Atocha: La nebulosa de un topónimo." Centro Virtual Cervantes, 13 November 2008. https://cvc.cervantes.es/el_rinconete/anteriores/noviembre_08/13112008_01.htm.

Lozano Bartolozzi, María del Mar. "Artistas plásticas españolas entre las dos guerras europeas: Pitti (Francis) Bartolozzi, Delhy Tejero, Remedios Varo." In *Iconografía y creación artísticas: Estudios sobre la identidad femenina desde las relaciones de poder*, edited by Rosario Camacho Martínez and Aurora Miró Domínguez, 289–328. Málaga: Diputación Provincial de Málaga–Centro de Ediciones de la Diputación Provincial de Málaga, 2001.

Lozano Miralles, Rafael, ed. *Crónica de una amistad. Epistolario de Federico García Lorca y Melchor Fernández Almagro*. Granada: Fundación Federico García Lorca/Caja de Ahorros de Granada, 2006.

Lozano Úriz, Pedro Luis. "Una vida entre el arte y la familia." In *Homenaje a Francis Bartolozzi. Exposición de una selección de sus obras*, edited by Pedro Luis Lozano Úriz, 7–12. Navarra: Museo de Navarra, 1999.

– *Un matrimonio de artistas. Vida y obra de Pedro Lozano de Sotés y Francis Bartolozzi*. Pamplona: Gobierno de Navarra–Departamento de Cultura y Turismo/Institución Príncipe de Viana, 2007.

Luengo López, Jordi. "Tazas calientes manchadas de carmín. Mujeres de cafés en la bipolaridad moral del espacio público (1890–1936)." *Asparkía. Investigació Feminista*, no. 17 (2006): 81–105.

L.R. "Los primeros pasos de una artista que llegará lejos. Con sus lápices y sus pinceles, Adelita Tejero, que aún es casi una niña, lucha bravamente por el arte y por la vida." *Crónica* 2, no. 18 (16 March 1930): n.p.

Mallo, Maruja. "Huella." "Cloaca." *La Gaceta Literaria* 3, no. 61 (1 July 1929): 1.

– "Wallace Beery, Detective," and "Charles Bower, Inventor." *La Gaceta Literaria* 3, no. 65 (1 September 1929): 3.

– "Las bodas de Ben Turpin," and "Farina y los fantasmas." *La Gaceta Literaria* 3, no. 66 (15 September 1929): 5.

– *Lo popular en la plástica española a través de mi obra, 1928–1936. Con 48 grabados y una lámina en color*. Buenos Aires: Losada, 1939.

– *59 grabados en negro y 9 láminas en color. 1928–1942*. Buenos Aires: Losada, 1942.

– "Ortega y Gasset," "Dalí," and "La Escuela de Vallecas." In *Maruja Mallo*, edited by Pilar Corredoira López, 221, 223, 225. Buenos Aires: Museo Nacional de Bellas Artes; Santiago de Compostela: Xunta de Galicia, 1994.

Manaut Viglietti, Juan. "Carlos Sáenz de Tejada. Evocación." ABC, 24 February 1962, 25.

Manegat, Luis G. "Tres artistas amigos." *El Noticiero Universal*, 30 June 1961.

Mangini, Shirley. *Maruja Mallo y la vanguardia española*. Barcelona: CIRCE, 2012.

Mannheim, Karl. *Essays on the Sociology of Culture*. Edited by Ernest Manheim with Paul Kecskemeti. London: Routledge and Kegan Paul, 1956.

Manuel Ángeles Ortiz en Granada. Granada: Junta de Andalucía–Consejería de Cultura, 1998.

Marchand, J.-J., ed. "Propos de l'artiste." In *Borès*, edited by Jacques Lassaigne, 15–25. Paris: Louis Carré Éditeur, 1957.

Marín-Medina, José, ed. *Delhy Tejero. Representación. Exposición antológica.* Valladolid: Junta de Castilla y León/Caja España, 2009.

Marrast, Robert. *Aspects du théâtre de Rafael Alberti.* Paris: Société d'Édition d'Enseignement Supérieur, 1967.

Martín Gijón, Mario. *Una poesía de la presencia: José Herrera Petere en el surrealismo, la guerra y el destierro.* Valencia: Pre-Textos, 2009.

Martínez Martín, Jesús A. *Vivir de la pluma. La profesionalización del escritor, 1836–1936.* Madrid: Marcial Pons, 2009.

Martínez Rus, Ana. "La Librairie Espagnole de León Sánchez Cuesta en Paris (1927–1936)." In *Prensa, impresos, lectura en el mundo hispánico contemporáneo. Homenaje a Jean-François Botrel,* edited by Jean-Michel Desvois, 109–21. Bordeaux: Université Michel de Montaigne Bordeaux 3/PILAR [Press, Imprimés, Lecture dans l'Aire Romane], 2005.

Martínez Sierra, Gregorio. *Un teatro de arte en España, 1917–1925.* Madrid: Ediciones de la Esfinge, 1926.

Mateo, María Asunción. "Introducción." In Rafael Alberti, *Antología comentada (Poesía),* vol. 1, edited by María Asunción Mateo, 13–164. Madrid: Ediciones de la Torre, 1990.

– *Rafael Alberti: de lo vivo y lejano.* Madrid: Espasa-Calpe, 1996.

Mateos Miera, Eladio. "Introducción." Segunda parte. *Auto de fe (Dividido en un gargajo y cuatro cazcarrias).* In Rafael Alberti, *Correspondencia a José María de Cossío, seguido de "Auto de fe" y otros hallazgos inéditos,* edited by Rafael Gómez de Tudanca and Eladio Mateos Miera, 111–41. Valencia: Pre-Textos, 1998.

– "Poesía y ballet: *El colorín colorado* de Rafael Alberti." In *Campos interdisciplinares de la musicología,* vol. 1, 571–82. Madrid: Sociedad Española de Musicología, 2001.

– "Rafael Alberti y la música." PhD diss., University of Granada, 2003.

– "Alberti en el teatro de las vanguardias: vida y fortuna de *La pájara pinta.*" *Papeles del Festival de Música Española de Cádiz,* no. 1 (2005): 61–81.

Maurer, Christopher. "De la correspondencia de García Lorca: Datos inéditos sobre la transmisión de su obra." *Boletín de la Fundación Federico García Lorca* 1, no. 1 (January 1987): 58–85.

– "¡Ay, Maroto!: Noticias de una amistad." In *Gabriel García Maroto y la renovación del arte español contemporáneo,* edited by Angelina Serrano de la Cruz Peinado, 31–9. Toledo: Junta de Comunidades de Castilla-La Mancha, 1999.

Meléndez Táboas, Amelia. "Formación y primeros trabajos de Maruja Mallo en España (1902–1931)." In *XV Congreso nacional de historia del arte (CEHA). Modelos, intercambios y recepción artística (de las rutas marítimas a la navegación en red),* vol. 2, 1619–28. Palma de Mallorca: Universitat de les Illes Balears, 2008.

– "Maruja Mallo entre sus condiscípulas de San Fernando." In *La mujer en la historia de la universidad. Retos, compromiso y logros,* edited by Yolanda Romano Martín, Sara Velázquez García, and Mattia Bianchi, 117–29. Salamanca: Universidad de Salamanca, 2018.

Méndez, Concha, and Paloma Ulacia. *Memorias habladas, memorias armadas.* Madrid: Mondadori, 1990.

Méndez, Rafael. *Caminos inversos. Vivencias de ciencia y guerra*. Mexico City: Fondo de Cultura Económica, 1987.

Méndez Bejarano, Mario. *Diccionario de escritores, maestros y oradores naturales de Sevilla y su actual provincia*, vol. 2, primera parte. Sevilla: Tipografía Gironés, 1923.

Menéndez-Onrubia, Carmen. "Galdós y el 'prodigioso invento' del cinematógrafo." In *La hora de Galdós*, edited by Yolanda Arencibia, Germán Gullón, and Victoria Galván González, 595–610. Las Palmas de Gran Canaria: Cabildo de Gran Canaria, 2018.

Mestre, Irene, Maria Abando, Antoni Alcover, Carme Estivill, and Mercedes Prieto, "Los estudios superiores de diseño en la convergencia europea." *V Congreso Internacional Virtual de Educación* (2005): 1–18.

M.G.O. "Delhy Tejero–Adela Tejero Bedate (Toro, Zamora, 1904–Madrid, 1968)." In *Dibujantas*, edited by Josefina Alix and Marta González Orbegozo, 328–36. Madrid: Museo ABC, 2019.

Milroy, Lesley, and James Milroy. "Social Network and Social Class: Toward an Integrated Sociolinguistic Model." *Language in Society* 21, no. 1 (March 1992): 1–26.

Mitchell, J. Clyde. "Network Procedures." In *Quality of Urban Life*, edited by Dieter Frick, Hans W. Hoefert, Heiner Legewie, Rainer Mackensen, and Rainer K. Silbereisen, 73–92. Berlin: De Gruyter, 1986.

Monte-Cristo [Eugenio Rodríguez Ruiz de la Escalera]. *Los salones de Madrid*. Madrid: Publicaciones de "El Álbum Nacional," ca 1898.

Montes López, Estrella, and Nazareth Gallego Morón. "María Luisa González, de la Universidad de Salamanca a ocupar cátedras en universidades extranjeras." In *La mujer en la historia de la universidad. Retos, compromiso y logros*, edited by Yolanda Romano Martín, Sara Velázquez García, and Mattia Bianchi, 217–29. Salamanca: Universidad de Salamanca, 2018.

Mora Guarnido, José. *Federico García Lorca y su mundo*. Buenos Aires: Losada, 1958.

Moreiro, José María. "Arte. Maruja Mallo: Casi cuanto sé de mí … " *Blanco y Negro*, no. 3402 (13 July 1977): 75–6.

Morelli, Gabriele, ed. *Gerardo Diego y el III Centenario de Góngora. (Correspondencia inédita)*. Valencia: Pre-Textos, 2001.

Moreno, Mati, ed. *José María Hinojosa. Entre dos luces 1904–1936*. Málaga: Centro Cultural de la Generación del 27, 2004.

Moreno Villa, José. *Vida en claro. Autobiografía*. Mexico City: El Colegio de México, 1944. Reprint, Mexico City: Fondo de Cultura Económica, 1976. Page references are to the 1976 edition.

– *Temas de arte. Selección de escritos periodísticos sobre pintura, escultura, arquitectura y música (1916–1954)*. Edited by Humberto Huergo Cardoso. Valencia: Pre-Textos; Málaga: Centro Cultural de la Generación del 27, 2001.

– *Memoria*. Edited by Juan Pérez de Ayala. Mexico City: El Colegio de México; Madrid: Residencia de Estudiantes, 2011.

Morla Lynch, Carlos. *En España con Federico García Lorca. (Páginas de un diario íntimo, 1928–1936)*. Edited by Sergio Macías Brevis. Sevilla: Renacimiento, 2008.

Moya Morales, Javier. "Los nombres de Manuel Ángeles Ortiz." In *Manuel Ángeles Ortiz en Granada*, 9–16. Granada: Junta de Andalucía–Consejería de Cultura, 1998.

Muñoz Alonso, María Dolores. "De hospital a museo: Las sucesivas transformaciones de un hospital inacabado. El Hospital General de Madrid." PhD diss., Escuela Técnica Superior de Arquitectura, Universidad Politécnica de Madrid, 2010.

Murga Castro, Idoia. "Muros para pintar: Las artistas y la Residencia de Señoritas." In *Mujeres en vanguardia. La Residencia de Señoritas en su centenario (1915–1935)*, edited by Almudena de la Cueva and Margarita Márquez Padorno, 86–127. Madrid: Residencia de Estudiantes, 2015.

Murga Castro, Idoia, and Carmen Gaitán Salinas. "Introducción." In *Mi vida*, vol. 1, *Sucedió*, by Victorina Durán, 11–104. Madrid: Residencia de Estudiantes, 2018.

Navarrete Navarrete, María Teresa, and Laura Lozano Marín, eds. *Redes literarias en la poesía española del primer tercio del siglo XX*. Madrid: Visor Libros, 2021.

Navascués Palacio, Pedro. "La creación de la Escuela de Arquitectura de Madrid." In *Madrid y sus arquitectos: 150 años de la escuela de arquitectura*, 23–34. Madrid: Comunidad de Madrid–Dirección General de Patrimonio Cultural–Consejería de Educación y Cultura, 1996.

Neira, Julio. "Epistolario de la Casona de Tudanca (Cartas de Emilio Prados y Manuel Altolaguirre a José María de Cossío y Rafael Alberti, 1927–1928)." *Ínsula*, no. 594 (Junc 1996): 15–16.

– *Viajero de soledades. Estudios sobre José María Hinojosa*. Sevilla: Fundación Genesian, 1999.

Nistal Ramón, Teresa, and Noemí Yuste López. "Fondos de la Escuela Central de Idiomas en el Archivo Central de la Secretaría de Estado de Educación (1945–1970)." Madrid: Ministerio de Educación, Cultura y Deporte, 2016.

Nooy, Wouter de. "Fields and Networks: Correspondence Analysis and Social Network Analysis in the Framework of Field Theory." *Poetics*, no. 31 (2003): 305–27.

Nuevo Cal, Carlos, and Emilio Ínsua López. *Maruja Mallo: De prometedora pioneira a artista universal. Materias para una biografía exacta e completa da pintora viveiresa entre 1902 e 1936*. A Coruña: Fundación CaixaGalicia, 2010.

Nuevo Cal, Carlos, Emilio Ínsua López, and Analía Álvarez González. *Maruja Mallo. Vida e exilio dunha artista universal*. Monographic special issue, *Cadernos de Estudos Xerais*, no. 9 (21 April 2017). Sada: Asociación Cultural Irmáns Suárez Picallo.

Núñez Jiménez, Antonio. *Wifredo Lam*. Havana: Fundación Antonio Núñez Jiménez de la Naturaleza y el Hombre, 2017.

Olmos, Víctor. *Ágora de la libertad. Historia del Ateneo de Madrid*. Vol. 1, *1820–1923*. Madrid: La Esfera de los Libros, 2015.

Ontañón, Elvira. "El Instituto-Escuela, experiencia educativa de la Junta para Ampliación de Estudios." In *1907–1987. La Junta para la Ampliación de Estudios e Investigaciones Científicas 80 años después*, vol. 2, edited by José Manuel Sánchez Ron, 201–38. Madrid: Consejo Superior de Investigaciones Científicas, 1988.

Ortiz Ballesteros, Consuelo. *Paseando por Madrid con el Real Conservatorio Superior de Música de Madrid. Recorrido histórico y documental a través de las distintas sedes ocupadas por el Real Conservatorio Superior de Música de Madrid.* Madrid: Real Conservatorio Superior de Música de Madrid. https://rcsmm. eu/general/files/biblioteca/otraspublicaciones/sedes_rcsmm.pdf.

Ortiz Saralegui, Juvenal. "Federico García Lorca y Rafael Barradas." *Romance. Revista Popular Hispanoamericana* (Mexico City) 1, no. 19 (18 December 1940): 9.

Osma, Guillermo de. "Bores: Años veinte y treinta." In *Bores nuevo. Los años veinte y treinta*, 5–6. Madrid: Guillermo de Osma; Barcelona: Oriol Galeria d'Art, 1996.

Otero Carvajal, Luis Enrique. "Ciencia y cultura en Madrid, siglo XX, edad de plata, tiempo de silencio y mercado cultural: Las tertulias de café. Espacio de sociabilidad cultural." In *Historia de Madrid*, edited by Antonio Fernández García, 697–737. Madrid: Universidad Complutense de Madrid/Editorial Complutense, 1993.

Padró Nieto, Bernat. "El banquete a Luis Araquistáin: Un caso de escenificación de políticas literarias." *Revista Canadiense de Estudios Hispánicos* 41, no. 3 (2017): 621–42.

Palencia, Benjamín. In "Juan Ramón Jiménez, juzgado por sus contemporáneos y discípulos." *ABC*, 26 October 1956, 36–8.

Palomares-Salas, Claudio. *The Spatiality of the Hispanic Avant-Garde. Ultraísmo & Estridentismo, 1918–1927*. Leiden: Brill; Boston: Rodopi, 2020.

Palomera Parra, Isabel. "La organización académica y administrativa de la facultad: Legislación y fuentes documentales." In *La Facultad de Filosofía y Letras de Madrid en la Segunda República. Arquitectura y Universidad durante los años 30*, edited by Santiago López-Ríos Moreno and Juan Antonio González Cárceles, 179–91. Madrid: Sociedad Estatal de Conmemoraciones Culturales/Ayuntamiento de Madrid/Ediciones de Arquitectura/Fundación Arquitectura COAM, 2008.

Parsons, Deborah L. *A Cultural History of Madrid: Modernism and the Urban Spectacle*. Oxford: Berg, 2003.

Pavlova Todorova, Polina. "Consola, 1905, de Joaquín Sorolla." *Pieza del mes.* Madrid: Museo Sorolla, April 2013. https://www.culturaydeporte.gob.es/dam/ jcr:d9eac3e5-69be-4693-81bd-027b3e889955/consola.pdf.

Pedro, Valentín de. *España renaciente. Opiniones. Hombres. Ciudades. Paisajes.* Madrid: Calpe, 1922.

Pekacz, Jolanta T. *Conservative Tradition in Pre-Revolutionary France: Parisian Salon Women*. New York: Peter Lang, 1999.

Peláez, Manuel J. "Epistolario selectivo del jurista y político Fernando de los Ríos Urruti (Cuarta parte)." *Contribuciones a las Ciencias Sociales*, no. 10 (December 2010). www.eumed.net/rev/cccss/10/.

Peláez Martín, Andrés. "Barradas en el teatro de arte: Tradición y vanguardia (1917–1925)." In *Barradas. Exposición antológica, 1890–1929*, edited by Jaime Brihuega and Concha Lomba, 83–97. Zaragoza: Gobierno de Aragón; Barcelona: Generalitat de Catalunya; Madrid: Comunidad de Madrid, 1992.

Peña Hinojosa, Baltasar. "Nota previa." In *Obras completas*, by José María Hinojosa, 13–20. Málaga: Diputación Provincial–Instituto de Cultura, 1974.

Penagos, Rafael de, and Alicia Navarro, eds. *Penagos (1889–1954)*. Madrid: Fundación Cultural Mapfre Vida/Centro Cultural del Conde Duque, 1989.

Peralta Ortiz, María Dolores. "Orígenes y características de una residencia para universitarias en 1914. La Residencia Teresiana de Madrid." In *La Residencia de Señoritas y otras redes culturales femeninas*, edited by Josefina Cuesta, María José Turrión, and Rosa María Merino, 313–35. Salamanca: Universidad de Salamanca/ Fundación José Ortega y Gasset–Gregorio Marañón, 2015.

Pereda, Raquel. *Barradas*. Montevideo: Galería Latina, 1989.

Pereda Valdés, Ildefonso, ed. *Antología de la moderna poesía uruguaya, 1900–1927*. Buenos Aires: El Ateneo, 1927.

Pérez, Darío. "Rafael Cansinos Assens." In *Figuras de España*. Prologue by Santiago Alba, 209–23. Madrid: CIAP, 1930.

Pérez Bazo, Javier. *Juan Chabás (Denis, 1900–La Habana, 1954)*. Denia: Ayuntamiento de Denia, 1985.

– *Juan Chabás y su tiempo. De la poética de vanguardia a la estética del compromiso*. Barcelona: Anthropos, 1992.

Pérez Calero, Gerardo. *José Jiménez Aranda*. Sevilla: Diputación Provincial de Sevilla, 1982.

– "La Academia Libre de Bellas Artes de Sevilla (1872-1888)." *Laboratorio de Arte*, no. 11 (1998): 275–300.

Pérez de Ayala, Juan, ed. "La Residencia de Estudiantes." Special issue, *Poesía. Revista Ilustrada de Información Poética*, nos 18–19 (1984).

–, ed. *José Moreno Villa (1887–1955)*. Madrid: Ministerio de Cultura–Dirección General del Libro y Bibliotecas, 1987.

– "Miscelánea biográfica (Siguiendo *La vida en claro* de José Moreno Villa)." In *José Moreno Villa (1887–1955)*, edited by Juan Pérez de Ayala, 93–132. Madrid: Ministerio de Cultura–Dirección General del Libro y Bibliotecas, 1987.

– "Álbum biográfico. Maruja Mallo." In *Maruja Mallo*, edited by Juan Pérez de Ayala and Francisco Rivas, 77–91. Madrid: Guillermo de Osma/Fundación Cultural Banesto, 1992.

– "Joaquín Peinado escribe a Francisco García Lorca." *ABC Cultural*, 27 October 2001, 6–9.

Pérez de Ayala, Juan, and Francisco Rivas, eds. *Maruja Mallo*. Madrid: Guillermo de Osma/Fundación Cultural Banesto, 1992.

Pérez Ferrero, Miguel. "Baraja de estampas." *Parábola* (Burgos), no. 4 (February 1928), 1. Reprinted in *1928. Revista de Avance* 2, no. 25 (15 August 1928): 220–2.

– *Unos y otros*. Madrid: Editora Nacional, 1947.

– "Sáenz de Tejada, recuerdos de otros días." *ABC*, 23 February 1958, 54.

– *Tertulias y grupos literarios*. Madrid: Cultura Hispánica, 1974.

– "El largo exilio del pintor Bores." *ABC*, 29 June 1975, 7.

Pérez Marqués, Fernando. "Cartas a J. López Prudencio, crítico literario." *Revista de Estudios Extremeños* 33, no. 2 (1977): 779–88.

Pérez Segura, Javier. "Cronología." In *Joaquín Peinado desde 1918 hasta 1945*, edited by Javier Pérez Segura, 89–90. Granada: Huerta de San Vicente, 2001.

–, ed. *Joaquín Peinado desde 1918 hasta 1945*. Granada: Huerta de San Vicente, 2001.

– "Joaquín Peinado en los escenarios del arte moderno." In *Joaquín Peinado desde 1918 hasta 1945*, edited by Javier Pérez Segura, 31–55. Granada: Huerta de San Vicente, 2001.

–, "La sociedad de artistas ibéricos (1920–1936)." PhD diss., Universidad Complutense de Madrid, 2003.

–, ed. *Tejada y la pintura. Un relato desvelado, 1914–1925*. Segovia: Caja Segovia–Obra Social y Cultural, 2003.

– "Tejada y la pintura moderna en España, entre la renovación formal y la vanguardia." In *Tejada y la pintura. Un relato desvelado, 1914–1925*, edited by Javier Pérez Segura, 13–61. Segovia: Caja Segovia–Obra Social y Cultural, 2003.

Pérez-Villanueva Tovar, Isabel. "La Residencia de Estudiantes." In *El laboratorio de España. La Junta para Ampliación de Estudios e Investigaciones Científicas, 1907–1939*, edited by José Manuel Sánchez Ron, Antonio Lafuente García, Ana Romero, and Leticia Sánchez de Andrés, 433–63. Madrid: Sociedad Estatal de Conmemoraciones Culturales/Residencia de Estudiantes, 2007.

– *La Residencia de Estudiantes. Grupos universitario y de señoritas. Madrid, 1910–1936*. Madrid: Ministerio de Educación y Ciencia, 1990. Revised as *La Residencia de Estudiantes 1910–1936. Grupo universitario y Residencia de Señoritas*. Madrid: Acción Cultural Española/CSIC/Residencia de Estudiantes, 2011.

– "La Escuela del Hogar y Profesional de la Mujer y las enseñanzas domésticas (1911–1936)." *Arenal: Revista de Historia de Mujeres* 22, no. 2 (2015): 313–45.

– "María de Maeztu en la Residencia de Señoritas. Educación y feminismo." In *Mujeres en vanguardia. La Residencia de Señoritas en su centenario (1915–1935)*, edited by Almudena de la Cueva and Margarita Márquez Padorno, 234–52. Madrid: Residencia de Estudiantes, 2015.

– "La Residencia de Señoritas. Mujeres y Universidad." In *La Residencia de Señoritas y otras redes culturales femeninas*, edited by Josefina Cuesta, María José Turrión, and Rosa María Merino, 131–59. Salamanca: Universidad de Salamanca/Fundación José Ortega y Gasset–Gregorio Marañón, 2015.

Pestana Nóbrega, Ernesto. "Maruja Mallo." *La Rosa de los Vientos* 2, no. 5 (January 1928): 9–11.

Piñer, Luis Á. *Memoria de Gerardo Diego. (De los cuadernos de Luis Á. Piñer)*. Edited by Juan Manuel Díaz de Guereñu. Madrid: Residencia de Estudiantes, 1999.

Piñón, Pilar. "El Instituto Internacional en España y la Residencia de Señoritas." In *Mujeres en vanguardia. La Residencia de Señoritas en su centenario (1915–1935)*, edited by Almudena de la Cueva and Margarita Márquez Padorno, 256–67. Madrid: Residencia de Estudiantes, 2015.

Pinsker, Shachar M. *A Rich Brew: How Cafés Created Modern Jewish Culture*. New York: New York University Press, 2018.

Pinto Crespo, Virgilio. *Madrid en 1898. Una guía urbana*. Madrid: La Librería, 1998.

Prado, Benjamín. *Los nombres de Antígona*. Madrid: Aguilar, 2001.

Prado Herrera, María Luz de. "Universitarias en Salamanca en el primer tercio del siglo XX: Cuantificación y perfiles." *Culture and History Digital Journal* 8, no. 1 (2019). https://doi.org/10.3989/chdj.2019.005.

Prieto, Gregorio. *Lorca y la generación del 27*. Madrid: Biblioteca Nueva, 1977.

Puertas de Raedo, Antonio Cleofé. *Flores de luna*. Bilbao: n.p., 1921.

Quesada Dorador, Eduardo. *Juan Cristóbal (1896–1961)*. Granada: Junta de Andalucía/Patronato de la Alhambra y Generalife, Consejería de Educación, Cultura y Deporte, 2013.

– "Juan Cristóbal (1896–1961)." In *Juan Cristóbal (1896–1961)*, edited by Eduardo Quesada Dorador, 15–23. Granada: Junta de Andalucía/Patronato de la Alhambra y Generalife, Consejería de Educación, Cultura y Deporte, 2013.

Quiroga Pla, José María. "Ulises adolescente." *Revista de Occidente* 7, no. 69 (March 1929): 403–8.

R. "En la Residencia de Niños. Los hombres del porvenir." *La Esfera* 13, no. 634 (27 February 1926): 13–16.

Rafael Barradas. Madrid: Galería Jorge Mara, 1992.

Rafael Barradas. Buenos Aires: Galería Palatina, 1997.

Ramírez de Lucas, Juan. "Arquitectura y urbanismo. Plaza nueva en el centro de Madrid." *ABC*, 10 October 1985, 105.

Ramos, Carlos. *Construyendo la modernidad. Escritura y arquitectura en el Madrid moderno (1918–1937)*. Lleida: Universitat de Lleida, 2010.

Ramos Altamira, Ignacio. *Ricardo Vilar i Negre y el Jardín-Escuela Altamira de Alicante*. Alicante: Ayuntamiento de Alicante/Publicacions Universitat d'Alacant, 2019.

Recio Aguado, Rosa María. "Arte en la academia. Pintores en la Real Academia de Bellas Artes de San Fernando (siglo XX)." PhD diss., Universidad Complutense de Madrid, 2018.

Reyero Hermosilla, Carlos. *Gregorio Martínez Sierra y su teatro de arte*. Madrid: Fundación Juan March, 1980.

Reyes, Alfonso. *Tertulia de Madrid*. Buenos Aires: Espasa-Calpe Argentina, 1949.

R.G. [Joaquín Rodríguez de Gortázar]. "En San Sebastián. Una Exposición de Arquitectura y Pintura Modernas." *La Gaceta Literaria* 4, no. 91 (1 October 1930): 13.

Ribagorda, Álvaro. "Una historia en la penumbra: las intelectuales de la Residencia de Señoritas." *Sistema: Revista de Ciencias Sociales*, no. 188 (2005): 45–62.

– *El coro de Babel. Las actividades culturales de la Residencia de Estudiantes*. Madrid: Residencia de Estudiantes, 2011.

– "La Fundación Del Amo y las residencias de la Ciudad Universitaria." In *La Universidad Central durante la Segunda República: Las Ciencias Humanas y Sociales y la vida universitaria*, edited by Eduardo González Calleja and Álvaro Ribagorda, 107–35. Madrid: Universidad Carlos III, 2013.

– "La vida cultural de la Residencia de Señoritas en el Madrid de la Edad de Plata." In *La Residencia de Señoritas y otras redes culturales femeninas*, edited by Josefina Cuesta, María José Turrión, and Rosa María Merino, 161–96. Salamanca: Universidad de Salamanca/Fundación José Ortega y Gasset–Gregorio Marañón, 2015.

Rico, María Luisa. "La mujer y las Escuelas de Artes y Oficios en la España de la Restauración." *Cuadernos Kóre. Revista de Historia y Pensamiento de Género*, no. 6 (primavera/verano 2012): 83–113.

Rico Carabias, Mercedes. "Josefina Carabias y la Residencia de Señoritas Estudiantes." *Boletín de la Institución Libre de Enseñanza* 2ª época, no. 68 (December 2007): 77–82.

– "Josefina Carabias y la Residencia de Señoritas Estudiantes." In *Ni tontas ni locas. Las intelectuales en el Madrid del primer tercio del siglo XX*, edited by Paloma Alcalá Cortijo, Capi Corrales Rodrigáñez, and Julia López Giráldez, 242–7. Madrid: Fundación Española para la Ciencia y la Tecnología, 2009.

Río López, Ángel del. *Los viejos cafés de Madrid*. Madrid: La Librería, 2003.

Rittner, Leona, W. Scott Haine, and Jeffrey H. Jackson, eds. *The Thinking Space: The Café as a Cultural Institution in Paris, Italy, and Vienna*. Farnham, UK: Ashgate, 2013.

Rivas, Francisco. "Maruja Mallo, pintora del más allá." In *Maruja Mallo*, edited by Juan Pérez de Ayala and Francisco Rivas, 15–29. Madrid: Guillermo de Osma/ Fundación Cultural Banesto, 1992.

R.M. [Rafael Marquina]. "María Teresa León." *La Gaceta Literaria* 4, no. (15 July 1930): 12.

Ródenas de Moya, Domingo. "Benjamín Jarnés, del vanguardista afable al escriba consumido." In *Elogio de la impureza. Invenciones e intervenciones*, by Benjamín Jarnés, ix–lxi. Madrid: Fundación Santander Central Hispano, 2007.

Rodrigo, Antonina. *Memoria de Granada: Manuel Ángeles Ortiz–Federico García Lorca*. Barcelona: Plaza & Janés, 1984.

– "*El pescador de maravillas submarinas*. Barradas y Gutiérrez Gili." In *Rafael Barradas y Juan Gutiérrez Gili (1916–1929)*, edited by Belén Alarcó, 11–25. Madrid: Residencia de Estudiantes, 1996.

Rodríguez Rubio, Raquel. "Historia de las Escuelas Oficiales de Idiomas bajo el prisma de su legislación." MA thesis, Universidad de Alcalá/UNED, 2016.

Rodríguez Ruíz, Delfín, and Blanca Sánchez, eds. *El Círculo de Bellas Artes de Madrid, ciento veinticinco años de historia (1880–2005)*. Madrid: Círculo de Bellas Artes, 2005.

Rogers, Paul Patrick. "García Lorca and His Friends: Some Anecdotes Recalled by Pictures." *The Library Chronicle of the University of Texas at Austin*, new series, no. 13 (1980): 13–26.

Romano, Julio. "Las Escuelas de Artes y Oficios, en España. Donde se forja el gran ejército de los buenos artesanos y artistas." *La Esfera* 15, no. 776 (17 November 1928): 21–2.

Romero de Pablos, Ana, and José Manuel Sánchez Ron. "Cronología." In *El laboratorio de España. La Junta para Ampliación de Estudios e Investigaciones Científicas, 1907–1939*, edited by José Manuel Sánchez Ron, Antonio Lafuente García, Ana Romero, and Leticia Sánchez de Andrés, 29–59. Madrid: Sociedad Estatal de Conmemoraciones Culturales/Residencia de Estudiantes, 2007.

Rueda, Germán. "Gregorio del Amo entre los 'californios' españoles en EE. UU."
Hispania Nova, no. 10 (2012). http://hispanianova.rediris.es.

Ruiz Salvador, Antonio. *El Ateneo Científico, Literario y Artístico de Madrid (1835–1885)*. London: Tamesis, 1971.

– *Ateneo, dictadura y república*. Valencia: Fernando Torres, 1976.

Ruiz Silva, Carlos. "Música y literatura en la Generación del 27: La relación Alberti–Esplá." *Cuadernos de Música* 1, no. 1 (1984): 35–43.

Sabio, Begoña, "Las escuelas de arte a través de la historia." *Paperback*, no. 1 (December 2005): 1–10.

Sáenz de la Calzada, Margarita. *La Residencia de Estudiantes 1910–1936*. Madrid: CSIC, 1986. Revised as *La Residencia de Estudiantes. Los residentes*. Madrid: Acción Cultural Española/CSIC/Residencia de Estudiantes, 2011.

Sáenz de Tejada Benvenuti, Carlos. "Cronología." In *Carlos Sáenz de Tejada. Los años de "La Libertad,"* edited by María Escribano, 265–82. Madrid: Fundación Cultural MAPFRE VIDA, 1998.

Sáez Delgado, Antonio. "*El almanaque de las artes y las letras para 1928*, lugar de encuentro ibérico." In *Como el camino empieza. Palabra e imagen para Perfecto E. Cuadrado*, edited by Antonio Bernat Vistarini, Almudena del Olmo Iturriarte, Francisco J. Díaz de Castro, and María de Lourdes Pereira, 316–28. Palma de Mallorca: José J. de Olañeta, 2020.

Sáiz Carrero, Ataulfo. "Historia del Hospital General o Provincial de Madrid, cuna de un servicio de urología centenario." *Archivos Españoles de Urología* 59, no. 7 (2006): 663–73.

Salaberria Lizarazu, Ramón. "La larga marcha de Juan Vicens (Zaragoza, 1895–Pekín, 1958)." *Educación y Biblioteca* 12, no. 108 (2000): 5–16.

Salcedo, Nacho. "Los orígenes del CBA: De tertulia de café a Casa de las Artes." BlogdelCírculo, 13 July 2017. https://www.circulobellasartes.com/blog/los-origenes-del-cba-de-tertulia-de-cafe-a-casa-de-las-artes/.

– "El edificio del CBA, una historia escrita en piedra." BlogdelCírculo, 25 August 2017. https://www.circulobellasartes.com/blog/el-edificio-del-cba-una-historia-escrita-en-piedra/.

Salinas, Pedro, and Jorge Guillén. *Correspondencia (1923–1951)*. Edited by Andrés Soria Olmedo. Barcelona: Tusquets, 1992.

Sampelayo, Juan. "El Pasaje de la Alhambra se va." *ABC*, 10 October 1972, 53.

Sánchez, Alberto. "Sobre la Escuela de Vallecas. Texto dictado por el escultor Alberto, en el verano de 1970." *Litoral*, nos 17–18 (March 1971): 47–56.

– *Palabras de un escultor*. Valencia: Fernando Torres, 1975.

Sánchez, Juan. "El artista adolescente. Lam antes de Lam." *Bohemia* 81, no. 31 (4 August 1989): 5–7.

Sánchez Blanco, Laura, and José Luis Hernández Huerta, "La Asociación para la Enseñanza de la Mujer. Una iniciativa reformista de Fernando de Castro (1870–1936)." *Papeles Salmantinos de Educación*, no. 10 (2008): 225–41.

Sánchez Cuesta, León, Pedro Salinas, and Jorge Guillén, *Correspondencia*. Edited by Juana María González. Madrid: Residencia de Estudiantes, 2016.

Sánchez de Andrés, Leticia. "La Junta para Ampliación de Estudios dentro del proyecto institucionista de Francisco Giner de los Ríos y Manuel B. Cossío." In *100 años de la JAE. La Junta para Ampliación de Estudios e Investigaciones Científicas en su centenario*, vol. 1, edited by José Manuel Sánchez Ron and José García-Velasco, 49–93. Madrid: Fundación Francisco Giner de los Ríos/Residencia de Estudiantes, 2010.

Sánchez Felipe, Alejandro. *Dibujos, pluma y lápiz. Rincones coloniales, retratos, composiciones.* Havana: J. Hurtado de Mendoza, 1926.

– *Dibujos: España, Francia, Venezuela, Colombia.* Introduction by Benjamín Jarnés. Madrid: El Autor, 1932.

Sánchez García, Raquel. "Juan Ramón Jiménez y el mercado editorial." *Dicenda. Cuadernos de Filología Hispánica*, no. 21 (2003): 301–18.

Sánchez Rodríguez, Alfonso, ed. *Este film inacabado. Diez entrevistas con familiares, amigos y contemporáneos de José María Hinojosa (1993–1998).* Málaga: Centro Cultural de la Generación del 27, 2002.

– "José María Hinojosa y la calavera de Rimbaud." *Clarín. Revista de Nueva Literatura*, no. 73 (4 June 2008): n.p.

Sánchez Ron, José Manuel, ed. *1907–1987. La Junta para la Ampliación de Estudios e Investigaciones Científicas 80 años después.* 2 vols. Madrid: Consejo Superior de Investigaciones Científicas, 1988.

– "La Junta para Ampliación de Estudios e Investigaciones Científicas ochenta años después." In *1907–1987. La Junta para la Ampliación de Estudios e Investigaciones Científicas 80 años después*, vol. 1, edited by José Manuel Sánchez Ron, 1–61. Madrid: Consejo Superior de Investigaciones Científicas, 1988.

– "La Junta para Ampliación de Estudios e Investigaciones Científicas (1907–2007)." In *El laboratorio de España. La Junta para Ampliación de Estudios e Investigaciones Científicas, 1907–1939*, edited by José Manuel Sánchez Ron, Antonio Lafuente García, Ana Romero, and Leticia Sánchez de Andrés, 65–133. Madrid: Sociedad Estatal de Conmemoraciones Culturales / Residencia de Estudiantes, 2007.

– "Encuentros y desencuentros: Relaciones personales en la JAE." In *100 años de la JAE. La Junta para Ampliación de Estudios e Investigaciones Científicas en su centenario*, vol. 1, edited by José Manuel Sánchez Ron and José García-Velasco, 95–215. Madrid: Fundación Francisco Giner de los Ríos/Residencia de Estudiantes, 2010.

Sánchez Ron, José Manuel, and José García-Velasco, eds. *100 años de la JAE. La Junta para Ampliación de Estudios e Investigaciones Científicas en su centenario.* 2 vols. Madrid: Fundación Francisco Giner de los Ríos/Residencia de Estudiantes, 2010.

Sánchez Ron, José Manuel, Antonio Lafuente García, Ana Romero, and Leticia Sánchez de Andrés, eds. *El laboratorio de España. La Junta para Ampliación de Estudios e Investigaciones Científicas, 1907–1939.* Madrid: Sociedad Estatal de Conmemoraciones Culturales/Residencia de Estudiantes, 2007.

Sánchez-Santiago, Tomás, ed. *Delhy Tejero. "Una muchacha y una maleta."* Zamora: Ayuntamiento de Zamora/Diputación Provincial, 1998–1999.

Santeiro, José Ramón. "Nueva humanización del arte." *Alfar* 8, no. 67 (July 1930): n.p.

Santonja, Gonzalo. *Del lápiz rojo al lápiz libre. La censura de prensa y el mundo del libro.* Barcelona: Anthropos, 1986.

Santos Torroella, Rafael. "Barradas–Lorca–Dalí: Temas compartidos." In *Dibujos*, by Federico García Lorca, edited by Mario Hernández, 39–53. Madrid: Museo Español de Arte Contemporáneo, 1986.

– ed. "Las cartas de Salvador Dalí a José Bello Lasierra." *ABC Literario*, 14 November 1987.

–, ed. "Salvador Dalí escribe a Federico García Lorca." Special issue, *Poesía. Revista Ilustrada de Información Poética*, nos 27–8 (1987).

– "Barradas y el clownismo con Dalí y García Lorca al fondo." *Guadalimar*, no. 116 (April–May 1992): 22–5.

– "Barradas y el *clownismo* con Dalí y García Lorca al fondo." In *Rafael Barradas*, 25–33. Madrid: Galería Jorge Mara, 1992.

– *Dalí residente.* Madrid: Residencia de Estudiantes, 1992.

Sanz Esteban, Isabel. "Historia del caserón de San Bernardo. Breve historia del edificio y de las instituciones. II. – Instituciones que se instalaron después de su adaptación a espacio docente durante los siglos XIX y XX." *Participación Educativa. Revista Cuatrimestral del Consejo Escolar del Estado*, no. 3 (November 2006): 102–5.

Sapiro, Gisèle. "Réseaux, institution(s) et champ." In *Les Réseaux littéraires*, edited by Daphné de Marneffe and Benoît Denis, 44–59. Brussels: Le Cri/CIEL, 2006.

Sarget Ros, María Ángeles. "Rol modélico del Conservatorio de Madrid I (1831–1857)." *Ensayos: Revista de la Facultad de Educación de Albacete*, no. 16 (2001): 121–48.

– "Rol modélico del Conservatorio de Madrid II (1868–1901)." *Ensayos: Revista de la Facultad de Educación de Albacete*, no. 17 (2002): 149–76.

Sarto, Juan del, "La Escuela Especial de Pintura, Escultura y Grabado." *Crónica* 1, no. 7 (29 December 1929): n.p.

Serrano de la Cruz Peinado, Angelina, ed. *Gabriel García Maroto y la renovación del arte español contemporáneo.* Toledo: Junta de Comunidades de Castilla–La Mancha, 1999.

– "Hacia el reconocimiento debido: Gabriel García Márquez, promotor e impulsor de las artes." In *Gabriel García Maroto y la renovación del arte español contemporáneo*, edited by Angelina Serrano de la Cruz Peinado, 139–93. Toledo: Junta de Comunidades de Castilla–La Mancha, 1999.

– "Por tercera vez, y … ¿definitiva?: 'El mito de Maroto.'" In *Gabriel García Maroto y la renovación del arte español contemporáneo*, edited by Angelina Serrano de la Cruz Peinado, 11–20. Toledo: Junta de Comunidades de Castilla–La Mancha, 1999.

Seseña, Natacha, ed. *Eduardo Vicente.* Madrid: Museo Municipal de Madrid, 1999.

Sinclair, Alison. "'Telling It Like It Was'? The 'Residencia de Estudiantes' and Its Image." *Bulletin of Spanish Studies* 81, no. 6 (2004): 739–63.

– *Trafficking Knowledge in Early Twentieth-Century Spain. Centres of Exchange and Cultural Imaginaries.* London: Tamesis, 2009.

Sirinelli, Jean-François. "Le hasard ou la nécessité? Une histoire en chantier: L'histoire des intellectuels." *Vingtième Siècle. Revue d'Histoire*, no. 9 (January–March 1986): 97–108.

Soler Serrano, Joaquín. "Benjamín Palencia: A fondo." TVE program *Grandes Personajes. A fondo*, broadcast 12 March 1976.

Soria Olmedo, Andrés, with Almudena de la Cueva, ed. *Alberti. "Sobre los ángeles."* Madrid: Residencia de Estudiantes; Sevilla: Fundación El Monte, 2003.

Soto Cano, María, ed. *Homenaje a Paulino Vicente en el XXV aniversario de su muerte*. Oviedo: Museo de Bellas Artes de Asturias, 2015.

Tagore, Rabindranath. *Sacrificio. (Poema dramático)*. Translated by Zenobia Camprubí de Jiménez. Madrid: Tip. Lit. de Ángel Alcoy, 1919.

– *Obras de Rabindranath Tagore. La hermana mayor (y otros cuentos)*. Translated by Zenobia Camprubí de Jiménez. Madrid: Juan Ramón Jiménez y Zenobia Camprubí de Jiménez, 1921.

Tedeschini Lalli, Biancamaria. "A Knot of Salons." In *Networking Women: Subject, Places, Links Europe-America. Towards a Re-Writing of Cultural History, 1890–1939*, edited by Marina Camboni, 79–113. Rome: Edizioni di Storia e Letteratura, 2004.

Tejada, José Luis. "Una entrevista con Rafael Alberti." *Gades*, no. 12 (1984): 5–28.

Tejero, Delhy. *Los Cuadernines (Diarios 1936–1968)*. Edited by María Dolores Vila Tejero and Tomás Sánchez Santiago. 2nd ed. León: EOLAS ediciones, 2018.

Temes, José Luis. *El Círculo de Bellas Artes: Madrid, 1880–1936*. Madrid: Alianza, 1999.

Thacker, Andrew. *Moving Through Modernity: Space and Geography in Modernism*. Manchester: Manchester University Press, 2003.

Tinnell, Roger. "Epistolario de Emilio Prados a Federico García Lorca." *Boletín de la Fundación Federico García Lorca* 11, nos 21–2 (1997): 25–72.

Toral Madariaga, Gotzon. *Tertulias, mentideros y programas de radio*. Irún: Alberdania, 1998.

Torre, Guillermo de. "Desde Buenos Aires. Adiós a Barradas." *La Gaceta Literaria* 3, no. 58 (15 May 1929): 5.

– "Guillaume Apollinaire. Su vida, su obra, las teorías del cubismo." In *Guillaume Apollinaire: Estudio preliminar y páginas escogidas*, edited by Guillermo de Torre, 7–86. Buenos Aires: Poseidón, 1946.

– "La polémica del creacionismo. Huidobro y Reverdy." *Ficción* (Buenos Aires), nos 35–7 (January–June 1962): 112–20.

– *Tan pronto ayer*. Edited by Pablo Rojas. Sevilla: Renacimiento, 2019.

Torre, Guillermo de, Miguel Pérez Ferrero, and E. Salazar y Chapela, eds. *Almanaque literario 1935*. Madrid: Plutarco, 1935.

Torres, Rosana. "Rafael Alberti, en el 'lecho del torero herido.'" *El País*, 22 July 1987.

Trapiello, Andrés. *Imprenta moderna. Tipografía y literatura en España*. Valencia: Campgràfic, 2006.

Trebitsch, Michel. "Avant-propos: La chapelle, le clan et le microcosme." *Les Cahiers de LIHTP. Sociabilités intellectuelles. Lieux, milieux, réseaux*, no. 20, edited by Nicole Racine and Michel Trebitsch (March 1992): 11–21.

Tuan, Yi-fu. *Space and Place: The Perspective of Experience*. Minneapolis: University of Minnesota Press, 1977.

Tudela, Mariano. *Aquellas tertulias de Madrid*. Madrid: El Avapiés, 1984.

Tudela, Mariano, José Esteban, Charles David Ley, and José María Kaydeda. *Café Gijón. 100 años de historia. Nombres, vidas, amores y muertes*. Madrid: Kaydeda, 1988.

Tusell, Javier. "Francisco Bores. El pintor de la generación de 1927." In *Francisco Bores. El ultraísmo y el ambiente literario madrileño 1921–1925*, 89–106. Madrid: Residencia de Estudiantes, 1999.

Ugarte, Michael. *Madrid 1900: The Capital as Cradle of Literature and Culture*. University Park: Pennsylvania State University Press, 1996.

Ulacia, Paloma. "Concha Méndez y Luis Buñuel." *Ínsula*, no. 557 (May 1993): 12–15.

Umbral, Francisco. *La noche que llegué al café Gijón*. Barcelona: Destino, 1977.

Valender, James. "García Maroto y los Contemporáneos." In *Los Contemporáneos en el laberinto de la crítica*, edited by Rafael Olea Franco and Anthony Stanton, 417–30. Mexico City: Colegio de México, 1994.

– "García Maroto y el *Libro de poemas* de García Lorca." *Nueva Revista de Filología Hispánica* 44, no. 1 (1996): 155–65.

– "Concha Méndez escribe a Federico y otros amigos." *Revista de Occidente*, no. 211 (December 1998): 129–49.

Valverde, José María. "Rafael Alberti and Luis Felipe Vivanco." *Malahat Review*, no. 47 (July 1978): 62–4.

Varo, Beatriz. *Remedios Varo: En el centro del microcosmos*. Mexico City: Fondo de Cultura Económica, 1990.

Vázquez Astorga, Mónica. "El diario madrileño ABC y los humoristas españoles. El concurso 'del ingenio español' de 1928." *Artigrama*, no. 17 (2002): 419–45.

Vázquez Ramil, Raquel. "La Residencia de Señoritas dentro del esquema de la Junta para Ampliación de Estudios." In *100 años de la JAE. La Junta para Ampliación de Estudios e Investigaciones Científicas en su centenario*, vol. 2, edited by José Manuel Sánchez Ron and José García-Velasco, 507–29. Madrid: Fundación Francisco Giner de los Ríos/Residencia de Estudiantes, 2010.

– *Mujeres y educación en la España contemporánea: La Institución Libre de Enseñanza y la Residencia de Señoritas de Madrid*. Tres Cantos: Akal, 2012.

Vehi, Pere, ed. *Del primer Dalí al Manifest Groc. 1914–1928*. Cadaqués: Adjuntament de Cadaqués/Museu de Cadaqués, 2011.

Velasco Zazo, Antonio. *Panorama de Madrid. Florilegio de los cafés*. Madrid: Librería General de Victoriano Suárez, 1943.

– *Panorama de Madrid. Tertulias literarias*. Madrid: Librería General Victoriano Suárez, 1952.

Vian Herrero, Ángeles. "La biblioteca de la Facultad de Bellas Artes." In *Historia de la biblioteca de la Universidad Complutense de Madrid*, edited by Juan Antonio Méndez Aparicio and Cristina Gállego Rubio, 255–72. Madrid: Editorial Complutense, 2007.

Vicent, Manuel. "Maruja Mallo, la diosa de los cuatro brazos." *El País*, 12 September 1981, 11–12.

Vicente, Eduardo. "Credo pictórico de Eduardo Vicente." In *Eduardo Vicente*, edited by Natacha Seseña, 235–7. Madrid: Museo Municipal de Madrid, 1999.

Vila Tejero, María Dolores. "Adela Tejero Bedate (Delhy Tejero 1904–1968)." In *Ni tontas ni locas. Las intelectuales en el Madrid del primer tercio del siglo XX*, edited by Paloma Alcalá Cortijo, Capi Corrales Rodrigáñez, and Julia López Giráldez, 165–7. Madrid: Fundación Española para la Ciencia y la Tecnología, 2009.

– "Delhy Tejero. Biografía." In *Delhy Tejero. Representación. Exposición antológica*, edited by José Marín-Medina, 281–5. Valladolid: Junta de Castilla y León/Caja España, 2009.

Villacorta Baños, Francisco. *El Ateneo Científico, Literario y Artístico de Madrid (1885–1912)*. Madrid: CSIC–Centro de Estudios Históricos, 1985.

Villalba Salvador, María. "El crítico de arte José Francés. Una aproximación a su figura y su obra crítica." *Goya. Revista de Arte*, no. 285 (2001): 368–78.

– "Arte entre líneas. La memoria personal y la novela del arte en la literatura femenina española contemporánea." In *Estudios de narrativa contemporánea española. Homenaje a Gonzalo Hidalgo Bayal*, edited by Ana Calvo Revilla, Juan Luis Hernández Mirón, and María del Carmen Ruiz de la Cierva, 94–106. Madrid: Fundación Universitaria San Pablo-CEU, 2011.

Villarejo Hervás, Vanesa. "'Adorno' y profesionalización artística femenina. El caso de la Escuela Especial de Pintura, Escultura y Grabado de Madrid desde un enfoque histórico-social y con perspectiva de género. Breve historia de un olvido reconocido (1903–1936)." MA thesis, Universidad Complutense de Madrid, 2019.

Vivanco, Luis Felipe. "Rafael Alberti en su palabra acelerada y vestida de luces." *Papeles de Son Armadans* 2, no. 16 (July 1957): 11–30.

V.X., "La más joven poesía." *Nueva Revista. Notación Literaria*, no. 2 (24 December 1929): 1.

Ybarra, Lucía, ed. *La Sociedad de Artistas Ibéricos y el arte español de 1925*. Madrid: Museo Nacional Centro de Arte Reina Sofía; Barcelona: Àmbit Servicios Editoriales, 1995.

Young, Howard. "The Invention of an Andalusian Tagore." *Comparative Literature* 47, no. 1 (Winter 1995): 42–52.

Zulueta, Carmen de. *Misioneras, feministas, educadoras. Historia del Instituto Internacional*. Madrid: Castalia, 1984.

Zulueta, Carmen de, and Alicia Moreno. *Ni convento ni college. La Residencia de Señoritas*. Madrid: Residencia de Estudiantes, 1993.

INDEX